Additional Praise for *The Real Crash*

"Peter Schiff has written the most compelling argument against central economic planning and debt-financed consumption to come along since our present woes were exacerbated in 2008. His explanations of how unfettered free choices will produce prosperity, and how ending the Federal Reserve, abolishing the IRS, and returning to the gold standard will tame the federal beast, are among the most forceful and cogent I have seen."

—Judge Andrew P. Napolitano, senior judicial analyst, Fox News

"Peter Schiff understands the marketplace, and he understands the consequences that occur when government attempts to manage that marketplace. Pay attention, America!"

—Gary Johnson, former governor of New Mexico and presidential candidate

"Peter Schiff has been painfully right about the downward spiral of the U.S. economy over the last four years. Easy money, rising tax rates, and unbridled debt are a prescription for economic disaster. Let's hope Barack Obama reads this."

—Stephen Moore, economist and Fox News commentator

"As we continue grappling with the monster of a runaway federal government, this book is one of the best assets conservatives can turn to in making the case for fiscal responsibility and capitalism."

—Grover Glenn Norquist, president of Americans for Tax Reform

"Peter Schiff makes a compelling case in a highly readable book that the day will come when the world stops trusting the dollar and the ability of the U.S. government to pay its debts."

—Marc Faber, editor, the Gloom, Boom & Doom Report

Also by Peter D. Schiff

Crash Proof

Crash Proof 2.0

The Little Book of Bull Moves

How an Economy Grows and Why It Crashes
(coauthored with Andrew J. Schiff)

How an Economy Grows and Why It Crashes:
Collector's Edition

The Real
CRASH

America's Coming Bankruptcy—How to
Save Yourself and Your Country

Revised and Updated

Peter D. Schiff

St. Martin's Press ⚏ New York

The advice and strategies in this book constitute the opinions of the author and may not be appropriate for your personal financial situation. You should therefore seek the advice and services of a competent financial professional before utilizing any of the investment strategies advocated in this book.

THE REAL CRASH: REVISED AND UPDATED EDITION. Copyright © 2012, 2014, 2016 by Peter D. Schiff. All rights reserved. For information, address St. Martin's Press, 175 Fifth Avenue, New York, N.Y. 10010.

www.stmartins.com

The Library of Congress Cataloging in Publication Data is available upon request.

ISBN 978-1-250-11659-8 (hardcover)

Our books may be purchased in bulk for promotional, educational, or business use. Please contact your local bookseller or the Macmillan Corporate and Premium Sales Department at 1-800-221-7945, extension 5442, or by e-mail at MacmillanSpecialMarkets@macmillan .com.

Revised and Updated Edition: April 2016

10 9 8 7 6 5 4 3 2 1

Unfortunately my father did not survive to see his prison release date, or the publicaiton of this edition. After serving ten years of a thirteen-year sentence, he passed away at the age of eighty-seven on October 16, 2015, shackled to a hospital bed in a guarded room in intensive care. Though the official cause of death was lung cancer, the real cause was skin cancer that went undiagnosed and untreated for years by prison doctors, allowing it to metastasize to his lungs and other organs.

If all goes well, his fifth grandchild, my daughter Lilyan Ruth will be born in April 2016. Although he will never know her, I will make sure that she knows him, and the principles he lived and died for. Hopefully her generation will not only come to know those principles too, but experience them as well.

Although there were many people and groups that I had considered for this dedication, I feel compelled to risk redundancy and once again credit my father, Irwin Schiff. As I re-read the material, the echo of his voice clearly resonates throughout. It would be disingenuous to avoid the fact that no single individual had a greater influence on the development of this material. Unfortunately, as a quasi-political prisoner, he can't speak for himself. I'm happy to be able to do it for him. Hopefully his courage and idealism will play a part in restoring the American spirit that once beckoned people like my grandparents to come to these shores in the first place, so that my sons, Spencer and Preston, their generation, and those that follow might also enjoy the blessings of liberty.

Contents

New section appearing for the first time is indicated by 2.0

Acknowledgments

This book would not have been possible without the help and support of many people.

I am grateful to the team at St. Martin's Press—Sally Richardson, George Witte, the late Matthew Shear, Laura Clark, and Joe Rinaldi—for immediately recognizing the importance of this book and publishing it with such skill and energy. Once again, I am indebted to my brother, Andrew Schiff, a crucial member of the Euro Pacific team, for his marketing savvy and dedication to getting my message out. And I want to thank Tim Carney and David Freddoso for their invaluable and steadfast help in crafting the text through many revisions as well as my agent, Lynn Sonberg, for her professionalism and editorial support.

Disclosure

Data from various sources was used in the preparation of this book; the information is believed to be reliable, accurate, and appropriate; but it is not guaranteed in any way. The forecasts and strategies contained herein are statements of opinion, and therefore may prove to be inaccurate. They are in fact the author's own opinion, and payment was not received in any form that influenced his opinion. Peter Schiff and the employees of Euro Pacific Capital implement many of the strategies described in the book. This book contains the names of some companies used as examples of the strategies described, as well as mutual funds that can only be sold by prospectus; but none can be deemed recommendations to the readers of this book. These strategies will be inappropriate for some investors, and we urge you to speak with a financial professional and carefully review any pertinent disclosures before implementing any investment strategy.

In addition to being the CEO, Peter Schiff is also a registered representative and owner of Euro Pacific Capital, Inc. (Euro Pacific). Euro Pacific is a FINRA registered Broker-Dealer and a member of the SIPC. This book has been prepared solely for informational purposes, and it is not an offer to buy or sell, or a solicitation to buy or sell any security or instrument, or to participate in any particular trading strategy. Investment strategies described in this book may ultimately lose value even if the opinions and forecasts presented prove to be accurate. All investments involve varying amounts of risk, and their values will fluctuate. Investments may increase or decrease in value, and investors may lose money.

Investors should carefully consider the information about Euro

Pacific Funds, including investment objectives, risks, and charges and expenses, which can be found in the Euro Pacific Funds' prospectus or summary prospectus. Copies of the prospectus or summary prospectus are available at the Fund's Web site, www.europacificfunds.com. You should read the prospectus or summary prospectus carefully before investing or sending funds.

Foreword to the 2016 Edition

On May 1, 2003, on the flight deck of the USS *Abraham Lincoln,* then President George W. Bush, after becoming the first U.S. president to land on an aircraft carrier in a fixed wing aircraft (in a dashing olive drab flight suit), declared underneath an enormous "Mission Accomplished" banner that "major combat operations" in Iraq had been concluded, that regime change had been effected, and that America had prevailed in its mission to transform the Middle East. Thirteen years later, after years of additional combat operations in Iraq, and a Middle East that is spiraling out of control and increasingly disdainful of America's influence, we look back at the "Mission Accomplished" event as the epitome of false confidence and premature celebration.

The image of W on the flight deck comes to mind in much of the reaction to the December 16, 2015, decision by the Federal Reserve to raise interest rates for the first time in nearly a decade. While many in the media and on Wall Street talked of a "concluded experiment" and the "dawning of a new era," few realized that we were just as firmly caught in the thickets of failed policy as were Bush, Cheney, and Rumsfeld in the misunderstood quagmire of 2003 Iraq.

The Fed's decision to finally raise interest rates to one quarter of one percent, after having held them near zero for almost seven years, was heralded as official confirmation of their victory over the financial crises of 2008 and the great recession. The emergency was finally over and the Fed's confidence to begin normalizing interest rates proved it.

In its initial story written that day, *The Washington Post* declared that by raising the Fed Funds rate to one quarter of a percent, the Fed is "ending an era of easy money that helped save the nation from another Great Depression." Putting aside the fact that 25 basis points was still 175 points below the near 2.0 percent trailing twelve-month core inflation rate that the government had reported over the preceding twelve months (and should therefore be considered undeniably easy), the more important question that should have been asked was into what environment the Fed had apparently turned this page.

Historically, the Fed had begun its tightening cycles during the early stages of expansions, when the economy had enough forward momentum to absorb the headwinds of higher rates. But that was certainly not the case this time.

In the six recessions since 1969 that preceded the Great Recession, an average of 13.3 months passed from the time each recession ended to when the Fed felt confident enough in the ensuing recovery to raise rates. (The lag time was just 3.5 months in the four recessions between 1971 and 1991). But following the end of the great recession of 2008–2009, the Fed waited a staggering 78 months before its first interest rate hike! Those prior tightening cycles also occurred at times when GDP was much higher than it was then. Over the prior six occasions, GDP in the quarters when the Fed first moved averaged a robust 5.3 percent. Yet according to its original estimate released on January 29, 2016, fourth quarter GDP growth was a meager .7 percent.

Another key difference is the level of unemployment at the time the hikes occurred. As they started tightening much earlier in prior expansion cycles, unemployment at the times of those recoveries tended to be high, but falling. The average unemployment rate at the onset of the six prior tightening cycles was 7.5 percent. But that rate fell to an average of 5.1 percent (a level that most economists consider to be "full employment") on average forty-two months after the initial rate hike. In other words, those expansions were young enough and strong enough to create additional jobs to substantially reduce unemployment even while the Fed was tightening substantially.

But by the time of the Fed's December 2015 rate hike, the unemployment rate had already fallen to 5.0 percent (mostly because so many workers had either dropped out of the labor force completely, or settled for part-time jobs). Few economists allowed for the possibility that it would fall much lower. This was particularly true if one acknowledged the rapidly deteriorating economic conditions that were apparent at that time.

In the weeks and months leading up to that December rate hike, while the Fed maintained its decision to raise rates was "data dependent," the data clearly showed a recovery rapidly losing momentum. While it was obvious that the manufacturing sector was already in recession, (proving that the promised "manufacturing renaissance" never left the dark ages), data on retail sales and wholesale inventories were showing signs that the service sector was not too far behind.

Given that the U.S. economy has, on average, experienced a recession every six years, the 6.5-year longevity of the most recent "expansion" should have raised eyebrows, even if the data wasn't falling faster than a bowling ball with wings.

So what kind of outcome should we expect when the Fed postpones its first rate hike until the death throes of a tepid recovery rather than doing so at the onset of a strong one? If unemployment starts ticking up during the election year of 2016, can anyone really expect the Fed to follow through with its projected additional rate hikes, potentially allowing a full-blown recession to take hold prior to voters casting their ballots? All of this strongly suggests that this tightening cycle could be the shortest on record. In fact, it's even possible that the Fed's first hike is also its last. But a "one-and-done" scenario does nothing to extricate the Fed from the monetary trap it has created for itself, and hardly merited the fanfare with which it was first received.

Another big question is why the Fed decided to move in December 2015, after doing nothing for so long. Clearly the markets were surprised and confused by the Fed's failure to pull the trigger that September, when the economy appeared, at least to those who chose to ignore the bad data, to be on more solid footing than it was in December. In September, the Fed suggested that it needed to see more improvement before green lighting liftoff. And while I tended not to place much stock in the pronouncements of most economists, one would have been hard-pressed to find anyone who would claim that the data in December looked better than it did in September.

A much more likely explanation is that through its rhetoric the Fed had inadvertently backed itself into a corner. Even though the Fed would have preferred to leave rates at zero, it felt that failure to raise them would have damaged its credibility. After having indicated for all of 2015 that the economy would improve enough to merit a rate increase later in year, to have done nothing in December would have suggested that the Fed did not actually believe what it had been saying. But such an outcome surely frightened the Fed. If the markets began to doubt the Fed's economic pronouncements, perhaps they would also question their professed ability to shrink their balance sheet over the next few years, contain inflation if it ever reared its ugly head, or prevent financial contagion from spreading during a new recession.

In truth, there should have been very little confidence that a new era had begun. A symbolic 25 basis point face-saving gesture, coming just two weeks before year-end, was a non-event. It was the equivalent of a credibility Hail Mary, with the Fed desperately trying to infuse confidence into a "recovery" that for all practical purposes was already over.

The question is whether this small move on its own will be sufficient to push the economy into recession, or whether any additional hikes will be required? Over the past seven years the U.S. economy has become completely dependent on zero percent interest rates. But as with Warren Buffet's famous bathing suit maxim, these dependencies won't be fully revealed until the tide rolls out and those zero percent rates are taken away.

The bigger question is how quickly the Fed will reverse course. Will it do so once it becomes painfully obvious to everyone that we are headed into another recession, or will it wait until we are officially knee deep in a contraction that is even bigger than the last one?

The new rounds of rate cutting and Quantitative Easing that the Fed will have to unleash will echo the military "surge" in Iraq in 2007. Those fresh troops were needed to roll back the chaos that the administration had ignored for so long. But just as that surge only bought us a few years of relative calm, look for the gains brought about by our next monetary surge to be even more transitory. That is a development for which virtually no one on Wall Street is preparing.

The dollar lost considerable ground as a result of the first two rounds of quantitative easing, but by the time the Fed launched its third round, the dollar recovered those losses as markets began pricing in the successful end of the program, the normalization of interest rates, and the unwinding of the Fed's $4.5 billion dollar balance sheet, all without endangering the QE induced recovery.

Now while I long argued that such a feat was impossible, the markets seemed oblivious to the simple fact that knocking the artificial supports out from underneath the economy would not allow it to levitate in midair. But when a faltering economy and markets unexpectedly result in a fourth round of quantitative easing, I expect the dollar's fortune to reverse sharply.

In fact the decline should be particularly sharp, as foreign currencies have a lot of lost ground to recover. QE 3 should have caused foreign currencies to rise against the dollar, but it did not based on false assumptions about the effectiveness and successful conclusion of those programs. Once those false hopes are dashed, not only will the dollar's ill-gotten gains be surrendered, but its forestalled decline will resume in earnest.

However, while foreign central banks provided significant support to the dollar during the early stages of QE, often referred to as a currency war, I do not expect them to make the same mistake twice. The problems recently experienced by many economies due to dollar strength, and the fact that 2015 was the first year in the past fifteen that foreign central bank holdings of U.S treasuries declined, means that a currency World War II looks unlikely to be waged.

This will be a huge problem for the U.S. as just as a renewed recession will cause a huge spike in new debt issuance, foreign central banks will not be there to help finance it. This was not a problem the last time foreign central banks were reducing their holdings of U.S. treasuries, as the U.S. had enjoyed budget surpluses. Also the surpluses themselves would have resulted in such declines, where as this time around they result from deliberate policy decisions, the adverse implications of which for the dollar cannot be ignored.

At the time I wrote the first edition of the book you are about to read, I thought that more of the events that I was forecasting would already have occurred. That was also the case when I revised and updated the original version two years later. However, some four years after its initial publication, those warnings are actually timelier than ever.

This is similar to my experience warning about the housing bubble, and the financial crisis and great recession that would ensue once it burst, events that also took much longer to play out than I first thought. During the intervening years my early warnings about a crisis that had yet to materialize provided great fodder for my critics. To them I was not early, just plain wrong. In fact, my warnings were so early that once the events I had been foretelling for years finally occurred, those same critics were able to dismiss me as being a stopped clock. Warn often enough about a crisis and you will eventually be right, is the way most who were blindsided by the crisis sought to rationalize my ability to see it coming.

But there is ample evidence online, both in articles written by me, or interviews and presentations I gave on the subject, to show that I did not simply warn of a looming disaster in general, but that I described in specific detail the precise nature of the problem, the factors that were creating it, the elements that made a disaster inevitable, and the manner in which the crisis would unfold.

That is why readers should take my current warnings seriously, and not feel that somehow that the passage of a few extra years, that in the scheme of things will be meaningless, invalidates my arguments. Those who did not read the earlier edition of this book are fortunate in that there is still time to prepare, and that the investment strategies I outlined then provide even better entry prices now. Just don't press your luck!

When I wrote my first book, *Crash Proof: How to Profit from the Coming Economic Collapse*, I warned that the bursting of the housing bubble, and that the events that would initially ensue once it burst would not be the end of the financial crisis but the beginning. The end is what is coming next, and this book will help make sure that this time you are prepared.

Preface

By the time this second edition of *The Real Crash* becomes available for sale and reaches your hands, the government shutdown of October 2013 will probably feel like a distant memory. As you read this, you may have already forgotten the conversations of that time; the fights in Congress between Texas Republican senator. Ted Cruz and his colleagues; and the Obama administration's push to make the shutdown as painful as possible for as many as possible—even if it meant spending more money during the shutdown than it would have spent had the government remained open.

You may also forget what brought about the eventual resolution of that manufactured mini-crisis. It was not the shutdown itself, which was only partial and affected relatively few Americans. It was not a sudden agreement on ObamaCare. Rather, it was the mid-October deadline for raising the government's debt limit. What finally forced an agreement to fund the government was the ominous threat of default—the danger that the federal government, because of Congressional inaction, might suddenly stop servicing its debt.

If this happened, we were told, the consequences would be catastrophic. Interest rates would skyrocket. Home values would plummet. Jobs and foreign investment would disappear. The dollar would crash. Governments would seize up and cease providing basic services, for lack of borrowing power. Some said it could be worse than the crash of 2008 or even the Great Depression itself

President Obama also repeated the lie that the debt ceiling had to be raised because "America always pays its bills." Yet the truth is that Congress had to raise the debt ceiling precisely because our government neither does nor can pay its bills.

We had approximately $17 trillion of unpaid bills, and the president wanted to make sure that the stack kept growing. If America actually paid its bills, we would not have been $17 trillion in debt, and the debt ceiling would not have been an issue. You don't pay your bills by going deeper into debt. If you pay your bills, there is no debt, as your obligations are extinguished.

You avoid paying your bills by going into debt, and that is precisely what the president wanted to do. His even bolder lie was that raising the debt ceiling would not increase our debt. But the only thing standing between America and more debt was the ceiling. Had it not been raised, the government would have been legally barred from borrowing any more money. So what Obama advocated was to go deeper into debt, and this, he claimed, was more fiscally responsible than instead paying the bills.

Had Obama really been in favor of paying our bills and not adding debt, he would have been leading the charge not to raise the debt ceiling. He had once done so as a U.S. senator with higher political aspirations. He would have advocated spending cuts or tax hikes so we could actually pay our bills instead of postponing payment further by taking on even more debt.

His willing partner, the Congress, doesn't just refuse to pay what it owes—it also refuses to live within its means. Congress is the drunk who thinks he's being a responsible citizen because he asks the barkeep for more credit before ordering his next drink.

By the time of the shutdown, the United States federal government not only had $17 trillion in unpaid bills, but more than five times that amount in long-term unfunded liabilities, which will require still further borrowing in the coming decades.

This is the result of big government gone wild. Over the years, American politicians have heaped program upon program, entitlement upon entitlement. Government is becoming too big to fail.

Ironically, the Communist Chinese are just now seeing the light. As Bloomberg News reported, their 2013 economic summit produced recommendations in favor of "curbing the government's role in the economy, adjusting the fiscal system and spurring foreign investment."

Our politicians, on the other hand, cannot see beyond the end of their egos. They have refused for so long to set priorities and to put spending on a sustainable trajectory that it would take draconian, politically impossible spending cuts to get us anywhere close to a balanced budget. And after that, in order to pay off the debt, Congress would have to hold spending in check and run annual surpluses for decades.

That just isn't going to happen. We're well past the point where it could have happened. Even when Congress puts a small dent in its projected spending—as it did with sequestration—it manages to undo that progress as quickly as it can. Both parties are guilty of this. Republican hypocrisy was on full display with the quick, easy adoption of the December 2013 budget agreement—and the ease with which that came off does not bode well for the approaching debt ceiling rematch in February 2014.

Entitlements, debt service, and other "mandatory" spending programs, all taken together, consumed just over 100 percent of federal revenues in 2012. The rest of the government is paid for through borrowing. Congress could have completely shut down every single one of the programs and departments it funds annually—laying off hundreds of thousands of bureaucrats and even leaving military servicemen stranded in hostile foreign countries—and the federal budget still would have failed to balance in 2012.

That's how bad things have become.

America's consumers and its government have quite a bit in common. Each time the federal government runs up against its debt limit, it does what any financially irresponsible American would do: It applies for another credit card, does a balance transfer at a low teaser rate, borrows more, spends more, and repeats the process.

In October 2013, we were being warned that Congress had to repeat the process again, or else Armageddon would result. And that's also why, even if we've avoided it for now, Armageddon is inevitable.

All of the negative consequences of a federal default that we were warned about in October are still coming. It's just that the disaster will be that much worse, because we took on even more debt, and exacerbated the underlying economic problems producing that debt, in order to postpone the consequence.

That's what this book is about. I anticipated the housing crash of 2008 and tried to help investors prepare for the consequences. But I had expected and continue to expect a much bigger crash. We've temporarily put it off, but it's still coming. We saw the housing bubble pop, and the government step in to mitigate its effects. When the government bubble pops, there will be no one big enough to offer a bailout.

The next government shutdown will not be theoretical, but real. Significant parts of government will actually shut down because we will no longer be able to borrow enough money to keep them open. Millions of government workers will actually be fired, not just given paid vacations, supplemented with unemployment benefits. Agencies and departments will close and entitlements will be cut.

The Real Crash made waves upon its original release because in these very pages I recommend that the U.S. government avoid this by defaulting on its debt. Again, if Obama was correct in saying failure to raise the debt ceiling would result in default, then default is truly inevitable. So the sooner we do it, the less painful it will be.

If the only way to avoid default is to borrow more money, then eventually the day will come when we run out of fools willing to lend to us. Sure, we can raise the debt ceiling as often as we want, but when the lenders erect their own ceiling, there is nothing we can do to raise it.

The first edition of *The Real Crash* also made suggestions on how you could brace yourself against the day that happens. I have updated those suggestions for this new edition. But nothing has happened since the original publication of this book to change my attitude toward default. In fact, the need to default quickly, before things become much worse, has only become more urgent.

It is not lost on me—nor should it be on you—that default would be very painful for many Americans. All of the things people said during the debt-limit debate on this subject were true. What they didn't say was that all of those bad things are going to happen anyway—not because we failed to raise the debt ceiling, but precisely because we casually raised it every time it was approached. Eventually we will have to face reality: America is bankrupt and beyond any hope of repaying its debts. The pain is coming, one way or another.

A prompt and orderly default—before the debt becomes even larger and the pain even worse—is needed to minimize the damage. Raising the debt ceiling merely allows Congress to kick the can down the road. The price ultimately paid for their political expediency will be steep once the road comes to an end.

This is not a pretty thought, but the day is coming fast when we won't have a choice. Once the illusion that we can ever repay the national debt has receded into the mists of time—along with "I am not a crook," "read my lips," and "If you like your health plan you can keep it"—the only other way out will be to debase the dollar in an unprecedented and destructive manner, unlike anything you've seen in your lifetime. This would have many of the same ill effects as default, but on top of these it would also destroy whatever savings Americans have left and do much more damage to their standard of living.

From many corners, we get hollow reassurances that the economy is recovering. Many of them came from Chairman Ben Bernanke's Federal Reserve, which failed to see the housing bubble even after it was bursting. Bernanke's fellow Fed governors, including his successor, Janet Yellen, saw it no more clearly than he did.

And in fact, having learned nothing from the mistakes that led to the crisis of 2008, Yellen is almost certain to follow in Bernanke's footsteps with a monetary policy that amounts to a ticking time bomb, placed at the base of an extremely fragile economy.

The Fed's policy of "quantitative easing" has had its expected effect so far. It has kept mortgage rates low and supplied the government with a willing lender at near-zero interest rates. The Fed is thus helping reflate the same housing bubble that burst in 2008, and also continuing to inflate the government bubble that's been growing all along.

This book describes in greater detail how the policy of quantitative easing has helped keep the economy just reasonably lousy but not officially recessionary throughout the Obama era. America's wealth is recovering on paper as assets appreciate, but businesses are struggling and dying, little new wealth is being created, and jobs remain scarce. It's all there in the data.

Quantitative Easing is temporarily preventing the inevitable. But when the Fed loses its grip on interest rates, then it's game over. All it takes is a return to historically average interest rates, and the government will suddenly find it nearly impossible to service the mountain of debt that quantitative easing allowed it to accumulate

And as we shall see, Yellen is bound to continue this easy monetary policy indefinitely. Even the December 2013 announcement of a modest "taper" had to be accompanied by a promise that interest rates will be held near zero indefinitely. In fact, the taper itself will likely be abandoned as well, since the economy depends on it. I think the Fed has figured out that unlike previous bubbles, this one is just too big to pop.

Yet at the same time, QE cannot make America truly prosper, nor can it go on forever. In November 2013, just as this second edition went to press, former Fed manager Andrew Huszar wrote an op-ed in *The Wall Street Journal* regretting his own personal role in QE. He called it "the largest financial-markets intervention by any government in world history." And he added:

> Because QE was relentlessly pumping money into the financial markets during the past five years, it killed the urgency for Washington to confront a real crisis: that of a structurally unsound U.S. economy. . . . Meanwhile, the country remains overly dependent on Wall Street to drive economic growth.

He could have added that the country is overly dependent on the Fed for its growth. He concluded by calling quantitative easing "Wall Street's new 'too big to fail' policy."

But it's really even worse than that. Between our government's fiscal recklessness and the central bankers' willingness to accommodate it, we're not just putting off the crash—we're actively worsening its eventual effects. We're winding up the spring each day for a more powerful recoil. This book explains how.

That's why it's time to prepare for The Real Crash. I hope this second edition helps you do so.

Introduction

"I GUESS YOU WERE RIGHT about the crash, Peter."

I hear that a lot, in reference to my 2007 book, *Crash Proof,* where I predicted an economic catastrophe in the United States. Since late 2008, when the housing market had collapsed and major banks went to the brink of failure, whenever people credit me with calling the crash, it pains me to tell them that what they saw in 2008 and 2009 wasn't the crash—that was a tremor before the earthquake.

The real crash is still coming.

Just as the housing bubble delayed the economic collapse for much of the last decade on the strength of imaginary wealth, today twin bubbles in the U.S. dollar and Treasury bills and bonds are providing a similar prop. But the day will come when the rest of the world stops trusting America's currency and our credit. Then we'll get the real crash.

During my run for Senate in 2010, I constantly encountered politicians and journalists who blamed the current economic troubles on capitalism and free markets, arguing that more government was needed. When the bigger crash comes, the attacks on capitalism will become louder, and the proposed government interventions will become even more extreme. This makes sense—politicians want more power, and they know that crises and panics are the best opportunities to get people to surrender their freedom for the promise of security. That's what Rahm Emanuel meant when he said, after the 2008 election, "You never want a serious crisis to go to waste."

But the government was a chief architect of the mess that we're in, and every day, the government is making it worse.

I invest for a living. I look for where other people are making mistakes. I look for companies or commodities that are mis-valued by the market, and I study who is investing where. It's glaring that American companies are still not making capital investments. American families—after a brief period of paying down debt and increasing savings—are borrowing more than they're saving.

Just as in 2008, we have too much consumption and borrowing, and too little production and saving. Since the depths of the economic downturn in early 2009, most of the "wealth" we've created has—once again—been imaginary.

Real estate is still grossly overpriced. Most stocks are still overpriced as valuations are based on earnings and artificially low interest rates, and both are unsustainable. Companies that are hiring are probably making mistakes they will soon regret. The fundamentals of the economy are not sound—not even close.

Four years ago, I said that the disease in the economy is debt-financed consumption, and that the cure would require a recession. But the medicine I prescribed—Americans consuming less and saving more while companies invest for the long term and the government tightens its belt—was deemed too bitter a pill to swallow by the Bush and Obama administrations. Instead, they fed us bailouts and stimulus to blow the bubble back up. This political aversion to austerity has set us up for an even bigger crash.

Not only did I predict the recent collapses of the housing bubble and the stock market in *Crash Proof,* I also predicted the government reaction. I was the original opponent of the 2008 Wall Street bailout, because I was opposing it in 2007, a year before the Bush administration even proposed it.

In 2006 and 2007, when I made all these predictions, the "experts" laughed at me (literally—search for "Peter Schiff was Right" on YouTube, and you'll see). I was dubbed "Dr. Doom" for my dire—and ultimately correct—predictions. While the laughter and the names never hurt my feelings, this time I have decided that rather than simply predicting doom, I would lay out a comprehensive set of solutions. That's why I wrote this book.

My prescription, at heart, is this: We need to stop bailouts, government spending, government borrowing, and Federal Reserve manipulation of interest rates and debasement of the dollar. We need to reduce government spending so we can offer real tax relief to the productive sectors of our economy. We need to repeal regulations, mandates, and subsidies that create moral hazard, lead to wasteful and inefficient allocation of resources, and artificially drive up the cost of doing business and hiring workers. We need to let wages fall, allow people to pay down debt and start saving, and allow companies to make capital investments so that America can start making things again.

And regarding our national debt, there is only one good solution, and it's the one that no politician, debt commission, or TV talking head is proposing: America needs to restructure its debts. We're already bankrupt, it's time we declared it. The U.S.A. is insolvent, and should enter the sovereign equivalent of Chapter 11 bankruptcy. Then, like a bankrupt company, we can pay off some fraction of our debts—to China, to social security recipients, and other debt-holders—and then reorganize.

Nobody wants to hear this news, and politicians certainly don't want to deliver it. But Americans will like it even less when the real crash comes—when unemployment skyrockets, credit dries up, home prices plummet again, or worse, the dollar collapses, wiping out all savings and sending consumer prices into the stratosphere. My proposal is to soften the blow. Instead of a violent crash, my plan would give us a painful, but limited, recession.

In addition to saving us from economic ruin, my plan would have immediate benefits for Americans. Lower taxes and less regulation would mean more freedom, and more room for small businesses. Savers would benefit from sound monetary policy and from realistic interest rates.

I don't expect policymakers to adopt my plan any time soon. I think it will take some serious economic pain before politicians are willing to do anything outside of the ordinary. When the situation is ugly, Washington will have to consider the sorts of ideas I prescribe.

The unprecedented dangers our economy faces also mean you need to completely change the way you handle your money. Even if you don't think of yourself as an investor, you need to start paying more attention to your wealth, because our economic predicament means there will be no easy way to protect your money.

Conventional wisdom about investing doesn't work anymore, because we are in unconventional times. The Fed will be printing so much money that your dollars could become worthless. Our government is so profligate that your U.S. Treasuries could become subprime assets. You need to look to overseas assets and invest with the knowledge that the U.S. of the future will not be anything close to the economic powerhouse it was in the past.

But in the long run, my proposals could turn things around. We'd have a firmer foundation for our economy, a constrained government, a better education system, a more sustainable financial sector, and more room for innovation, meaning a more prosperous world.

Right now, though, we're in a car, out of control, speeding down an icy hill. Our politicians pretend they're in control, and so we just keep accelerating toward the bottom. We need a grown-up to grab the wheel and steer us into the ditch on the side of the road. That won't be pretty, but it's better to go into the ditch at 80 miles an hour than crash into a brick wall at the bottom of the hill at 120.

This book shows the way out of our mess with as little suffering as possible. The proposals are drastic and sound painful, but the alternative is worse. The time for a so-called soft landing has passed. All we can do now is prepare for the crash. If we brace ourselves properly and control the impact, at least we will survive it.

PART I

The Problem

I

Where We Are and Where We Are Headed

As I stated in the introduction, the real crash I predicted in my first book is still coming.

You see, before 2006, I had been predicting an economic catastrophe in the United States, with the bursting of the housing bubble being the catalyst. Once that bubble burst and major banks went to the brink of failure, people began crediting me with "calling the crash." But what we saw in 2008 and 2009 wasn't the crash. That was the overture. Now we have to sit through the opera.

The economic unpleasantness of those days was definitely part of the real crash, but only because of the way our politicians responded—replacing one government-created bubble with another, thus putting our economy at even greater risk.

The same bubble machine that fueled the last two boom-bust cycles—the Federal Reserve—is already back in high gear, and we must turn it off. The Fed needs to stop fueling inflation and start sucking dollars back out of the economy. It also needs to let interest rates rise. When the Fed does these two things, Washington's free ride will end—it will no longer be able to borrow at near-zero interest. As a result, Congress will have to slash spending, fix our entitlements, and generally shrink government.

These are the right things to do today—they were the right things to do ten years ago. But soon they will become inevitable. We will have no choice.

My past books predicted the crash. This book goes a step further and lays out the steps we need to take in order to make this crash as painless as possible and to rebuild in the aftermath. We need to wind down entitlements, eliminate many government functions, and stop play-ing with the money supply and interest rates. America needs to start mak-ing things again, and the government needs to stop taking. As individuals and as a nation, we need to get out of debt.

And ultimately, we'll have to face up to the fact that we can't pay off all our debts.

Later chapters spell out the solutions, but these first two chapters de-scribe the problem.

Our economy today is once again built on imaginary wealth. Like the proverbial house built on sand, it will collapse. When that happens, when America's tab finally comes due, it will probably be as bad as or worse than the Great Depression. You'd better be ready for it.

From a Dot-Com Bubble to a Housing
Bubble to a Government Bubble

To understand how bad things are and where we're headed, let's quickly go back a decade or so, and retrace the steps that brought us here.

Throughout the 1990s, the Federal Reserve injected tons of money into the economy, which fueled a stock bubble, focused particularly on dot-com companies. In 2000 and 2001, when the stock market turned down and un-employment started to creep up, that was a correction.

Assets that had been overvalued (such as stocks) were returning to a more appropriate price. The dot-com and stock market bubble had misal-located resources, and while investment was fleeing the overvalued sectors, inevitably the economy shrunk and unemployment rose while wealth be-came more rationally allocated around the economy.

Readjustments in the economy involve short-term pain, just as the cure to a sickness often tastes bitter. Short-term pain, however, was unacceptable to the politicians and central bankers in 2000 and 2001.

Federal Reserve Chairman Alan Greenspan manipulated interest rates lower. This made borrowing cheaper, inspired more businesses to invest, and softened the employment crunch. But the economy wasn't really get-ting stronger. That is, there weren't more businesses producing things of value. As there were few good business investments, all this cheap capital flowed into housing.

As housing values skyrocketed, Americans were getting richer on paper. This made it seem as if things were okay. In other words, Greenspan accomplished his goal of forestalling any significant pain. By the same token, he also kept the economy from healing properly, which would have laid the foundation for a stronger and lasting recovery.

When market realities started to bear down on the economy, and the housing bubble popped, with the broader credit bubble right behind, the government was running out of things to artificially inflate. So the Fed and the Obama administration decided to pump money desperately into government.

I'll explore this "how-we-got-here" story in more depth in chapter 2, but for now, I'll make this point:

Just as the housing bubble delayed the economic collapse for much of last decade on the strength of imaginary wealth, the government bubble is propping us up now. The pressure within the bubble will grow so great that the Federal Reserve will soon have only two options: (a) to finally contract the money supply and let interest rates spike—which will cause immensely more pain than if we had let this happen back in 2002 or 2008; or (b) just keep pumping dollars into the economy, causing hyperinflation and all the evils that come with it.

The politically easier choice will be the latter, wiping out the dollar through hyperinflation. The grown-up choice will be the former, electing for some painful tightening—which will also entail the federal government admitting that it cannot fulfill all the promises it has made, and it cannot repay everything it owes.

In either case, we'll get the real crash.

The National Debt

As a professional investor, when I study the American economy today, I see debilitating weaknesses. Most obvious is the debt. As this book went to press, the national debt was over $17 trillion. That works out to approximately $151,000 per taxpayer.* Let's talk a bit about what this means.

Whenever the government wants to spend money it doesn't have, it

---

* When *The Real Crash* was first published, it was $133,000 per taxpayer.

borrows. Our government borrows by selling T-bills and Treasury bonds, or "Treasuries." The buyer gets an IOU, and the government gets cash. So, various bondholders—individual investors, U.S. banks, the Chinese government, the Federal Reserve, even parts of the U.S. government—hold in aggregate $17 trillion in IOUs. These bonds and bills come due all the time, and typically, the Treasury pays them off by borrowing again.

Every day, the debt grows. First, it grows because it accumulates interest. In 2010, taxpayers paid $414 billion in interest on the national debt. Another reason the debt keeps growing: our government keeps borrowing more in order to spend more.

Barack Obama's $800 billion stimulus in 2009, for instance, was entirely funded by borrowing. In fiscal year 2011, the U.S. Government spent $3.6 trillion, but brought in only $2.3 trillion in revenues. The extra $1.3 trillion—the budget deficit for the year—was paid for through borrowing.

As a businessman or the head of a household, if you spend more than you earn in a given month, you're doing one of two things: you're either spending down your savings, or leaving a balance on your credit card. But the federal government has no net savings. That leaves only one option: every dime of deficit is added to our national debt—plus interest.

State governments are in the red, too. Nearly every state ran a deficit in 2010, and the aggregate of state debt is about $1.3 trillion. Local governments owe a combined $1.8 trillion. Add that $3.1 trillion in state and local debt to Uncle Sam's $17 trillion, and our public debt tops $20 trillion. Much worse, when off-budget and contingent liabilities are thrown in, total government debt tops $100 trillion!

State of Bankruptcy

In some ways, our state governments are in worse shape than the federal government. While most states don't have huge ticking time bombs like Medicare, they have just as much—or more—trouble breaking even.

For fiscal year 2012, more than forty states were in the red. Twenty-seven states (a majority of states and a vast majority of the country) were running deficits of 10 percent or more, according to data from the Center on Budget and Policy Priorities.

California is probably the most famous of the insolvent states because of the massive size of its annual shortfall: more than $25 billion in 2012.

To poison the fiscal waters so completely, it took a special brew of big-government liberalism, anti-tax-hike ballot measures, powerful public employee unions, and ridiculous public pension laws. These factors created what former Manhattan Institute scholar Josh Barro called "California's permanent budget crisis."

Indeed, since 2005, the California state legislature has been fighting an annual "crisis." Barro explains:

> California's permanent budget crisis stems from institutional failures. Ballot measures have made it nearly impossible to raise taxes or cut spending, and have cemented the idea in voters' minds that they can get government services without paying for them. The state has repeatedly failed to reform its inefficient tax code (which relies too much on highly volatile taxes on high-income people, and not enough on property taxes) or to tackle the problem of runaway public employee compensation.

California is special in many regards. (For instance, no other state has city managers paying themselves nearly a million dollars a year, as the folks of Bell, California, were caught doing.) But many of the problems with California are present elsewhere.

One is the tendency of states to go wild during boom years in revenue. Many individuals who did well during the boom years bought McMansions with huge mortgages on the assumption that every year would be just as good. Many states did the same thing. Nevada is a classic example. Nevada enjoyed faster population growth than any other state in the 1990s and most of the 2000s. This coincided with the nationwide housing bubble, and sent home prices through the roof. As a result, property tax receipts went way up. State and local politicians spent all this money on the crazy theory that Las Vegas—in the middle of a desert—was being "Manhattanized."

You might recall that Nevada was hit harder by the housing bust than any other state. Record foreclosures both sent people out of the state and dragged down property values. Revenues dropped, but expenditures didn't keep pace. The result: huge deficits.

Public employee unions are another central cause. Like any union, the American Federation of State, County & Municipal Employees, the American Federation of Teachers, and their cohorts exist to get as much pay and benefits as possible for their members.

But unlike most unions, government unions are negotiating with people who are spending someone else's money: politicians. Often, those politicians were elected thanks to campaign contributions from the unions. This is a vicious cycle: taxpayers pay government workers whose money goes to government unions, whose money goes to the campaigns of politicians, who approve more taxpayer money for the unions, who then contribute more to the politicians.

How has Washington responded to the budget crises in the states? Mostly by making things worse.

The 2009 stimulus bill included hundreds of billions of dollars in aid to states, allowing them to continue their spending binges. Had federal money not been available, states would have been forced to do the right thing and cut their spending.

Congress even took up a bill in 2011, the Public Safety Employer-Employee Cooperation Act, that gives special bargaining privileges to the unions of police officers, firemen, and emergency medical personnel. Many Republicans even backed the measure, probably because these public safety unions are far more supportive of Republicans than other government unions.

Bankrupt states are one more virus in our sick economy.

Government Driving People Deeper into the Red

The American people are pretty deep in hock, too.

Thanks to a housing bubble and artificially low interest rates, a lot of people borrowed money that they could not pay back in order to pay inflated prices for houses they could not afford. All told, Americans are laboring under about $13 trillion in mortgage debt.

But it's not in the past. After a brief period of paying down debt and increasing savings, thanks to the Fed, American families are once again borrowing more than they're saving.

Total consumer debt is $2.8 trillion, while credit card debt is $807 billion.* That's a grand total of $16.6 trillion in personal debt, or $200,000 per family. In addition, federally backed student loans now top $1 trillion, exceeding total credit card debt for the first time in 2011. On the other side of the ledger is approximately $7,000 in savings per family.

In the next chapter, I'll talk more about how private indebtedness got so bad, but for now let me just note that bad government policy and the bad economics of the chattering class have contributed to this situation. Government rewards borrowing (the biggest tax deduction for most families is the deduction for mortgage interest) but often punishes saving (by taxing investment gains and interest on CDs and savings accounts).

The biggest culprit in discouraging savings, though, is the Federal Reserve. For one thing, the Fed creates new dollars, driving up prices. That means the dollars you sock away today are worth less when you pull them out next month. Better to spend them today.

Even when there has not been a significant increase in consumer prices—as between late 2008 through 2011—the Federal Reserve deliberately warded off falling prices by inflating the dollar supply. Put another way: the Federal Reserve is putting upward pressure on prices, and thus keeping the dollar from gaining in value.

The Fed also keeps interest rates artificially low. Were interest rates as high as the market would set them, and were dollars not being cheapened, people would have more incentive to save and less incentive to borrow.

Spending Is Patriotic

Part of the problem, peddled by the media and politicians, is the notion that prosperity comes from consumer spending.

Listen to any TV or radio newscaster discuss economic news, especially during a downturn, and there's one hard and fast rule for them: *consumers spending more money is good, and consumers spending less money is bad. Shopping is good for the country. Paying down debt or saving is bad for the country.*

That's not just overly simplistic, it's almost completely wrong. If people

---

* When the first edition of *The Real Crash* was published in 2012, total consumer debt was $2.5 trillion and revolving consumer debt was $789 billion.

are spending money they don't have, that may be good in the short term for stores and manufacturers, but it's often bad in the long term for the whole economy.

Sure enough, this isn't the first time Americans have borrowed lots of money. But in the past, we borrowed money to invest in productive capacity, such as building a factory. That factory makes goods at a profit, and that profit then pays off the loan. If people are borrowing as a way to finance productivity, then indebtedness isn't bad, and it is often beneficial.

Today's borrowing and debt, however, isn't primarily for *investment*.

These days, because people are going into debt for the sake of *consumption*—buying a fancy dress or tickets to a basketball game This means U.S. indebtedness grows while productive capacity doesn't. That credit card debt doesn't go away. The dollar a person charges today is 1.10 he'll have to pay off tomorrow.

Imagine a rational, well-informed owner of the general store in a small town. If he sees all his customers running up credit card debt, what is he going to do? He'll stop stocking the shelves as much, because he knows the day will come when his customers will max out their cards. Not only will the customers no longer be able to spend more than they earn, they won't be able to spend even *as much* as they earn, because some of their income will go toward paying off debt, plus interest.

When that day comes, the prudent storeowner might be fine—if he saved up his surplus from the boom days. Many downtown businesses will suffer: if they believed this boom in spending represented real wealth and so they expanded or hired more employees, those higher overhead costs will not be sustainable when the town's shoppers become more austere.

Yet whenever the economy slowed down in the past decade, politicians always looked for ways to get people borrowing and spending as much as before. In other words, Washington wouldn't let people recover from their spending binges.

On September 20, 2001, nine days after terrorists took down the twin towers, President Bush told average Americans how they could help the economy: "Your continued participation and confidence in the American economy would be greatly appreciated." Bush urged Americans to go out and spend. (In contrast, when World War II broke out Americans were urged to save. The public purchased war bonds and consumer goods were rationed.)

Barack Obama rightly mocked Bush's version of civic duty, saying on the 2008 campaign trail of Bush after 9/11, "when he spoke to the American people, he said, 'Go out and shop.'"

But Obama was no different during the recession in 2009. A month into his presidency, he declared it his goal "to quicken the day when we re-start lending to the American people and American business." One of Obama's programs, "Cash for Clunkers" was designed to get Americans to buy cars they otherwise could not afford. So we destroyed fully paid-for cars that still worked, to go deeper into debt to buy newer ones, many of them imports, saddling car owners with additional debts at times when they should have been rebuilding their savings.

He put it more forcefully elsewhere in the same speech: "We will act with the full force of the federal government to ensure that the major banks that Americans depend on have enough confidence and enough money to lend even in more difficult times."

Of course, banks' lending more means consumers' *borrowing* more. Both Bush and Obama told the American people that when times are bad, they should run up credit card debt—it's the patriotic thing to do.

Saving Is Unpatriotic

While Obama was "act[ing] with the full force of the federal government" to get Americans borrowing and spending more, many people were—smartly—going in the other direction. In the second quarter of 2009, personal savings hit a seventeen-year high of 7.2 percent as a percentage of disposable income.

According to the Bureau of Economic Research, the American people saved $793 billion that quarter. This was at a time that personal income, at $12.2 trillion, was far lower than it had been during any point in 2008. People were behaving rationally. The economy had turned down, their friends and neighbors were losing jobs, and so people with income started saving it.

This had to stop, according to President Obama. Sure enough, artificially low interest rates and subsidies for home purchases helped discourage people from saving, and the savings rate quickly dropped.

By the end of 2010, consumer debt was rising again, according to data from the Federal Reserve,[1] and the contraction of overall household debt had ended. We were back on the road to "normal levels of lending," that is, normal levels of indebtedness. Mission accomplished.

Of course, the biggest problem is that savings is the key to economic growth, as it finances capital investment, which leads to job creation and increased output of goods and services. A society that does not save cannot grow. It can fake it for a while, living off foreign savings and a printing press, but such "growth" is unsustainable—as we are only now in the process of finding out (more on that later).

Why Our Trade Deficit Isn't Harmless

Just as politicians and liberal economists will tell you that savings are bad and borrowing is good, conservative economists are likely to tell you that trade deficits are a *good thing*.

Why should we care, they ask, *if our goods are coming from outside the U.S.?* They rightly point out that money isn't a good in itself, and, all else being equal, we'd all rather have the stuff money can buy than have the money itself. So, if we're importing more than we're exporting, we end up with goods, and the other guys—such as the Chinese—end up with dollars. The only thing the foreigners can do with dollars, ultimately, is to buy stuff from us. Ultimately, the argument goes, it all evens out.

Here's the problem with that argument: we're not making enough stuff for our trading partners to buy with all those U.S. dollars they have been accumulating. But foreigners aren't simply sitting on those surplus dollars—they're buying the one thing we are producing prodigiously: debt.

The idealized story of international trade says we buy Chinese televisions with dollars, then the Chinese use those dollars to buy U.S. cars. Ultimately, it's a trade of goods-for-goods (TVs-for-cars), with currency merely smoothing out the transactions.

But the real story of our international trade ends not with our selling physical goods overseas, but with our selling U.S. Treasuries. We end up with Chinese TVs and the Chinese end up with our IOUs. Put another way, we borrowed to buy the TV.

Our Trade Deficit by the Numbers

I'll go into this issue more later on, but for now, let's look at the lay of the land on trade. In early 2013, we were averaging about $185 billion in exports every month and about $227 billion in imports.

That's a trade deficit of $42 billion a month, or $500 billion a year. *
Put another way, we would need to boost our exports by 23 percent in order to reach balance. Vis-à-vis China, we typically run a goods deficit of about $20 billion per month.

Much of our exports to China are coal and iron ore, which the Chinese use to make steel—steel which they then sell. On the other hand, most of what we buy from the Chinese are electronics, toys, and sporting goods. In other words, Chinese imports are largely *investment,* and our imports are largely *consumption.* (Electronics, of course, can be investment, but only if we're not talking about Xboxes, but about computers that businesses use to be more productive.)

The same is true with all our trading partners. One third of our exports, according to the Census Bureau, are "capital goods"—machinery or other things businesses buy in order to be productive.[2] Another third are "industrial supplies"—again, investment in things to which foreign businesses will add value.

Crashproof Yourself: Don't Count on the American Consumer

Americans aren't making things, and they're not saving. That doesn't bode well for their future purchasing power. If my business depended on selling things to Americans, I'd be worried.

Think about this issue as an investor. It's no good to invest in a company that's in a growing economy if that company depends on

---

* When the first edition of *The Real Crash* was published, exports were $160 billion and imports were $210 billion, for a trade deficit of $50 billion per month or $600 billion per year.

selling things to Americans. Many Chinese manufacturers who don't adjust will find themselves running out of paying customers.

When you're investing, avoid companies that depend on Americans' continued ability to consume or repay their debts, and look for companies whose customers will have greater purchasing in the future. Who is selling washing machines to the Chinese? Who is selling cars to India?

When foreigners buy from us, they are laying the groundwork for productivity. The converse is not true.

One quarter of what we import are consumer goods, slightly more than what we spend on capital goods. Again, we're consuming more than we're investing. While our "industrial supplies" imports are proportionally equal to our exports in that category (about one third of our total imports), there's a key imbalance on this score: half of those imports are foreign oil—most of which is used by vehicles.

So, generally, we're importing to consume. Other countries are importing to produce.

Consumerism Does Not Equal Capitalism

These problems go unappreciated in part because some of the regular watchdogs of government folly give Uncle Sam a pass here.

Those who profess belief in the free market often confuse free markets with Wall Street, profit, and perceived economic growth. They dismiss worries about a trade deficit as protectionist carping. They see massive consumer spending as a sign of prosperity, and rising gross domestic product as the only measure of economic health.

This is wrong. In a free market, our economy wouldn't have the sort of indebtedness and leverage it has had. The housing bubble was one instance of the government's tendency to foster debt and create inefficiency.

Inflated home values—both their absurd climb before 2006 and the lack of a full correction afterward—are clearly the result of big government rather than the result of the free market. Everyone knows that Fannie Mae,

Freddie Mac, and the Community Reinvestment Act helped pump up the housing bubble. High income tax rates combined with the deduction for mortgage interest helped, too.

But the main problem was the Federal Reserve keeping interest rates artificially low.

The Fed's manipulation of interest rates not only artificially boosts the housing market, it also boosts all borrowing and indebtedness. Without the Fed, our indebtedness and consumption would both be much lower. Of course, in the long run, with sound money and limited government, our consumption would be even higher, but it would result from increased production rather than debt.

Government interference is often behind consumption. State and local governments subsidize shopping centers because they "create jobs." Banks— and thus credit cards—are all subsidized by the federal government. Fractional reserve banking, which would be fraud if it wasn't explicitly endorsed by the Fed, allows banks to lend out the same dollar many times.

Now, don't take me for some sort of anticonsumerist hippie. There's no such thing as too much spending or too much borrowing in the abstract— it's only a problem when spending and borrowing outstrip productive activity.

As it happens, a huge portion of our economy is simply about helping us consume—the service sector largely fits this bill. A shrinking portion is about helping us produce: Out of $15.3 trillion in GDP (gross domestic product) in 2011, about $1.23 trillion was capital investment. A decade before, capital investment was $965 billion out of a gross domestic product[3] of $9.4 trillion. Capital investment as a share of our economy fell by 20 percent in a decade.*

In other words, we have been trading production for consumption.

Fighting the Cure

Just as in 2008, we have too much consumption and too much borrowing. We also have too little production and too little savings. Since the depths

---

* When the first edition of *The Real Crash* was published, GDP was $14 trillion and $1.1 trillion of that was capital investment.

of the economy in early 2009, most of the "wealth" we've created has been—once again—imaginary wealth.

Judging by their actions, it's clear the politicians thought the problem was simply that all our pre-2008 imaginary "wealth" disappeared. Thus, they think it's their job to re-create the illusion.

The Troubled Asset Relief Program (TARP), the stimulus, the auto bailouts, and the inflationary actions of the Federal Reserve all treat the *symptoms* of our 2008–2009 downturn. It's all superficial.

Government *can* slow the fall of housing prices, and so our politicians make sure that it does. For example, Obama has used TARP to keep people in their homes—often only delaying foreclosure and thus making homeowners even poorer. Fannie Mae and Freddie Mac ramped up their subsidies, thus keeping demand for homes higher than it would be. The Federal Housing Authority is subsidizing mortgages to the point that people are once again putting down zero percent—this applies upward pressure to home prices, slowing their fall.

But falling housing prices are part of the *cure*. Inflated prices are part of the disease. It's as if a doctor saw a patient had an inflated count of white blood cells—the cells that respond to and fight infections—and so he decided to remove the white blood cells.

Along the same lines, government can keep interest rates low, and so it does. But low interest rates contributed to the disease. High interest rates are part of the cure that we need. Again, government makes sure that we never get the cure.

Falling prices and wages are another cure the government won't let us swallow (more on this in chapter 4). Ask an economics writer today, and "deflationary death spiral" is the biggest threat facing our economy. This is bogus. In the Depression, falling prices were a rare boon. They were a saving grace for anyone who lost his job and was spending down savings.

Today, Washington does everything it can to prevent falling prices. Mostly this means (1) Keynesian stimulus to drive up demand for goods and services, and (2) inflating the money supply.

Falling prices would be a cure, but government pumps up prices.

In other words, the market is trying to cure the economy, and the government won't let it. The government's "cure" for the market's cure is more imaginary wealth.

Government doesn't exactly pull this imaginary money out of a hat, but it does create it out of nowhere. Where did the $700 billion to bail out Wall Street and Detroit come from? That money was created by the Federal Reserve. Literally, the Fed just credited banks with money. Those dollars didn't come "out of" anywhere. The Fed simply declared that more dollars existed.

The stimulus? None of that was paid for with tax dollars. All of that money was borrowed. That means the U.S. Treasury sold bonds and treasury bills, and then spent all the money it borrowed.

Because the federal government runs a deficit, every year it is borrowing more. Everyone who owns U.S. debt today knows that if they redeem their bond or cash in their T-bill, the government will pay for it by borrowing again.

So every dollar with which our government tries to save banks, create jobs, and keep interest rates low comes either through (a) inflation (new dollars that dilute the value of existing dollars) or (b) revolving debt.

The Government Bubble

Throughout the 1990s, we had the stock bubble and the dot-com bubble. The Fed replaced that with the housing bubble and the credit bubble. Now, the Fed and the administration are replacing those bubbles with the government bubble.

The Fed is creating money that banks are then lending to the Treasury to pay for ever-expanding government. The same artificially low interest rates that made it easy to buy a house in the last decade are making it easy for the government to borrow in this decade.

Of course, the government isn't borrowing for investment, it's borrowing for consumption. That means Uncle Sam is simply going deeper into debt, and the only way we're going to pay off our current loans is by borrowing again.

How do we get away with this? Why does anyone lend us money when they know we're only going to pay it back by borrowing, and that we're going to pay it back with dollars that are worth less than they are today?

We get away with it because the dollar is considered the "reserve currency" of the world. In other words, all major governments in the world hold dollars. Global commodities, like gold and oil, are typically priced in dollars.

As of 2010, 60 percent of foreign exchange reserves are in U.S. dollars. That means, as a foreign country, you're willing to take dollars because you know some other country will be willing to take dollars. That other country will take dollars because some third country will take dollars. If this sounds familiar, it's because we've seen it before.

In 1999, people were investing in dot-coms not because they thought these companies might make a profit, but because they thought someone else would be willing to buy the stock at an even higher price.

In 2006, people were buying houses not because they thought the house was worth that much, but because they thought they'd be able to flip it for more money to someone else.

This is only slightly different from a Ponzi scheme. It all depends on the existence of a greater fool. Eventually you run out of fools and the bubble pops.

When the dot-com bubble popped, companies evaporated and retirement accounts shrank. When the housing bubble popped, foreclosures ran rampant and credit dried up. When the government bubble pops, the consequences will be worse.

Government Spending Is the Opposite of Investment

Economists and politicians point to government spending as economic growth. After all, it counts in our GDP, right?

But our government spending doesn't actually create wealth, because it's not really investment. In fact, government spending often *destroys* wealth by allocating resources to unproductive sectors of the economy.

The government bubble inflates housing values, which are still being propped up by Fannie Mae, Freddie Mac, housing bailouts, artificially low interest rates, and other government policies.

Much government spending goes to government-favored technologies that do not add value to the economy, such as subsidized wind turbines or solar panels. Republicans and Democrats alike have increased subsidies for whatever they consider to be cutting-edge technology.

These subsidies create very narrow booms: some solar-panel maker gets rich, or some company that makes windows expands and adds another plant. Politicians point to these successes as proof that their subsidies help the economy.

But these subsidy-induced booms actually hurt the economy. The tax credits and handouts draw rational businessmen to invest in technologies that don't really add value. If these technologies were valuable, they wouldn't need subsidies in order to draw investment. Government turns these useless or inefficient technologies—like ethanol, or solar power—into profitable undertakings.

Every dollar invested in these unproductive activities is drawn away from something that people would value more—and that would be able to grow on their own. This makes us poorer, and it is unsustainable in the long run. When people get rich from making things that don't have real value, they are just reenacting the housing and dot-com bubbles by other means.

Since investment has a positive connotation, government likes to describe spending as investment. When it comes to transfer payments, at least the government is more honest. But spending that results from transfer payments comes at the expense of spending or investments that otherwise could have occurred. While diverting spending from those who earn money to those who receive benefits has adverse moral consequences, the economic consequences are far greater if the money diverted is money that otherwise would have been saved. Such transfers convert savings to consumption, undermining investment and stifling economic growth.

Hair of the Dog

You probably see by now how the 2008–2009 crisis was merely the overture to a coming crash. The collapse of housing prices, the downturn in the stock market, the tightening of credit, and rising unemployment all triggered a government reaction that caused a far worse sickness.

Why do the politicians do this? I think there are two reasons.

The first is that they mistake the cures I discussed above—falling prices, rising interest rates—for the disease. They don't realize that our economy was sick for years beforehand. They mistake our decade-long sickness for health.

The second reason is less about bad economics and more about good politics. Politicians refuse to allow the short-term pain that the cure entails. They're like a doctor who won't give a patient any bitter medicine, or like a rehab counselor who won't let the addict go through withdrawal.

The politicians might be behaving rationally—that is, acting in their own political interests. If people face higher interest rates, smaller 401(k)s, falling wages, or foreclosure, they get upset. Presidents, governors, and congressmen know they will get blamed.

So, like Enron executives trying to hide losses off the books so that shareholders are happy, Congress, the White House, and the Fed take short-term gain, even though the price is long-term pain.

Put another way: throughout the 1990s, the Federal Reserve created a stock bubble. To cover up for this downturn, Washington created a credit and housing bubble. When that popped, government started papering it over with a government bubble. What will we do when this bubble pops?

Thus we are pushed toward an awful decision.

When the Government Bubble Pops

"In the long run, we are all dead."

That was the foundation of John Maynard Keynes's economics. The idea is that you can keep blowing up bubble after bubble, regardless of the long-term consequences. Who cares about long-term consequences, as long as we can put them off until after we're in the grave, or in the case of a politician, until after the next election?

But the moment of crisis can be pushed off only so long. Imaginary wealth cannot indefinitely mask a weak economy. If you keep replacing one bubble with another, you eventually run out of suds. And the government bubble is the final bubble.

The bedrock of our bubble economy had always been the full faith and credit of the United States government. At some point, the lenders of the world begin to lose their faith in us, and that credit dries up.

Those who lend to the U.S. government these days don't expect that *tax* revenues will pay them back—they know they will get paid back with more borrowed funds. Once would-be creditors begin to see the risk in this Ponzi scheme, they'll start demanding a higher risk premium. In other words, Uncle Sam will need to pay higher interest rates on his Treasury Bonds.

Lenders will also be tired of getting repaid in dollars that are worth less than the dollars they loaned. In order to borrow again—and to be able to buy anything with dollars—the Fed will have to start swallowing up those extra dollars it created in its bouts of quantitative easing and bailouts.

Tightening money supply and higher interest rates on Treasuries will drive up interest rates across the economy.

Normally, rising interest rates aren't disastrous—they're a market response to a high demand for capital and low supply. In the early 1980s, the Fed raised interest rates, and there was pain, but it was not devastating. But back then we were the world's greatest creditor nation. Today we're the greatest debtor nation.

So this time around, companies, homeowners, and banks are so highly levered, as the numbers earlier in this chapter showed, that rising interest rates will be devastating.

Anyone with an adjustable-rate mortgage will see his monthly payments skyrocket. This will cause more foreclosures, triggering another collapse in the housing market. Higher mortgage payments will be even more problematic for those who lose their service sector jobs, which will vanish as rates rise.

The tidal wave will also hit the banks and hedge funds that have already returned to the pre-2008 game of risky bets and massive leverage. In fact, most of our banks are only "solvent" as a direct result of these extremely low rates. If rates merely return to historic norms, many of the banks we bailed out in 2008 will be wiped out again when the real crash comes, only this time around the losses will be even bigger.

As to the nightmare scenarios fabricated by the Bush administration officials selling the TARP—some of them will become reality this time around, because government will have made us so much more vulnerable.

Of course, the biggest debtor of us all, the Federal government, has the mother-of-all adjustable-rate mortgages. Most of the national debt is financed with short-term paper, much of it maturing in less then one year. Rising rates would send debt-service costs soaring, and at a time when the deficits themselves were rising due to the economic contraction that higher rates would surely produce.

And the federal government would have to spend less. This is a good thing, of course, but it will certainly impose short-term economic pain, especially on those whose benefits are cut. Many of our biggest companies—Boeing, General Electric—are government contractors. Many others depend on government spending, either through subsidies or government consumption.

When the biggest spender takes up an austerity budget, a lot less money gets spent. Initially, this will cause some companies to go under and unemployment to rise. Other companies will expand and new ones will form as resources formerly used to support government spending are freed up for more productive purposes. But this transition will take time to play out.

The Alternative: Devalue the Dollar

Instead of this scenario of excruciating tightening, politicians could opt to try to cover up reality one last time by pumping even more dollars into the economy.

Need to pay off the national debt? Fine, just print more money, and pay it off with that money.

Need to pay for unsustainable entitlements like Medicare and Social Security? Fine, just print more money, driving up nominal wages and thus tax revenue. Of course, the real value of these benefits would collapse, but maybe politicians could maintain a pretense of keeping up benefits.

Some politicians might prefer this route, because it could deflect some blame: they could blame businesses and service providers for raising prices (even though the price hikes would be a necessary and natural response to inflation). For example in 2011, as oil prices rose as a result of the inflation created by the Fed, Ben Bernanke and President Obama blamed the rise on oil speculators, and commissions were convened to investigate the wrongdoing.

But this path leads to hyperinflation, which will be even more economically destructive for the average American. Anyone on a fixed income would starve. Price and wage unpredictability would cause chaos even more harmful than what would result from soaring interest rates.

Devastation as the Cure

While tightening the money supply, raising interest rates, and slashing of government services and spending will cause immense economic pain, it will be the right thing to do.

With high interest rates and tight credit, borrowing will slow down. Slowly, people will start to pay down their debt. High interest rates will also incentivize savings. Those savings will eventually become investment capital—the foundation for new enterprises. A shrinking government, of course, will open up the economic playing field for market actors, who will invest in what's promising rather than what's politically favored.

The process will simply be the delayed—and more painful—cure that should have come in 2001 or 2008. It will be the crash we should have had in 2002 or 2009, but it will be worse, because the imbalances are now greater as a result of the extra debt the government has accrued for itself and induced in financial institutions and individuals.

There will be plenty of politicians who call on government to avoid the painful tightening and cutting, and when people like me say, "bring on the pain," we'll be called heartless, just as we were heartless to oppose bailouts in 2008.

But pain will come one way or another, either through contraction or through hyperinflation. The difference is that tightening money supply and rising interest rates will be productive pain—like medicine—while hyperinflation will be destructive pain.

As a nation, we're going to have to accept a lower standard of living than we may be accustomed to enjoying. For one thing, with tighter credit and tighter monetary policy, it will be harder to live beyond our means. Along the same lines, the United States will no longer be able to consume more than we produce—we will have to start making things, too. In other words, we'll lose that credit card that we were never paying off.

But for the short term, things will be even worse. The economy will need to regain balance, and this will involve plenty of displacement.

People working in bubble industries—solar panels, banking, real estate, and government—will lose their jobs and need to find new ones. This is not a painless process.

Most costly might be the loss of our role as the issuer of the reserve currency of the world. Most people don't understand the value of the United States dollar being the reserve currency. It's what allows us to buy things without really paying for them. Once we lose that status, the free ride ends. The dollar will dramatically lose its value vis-à-vis other currencies, and it will become more expensive for us to buy things.

But for many people, especially in the long run, the crash and what follows will be beneficial. For one thing, this crash might finally bring about tax cuts. Government will be forced to shrink, thus freeing up more space in the economy for entrepreneurs. Maybe when the debt is paid down, we can keep government small. Also, those who have saved, and who have low debt and hard assets, such as farmland, gold, or natural resources, will benefit from a contracted money supply. The contraction will clean out the malinvestment and government bloat, sort of like the Old Testament flood cleansing the world's iniquity. When the floodwater recedes, there will be an opportunity for a sensible economy to take root. As long as we don't just repeat the mistakes that brought on the flood in the first place.

2

How We Got Here:
Government Is the Problem

THE FINANCIAL CRISIS OF 2008 was a nail in the coffin of capitalism, we're told.

Journalists and politicians agreed that "unfettered free markets" caused the crash and the ensuing suffering. This became an excuse for more laws and regulations, meaning more power for politicians, bureaucrats, and central bankers. Regulation, we were told, would make the economy safe. And when the real crash comes in the near future, those same politicians will once again blame capitalism and a lack of regulation.

In truth, big government played a central role in blowing the bubbles and is chiefly responsible for the resulting misallocation of resources. On the other hand, too many conservatives and proponents of limited government come up with overly simplistic explanations. They pick on a couple of liberal big-government programs that distorted the mortgage market. We need to understand that many of the bubble-making programs and institutions were touted not on the terms of equality or regulation, but as "pro-growth" policies creating an "ownership society." At the heart of these "pro-business" bubble machines is the Federal Reserve.

So, as we stand in the shadow of the 2008 downturn and on the precipice of an even greater crash that could be worse than the Great Depression, it's crucial to recount the steps that brought us to this point. Most of this book will be forward-looking, laying out solutions to our problems, but first, let's study how we got here.

The Fed: The Central Problem

You cannot speak intelligently about the root causes of the 2008 crash—or about our current instability—without speaking about the Federal Reserve System of the United States (the Fed).

The Fed sets interest rates. It controls the money supply. It is effectively the main lender to the United States Government and the lender of last resort to the banks. It is the core of the Bush-Obama bailout machine. The Fed has always been quietly at the heart of the economy's ups and downs, but since bailout mania began in March 2008 with the Fed's bailout of Bear Stearns, there's no ignoring it anymore.

And if you study all the facts, there's also no ignoring that the Fed, rather than the agent of stability it was supposed to be, is an inflation machine and a facilitator of big government, creating bubbles, causing waste, and now, setting us up for an economic downturn that could be worse than the Great Depression.

So if we are to trace the recent economic troubles back to their roots, we need to start in 1913 with the creation of the Fed.

The original intention of the Fed was something I might have supported, had I been around back then. In theory, it was an agent of stability that could also promote economic growth.

Before 1913, banks were, in effect, issuing their own currencies. To put it simplistically, banks would issue bank notes that were backed by assets, such as gold, and by the banks' loan portfolios. The bank notes were perfectly transferable, and so you could pay someone with a bank note, and that person would know he could redeem the note for gold at the issuing bank.

But banks, of course, could only issue bank notes against their own assets. As a result, each bank was effectively issuing its own currency. While Bank A could honor the notes from Bank B, this required some coordination and trust. If you traveled to California, your bank note from Connecticut might not be honored by other merchants or the California banks.

It was natural, then, for bankers to hatch an idea of a "banks' bank." Banks could deposit some of their assets—commercial paper or gold— with the Fed, and the Fed in return would issue its own bank notes to the individual bank. (Look at the top of your dollars today, and you'll see the words "Federal Reserve Note.")

The Fed, as it does today, controlled how much currency was in circulation, but back then, it operated within constraints, and without such ambitious goals. To begin with, the Fed couldn't issue indefinite currency as it does today; each Federal Reserve Note was backed 40 percent by gold and 100 percent by commercial paper (loans from other banks), meaning the Fed was limited in how much currency it could issue.

Just as important, the Fed wasn't trying to carry out a delicate balancing game between unemployment and interest rates—it was simply trying to match the supply of money to the demand for money. When the economy was expanding and there was more to invest in and spend money on, the Fed would pump in dollars. When there was less demand for money, the Fed would take dollars out of the economy. The architects of the Fed referred to this as an "elastic money supply." The Fed would increase the money supply as the economy expanded, and then reduce the money supply as the economy contracted.

Today, the Fed increases the money supply when the economy grows, then expands it even faster as it contracts. Not only is this the exact opposite of what it was intended to do, but had such a harebrained scheme been proposed in the beginning, the Federal Reserve never would have seen the light of day.

The role of a central bank is limited: to control the currency so as to keep prices and interest rates fairly stable. Job creation and economic growth were not part of the Fed's original mandate. Saving failed banks was certainly not part of the job. And the Fed's main role today—propping up government spending with money made out of thin air—was certainly not part of the original pitch, because the Fed was at first prohibited from buying government debt.

This sort of central bank is one I could have supported. But the Federal Reserve Bank of the United States never functioned this way, and it probably was never meant to. For the same reason one should never allow the camel to get its nose under the tent, we never should have trusted the Fed to respect its boundaries.

Fighting a War with Imaginary Money

Wars involve huge new costs to government. Governments can cover these wartime costs with cuts to domestic spending. They can also raise taxes, calling on a sense of common sacrifice. As a third option, governments can borrow, selling "war bonds" to investors.

Woodrow Wilson, when he thrust the U.S. into World War I, did all of the above, but he also had a novel way of financing the fight: selling bonds to the Fed. This would have violated the Fed's original charter, but wars and other crises give presidents hefty political capital. Wilson got Congress to change the law, and suddenly, the U.S. government had its own magic piggy bank.

Let's pause for a second to discuss just what happens when the Fed buys U.S. bonds. On one level, it's like any other sale: the Fed gets bonds, and the Treasury gets money. The difference is that the Fed doesn't have any less money than before it paid for the bonds. You see, the Fed "pays" a bank by crediting that bank's account at the Federal Reserve. There's no balance from which the Fed deducts that money. It comes out of thin air. The dollars aren't even printed. They exist only as numbers on a piece of paper or in a computer database.

Put another way: when the Fed buys $1 million in bonds, there is simply another $1 million in circulation. If the Fed sells $1 million in bonds, $1 million ceases to exist.

So, the Fed spent World War I lending to the government, and increasing the monetary supply.

However, to maintain some semblance of discipline, the Fed was not allowed to loan directly to the government. Instead it was given the ability to buy government bonds on the open market, or accept them as collateral for its notes. This little gimmick has merely acted to enrich the brokers acting on the Fed's behalf.

On a related note, the same year that Congress amended the Federal Reserve Act to allow the Fed to hold Treasuries, as part of the Liberty Bond Act, it imposed for the first time a national debt ceiling (the one modern politicians always use as an excuse to feign outrage about fiscal irresponsibility just before they vote to raise it). It seems that Congress at least saw the potential threat that such an unholy alliance of politicians and central bankers represented and tried to impose a safeguard to protect taxpayers. The problem is that the initial debt ceiling of $11.5 billion has been raised every time it has been approached. A movable ceiling is tantamount to no ceiling at all.

Popping the War Bubble

The war ended in 1919, and in 1921, Warren Harding replaced Woodrow Wilson in the White House. We were about to witness one of the United States' last bouts of monetary and fiscal sanity.

The end of World War I brought a recession. In 1920, as soldiers and sailors came home from war, 1.6 million people entered the labor force, at that point the largest single-year leap ever. Naturally, this drove up unemployment and drove down wages.

From January 1920 to August 1921, the Dow fell from 119.6 to 63.9—a massive 47 percent drop. Unemployment skyrocketed. Government economist Stanley Lebergott puts 1919 (wartime) unemployment at 1.9 percent, rising to 5.2 percent after the war in 1920, and 11.7 percent in the worst of the mini-depression in 1921. (Christina Romer calculates a more modest rise, from 3 percent in 1919 to 8.7 percent in 1921.)[1]

Companies had to adjust from a wartime economy to a peacetime economy. During this adjustment period, hiring was slow. In short, the economy was undergoing a dramatic shift, and there were growing pains.

Warren Harding addressed the unemployment and lack of growth with a response America would never see again. "We will attempt intelligent and courageous deflation," he said at the 1920 Republican Convention, "and strike at government borrowing which enlarges the evil."

The rest of the passage is astounding to the modern ear:

> We promise that relief which will attend the halting of waste and extravagance, and the renewal of the practice of public economy, not alone because it will relieve tax burdens but because it will be an example to stimulate thrift and economy in private life.
>
> Let us call to all the people for thrift and economy, for denial and sacrifice if need be, for a nationwide drive against extravagance and luxury, to a recommitment to simplicity of living, to that prudent and normal plan of life which is the health of the republic. There hasn't been a recovery from the waste and abnormalities of war since the story of mankind was first written, except through work and saving, through industry and denial,

while needless spending and heedless extravagance have marked
every decay in the history of nations.[2]

So Harding paid off the war bonds, slashing the national debt by one
third. Those dollars used to pay off debt held by the Fed just disappeared.
There were fewer dollars circulating in the economy.

Decreasing the money supply put a downward pressure on prices. With
the Fed no longer spurring lending through demand for bonds, there was
a shrinking supply of money for those who wanted to borrow, resulting in
higher interest rates.

This was part of the cure, in Harding's eyes. Higher interest rates meant
less borrowing and more saving. It was the "industry and denial" necessary
for "recovery from the waste and abnormalities of war."

Scholar Thomas Woods writes:

> The Federal Reserve's activity, moreover, was hardly noticeable.
> As one economic historian puts it, "Despite the severity of the
> contraction, the Fed did not move to use its powers to turn the
> money supply around and fight the contraction." By the late sum-
> mer of 1921, signs of recovery were already visible. The following
> year, unemployment was back down [from 11.7 percent in 1921]
> to 6.7 percent and it was only 2.4 percent by 1923.

Woods's point is that the Fed didn't aim for "countercyclical" policy as
it does today—injecting more liquidity when the demand for money is
down. Instead of trying to fix the lagging economy through stimulus, the
Fed responded to the economic contraction with monetary contraction.

Compare the 1920–21 depression to the Great Depression. From 1920 to
1921, the stock market dropped 47 percent, and unemployment doubled.

Harding and his Fed let the fever do its work, and soon the patient
(the economy) was much better. Woods mentioned the employment recovery; by the end of 1922, the Dow was back above 100. In the eyes of
Keynesian economists, this was a weird fluke. Woods quotes Keynesian
Robert Gordon:

> [G]overnment policy to moderate the depression and speed re-
> covery was minimal. The Federal Reserve authorities were largely

passive, and despite the absence of government stimulus, the recovery was not long delayed.[3]

In fact, it wasn't despite the absence of government stimulus that the
economy recovered so quickly, but because of its absence! This would be
just about the last time the Fed would behave with such restraint and such
wisdom.

Inflation Through the 1920s

After World War I, Britain's economy was a bit of a basket case. The Federal Reserve Bank of the United States decided to help. Alan Greenspan,
in a 1966 essay, wrote about this "disastrous . . . attempt to assist Great
Britain who had been losing gold to us because the Bank of England refused to allow interest rates to rise when market forces dictated (it was
politically unpalatable)."

Greenspan wrote:

> The reasoning of the authorities involved was as follows: if the
> Federal Reserve pumped excessive paper reserves into American
> banks, interest rates in the United States would fall to a level
> comparable with those in Great Britain; this would act to stop
> Britain's gold loss and avoid the political embarrassment of hav-
> ing to raise interest rates. The "Fed" succeeded; it stopped the
> gold loss, but it nearly destroyed the economies of the world, in
> the process. The excess credit which the Fed pumped into the
> economy spilled over into the stock market—triggering a fantas-
> tic speculative boom.

From mid-1921 to mid-1929, the Fed increased the money supply by 55
percent.[4] This extra money was the air that filled the stock and real estate
bubbles.

In official versions of history, the Fed and Herbert Hoover are blamed
for not doing enough to save the economy. But the official spin amounts to
revisionist history at best, and outright propaganda at worst. Either way,
this misunderstanding of history has formed the basis for a litany of policy

mistakes that have led us to the dire predicament we find ourselves in today.

Hoover's New Deal

You've probably been taught that Herbert Hoover was a laissez-faire ideologue. The opposite is true.

Historian Benjamin Anderson describes Hoover's reaction to the 1929 crash as being "Hoover's New Deal." Here's how Hoover spoke of his efforts, during his reelection bid in 1932, as quoted in Murray Rothbard's excellent history of the Great Depression:

> We might have done nothing. That would have been utter ruin. Instead we met the situation with proposals to private business and to Congress of the most gigantic program of economic defense and counterattack ever evolved in the history of the Republic. We put it into action . . . No government in Washington has hitherto considered that it held so broad a responsibility for leadership in such times. . . . For the first time in the history of depression, dividends, profits, and the cost of living, have been reduced before wages have suffered. . . . They were maintained until the cost of living had decreased and the profits had practically vanished. They are now the highest real wages in the world.
>
> Creating new jobs and giving to the whole system a new breath of life; nothing has ever been devised in our history which has done more for . . . "the common run of men and women." Some of the reactionary economists urged that we should allow the liquidation to take its course until we had found bottom. . . . We determined that we would not follow the advice of the bitter-end liquidationists and see the whole body of debtors of the United States brought to bankruptcy and the savings of our people brought to destruction.[5]

As Commerce Secretary, Hoover and his allies in industry pushed laws to keep wages high and work hours short. They called for housing subsidies.

The main reason unemployment rose so high was Hoover's insistence that wages not be reduced. Instead of lowering wages in line with falling prices, companies laid off workers. So we maintained high wages in name only, as few people were actually employed and earning them. Keeping wages artificially high, while other prices collapsed, meant that real wages were rising. This greatly reduced the demand for labor, causing the big spike in unemployment.

Once in the White House, Hoover intervened aggressively. He brought together leading industrialists, and won from them pledges to slow the drop in wages and to undertake new building projects.

Blaming the Fed for contracting the money supply, and thus causing destructive deflation, is also wrong. Hoover's Fed actually boosted the money supply by 10 percent in the two weeks following the 1929 crash. Repeatedly throughout Hoover's term, the Fed created more money. But the money supply fell because people began hoarding cash, and banks stopped lending out their money.

In other words, the money supply shrank despite the Fed's interventions, not because of its inaction.

The truth is that had Hoover not acted so boldly, but instead followed the advice of his own secretary of the treasury Andrew Mellon (perhaps the last time a secretary of the treasury gave any good advice) and Harding's example from the depression of 1920, the Great Depression would not have been so great. In fact, had Hoover simply allowed the free market to function, the recovery would have been so strong that he likely would have been elected to a second term, and Teddy would have been the last Roosevelt to occupy the White House. Instead he handed the Keynesian baton to Franklin Delano Roosevelt, who carried it for an unprecedented four terms in office. Hoover may have helped cause the Depression, but it was Roosevelt, expanding on Hoover's failed approach, who made it great.

Sound familiar?

Despite the facts, the official lesson of the Great Depression was that government needs to play a bigger role in battling downturns, and the Fed needs to pump in cash to jump-start the economy. This bad lesson stays with us today, and beginning in the early 1990s, this way of thinking started the cycle of bubbles that put us where we are now.

The Creation of the Dot-Com Bubble

During the 1990s, every time there was an economic problem—like the "Asian Contagion," the Russian debt default, the collapse of Long-Term Capital Management, the Orange County default, or worries about Y2K—the Fed stepped in with more cheap money, in an effort to postpone any kind of correction.

A look at money supply data is striking. In April 1995, there was barely more than $3.5 trillion in circulation, counting all currency and bank accounts (this number is known as M2). In the next eleven years, the money supply would double. By the middle of 2011, we were pushing $9 trillion in money supply.

When the big pump began in mid-1995, this new money had to find a place to go. The Fed was keeping interest rates artificially low, thus discouraging savings.

So the new money went into the stock market. The average close of the Dow Jones Industrial Average in May 1995 was under 4,500. Four years later, it was above 11,000. Most notoriously, the money poured into dot-com stocks. The Nasdaq, the epicenter of the dot-com boom, began in 1996 at 1033. In March 2000, the Nasdaq broke 5,000.

Many liberal economists and Fed defenders will argue that the Fed didn't create the stock market and dot-com bubble of the late 1990s. They blame "greed" and "manias." There's a small degree to which they are right: the Fed did not specifically steer capital toward dot-com stocks. The Fed just created the excess capital that needed a home, and market forces and other government policies determined where that money went.

It's worth addressing this excuse by Fed defenders, because it will pop up again. So let's be precise here: It's not quite correct to say the Fed caused the dot-com bubble. It's also not completely incorrect to blame groupthink, a dot-com mania, and greed for the bubble.

But greed, groupthink, and bad ideas always exist. The Fed's creation of excess capital and artificially low interest rates empower greed and bad ideas, which have always been present since the beginning of history, to turn into destructive bubbles.

By 1999, the ongoing inflation (increase in the money supply) led to noticeable price increases. From December 1998 until December 2000, the

Consumer Price Index (CPI) rose by 6.8 percent (3.4 percent annually). And the CPI doesn't totally reflect higher costs of living. Gasoline prices rose about 50 percent in eighteen months around then.

The Fed began to worry that its loose money was about to spur runaway inflation. In response, the central bank began raising interest rates. We're not talking drastic rate hikes—just a few quarter-point increases in the target fed funds rate. Greenspan boosted this rate from 4.75 percent on June 29, 1999, to 6.5 percent on May 16, 2000.

This sort of interest-rate boost might not sound like much, but when an economy is so levered—the price-to-earnings ratio of the S&P 500 was 46:1 at one point in 2001—slightly more-expensive credit can evaporate profits for hedge funds and investment banks.

Before the 2000–2001 downturn, everyone had been living as if the good times would never end. Dot-com companies invested in buildings, their employees invested in expensive houses, and their executives invested in yachts. Cities and states that saw booms in tax revenue also started spending like the boom would never end—government employees got raises, new entitlement programs and new spending initiatives were created.

So when interest rates went up, it wasn't just a slowdown. People, businesses, and governments had become addicted to the boom. Without the boom, they crashed.

We shouldn't overstate what happened a decade ago. The result of Greenspan's interest-rate increases in 1999 and 2000 was just a brief economic contraction. The recession was neither long nor deep, but it sparked a chorus of criticism of Greenspan. According to facile commentary from politicians and pundits, raising interest rates impoverished an economy that had been benefiting from loose money.

So Greenspan learned his lesson: never tighten; always loosen; the problem isn't the bubble, it's the popping of the bubble; in the long run, we're all dead.

And that was a fatal mistake. The bursting of a bubble is bad politics, but it's great economics. Bubbles have to burst, and the sooner they do, the less damage they create. The mistakes—malinvesments, as Ludwig von Mises referred to them—are made during the *booms*. During the Internet mania, we made some doozies. It's during the *busts* when those mistakes are corrected. A severe correction, in proportion to the mania that preceded it, was just what the economic doctor ordered. Instead, Witch Doctor Greenspan conjured up a housing bubble.

As I wrote in *Crash Proof* in 2006, the dot-com bubble was just the warm-up act. The real estate bubble would be the main event. All the same themes would resurface, with some different characters, and much larger consequences.

Replacing the Dot-com Bubble with a Housing Bubble

Alan Greenspan wasn't the only one in 2001 who thought we needed people to spend more money. At this time, President Bush gave his "go out and shop" exhortation. The only question was, how to get people to hit the malls? The answer was cheap money and low interest rates that encourage indebtedness and discourage savings. Thus began the Federal Reserve policy of perpetually cheap money—continued inflation of the money supply and near-zero interest rates. This wasn't prudent economically, but it was politically prudent for Greenspan. So the Fed brought the rate down to 1.0 percent by the middle of 2003.

The money supply continued to grow unabated, and so, once again, we had excess money and a disincentive to save. The stock market again swallowed much of that, and stock prices again began to rise. However, this time around, the real action was in real estate. To be more precise, the housing bubble didn't start after the brief 2001 recession. It actually started during the dot-com bubble. But back in the 1990s, the housing bubble played second fiddle. When the brief recession came, prices never fell. When the recession ended, housing became the prime place for excess speculation and paper wealth.

The Case-Shiller Indices are the preeminent measures of home prices. The Case-Shiller national index has been calibrated so that home prices in the first quarter of 2000 are set at 100—a point when home values were already rising at an accelerated rate. From there, it skyrocketed.

From 1997 through 2004, housing prices doubled, according to the national Case-Shiller index. After 2004, they would increase another 10 percent until the peak came in the middle of 2006. All told, from 1997 to 2006, Case-Shiller rose from 80 to 190, with most of that rise occurring after 2002.

Krugman: We Need a Housing Bubble

Don't think this was an accident. Nobody at the Fed publicly said, "we're going to cause a housing bubble," but other economists were urging capital toward that sector. Most notably, the *New York Times* columnist Paul Krugman, the leading voice of Keynesians, kept pushing Greenspan to cut rates even faster, citing a housing boom as one of the virtues.

Mark Thornton at the Ludwig Von Mises Institute has collected some Krugman quotes from early last decade.

"[L]ow interest rates act through several channels," Krugman said in one May 2001 interview. "For instance, more housing is built, which expands the building sector. You must ask the opposite question: why in the world shouldn't you lower interest rates?"

In July 2001, Krugman told Lou Dobbs, "I think frankly it's got to be—business investment is not going to be the driving force in this recovery. It has to come from things like housing."

The next month, talking to Dobbs again, Krugman said: "I'm a little depressed. You know, inventories, probably that's over, the inventory slump. But you look at the things that could drive a recovery, business investment, nothing happening. Housing, long-term rates haven't fallen enough to produce a boom there."

A week later, Krugman gave a more direct (if more long-winded) argument for Fed policy to drive up housing prices:

> Consumers, who already have low savings and high debt, probably can't contribute much. But housing, which is highly sensitive to interest rates, could help lead a recovery. . . . But there has been a peculiar disconnect between Fed policy and the financial variables that affect housing and trade. Housing demand depends on long-term rather than short-term interest rates—and though the Fed has cut short rates from 6.5 to 3.75 percent since the beginning of the year, the 10-year rate is slightly higher than it was on Jan. 1. . . . Sooner or later, of course, investors will realize that 2001 isn't 1998. When they do, mortgage rates and the dollar will come way down, and the conditions for a recovery led by housing and exports will be in place.

In October 2001, Krugman said, "economic policy should encourage other spending to offset the temporary slump in business investment. Low interest rates, which promote spending on housing and other durable goods, are the main answer."

After months of calling for inflation of housing prices, Krugman in 2002 came right out and said the Fed needed to create a housing *bubble*. Since 2007, Krugman has repeatedly and angrily denied that was what he was saying, so let me run his comments in their full context:

> A few months ago the vast majority of business economists mocked concerns about a "double dip," a second leg to the downturn. But there were a few dogged iconoclasts out there, most notably Stephen Roach at Morgan Stanley. As I've repeatedly said in this column, the arguments of the double-dippers made a lot of sense. And their story now looks more plausible than ever.
>
> The basic point is that the recession of 2001 wasn't a typical postwar slump, brought on when an inflation-fighting Fed raises interest rates and easily ended by a snapback in housing and consumer spending when the Fed brings rates back down again. This was a prewar-style recession, a morning after brought on by irrational exuberance. To fight this recession the Fed needs more than a snapback; it needs soaring household spending to offset moribund business investment. And to do that, as Paul McCulley of Pimco put it, Alan Greenspan needs to create a housing bubble to replace the Nasdaq bubble.[6]

Well, Krugman got exactly what he wanted. To his credit, at least he understood the initial effects that Fed policy would have on housing prices and consumer spending, even if he failed to comprehend the ultimate consequences. However, it's very disingenuous for him to deny his past statements and even more shocking for academia not to hold him accountable. In fact, if it were possible to lose a Nobel Prize on the grounds of economic idiocy, Krugman's housing bubble advocacy would be hard to beat.

Why Housing?

We should note, again, that the Fed didn't necessarily drive excess investment specifically into the housing market. The Fed merely created the excess capital that then went in search of somewhere to go.

So, why a housing bubble, and why not, say, a car bubble or a tulip bubble?

Some of it was just market forces. Crime was on the way down, and rich people were moving back into cities, driving up center-city prices. But much of it was government policy.

Politicians in both parties decided that government should promote homeownership. Democrats focused on helping poor people own homes by making mortgages easier to get. Republicans spoke of an "ownership society" that would promote personal responsibility.

Bankers and Realtors, two of the most powerful interest groups in Washington, both agreed, and they helpfully pointed out ways the government could subsidize mortgages.

The biggest subsidy for buying a home is the tax deduction for mortgage interest. If you rent your home, none of your rent is deductible. If you buy your home outright, your costs are not tax deductible. But if you borrow in order to buy your house, all of the mortgage interest—which is a majority of the monthly payment for many homeowners—is tax deductible.

This is the single biggest tax break most people get, and it's a huge reason to buy a home—especially one that costs a lot. If you borrow $250,000 for a 30-year mortgage at 6 percent, your monthly payments will be about $1,500. About $1,250 of that is interest. In the first year, you'd pay almost $15,000 in interest, and thus be able to reduce your taxable income by $15,000. In seven years, you will have paid $100,000 in interest, saving at least $25,000 on taxes.

Also, you can deduct the interest on your second home. The only limit is that you can only deduct the interest on $1 million worth of mortgage.

This is a huge mortgage subsidy. Even though it's just a tax deduction, it's still a subsidy, because it distorts the market in favor of homeownership (more precisely, leveraged homeownership).

Another reason the mortgage deduction counts as a subsidy: other taxpayers pay for it, at least indirectly. According to official estimates, the deduction reduces federal revenue by about $100 billion per year. Total revenue from individual income taxes is just above $1 trillion. So, if Congress abolished this deduction, and instead lowered all tax rates across the board, we could cut everyone's taxes by nearly 10 percent.

Put another way, almost 10 percent of your tax dollars go to benefit leveraged homeownership by Americans.

Even if you're one of those homeowners getting the deduction, there's a chance you're still losing out on net. It's important to remember that subsidizing something doesn't just benefit the people buying it. In fact, it often benefits the sellers more.

In the case of mortgage subsidies, there are plenty of "sellers" who benefit. A drop in the monthly cost of owning a home also drives up the price of buying a home. After all, you're not the only one with access to the mortgage-interest deduction. The deduction boosts demand, thus boosting price.

As a result of the home-mortgage deduction, homebuyers end up paying more for their homes. So while they get to deduct their interest payments, those payments are much higher due to the price effects of the deduction. Take away the excess demand generated by the deduction and home prices would fall. True, mortgage interest would no longer be deductible, but the payments would be much lower. Most homebuyers would be better off without the deduction.

The real beneficiary of the deduction is the seller, who sells his house at an inflated price. Of course, if he uses the proceeds to trade up to an even larger house, he loses out as well. The winners are those who sell and rent or who trade down to less expensive houses, and professional homebuilders, who sell houses for a living.

Realtors also profit. Greater demand for buying a home means more homes bought, meaning *more* commissions. Also, higher demand means higher home prices, meaning *higher* commissions.

Lenders profit as well from the home-mortgage interest deduction, which encourages people not only to buy, and thus take out mortgages, but also to take out bigger mortgages than they otherwise would.

The combined influence of Realtors and lenders ensured the home-mortgage interest deduction. The story of the deduction goes back to 1913, when the income tax was created. All interest—including personal loans and business borrowing—was tax deductible. After credit cards be-

came ubiquitous in the 1980s, Congress ended this deduction, but thanks
to the lobbying of the Realtors and mortgage lenders, mortgage interest
was spared, and it remained deductible.

It's probably significant that the National Association of Realtors has
been the single most generous political action committee (PAC) in terms
of donations to federal candidates in every election since at least 2000.
Since 2000, the Realtors PAC has spent $60 million, with $26.5 million of
that going directly to candidates, according to the Center for Responsive
Politics.

Homeownership gets other special tax breaks, and one big one drives
the idea of a home as an investment: the capital gains exclusion. Most investments you might make—say, you start a business, or invest in stock—
are subject to capital gains taxes when you sell and make money. Your home,
however, is not. If you live in your home for two years, you can sell it and
earn up to $500,000 in profit before paying a dime in capital gains taxes.
This is another huge subsidy to homeowners as compared to other investments. It encouraged serial home flipping during the bubble years.

Fannie and Freddie: "One of the Great Success Stories of All Time"

The greatest drivers of the housing bubble, after the Federal Reserve, were
the government-sponsored enterprises (GSEs) Fannie Mae and Freddie
Mac, which were supposed to make housing more affordable, but which
ended up creating a housing bubble instead.

In 2004, if you asked the average Washington politician about Fannie
and Freddie, you would have been told that these GSEs were sound, essential, and independent of government. In 2007, as the housing and
mortgage crisis became apparent, that same politician said that Fannie
and Freddie were doing just fine, and they wouldn't need a bailout. Come
late 2008, those very same politicians were crying that taxpayers needed
to bail out both.

I saw this all up close, because the man whose Senate seat I sought in
2010 was one of the biggest shills for Fannie and Freddie—Democrat Chris
Dodd of Connecticut. (The single biggest shill was probably Representative Barney Frank of Massachusetts). In 2004, when Alan Greenspan came

before the Senate Banking Committee, the issue of the GSEs came up. Dodd said of them, "I, just briefly will say, Mr. Chairman, obviously, like most of us here, this is one of the great success stories of all time." In July 2008, after *The New York Times* reported that the federal government might have to take over Fannie and Freddie, the stocks of both GSEs fell nearly 50 percent in a week.

Dodd chastised the sellers and those of us saying Fannie and Freddie were bankrupt. "There is no reason for the kind of reaction we're getting. These fundamentals are sound. These institutions are sound. They have adequate capital. They have access to that capital. And this is a reason for people to have confidence in these GSEs—in Fannie and Freddie." In the end, Fannie and Freddie collapsed, and rather than let them fail, the government bailed them out and took them over.

I focus on Dodd mostly because he was my senator. I wanted to run against him, but he declined to seek reelection. It really is too bad, because his opponents could have made some great campaign ads by playing clips of Dodd talking up housing and Fannie Mae, swearing there was no collapse coming. Of course, no one could have exploited this weakness better than I, as I not only predicted Fannie and Freddie's bankruptcy in my book *Crash Proof*, but I did so on television just as Dodd was declaring their solvency. Unfortunately, I never made it past the primary.

But Dodd is not the main point here. We need to spend a few pages talking about Fannie and Freddie, because other than the Federal Reserve, they are the biggest culprits in the housing bubble. When we see just how the two GSEs fueled the housing bubble, government's guilt in this most recent downturn becomes undeniable.

Fannie Mae and Freddie Mac, Bubble Machines

When you think of the 2008–2009 economic crisis, some words might come to mind: mortgage-backed securities, housing bubble, subprime mortgages, cronyism, moral hazard, derivatives.

When you think of these words, you should think of Fannie Mae and Freddie Mac.

Franklin Roosevelt created the Federal National Mortgage Association during the Great Depression in order to stimulate home buying ("FNMA" became "Fannie Mae"). In 1968, Congress privatized Fannie, and a couple of years later, created a competing agency, the Federal Home Loan Mortgage Corporation, or Freddie Mac.

These agencies buy mortgages from lenders. You can imagine how this opens up the mortgage market. Without someone buying up mortgages, a bank is limited in how many loans it can make—after all, even with fractional reserve banking and loose reserve requirements, your loans still need to be backed up by some amount of assets.

But once you have Fannie and Freddie buying mortgages, there's no limit. Bank of America can lend money to a homebuyer and then sell the mortgage to Fannie. Bank of America now has its cash back and can lend it out again—a loan the bank will then off-load.

Now, there's nothing wrong with mortgage securitization in itself—it's a financial innovation which is a bit risky, but that's what finance is about. The problem with Fannie and Freddie is that they knew that while their profits were real—and huge—their risk was not real. More precisely, the politically connected bigwigs who ran the halls at these GSEs knew that if their companies ever lost money, the taxpayers would bail them out.

This government guarantee was not explicit, but implicit. Of course, Fannie's biggest boosters denied there was any guarantee. Barney Frank, in 2003, famously said: "There is no guarantee. There's no explicit guarantee. There's no implicit guarantee. There's no wink-and-nod guarantee. Invest and you're on your own. Nobody who invests in them should come looking to me for a nickel. Nor anyone else in the federal government."

Fannie Mae officials also fiercely denied that they enjoyed any subsidy. But they did. Fannie Mae was able to borrow at lower interest rates because lenders realized that taxpayers would bail them out. Near-zero borrowing costs had two detrimental effects. First, it allowed Fannie and Freddie to buy up massive amounts of mortgages, and to buy up riskier mortgages. If Fannie or Freddie were willing to buy a loan, there was no reason not to issue it.

A second detrimental effect: it was impossible for anyone to compete with these GSEs. Nobody could approach Fannie and Freddie on operating costs, and so nobody could operate on such slim margins. That meant that there were only two players in the secondary mortgage market. This provided even more incentive, come the meltdown, for Congress and the Fed to bail out these entities.

So the net effect of Fannie and Freddie was to drive down lending standards and interest rates. Had there been no government-subsidized secondary mortgage market, mortgages would have been harder for banks to sell, and so lending standards and interest rates would have been higher.

This was exactly the point. Fannie was in "The American Dream Business," they would say. Their job was get people to buy homes they otherwise wouldn't buy, and to make *everyone* pay more.

Some like to point out that subprime loans were the real problem, and that Fannie and Freddie did not guarantee subprime loans. While that is technically true, they were the biggest buyers of these loans in the secondary market. In fact, without their lavish appetites, far fewer subprime loans would have been originated. Not only did their demand help fuel originations, but it helped legitimize the investment merit of the securities.

However, in a nod to Fannie and Freddie defenders I will acknowledge that the primary culprit behind subprime was the Fed. Without ultralow short-term interest rates, the low teaser rates that made subprime loans initially "affordable" never would have existed. In addition, ultralow interest rates and the excess trade deficits they fueled drove global demand for higher-yielding dollar assets. Because the private sector originated subprime loans without any official government backing, many like to blame capitalism, or more specifically Wall Street greed, for the problem. But take the Fed and Fannie and Freddie out of the picture, and subprime would have been a trivial part of the mortgage market.

Other Bubble Factors

Fannie Mae and Freddie Mac were the most important players in driving the Fed's excess capital into housing, but other policies helped, too. The Community Reinvestment Act (CRA) was one.

The CRA has changed plenty over its thirty years, but the general thrust was always the same: it empowered federal regulators to pressure banks to make more loans to low-income people.

George W. Bush pushed his "ownership society," too. Bush spoke at a black church in Atlanta in 2002 about "the American Dream," meaning homeownership. The president named some of the new homeowners he had just met and said, "what we've got to do is to figure out how to make sure these stories are repeated over and over and over again in America."

To this end, he proposed the American Dream Downpayment Initiative (ADDI); also, American Dream Downpayment Assistance Act to help folks buy homes even if they couldn't afford the down payments. The law, passed in 2003, provided grants of up to $10,000 to cover down payment, closing costs, and some home repair for first-time homebuyers of below-average means.

Of course, the tax preferences mentioned above drove the housing market, too. Housing prices soared. At the same time, the American Dream was hijacked. Instead of referring to the upward mobility made possible by American capitalism, it was redefined to mean getting rich just by buying a house and extracting equity as it magically appreciated.

Another Bubble, Another Pop

I saw it as a misallocation of resources. I called it "the worst speculative episode in American history." Others—and not just Paul Krugman—saw it as a great boon, helping the economy.

In 2006 and 2007, the housing bubble popped. At first, pundits said it was just a little crisis in subprime mortgages. It wasn't. I won't go through the entire story of what happened in the housing and credit markets in 2006 through 2009, but it was a replay (on a much larger scale) of the popping of the dot-com bubble.

When bubbles are built upon foundations of massive leverage, the bust brings real destruction. On the smallest level, consider the guy who took out an adjustable rate mortgage in 2005 to buy a big house with a very small down payment. When his home value dropped 30 percent, it wasn't just his on-paper net worth that suffered. His rate adjusted in 2010, and he couldn't refinance because his house was underwater. If he sold his house, he wouldn't be able to get enough money to cover his outstanding mortgage and the bank would take all his savings.

Banks also took a hit, when everyone realized the trillions investors and banks had spent on mortgage-backed securities were worth a fraction of what they were supposedly worth. All the financial institutions that had been providing credit to the economy were suddenly in trouble, and couldn't lend like they used to. Those businesses that depended on credit for their day-to-day operations were in trouble.

The stock market fell. From an October 2007 peak above 14,000, the Dow Jones Industrial Average staggered down to 11,000 before the collapse of Lehman Brothers in September 2008. In the next month, the Dow fell below 8,500, eventually bottoming out at 6,626 in early 2009. That's a 53 percent drop.

Housing prices collapsed. The June 2006 Case-Shiller index was 189.93. In March 2009, the index hit 129.2. That's a 32 percent drop. In many markets, it was worse. This was a correction, like the 2000–2001 correction, just deeper. Accordingly, our government reacted in the same stupid way it had at the beginning of the decade, but with much more force.

Rather than rehashing the dynamics of the housing bubble in this book, I will instead refer you to chapter 6 of my 2007 book *Crash Proof* titled "They Burst Bubbles Don't They? The Coming Real Estate Debacle." I wrote that chapter in early 2006, and it's as good an explanation of the housing bubble as any written post-collapse. In fact, the speech that I gave to three thousand mortgage bankers gathered at the Western Regional Mortgage Bankers conference in Las Vegas in 2006 (which is available on the Europac Web site or YouTube—just search "Peter Schiff Mortgage Bankers") is perhaps the best explanation of the housing bubble and the financial crisis of 2008, despite the fact that I gave it two years before the crisis occurred. I would also refer you to the dozens of articles archived on the europac.net Web site, which I wrote between 2004 and 2008, warning about the housing bubble and forecasting the financial crisis that would result when it burst.

The Bailouts

Remember the prime directive that transcends party lines at the Fed, in Congress, and the White House: minimize short-term economic pain at any cost.

Never was this directive on display as clearly as in 2008. In March, the Fed bailed out failed bank Bear Stearns. In July, Congress passed housing bailouts. In early September, the federal government took outright ownership of Fannie and Freddie (since then, according to Congressional Budget Office numbers, taxpayers have poured $317 billion into the two GSEs—$130 billion in cash and the rest in the form of guarantees).

In mid-September, the Federal Reserve, with no authorization from Congress, created brand-new Enron-like special-purpose entities to buy an 80 percent stake in insurance giant AIG. This was an attempt to bail out a collapsing financial sector. It wasn't enough.

By the end of the month, Federal Reserve Chairman Ben Bernanke and Treasury Secretary Henry Paulson had formulated the mother of all bailouts, which they named the Troubled Asset Relief Program, or TARP. At first, we were told the TARP would allow the Treasury, using money created out of thin air by the Fed, to buy up mortgage-backed securities and other financial assets whose value couldn't be ascertained.

The idea was to prevent a "disorderly" unwinding of troubled financial institutions, with debt and other financial instruments going at fire-sale prices, thus destroying the market prices of the assets on which other banks were sitting.

The reality, unsurprisingly, was something far bigger. The Bush and Obama administrations used TARP in all sorts of creative ways, like buying up auto companies and creating "Public-Private Investment Partnerships," paying banks to reduce the principal of underwater homes, and other innovative ways of injecting the government into the economy.

Most important, though, was the way this string of bailouts fit the government pattern: prevent the economy from correcting itself. Once again, rather than let an inefficient allocation of resources shake itself out, politicians and central bankers decided that the right cure for a drinking binge was "the hair of the dog that bit you."

That is, when confronted with a crisis caused by government-created moral hazard, cheap money, and central planning, Washington responded with more moral hazard, even cheaper money, and heightened central planning.

The Government Bubble

Since July 2007, the Fed has increased the money supply by about 45 percent.* Bernanke has been buying bonds from big banks as quickly as the

---

* When the first edition of *The Real Crash* went to press in early 2012, the Fed had increased the money supply by 23 percent since since July 2007.

Treasury can sell them to the banks, keeping interest rates absurdly low, and thus discouraging saving.

Crashproof Yourself: The Next "Big Short" Is Government

The greatest investment opportunity I've ever seen was shorting subprime mortgages in 2006 and 2007. Since we've replaced the housing bubble with a government bubble, the next big bet is shorting the U.S. government.

How do you short the U.S. government? By shorting the dollar. The only way Uncle Sam can pretend to repay his debts is to put the printing presses into overdrive. This will devalue the dollar, thus boosting the value of other currencies and gold.

So brace yourself for rapid inflation and the popping of the government bubble by buying physical gold, getting a diversified portfolio in dividend-paying global stocks and gold-mining stocks, and holding a good mix of strong foreign currencies like Chinese RMB, the Swiss franc, the Canadian dollar, and the Australian dollar.

Congress and the Obama administration have accelerated federal spending at a breakneck pace. Federal spending rose from $2.66 trillion in fiscal year (FY) 2007 to $3.82 trillion in 2010. Because tax revenues actually went down, the new federal spending was all borrowed money (the 2011 deficit was about $1.65 trillion). The national debt held by the public—a disgrace under George W. Bush at $4.82 trillion in 2007—skyrocketed to about $10 trillion in 2011.

Remember, this wasn't accidental on the part of the Fed and the federal government. It was an intentional plan: Keynesian stimulus, punctuated by Obama's $800 billion stimulus bill and the Fed's giant "quantitative easings" (episodes of pumping money into the economy).

Corporate welfare and business subsidies have always been around, but the Bush and Obama administrations gave government a role more central in the economy than it has ever played. The government owned insurance companies, mortgage companies, automakers, and more. Washington was giving handouts to power companies, banks, small businesses, big businesses, manufacturers, and every type of business imaginable.

Government had become a venture capitalist, an insurer, and even an owner of the private sector. If the private sector—even with prodding from Washington—wasn't going to step up and prevent a downturn, the government would. It was just one more step down the same path. When the dot-com bubble popped, they replaced it with a housing bubble. When the housing bubble popped, they replaced it with a government bubble. The greater problem is that while we at least have something to show for the first two bubbles—a few good Internet companies and some pretty nice McMansions—no such benefits will remain when the government bubble pops.

Setting Things Right

These first two chapters covered the state of the economy, and the bad line of thinking that got us here. As an investor, I often would stop here. If I know where the economy is headed, I've got the information I need to put my money in the right places.

But this book is different from my previous books, because I'm not just assessing the situation. In the next section of the book I will propose solutions.

People aren't working. I've got ideas to get them back to work.

Wall Street is dysfunctional. I've got proposals to fix it.

The health-care economy is a mess. I've got a chapter on that.

And because this is version 2.0 of *The Real Crash*, I've added the next chapter, plus new material to update other chapters.

My ideas aren't really "clever" or creative. They're almost the opposite. My solutions are based on the understanding that when economic actors are free to pursue their own self-interest, an economy will enjoy more prosperity than otherwise.

The rest of this book is the roadmap to getting the country back on track. Many of the proposals are far outside the political mainstream. But given the gravity of the crash that's coming, I think people will be ready for them.

3

The Problem 2.0:
We've Learned Nothing and
Things Are Getting Worse

How quickly we forget.

We're only five years away from the bursting of the housing bubble and the financial crisis, and people still have no idea why that crisis occurred. As a result, we are doing everything to recreate it.

As I write this new chapter for the second edition of *The Real Crash*, I am watching America attempt to reinflate its housing bubble, quietly prepare to monetize its debt, and continue to live in denial of its long-term debt problem. Spurred by misguided monetary policies, consumers are saving less and returning to the old habits of spending more than they earn. Investors are returning to their old habits of speculating instead of truly investing.

We're doing the very same things that led up to the 2008 experience— only this time the underlying structure of our economy is far weaker. We saw the weakness in 2008, and we had a chance to allow market forces to fix it. Instead of shaping up after Standard & Poor's downgraded America's credit, the federal government sued the ratings agency for $5 billion, in what S&P claims is simple political retaliation.

We fooled ourselves about why that crash happened. Instead of admitting that we brought it about with bad policies, we blamed the free market.

In order to stem widespread fear, we applied superficial solutions which, when they weren't making the problem worse, served chiefly to inspire a false confidence in our economic health.

This is why, even though the big crash that I first predicted in May

2012 hasn't happened yet, I'm even more confident in my prediction as I write this new edition, in late 2013, than I was then.

So why hasn't it happened yet? I never predicted a timetable—nor can I do so now—but some events have helped put off the day of reckoning. When *The Real Crash* was originally published, everyone was rightly worried about the European sovereign debt crisis. And a lot of politicians (including President Obama) took advantage of this by blaming the slow recovery here on the problems over there. But in fact, it's quite the opposite. Europe's problems were a boon for us. They caused money to flow in our direction, out of the Euro and into the supposed safe haven of U.S. dollars and Treasury bonds. People bought our government's debt out of fear, and that provided us with the extra rope we are now using—not as a lifeline, but to hang ourselves.

Even as I write today, people are still worried about Europe, Japan, and China. Europe remains a big mess as it tries to absorb the blowup of several member states' sovereign debt crises. Greece, having gorged itself for so long with other people's money, was on the point of letting more civil servants go in summer 2013 amid 27 percent unemployment (and youth unemployment above 60 percent) as a condition of receiving more bailout money.

That's bad, and so was the banking crisis in Cyprus that Greece's problems caused. But the European Union faced much bigger problems than those as larger nations like Portugal, Spain, and Italy sat on the knife's edge. Spain, with an astonishing 27 unemployment rate, suffered its first absolute population decrease in 2012 since at least the Franco era, and perhaps since the conquistadores headed west. That nation's young people—along with its many South American immigrants—began seeking opportunities elsewhere because there were simply no jobs to be had.

Americans are perhaps less cognizant of the problems in the Far East. Japan, whose government carries a debt burden more than twice as big as its economy, has been printing money as fast as possible in order to create more inflation and lower interest rates. Rates spiked anyway in the spring of 2013, and although Japan's central bank has since forced them back down out of necessity, inflation was causing some prices in Japan to jump by summertime. It's not just oil prices, which hit a five-year high. Inflation began buffeting finished goods as well. Apple suddenly increased the price of iPads sold in Japan by 19 percent, and McDonalds' raised the price of cheeseburgers by 25 percent. And as inflation accelerates, the government there will be powerless to stop it, because it holds too much short-term debt to survive higher interest rates.

To make matters worse, instead of claiming victory over the manufactured threat of deflation, Japan's government is moving the goal posts to argue that inflation is still too low. Japan's core measure of consumer prices excludes fresh food. During the summer of 2013, borrowing a page from the U.S., Japan introduced the concept of "core-core" inflation, which excludes energy. The new goal is for "core-core" inflation to rise 2 percent annually. The irony lost on everyone is that the goal is to use higher inflation to create purchasing power and economic growth. In fact, higher prices tend to destroy purchasing power and stifle growth. As with QE in the U.S., Japanese stock prices have surged, but real incomes have declined.

Japan has debased its currency and lowered its citizens' standard of living in hopes of rejuvenating its exports, and it just isn't working, to the amazement of Keynesian economists. The weaker Yen is causing the Japanese to pay more for imports, but exports can't keep up. The Land of the Rising Sun, once an export powerhouse, had its seventeenth consecutive monthly trade deficit in November 2013—its longest negative streak since 1980, and still getting wider. Since the sole purpose of exports is to pay for imports, a weaker yen means the Japanese now have to work that much harder to pay for their imports.

All of this benefits us because the dollar is still the world's economic port of choice in a storm. Even if the problems everywhere else in the world emanate from us—even if our inflation and malinvestments are being exported, creating or exacerbating the problems in Europe and Asia—we remain the big winner. It has us enjoying lower prices and the possibility of running up bigger deficits than we could otherwise. Crises elsewhere in the world leave us with fewer motives for restraint.

For this and other reasons, we have delayed the day of reckoning. But our problems keep becoming more acute. They are like a compressed spring that keeps tightening further and further, ready to fly apart and shatter everything in its path when the restraints are removed. Our economy is like a vat containing an unstable solution, whose concentration we keep increasing. It's harmless at the current low temperature, but when the sun rises and the temperature goes up a few degrees, it will erupt in a violent and toxic reaction.

The Slowest Recovery

They're calling this the slowest recovery ever—and I did predict that, but I wasn't sure how long it would last. We're five years past the 2008 crash, and we're still reeling from the blow. In fact, a more accurate GDP deflator, which is used to adjust nominal GDP growth for inflation, might reveal that the economy has actually been in a depression during the entire period. Perhaps the real reason this recovery doesn't feel like a recovery is that it's not a recovery at all, but an illusion created by government sleight of hand when it comes to reporting inflation. (More on this in the chapter about sound money.)

Meanwhile, government is also concocting creative ways of fooling us (and itself) about our economic growth and our debt problem. The Commerce Department changed the way it calculates GDP in the summer of 2013 to reclassify to kinds of expenses—film and television production costs and research and development—as "fixed investments." For the sake of consistency, the changes were applied to every year going back to 1929, but these changes are dodgy, and merely make the economy look bigger and more dynamic than it really is.

First of all, an awful lot of research and development money produces nothing. This happens routinely with drug companies, for example, which spend billions gambling on long-shot cures, most of which never pan out. That money is part of their cost of business—unlike real fixed investments (a factory machine, or computers that increase productivity) it doesn't necessarily reflect economic health.

The other change—the "Hollywood" GDP—is even worse because it bastardizes the very concept of GDP. The government will now count the cost of labor in film and television as an investment, whereas in all other fields, labor is treated as a cost. That is to say, as long as Kevin Costner is grossly overpaid for his next bomb of a film, that will make up statistically for hundreds or even thousands of small businesses forgoing minor capital investments because of an unsound economy.

Business investment in capital goods is important, and such goods increase our capacity to produce consumer goods in the future. Spending money to film movies, record music, or produce reality TV shows does nothing to increase the productive capacity of the nation. A movie is not capital equipment—it's a finished consumer product.

But now, thanks to these changes, the government will pretend other-wise. In its effort to make the U.S economy appear larger and faster grow-ing, the government has changed the very definition of GDP. It is no accident that the government has rejiggered the methodology used to com-pute GDP by overweighting the areas of the economy that are still grow-ing. This is the same sleight of hand they use to underreport inflation when they calculate the CPI. This is par for the course with government statistics and why they are completely worthless in understanding what is happening in the real economy. They make GDP look bigger, and inflation and unemployment appear lower, by constantly changing the methodol-ogy used to compute the numbers. What is amazing is that despite what amounts to a sweeping change to the very concept of GDP, not a single academic institution has called the government out on its error—although several respected business news pundits have raised questions.

These and a few other minor changes boosted U.S. GDP overnight by $526 billion. There is a purely psychological element of deception here, not unlike the government's tendency to annualize growth numbers but not in-flation numbers. But that's not the real problem. The real problem is that this new GDP calculation reduces the federal government's debt-to-GDP ratio by increasing the denominator. This will allow politicians more leeway to propose and pass budgets that borrow more money and put the nation in further peril. If you think that's crazy, just wait until 2017, when the U.S. government hopes to add to its statistical legerdemain the concept of "fac-toryless manufacturing." This would essentially turn American companies that outsource their factory units to foreign countries into America's next manufacturing juggernaut. This proposed statistical change would essen-tially count foreign workers as U.S. employees for trade and GDP purposes, so long as they make American-owned products.

This is more evidence that we're still just trying to devise new ways of fooling ourselves into prosperity. It's even clearer today than it was in early 2012 that our government learned nothing from the 2008 crash. Government continues to pursue policies that will make the real crash much worse when it comes. The national debt has increased by more than $1.1 trillion since the first edition of this book went to press. More than ever before, our federal, state, and municipal governments resemble overvalued suburban McMansions, whose adjustable rate mortgages could at any moment cause monthly payments to exceed their owners' ability to pay.

America's GDP for the first quarter of 2013 was revised downward, from an original estimate of a tepid 2.5 percent to a pathetic 1.1 percent annualized growth rate. (And that's only if you believe the government's claims that inflation during the quarter rose by an annualized rate of just 1.2 percent. In fact, the original 1.7 percent estimate of second quarter GDP growth assumed just 0.7 percent annualized inflation.) America's capital remains sidelined as investors and entrepreneurs fret over higher taxes and the uncertainty of new regulations—especially health-care regulations, still to be implemented, which make the cost of hiring unpredictable. The delay of ObamaCare's employer mandate until 2015 only makes matters worse because it extends the uncertainty.

With capital waiting in the wings, the productive people of America—ready and able workers who would normally be counted on to pay the bills—remain out of work. There were still six million fewer full-time jobs in the U.S. economy in July 2013 than there had been in late 2007, before the "Great Recession" began. Full-time work was being replaced by temp jobs (up 50 percent from before the recession) and part-time jobs (up 3.3 million).

The standard unemployment rate stood at 7.6 percent in June 2013. That's high by historical standards, but the rate would have been an astounding 11.1 percent if not for so many people giving up on finding work, thus falling out of the equation used to calculate unemployment. The rate seems low because workforce participation is at its lowest point since 1978.

The Department of Labor reported that in summer 2013, less than 59 percent of Americans were working for a living. The number had been stuck right around this historic low for about three years. The last time the number was this low, it lasted only briefly—during the recession in President Reagan's first term, when Fed chairman Paul Volcker had imposed high interest rates to fight rampant inflation. This time, interest rates are already at zero, and there's been no significant improvement since 2010.

Job creation isn't even keeping up with growth in the working-age population. In summer 2013, the measure of unemployment that includes the underemployed and discouraged job-seekers—known as U6—was still up over 75 percent from when the recession began. It's not just that it's a bigger number—it's a more descriptive number because it has remained high while the standard unemployment figure has fallen.

All of this has left the very people who should be building up our country instead depending on government for their sustenance. As of August 2013, food stamp rolls were up 2 million and disability rolls were up by about 500,000 just since the first edition of this book was published—both to all-time highs. The disability program is now so oversubscribed that its trust fund will officially run out in 2016, at which point its beneficiaries will see automatic benefit cuts.

Those still working are forced to settle for worse and worse jobs. Wages fell 4.4 percent between the recession's end in June 2009 and August 2013, according to a study by Sentier Research—twice as fast as they fell during the recession. When Obama talked about "change," most of his fans probably didn't think he intended to create a recovery that is even worse than the recession that preceded it. And if they think the Obama recovery is bad, just wait until they get a load of the Obama recession that lies ahead.

Meanwhile, the Fed has continued its policy of easy money—a policy that the markets now depend on for life support. On June 19, 2013, Fed Chairman Ben Bernanke announced that there would, at some point, be an end to "quantitative easing." This apparently obvious statement was enough to send stocks swooning, causing the Dow to lose hundreds of points instantly and nearly 5 percent of its value over the next three days. All he had to say was this:

> [O]ur basic forecast is one which is basically . . . a moderately optimistic forecast, where growth picks up as we pass through this period of fiscal restraint; where unemployment continues to fall at a gradual pace as it has been since last September—and we have made some progress since last September; and inflation rises slowly towards 2 percent. Those are the conditions that define this sort of baseline forecast. In that case then, as I described it, we would expect probably to slow or moderate purchases [of U.S. government debt] some time later this year, and then through the middle of—through the early part of next year, and ending, in that scenario, somewhere in the middle of the year.

In other words, if the economy continues to improve (as if it were really improving), he would begin a process of gradually slowing down the Fed's purchases of bad mortgage assets and government bonds. If such a subtle hint as this one is enough to erase so much wealth on paper, imagine what will happen when Fed policy actually stops quantitative easing altogether.

As if those losses in stocks weren't big enough, *The Wall Street Journal*'s Patrick McGroarty reported in June that Bernanke's little hint at possible "tapering" caused investors to flee emerging markets—including India, South Africa, and Brazil—on the expectation that U.S. bond yields would suddenly rise—which they did.

The only supposed positive sign in the economy in 2013 was real estate, which seemed to be recovering. But this was an illusion. The reinflation of the housing bubble is not a sign of economic health, but a mere indication that the Fed stimulus is having its predictable and intoxicating short-term effect—it inflates asset values and holds down interest rates for homebuyers, who are thus encouraged to take on larger and larger debts.

In his June 19, 2013 press conference, Bernanke showed shades of 2005 when he said he was not worried about a modest rise in mortgage rates, because housing prices will keep appreciating.

> Rates have tightened some, but, you know, other factors have been more positive—increasing house prices, for example. I think as far as the housing market is concerned, we're going to want to watch that, but one important difference now is that people are more optimistic about housing. They expect house prices to continue to rise . . . And that, you know, compensates to some extent for a slightly higher mortgage rate.

This is exactly what people were saying last time, before the crash of 2008. It is mind-numbing to watch it all happen again, and to see everyone pretend that everything is okay. It is painful to watch James Bullard, president of the St. Louis Fed, assert in September of 2013 that "The bubbles we had in the past were gigantic and obvious. I don't see anything like that going on right now." Of course they're "gigantic and obvious" in hindsight. But at the time those bubbles were growing, Bullard and all of his current Fed colleagues were clueless. In fact, Bernanke himself denied the existence of the gigantic housing bubble right up until 2008, long after it had already burst.

Bernanke's successor, Janet Yellen, was equally clueless. No, you wouldn't get that impression reading the newspapers. *The Huffington Post* wrote that Yellen "[w]arned early and often, starting at least in 2005, about the problems in housing and the looming economic catastrophe." On October 9, 2013, the *New York Times* editorial board wrote that Janet Yellen "sounded the warning about the housing bubble even as others praised the boom." President Obama himself repeated this lie when announcing Yellen's nomination by praising her for having "sounded the alarm early about the housing bubble, excess in the financial sector, and the risks of a major recession."

In reality, Yellen was blindsided by the housing crisis. In fact, she went out of her way to downplay the risks and dismiss the warnings made by others.

In an October 2005 speech at the fourth annual Haas Gala, she argued that there was no housing bubble, and that the rise in home prices, which she expected to continue, was fundamentally justified. She added that even if her assessment was wrong and there was a housing bubble about to burst, it would be no worse than "a good-sized bump in the road" and "the economy would likely be able to absorb the shock."

Yellen also praised the proliferation of cash-out refinancing and home equity extractions as being innovative and supportive of improving real estate fundamentals. In making her case that housing was not in a bubble, she confidently noted, "Another development, which may be making housing more like an investment vehicle in the U.S., is that it's now easier and cheaper to get at the equity—either through refinancing, which has become a less costly process, or through an equity line of credit. These innovations in mortgage markets make the funds invested in houses more liquid."

So the person most credited for having warned about the dangers of a housing bubble and a looming financial crisis, was one of the biggest supporters of the very credit excesses that not only fueled the bubble, but exacerbated the crisis after it burst.

In an April 2006 speech at the Bay Area Economic Conference, Yellen reiterated her expectation for continued housing appreciation, only at a more moderate pace. A few months later, at a Fed meeting in September, Yellen downplayed the slowdown in housing and the unexpected decline in prices: "The speed of the falloff in housing activity and the deceleration in house prices continue to surprise us . . . [but] housing is a relatively small sector of the economy, and its decline should be self-correcting."

By February 2007, as home values began their epic plunge, she was convinced the worst was over and that the housing correction had already finished. In a speech, she noted "signs of stabilization in the housing market." She was pleased to report that "housing's slowdown had [not] spilled into other parts of the economy," and that in fact she was far more worried about inflation than a housing downturn.

Mind you, these quotations come from the very speeches the left points to as proof of Yellen having warned about the crisis!* That's something to keep in mind as she takes the helm—no one is prescient, and especially no one at the Fed. In fact, near the peak of the gigantic NASDAQ bubble, Chairman Alan Greenspan said that it was impossible to detect a bubble until after it burst.

It seems when it comes to FOMC members, including Bullard and Yellen, Greenspan's observation was correct. And the failure to see gigantic bubbles is not limited to Federal Reserve members. Nearly everyone thought I was nuts when I warned about the housing bubble and the financial crisis that would ensue after it popped. (If you did not already watch the "Peter Schiff was Right" YouTube video referenced in the introduction, now would be a good time to do so.)

Do you want to know what a bubble looks like? *The New York Times* reported in June 2013 that the driving force behind the real estate "recovery" is not purchasers in need of homes, but speculators in search of profits. They were stepping into troubled markets like Phoenix and Las Vegas and bidding up houses so fast that ordinary buyers were being squeezed out. In Florida, more than 30 percent of home purchases were by investors, not homeowner occupants. This was another result of low interest rates. In a market where there was no decent conservative investment offering any return, housing speculation was becoming popular again.

But what happens when these investors can't find a greater fool—a buyer ready to pay even more, or a renter who can cover their carrying costs indefinitely, with a decent return?

If genuine demand for housing is so strong, then why haven't construction jobs—which reached a high of 7.7 million during the housing boom in 2007—shown any signs of recovering from their post-crash lows? As of

---

* For a more in-depth analysis, see my YouTube videos "Janet Yellen Exposed," parts 1 and 2.

June 2013, they were still stuck around 5.8 million, less than 10 percent above the low and still less than they had been sixteen years earlier.

These are just a couple signs of how, as before the 2008 crash, our economy finds itself dependent on speculation rather than investment—on increasing asset values instead of productive activities that create wealth. And as in the middle of the last decade, this is a recipe for disaster.

Doctor Ben

Bernanke had the economy on life support, and he spoke as if he could pull the plug at any moment and it would live on its own—if he just pulled it slowly enough through "tapering."

The Fed had already brought us to the point of zero percent interest rates when I originally wrote this book. With that dial already maxed out, it began "quantitative easing," reaching the second iteration, or QE2, by which the Fed pushed still more money into the economy by purchasing $600 billion in new long-term Treasury debt and buying $550 billion more from the proceeds of the sales of mortgage-backed securities on its balance sheet.

After the first edition of *The Real Crash* went to press, the Fed moved on to QE3—a monthly purchase of $40 billion in mortgage-backed securities. It then moved to "Operation Twist" (by which the Fed tried to lengthen the maturity of its debt to force down long-term interest rates—a process I jokingly referred to as Operation Screw, as taxpayers will lose big when long-term interest rates rise). Then came QE4, which added $45 billion in monthly Fed purchases of federal government debt and another $40 billion of government-guaranteed mortgages. As of August 2013, the Fed owned $2 trillion in U.S. government debt—more than four times what it owned at the end of 2008—and another $1.3 trillion in mortgage-backed securities.

Bernanke repeatedly denied that he was "monetizing" this debt—that is, inflating the currency by purchasing debt that will never be repaid or simply absorbing the losses on bad mortgage assets. The rationale for his denial in congressional testimony was that he intended to sell the debt before it matured. However, he later backed off of that assurance, making the more limited claim that the Fed will not only hold the bonds in its portfolio to maturity, but it will roll over the principal of any maturing debts into newly issued debt. Even measured by his own absurd criteria, Bernanke could no longer deny the obvious.

The reason Bernanke reversed course on his commitment to sell off the Treasuries he was buying (in other words, his original exit strategy) was that the markets rightly became concerned about the adverse effects such sales would have on the bond market, and the consequences rising interest rates would have on the housing market and the broader U.S. economy. To defuse these concerns, and with little regard for his prior commitment, Bernanke assured the markets that no Treasury sales were forthcoming. The Fed would hold all bonds to maturity and even reinvest any interest earned into more Treasuries.

What no one seemed to understand was that if the Fed held its bonds to maturity, where would the Treasury get the money to repay the Fed? It would have to sell additional treasuries into the market. The result for the bond market, interest rates, housing, and the economy would be identical to what would have happened had the Fed simply sold the bonds itself. In other words, the disaster the markets feared would not be averted at all, but merely postponed. My guess is that Bernanke understood this, but was confident in his ability to confuse the public.

In April 2013, Federal Reserve Bank of Atlanta president Dennis Lockhart pointedly denied that there was any connection between the Fed's activity and federal indebtedness. Bloomberg quoted him saying that "The accusation of intentional suppression of government financing costs is unfounded. . . . The Fed has to try to ease financial conditions . . . until the economy improves."

The absurdity of this statement is rivaled only but the fact that anyone believed it. Were it not for the Fed artificially holding interest rates at zero, and acting as the U.S. government's largest lender, trillion-dollar annual budget deficits would have been impossible to finance. The government would have been forced by the markets to dramatically curtail its spending. However, because of the Fed, and in direct contradiction to Lockhart's claim, the government did not have to make any of those politically difficult choices. As a result, the spending and the debt necessary to finance it continued to grow.

Of course, even if the economy improves, the Fed will never be able to sell all of the debt it has accumulated. Warren Buffett was actually trying to allay people's fears when he made the alarming comments covered in September 2013 by *Bloomberg News*:

> "The Fed is the greatest hedge fund in history," Buffett told students yesterday at Georgetown University in Washington. It's generating "$80 billion or $90 billion a year probably" in revenue for the U.S. government, he said. "And that wasn't the case a few years back."
>
> . . . The Fed "is under no pressure, none whatsoever to have to deleverage," Buffett said. "So it can pick its time, and if you have somebody wise there—and I think Bernanke is wise, and I certainly expect his successor to be—it can be handled. But it is something that's never quite been done on this scale. It will be interesting to watch."

Buffett is correct that Bernanke and his successor face an unprecedented task—what he glosses over is that they face an impossible task. It's been hard enough for the Fed to even reach the point at which it would scale back its asset purchases, i.e., taper them. What if the Fed actually started *selling off the debt it has accumulated*? The effect would be catastrophic.

The fact that the Fed manages a meager 2.5 percent annual return on its 3.5 trillion dollar balance sheet hardly qualifies it as being the greatest hedge fund in history. However, when interest rates rise, it will be the greatest hedge fund blow-up in history. Buffett is naïve to believe that the Fed is under no pressure to deleverage and that it can pick its time to do so. If offical measures of inflation flare up, the Fed will be forced to delever, and the losses will be horrific. In fact, the prospect of realizing hundreds of billions in losses on its treasury and mortgage portfolio, which U.S. taxpayers are on the hook to make good, is one reason the Fed will do nothing to restrain inflation. However, when the bond market figures this out, it will be a blood bath. Too bad it's not just Warren Buffett's money the Fed is playing with.

I argued in 2004, 2005, and 2006 that what seemed in those days like economic growth was really the result of Fed manipulation—low interest rates and artificially cheap money. At that time, the people who called me crazy at least tried to justify their position. They argued that the growth was somehow justified by economic fundamentals. We were creating an information economy . . . or something. Today, though, they've dropped that pretense. Everyone now *explicitly* credits the Fed for what little economic growth we seem to be enjoying.

Implicit in this admission is the fragility of the economy. The adage that "bad news is good news" remains truer than ever. That is to say, the stock market is more concerned with the cure—the Fed's manipulation—than it is with the economic health toward which this cure is supposed to lead us. Bad economic news is thus taken as good, because it suggests the cure will keep coming. And good economic news—as with Bernanke's optimistic comments in June 2013—is bad news, because it implies that the cure worked and that quantitative easing might stop.

How telling that by July 18, 2013, Bernanke had learned his lesson. In testimony before Congress, he went out of his way to downplay concerns that some members of the Fed had expressed about continued quanititative easing, and to play up (though not *too* much) the headwinds that might affect the economy, leading to more of it:

> "We will be waiting to see if the movement in mortgage rates has any material effect on housing. If we think the mortgage rate increases are thwarting the progress, we will have to take additional action . . . I emphasize that, because our asset purchases depend on economic and financial developments, they are by no means on a preset course. . . ."

Not only could QE4 go on forever, but now we're talking about *additional* action! The traders loved that. Bernanke's prepared remarks were disseminated the night before, and the Dow opened 30 points higher. It shot up still further as he testified, and it finished the day up 78 points, closing at a new all-time high.

They loved even more the September 2013 announcement—surprising to nearly everyone but myself—that the Fed would not begin tapering, which sent the Dow to another all-time high. Bernanke said he was delaying tapering on the grounds that mortgage rates had been rising. But of course, mortgage rates were only rising on the expectation that the Fed would taper its purchases. So by Bernanke's logic, there could never be an appropriate time to taper. The implication is that this lending by the Fed is forever—we're monetizing the debt.

The December 2013 announcement that tapering would begin did not really change this. Not only is Bernanke's successor likely to be forced into reversing the taper, but tapering itself is a mere scaling back of asset purchases, not a halt to them and certainly not a shift from buying to selling.

All the warning signs are there. And there exists the same complacency among the experts as there was in 2008. Once again, the media and Wall Street are missing it. No one has recognized the real nature of the crisis, and so we're doomed to repeat it.

We didn't fix our problem when we had the chance because we deluded ourselves. Self-serving politicians successfully sold voters the myth that this had been the result of overly-free markets at work. And acting from this myth, we passed new financial regulations that in fact made the situation even worse. Their chief effect has been to give big banks an advantage over smaller and better-run competitors when it comes to the cost of money.

The banks' creditors don't believe Obama (and rightly so) when he says that the "too big to fail" concept is over and done. So they're placing a bigger bet than ever on a bailout the next time things go south, because they're convinced they're going to get it. Meanwhile, better-managed, prudently run banks lack access to capital.

We Need Higher Interest Rates

No one wants to admit or even ponder what higher interest rates, whenever they arrive, are going to do to the housing market and the cost of government. The moment the bond market pulls away the punch bowl, this party is over.

The federal government's debt is not like your 30-year fixed-rate mortgage. Its interest rate more resembles a five-year adjustable-rate mortgage. On average, each dollar the U.S. borrows comes due again every 65 months. The government refinances that dollar of debt by borrowing another dollar at the lowest interest rate it can. The federal government is thus constantly refinancing in a process that will last as long as our nation continues to borrow (or more precisely, as long as our creditors are willing to lend).

At the moment, this is working out just great. It has helped the government to refinance nearly all of its debt at near-zero interest rates, and to run enormous new deficits with minimal debt service costs. But this is a very fragile situation, because the artificially low rates of today will not last forever, yet they are the only thing keeping the government solvent and home values high.

Low interest rates affect our entire economy, not just housing and government. They prompt large public U.S. companies to borrow money and buy back shares of their own stock. It makes sense for them to do this, because buybacks make their earnings per share go up. But it also means they have less cash on hand and are less invested in their own operations. It makes them more vulnerable to an increase in interest rates. Also, to the extent that corporations sell to each other, higher interest expenses for one corporation will mean less sales revenue for another.

Low rates also prompt speculators to borrow money to buy stocks. In September 2013, margin debt on the New York Stock Exchange was at $401 billion—exceeding the highs of summer 2007, right before the last crash.

Low interest rates thus encourage excess consumption, consumer debt, government debt, college debt, mortgage debt, and speculation—activities that produce no added value. (Some will defend the idea of college debt as a value-creator—I argue in a later chapter that this is usually not the case.) High interest rates, on the other hand, encourage savings and investment, which facilitates business lending. And that's the problem our economy faces. We need more investment and more savings, and that requires higher interest rates. But higher interest rates would create a massive crisis for government and for the millions engaged in speculations—large and small—because super-low rates have made it all possible.

In February 2013, the Congressional Budget Office published its ten-year fiscal outlook. CBO anticipated a four-point increase in the government's cost of borrowing on three-month Treasury Bills (from zero to 4 percent) by 2019, and a 3.4-point increase (to 5.2 percent) in the yield on 10-year Treasury notes.

Even that would leave yields well below where they were throughout the 1980s and much of the 1990s. But CBO also noted that rates could go higher than their estimates. And all other things being equal, they wrote, each additional point increase to government debt yields implies an extra

$1.1 trillion dollars in debt service spending over ten years, plus extra for debt service on that amount. The Bank for International Settlements estimated in June 2013 that if rates rise by just 2 points, then America's debt-to-GDP ratio would reach 200 percent of GDP, up from the current 100 percent.

In short, if interest rates go up substantially, it will endanger the federal government's ability to pay for anything beyond debt service and entitlements—and even the latter may suffer.

Higher interest rates won't just change how government functions. They will also end the current borrowing for stock-buybacks. And then there's housing. Imagine a world in which mortgage payments on the same house at the same price are 35 to 50 percent higher because of higher interest rates. What do you suppose that does to the pool of potential buyers, upon whose shoulders our apparent economic progress now rests? It sends home values plummeting, of course. And that creates problems not only for homeowners, but also for the federal government, which has been guaranteeing almost all new mortgages in recent years, through either Freddie Mac, Fannie Mae, the FHA, or the Veterans Administration.

And then there are the banks. The biggest banks are not only propped up by too big to fail, but their bloated balance sheets are loaded up with treasuries and mortgage paper—known as "Fannies and Freddies." We know the risks of the latter all too well, but both are subject to severe interest rate risk. In July 2013, *The Wall Street Journal* reported that between late May and mid-July, in the same time frame as Bernanke's "tapering" comments, as long-term mortgage rates rose, nearly $40 billion in unrealized gains from these assets had suddenly been erased at various banks. The paper also reported midsized lender Zions Bancorp's estimate that a three-point rise in interest rates would reduce the banks' capital by a quarter trillion dollars and their lending capacity by $2 trillion.

And since the banks are much bigger now than they were in 2007 and 2008, the losses if they were to fail would be staggering.

In the December 2013 announcement that the Fed would modestly reduce its quantitative easing, I sense overconfidence. The Fed will likely be forced to reverse course as interest rates rise and the economy heads south. Such an about-face on tapering would likely cause the Fed to lose face with the markets.

But acknowledging economic headwinds as justification to postpone the taper would eventually backfire as well. Any admission that this monetary stimulus has failed could ignite an enormous sell-off in the bond market. That would cause rates to rise anyway, and to levels that government cannot handle with its current level of debt.

There's no need to ask a question as dramatic as whether we are ready for an economic jolt. We are not even prepared for something as simple as a return to "normal" interest rates. The violent chemical reaction begins not at a boil, but at the moment room temperature is restored. Americans have much more debt now than they did the last time interest rates were "normal." The federal, state, and local governments have added trillions to their debts since the last time rates were normal. When the rates return to normal, everything falls apart.

Romney Was Right

Mitt Romney received a lot of bad coverage for his closed-door remarks about "the 47 percent." He asserted, in a fundraiser that was secretly filmed by one of the waiters, that with so many Americans no longer paying income taxes, fewer of them were receptive to ideas about cutting taxes. And with so many dependent on government, ideas about limited government are no longer popular.

As much grief as Romney got for these comments, he opened an important can of worms by bringing it up. Only 53 percent of Americans pay income taxes. And by 2012, the desperate economic situation had opened new doors for big government that previously remained closed. A politician willing to play the right cards (as Obama was) and stoke class envy could take advantage of it.

More and more Americans are now getting government help to purchase food. Nearly all Americans who want a college education nowadays are borrowing large amounts, guaranteed and perhaps also subsidized by the government. Most homebuyers are now government-subsidized, and many renters as well. People even complained that there were *only* 99 weeks of benefits available to the unemployed. (Only!)

Everyone wants a free ride on the government gravy train, and nobody wants to help pull it down the track. For all the bad publicity it brought him, Romney made a solid point. At some point, people figure out they can vote themselves free stuff, and perhaps that's when democracies die.

Everything that's wrong with democracy was epitomized in Obama's re-election. In his first term, his administration had helped facilitate greater government dependency, and he reaped the benefits. As a result, our nation may well have passed the point at which so many people depend on government it's virtually impossible to elect anyone good anymore.

What Obama proved is that the guy who tells you you're poor because that other guy is rich can win an election. The guy who tells you that he can lift you up by dragging other people down—he can win. And he can win re-election even if his first term brought about abysmal results.

PART II

The Solutions

4

Jobs, Jobs, Jobs: Government Can Improve Employment Only by Getting Out of the Way

BILL CLINTON, DURING HIS PRESIDENTIAL run of 1992, famously had a sign in his campaign headquarters to remind him of the issue that matters most to voters: IT'S THE ECONOMY, STUPID.

But most voters don't really care so much about the economy, per se. They really care about *jobs*. That's the root of the quip that the *real* definition of a recession is when your neighbor loses his job, while a depression is when *you* lose yours.

Politicians understand this, and that's why both parties have adopted "Jobs, Jobs, Jobs," as their unofficial mottoes. But they're doing it wrong.

Unstimulating

President Obama seems to think he can spend jobs into existence. His $827 billion stimulus bill was the prime example. Coming into office, Obama claimed the bill would create more than 4 million jobs.[1] A year and a half after the bill passed, the White House was claiming that it had "created or saved" somewhere between 2.5 million and 3.6 million jobs.[2]

We know that the administration's claims about stimulus jobs are false. A great example of the administration's false job claims and the general fruitlessness of government attempts at job creation is a "green jobs" program administered by the Department of Energy (DOE).

DOE's Web site lists the recipients of "green job" subsidies—solar panel makers, wind-power developers and so on—and how many jobs their subsidies supposedly created. As of March 2011, the DOE was still claiming that the $535 million stimulus loan guarantee from taxpayers to solar company Solyndra was creating 1,000 permanent jobs (in addition to construction jobs).

The Obama administration was so fond of Solyndra that they twice held it up as the model for the new economy as well as the model for stimulus "job creation." Vice President Joe Biden visited Solyndra's factory along with Energy Secretary Steven Chu, touting the plant to high heaven. President Obama visited in May 2010, saying, "The foundation of economic growth will always be companies like Solyndra."

The DOE loan guarantee (which meant taxpayers would pay back Solyndra's bank if Solyndra couldn't) helped finance a new plant to make solar panels. We'll discuss the folly of government loan guarantees later, but for now we'll grant that DOE made it easier for Solyndra to build the new factory. Still, this didn't "create jobs."

In 2010, as Solyndra was planning an initial public offering (IPO) of its stock, the company's paperwork with the Securities and Exchange Commission (SEC) spelled out a dire picture. Solyndra's auditor, PriceWaterhouseCoopers, wrote, "The company has suffered recurring losses from operations, negative cash flows since inception and has a net stockholders' deficit that, among other factors, raise substantial doubt about its ability to continue as a going concern."

Soon, Solyndra pulled the plug on its IPO, and also on adding 1,000 jobs. Instead of expanding, Solyndra decided to lay off 150 workers and close its original factory, moving all its remaining workers to the new subsidized factory. In 2011, Solyndra declared bankruptcy.

The Solyndra story is a good example of government efforts at "creating jobs." If the goal of the stimulus loan guarantee program was to help Solyndra build a new factory, then this could have been a success story. But for the broader goal of increasing the number of jobs in the economy, it failed.

What would have happened had DOE not shown up with a loan guarantee for Solyndra? There are two possibilities: (a) Solyndra still might have gotten financing favorable enough to build the new plant; or (b) without the guarantee, a bank would not have loaned Solyndra the money on terms good enough for Solyndra to justify building the plant.

If (a), then this loan guarantee was simply a giveaway, putting U.S. taxpayers on the hook for a project that would have gone ahead anyway.

If (b), then Solyndra's short-lived gain likely came at the expense of some other enterprise. Businesses often compete for loans, and the loan guarantee likely helped Solyndra beat out another customer for this loan. The loser was some company that would have gotten the loan if not for the government loan guarantee for Solyndra. That means there was some enterprise—or enterprises—that a bank saw as more financially promising than Solyndra, but the bank went with Solyndra because the government was passing the risk on to taxpayers.

So even if Solyndra hadn't failed, the government would have succeeded only at bringing a new solar panel factory into existence at the expense of more economically promising undertakings. Instead, the government effectively threw money into a pit and lit it on fire.

This is the nature of government "job creation." At best, it brings into being jobs that otherwise wouldn't exist—but at the expense of other jobs that would exist, and would probably create more value.

The problem isn't that the government bets on the wrong horses. It's that the government shouldn't be at the track in the first place. Government should not be in the "job creation" business at all. Because government can't create jobs, it can only shuffle them around the economy, usually with a loss of net employment and always with a loss of net prosperity for society.

The root of the problem is politicians' ignorance about where jobs come from. They believe that spending—either by government or by consumers—can "create jobs." The truth is less simplistic, but not complicated.

Where Do Jobs Come From?

Jobs do not exist in nature. All animals—all chimpanzees, dolphins, and turkeys—are self-employed. All cavemen were self-employed, too. It would be the same for today's humans if not for the ability of one person to employ another.

There are two parties involved in any job: the employer and the employee. To be an employee, a person needs the ability to work, which is no more than he needs in order to be self-employed. But being an employer requires more than being either an employee or self-employed. To be an employer, you need to be able to multiply the value of your employees' efforts. In most cases, you need to make their work more valuable under you than it would be were they to work on their own. You can only do this if you can bring some assets to the table: capital, ingenuity, and willingness to take risks.

Put another way: everyone has a choice, either to be self-employed or to work for someone else. Those who choose the latter do so because they conclude it is the best option available to them. In other words, they feel they can earn a better living working for someone else than by being self-employed. But employers will not hire unless doing so increases their own income. In addition, employers cannot provide jobs unless they have capital to offer their workers.

So to answer our question: Jobs come from (a) the incentive to earn a profit and (b) capital formation. The harder government makes it for employers to earn profits and the less we save to finance capital formation, the fewer jobs that will be created.

You probably can begin to sense why politicians and bureaucrats don't like this line of reasoning. The conclusion is that they cannot "create jobs."

Real Jobs versus Fake Jobs

Of course, if you define the aims narrowly enough, government can claim the ability to create jobs. Consider the Solyndra example above: certainly the construction workers building the new factory seem to have benefited from government spending. The same is true for Franklin Roosevelt's make-work programs like the Works Projects Administration. If the government is willing to pay people to build a dam—or heck, even to dig ditches and then fill them back in—it can theoretically employ the entire population.

Alternatively, the government could provide a huge subsidy to any business that hires workers to dig ditches with shovels and then fill them back in—that would "create jobs," too. With enough government employment and subsidies, we could have full employment.

But digging ditches and filling them back in is not valuable work. Except for maybe the diggers, nobody's life is better off because of the digging. This is the difference between *real* jobs and government jobs (and I include in this latter category those private sector jobs created by subsidies).

If you recall, the former Soviet Union used to boast that in contrast to the capitalist United States, they had no unemployment. This was true in the sense that all Soviet citizens had government jobs. The problem was that those jobs were so unproductive; workers had to wait in line for hours to buy the most basic goods or services with their government paychecks. Lots of people were working but few produced anything of value to consumers. So the Soviets had jobs, but those jobs did little to raise their living standards.

Real jobs provide something of value. Someone who works for Apple turned a bunch of wires into an iPad. Someone who works for FedEx brought something from where it was to where it was wanted. A gardener made a backyard more pleasing to the homeowner.

Government jobs can provide value, and they often do—think about garbage men or policemen. But almost all government jobs that provide value would be taken up by the private sector if the government ceased taking care of them. Government isn't creating those jobs, it's just taking them away from the private sector.

So what we really want when we say we want more jobs is more productive jobs. And on that score, if politicians want to help, the best they can do is to end the government policies that stultify job creation. In other words, on the jobs situation, the best our politicians can do is to get the heck out of the way.

Nancy Pelosi criticized the Republican Congress for its failure to produce a jobs bill, as if the way to create jobs is to pass more laws. The fact is that many Republicans were introducing bills to cut government spending, which Nancy Pelosi opposed. What Ms. Pelosi failed to see was that cutting government spending is one of the best jobs programs the government could devise. By cutting government spending, resources necessary for job creation are returned to the private sector.

A general shrinkage of government would help the jobs picture by ending the inefficient allocation of wealth caused by subsidies, high tax rates and complex tax codes, and other government interventions. But there are plenty of specific government policies that acutely hurt job creation. Many of them are politically popular, but any leaders who want to create jobs need to end these policies.

The Hiring Penalty

Hiring people costs money, as we discussed above—that's why businessmen with capital are a precondition to job creation. In any environment, an employer's costs include wages, but they also include other items: maybe more office space, another computer, more coffee grounds, bigger bathrooms at the office, plus the cost of recruiting, checking out, and deciding on a new hire.

So, in any environment, an employee costs more than just her wages. But our government today adds a huge cost to hiring an employee. I call it the "Hiring Penalty," and eliminating it or minimizing it should be Job No. 1 of any politician who wants employment to improve.

The Hiring Penalty takes many forms, and springs from federal and state laws and regulations. Some of the policies making up the Hiring Penalty are direct—I call them the "Hiring Tax"—and others are indirect, but still costly, and still the fault of government (I'll get into those later, too).

Many of these costly policies are lauded as "worker protection," but politicians have given workers so much protection, they have inadvertently protected many from getting jobs. Sure, those who promoted and passed the laws probably had more noble intentions, but as in most aspects of life, we understand that good intentions don't always lead to the desired outcome. They often produce unintended consequences that create worse problems than the ones well-intentioned legislators originally sought to solve.

We shouldn't give government policies a pass just because their sponsors' purported aims are noble. We all know the old adage "the road to hell is paved with good intentions," and our government has been laying down a lot of asphalt.

Many elements of the hiring penalty I'll discuss below are politically popular, but all of them have this in common: they are government interventions in the economy that add to the cost of hiring an employee.

The Hiring Tax

Let's start with the direct costs government imposes—the hiring tax.

The payroll tax is the most obvious example. It is unambiguously a penalty for hiring someone, and it increases as you pay workers more. Anyone who has never been in a position to sign the *front* of a paycheck might not realize the way payroll taxes work.

If you're not an employer, here's an eye-opening lesson for you: Look at your pay stub. See the line for FICA and MICA? Those are taxes that come out of your paycheck to fund Social Security and Medicare. They add up to 7.5 percent of your paycheck. No matter what, you never see this money. You can add to your exemptions, pile on the tax deductions, and claim all the tax credits you want—even if you receive welfare, you still pay 7.5 cents of every dollar you earn to the Social Security Administration and to Medicare.

But what you don't see, if you're an employee, is that your boss is also paying the same amount in FICA and MICA taxes. Yes, your paystubs only reflect half of the cut today's retirees take out of every dollar you earn.

If the gross on your paycheck is $1,000, MICA and FICA take $75 from you—and that's before you have paid a penny in income tax. But meanwhile, your employer also pays $75 in MICA and FICA. That means an employer is paying $1,075 and the employee (before income taxes) is pocketing only $925. That's a 16.5-percent hiring tax, and we're only getting started.

Federal law requires employers to pay for unemployment insurance for their workers. States administer this program, and so the rates vary and are based on complex formulae, but Intuit's Small Business Services says that this typically costs somewhere from 2 percent to 6 percent of wages, and that "4 percent is typical for new employers." (In New York and Maryland, it's 9 percent.) So for your $1,000-a-week employee, add $40 a week for unemployment insurance. Now you're paying $1,115 for him to take home $925 before income taxes.

Some states require employers to participate in the workers' compensation program, adding yet another hiring tax that averages about 5 percent, according to Intuit. But in many states, workers' comp is optional or market-based, and so we won't count this as part of the hiring tax—because it is often part of the hiring premium that the free market would impose.

Intuit estimates you'll pay 1 percent or 2 percent of your employee's wages in local employment taxes. Taking the low end of that estimate, you're now paying $1,125 to get your employee $925. That's a 21.6 percent hiring penalty, not counting legal liability and the nongovernment costs that come along with hiring someone.

Keep in mind, these are taxes a business pays before it has even made a dollar in revenue, much less in profit. A business incurs this tax for the simple crime of paying an employee. That's why I call it a hiring tax.

Most of these taxes are long-standing, but the hiring tax overall has been steadily growing. President Obama talks about creating jobs, but he has made things worse with his health-care bill. The bill includes an employer mandate, requiring businesses with more than fifty employees to provide employer-sponsored health insurance. Not only is this bad health-care policy (chapter 10 explains how the employer-based system is at the heart of our health-care problems), it's also another hiring tax.

To take a special case, can you imagine anyone with forty-nine employees today hiring a fiftieth? Even if the owner was already providing health insurance for her workers, she would fear forfeiting the right to end this benefit—to trade it out for higher wages, or some other benefit her workers might want—by hiring one more. The same goes for the boss with forty-five employees looking to hire a new division. Thanks to ObamaCare, she's now more likely to contract that out. And someone with fifty-two employees is going to fire three of them before the law goes into effect.

All aspects of the hiring tax discourage employment. If you tax something, you get less of it. At times, big-government politicians seem to understand this. Why do they propose tobacco taxes and soda taxes? They want to raise the price of behavior in order to discourage it. Taxing employment, of course, has the same effect.

An employee who wants to take home $30,000 a year (before income taxes, commuting costs, health care, 401(k), and so on) has to add $36,500 in value to a company just to cover his wages and the hiring tax. That huge tax depresses wages in all cases, and in many borderline cases, the employment tax convinces a boss not to make the hire. Instead he might outsource that function to a different firm. If he can automate the task—with an expensive software program, or a new machine for manufacturers—he will. Or, worse, the employer might decide simply not to expand operations at all.

This last case—where the hiring tax keeps small business from growing—hurts the employer (who forgoes the potential for more profits), the would-be employee (who is still out of work), and consumers, who now have one less option.

Solution: End the Hiring Tax

The biggest thing the government could do to stimulate hiring would be to abolish the payroll tax that pays for Medicare and Social Security.

The closest any politicians come to this is to propose brief payroll tax holidays, which are silly. They don't appeal to serious businessmen, who know that they'll be paying this tax for a vast majority of the employee's tenure—it's like a bank offering a one-month teaser rate on a long-term loan.

The ideal "fix" for the payroll tax is complete and permanent abolition. Of course, this requires abolishing Social Security and Medicare. That's not an easy move politically—many pundits and politicians think it's impossible. In chapter 8, I'll lay out in detail how and why we can abolish these entitlements. Even if we have to settle for a slow phase-out of these programs, a partial cut in the payroll tax would still stimulate hiring in the short term.

The other components of the hiring tax can be cut, too—including mandatory unemployment insurance, which should be fully privatized and made optional.

Now, of course, unemployment insurance is valuable—especially if you get laid off. But once you're unemployed, it makes it harder for you to get a good-paying job because it makes it more expensive for businesses to hire you. If unemployment insurance were optional for employers, some would offer it and some wouldn't. (Later, we'll talk more about why government unemployment insurance should be scrapped.)

As an employer, I might buy into an optional unemployment insurance program, and use that as a way to attract good workers who were looking for income security. My competition across the street, however, might not, opting instead to pay higher wages. A worker would weigh which pay package he valued most. Making unemployment insurance optional would expand the choices workers have, and make it easier for businesses to hire by giving them a way to reduce the hiring tax.

It will also enable employees to self-insure if they wish—to save some of each paycheck until they have a few months of living expenses in the bank. We'll discuss these options later in this chapter.

Alternatively, employees could purchase their own private unemployment insurance policy much the way they buy fire or auto insurance. There's no reason government has to be the sole provider of such coverage. Aflac could sell it to you along with casualty insurance. A private insurer would charge premiums based on risk—someone with a stable employment history would pay lower premiums than someone who keeps losing his job. This would provide positive incentives. Under the government system, all workers pay the same rate, regardless of risk.

State and local governments can and should abolish their other hiring taxes, too. But even if we get rid of all the hiring taxes, there are still other hiring penalties—indirect costs that government imposes on every new hire.

Other Hiring Penalties

Hiring a person will always bring extra costs, regardless of government policies. It's worth repeating that in a free market the cost of a new employee isn't merely his salary. You might need to add another parking spot, get some new office space, or buy a new computer, phone, and phone line. With more workers, your office will use more printer paper, toner, tissues, water, and coffee. You may need to pay more for the added human resources work.

But government adds significantly to the indirect costs. These indirect hiring penalties are usually described as "worker protection" laws, and sometimes they do protect workers from unscrupulous bosses. But often, "worker protection" laws don't protect anyone—they simply discourage employers from hiring in the first place.

Antidiscrimination laws are among the most obvious forms of hiring penalty—and the most harmful, because they hurt the very people they are supposed to protect. Antidiscrimination laws actually create incentives for discrimination.

Everyone I hire is someone I might have to fire someday. He's also someone whom I might pass over for a promotion or a pay raise. Certainly, at the time I hire someone, I'm not planning to fire him, but every boss knows that all hires come with massive uncertainty. We have to take that uncertainty into account when making a hiring decision.

Hurt feelings and even wounded morale are often the cost of any decision to fire or pass over a worker. But thanks to discrimination law, there are greater costs if the person you fire or refuse a raise is black, a woman, or disabled, Buddhist, elderly, or any other protected class. Many small employers are afraid that the Equal Employment Opportunity Commission (EEOC) could come after them for racial or sex discrimination. And being innocent of discrimination doesn't inoculate them: Even if the government finds no evidence of discrimination, the process is a painful and costly experience for any small business person to endure.

Not only does an employer's own conduct expose him to a potential antidiscrimination lawsuit, but he is also at risk for the conduct of his other employees. This is a significant risk, and much harder to mitigate, since it involves the actions of third parties. It makes it even easier for disgruntled employees to make false allegations, as employers have no direct knowledge of the facts. Under current law, employers are basically responsible for providing sexually or racially stress-free environments where no employee ever feels offended or uncomfortable. While this may be an admirable goal, it is very difficult to achieve, and many small employers simply do not want to pay for it, or risk not meeting the expectations of their minority or female employees.

So a rational employer reacts by being extra careful when hiring minorities and women. He's less willing to take a risk with a minority or woman hire—say a really bright kid just out of school but with no employment history—than he would be with a white employee, simply because of the risk of a discrimination suit.

In other words, hiring a minority brings added liabilities, in the form of a potential EEOC case, thus making these candidates less desirable. The perverse effect: antidiscrimination laws reward discrimination.

The irony is that a free market punishes discrimination.

If I refuse to hire women and blacks, I am omitting qualified workers from my hiring pool. If my competitor is simply buying up the best available talent regardless of color or sex, he'll have a more skilled team. Any employer who really does discriminate simply based on race or sex is putting his bigotry ahead of profit. Antidiscrimination laws, however, make it profitable to discriminate.

Also, while small employers can easily refrain from hiring members of protected groups, larger companies cannot. It would be easy for a black job applicant to allege discrimination if a company with one thousand employees, none of them black, refused to hire him. It's not so easy if it's a small company with just two white employees. So large companies incur great legal and human resources expenses to mitigate discrimination lawsuits, and are forced to pay out significant sums to settle claims, many of which are totally baseless. The result is that money that might have been used to hire is instead used to fend off lawsuits and pay off disgruntled employees. Another way larger companies can mitigate the risk is to hire as few workers as possible—which in turn affects employment numbers nationally.

Abolishing discrimination laws would reduce the hiring penalty, therefore benefiting women and minorities. We need to maintain antidiscrimination laws in public sectors, however, as there are no market-based safeguards to punish bad behavior by government employers.

Discrimination Law 2.0

In August 2013, a tentative agreement was reached on an eight-year-long racial discrimination lawsuit against Merrill Lynch. This wasn't really about pay—regardless of color, these brokers all depend on performance-based commissions. But black brokers, the suit alleged, had been given inadequate support, were excluded from servicing certain clients, and were badmouthed by the company's executives. (Incidentally, the company's CEO at the time the suit was filed was black.)

The settlement, expected to be approved in coming months, would pay $160 million to 1,200 of the company's current and former African American employees.

Even if it has more merit in some areas than meets the eye, the damage this suit will do to blacks in the financial industry is incalculable. To put it bluntly, this will make it a lot harder for young black brokers to be hired.

One of the claims in this case was that Merrill Lynch didn't do enough to make sure its black brokers succeeded. I'm in this business, and I can tell you firsthand that when you hire a broker, that's just not your responsibility. It's like Special Forces training. You hire brokers expecting most of them to fail and drop out. You might hire 100 people, and a year later, there are ten still there.

According to this theory, Merrill Lynch owed a special duty to black brokers that it did not owe to brokers of other races. If despite being on identical payout grids, black brokers on average earned less than white brokers, Merrill Lynch had a responsibility to remedy the disparity. This is not about equal pay for equal work. Again, brokers work on commission, and so pay varies by performance. Yet if black brokers fail to perform, it's because their employer is racist.

Another claim was that Merrill Lynch's practice of encouraging brokers to form teams disadvantaged black brokers, as white brokers were supposedly reluctant to team up with black brokers. But probably one of the most disturbing elements of the case was the supposed smoking gun admission by Merrill's former CEO Stanley O'Neal (who is black), who in discovery stated that "black brokers might have a harder time because most of the firm's prospective clients were white and might not trust their wealth to brokers who were not." So not only is Merrill Lynch supposedly liable for the silent, yet unproven prejudices of its brokers, but for those of its clients as well!

Customers have a legal right to discriminate. It's against the law for a restaurant to refuse service to a black customer solely because of his race, but if a white customer refuses to dine at a restaurant because the waiter is black, there is no legal recourse for the restaurateur or the waiter. But by the logic used in this case, the black waiter would be able to sue his employer to recover the lost tip!

And the most chilling aspect of the case is the certification of the class action status of the plaintiffs. Simply being black was all that was required to qualify. Even Merrill's top-producing black brokers, making far more than most white brokers, were entitled to compensation. Clearly, the most successful black brokers were not disadvantaged by discrimination, yet they were unjustly enriched simply by virtue of their race.

So what does this new legal precedent say to brokerage firms, or other companies that hire commission-based salespeople? It says that if they hire a white broker and he fails, they're fine, but if they hire a black broker and he fails, they might get sued. How do you think employers will react to that when making future hiring decisions?

Government has also made it harder for black brokers by cracking down on the old practices by which brokers once succeeded. Back when I started out in the business, it was a lot easier to break in because you could build your client list by cold-calling. Today, with the Do Not Call list and other regulations, there's too much regulatory risk in cold-calling, so most firms don't allow it, and many shy away similarly from other innovations such as social media, which tend to level the racial playing field.

Thanks to the regulations, brokers must rely much more on connections and relationships, which automatically favor people who are from affluent, well-connected families—on average, a crowd that is disproportionately white.

Thus, in multiple ways, government has made it harder for people from poorer and minority backgrounds to do well in the financial sector.

Hiring Penalty Hits Small Business the Most

The biggest hiring penalties usually come with a businessman's first hire.

Imagine a husband and wife that start a business making and selling picnic tables. At first, they simply work out of the workshop on their property, turning out tables. As demand grows, they realize they need to hire a full-time employee to process all the orders, pay the bills, and collect payments.

As always, there are costs that come with this hire. But the government-imposed costs are huge. Federal, state, and local governments all have workplace requirements regarding lighting, office furniture, restrooms, and so on. The government will require the couple to post all sorts of signs around the office—lighted EXIT signs, posters explaining minimum wage and workman's compensation laws. Then there are employment taxes and payroll withholding that not only cost money to collect, but require time to administer—time and money that otherwise could have been put to more productive use.

These costs might not matter to a business with tons of capital, but Mom & Pop will feel the pain.

Some regulations don't penalize the first hire, but affect some subsequent hire—such as the ObamaCare mandate for anyone who dares hire fifty people, and the Americans with Disabilities Act (ADA) for anyone who has the gall to employ fifteen people. Again, think about the incentives here. If you've got fourteen employees, the fifteenth hire comes with a huge hiring penalty.

In March 2011, the Obama administration, through regulations, expanded the ADA to the point where the law can be triggered by the slightest "disabilities," even temporary ones. In other words, a brief illness or injury, or some condition like asthma, claustrophobia, or obsessive-compulsive disorder, can count as a "disability," thus requiring employers to make often-expensive accommodations. The new regulations also place the burden of proof on an employer—that he *didn't* discriminate or that the employee *wasn't* disabled—rather than the other way around.

You can bet any attentive employer with fifteen employees in March 2011 hurried to fire someone so that they could get below the threshold before the new regs kicked in.

While many "worker-protection" regulations exempt smaller employers, in general, the costs of these rules all fall more heavily on smaller businesses. Providing ramps, bathrooms, or any benefit for one hundred employees does *not* cost one hundred times as much as providing them for one employee. Government regulations on employers reward economies of scale, and thus disproportionately punish small employers.

When the media does acknowledge the economic costs of these regulations, it always presents the debate as a trade-off between worker protection and economic growth. But even this framing is false. This section has shown that these "worker protection" laws often undermine their stated goal—for instance, antidiscrimination laws incentivizing discrimination.

So where can workers find protection? The answer is: the market. And the stronger the economy, the more protection the worker gets.

If an employer treats his workers poorly, he is asking his employees to leave. Sure, an abusive or thoughtless boss can get people to work for him, but he will always be overpaying them—if someone can get a less abusive boss for the same pay, he will quit and take the other job. On the flip side, many workers might opt for better work conditions over a higher salary, thus providing a discount for good bosses.

The net economic effect is lower costs for good bosses and higher costs for bad bosses. In other words, in a free market, it's profitable to treat your employees well. "Worker protection" regulation in some cases might protect workers, but mostly it just imposes new costs and kills jobs.

Wages Need to Fall

Hiring taxes and other hiring penalties add to the cost of employing someone. Their elimination means that more of the boss's outlays end up in the workers' hands. But improving the jobs situation will also require some pain for employees.

It's unpleasant to say it, but for unemployment to come down, wages will need to come down. Supply and demand is really quite simple. We have a surplus of workers. In order to increase demand for labor, the price of labor must fall. That means our government needs to end some policies that keep wages high, and resist the temptation to use regulation or the Federal Reserve to prop up wages.

America needs to start making things again. It's a pipe dream that we can keep buying everything from China and paying for it with our national credit card. In addition to labor and environmental regulations, the cheap wages of Asia and Mexico make it profitable for American companies to have their work done over there. If American wages were lower, many companies would start manufacturing here. Instead, marginally skilled American workers remain unemployed. Some turn to crime, and our trade deficit continues to balloon.

On a more elementary level: wages *are* going to come down one way or another. Wages are a function of worker productivity. Productivity is a function of capital and skills. Worker skills are falling in the United States, in part because of our horrific education system that keeps kids in worthless classes and out of the workplace (we'll address this in more depth when discussing the minimum wage). And free capital is basically nonexistent in the United States thanks to a punitive tax code, burdensome regulations, massive budget deficits, and reckless monetary policy.

So American workers simply cannot be as productive as they used to be, especially relative to the rest of the world. The natural consequence is falling wages, but the government can prevent this by printing more money. If the value of the dollar goes down faster than the value of an hour of work, your nominal wages will go up. But that's still a wage reduction, because this inflation will drive up the price of consumer goods even faster. If your wages rise slower than your cost of living, you're getting poorer, but you might not notice it as easily, which is good for the politicians.

Politicians will do everything they can in order to prevent nominal wages from falling—they're already doing plenty on that score. But if they're interested in the health of the economy, especially if they're really interested in job growth, our politicians will let wages fall, both by resisting the temptation to inflate the currency and by repealing those policies that artificially boost wages.

Repeal the Minimum Wage

The most elementary step to take is to eliminate the minimum wage. Although the minimum wage probably does boost wages for some workers, its primary effect is to deter businessmen from hiring. If I calculate an unskilled worker in a certain job would be worth $6 an hour to me, but minimum wage is $7.25, I just won't hire him. Of course, if nobody wants the job for $6 an hour, the law makes no difference. That means that the only effect of the law is to outlaw a mutually consensual agreement.

So, what effect does the minimum wage have on employment? It eliminates from the job market any job that an employer thinks is worth less than minimum wage. For a few borderline cases, it will mean slightly higher wages, but their benefit comes at the cost of the millions who are out of work because the job they would have is now illegal.

But there are longer-term consequences of a high minimum wage. Most important, outlawing entry-level jobs dries up opportunities for on-the-job training. Recall our earlier discussion about the elements needed for employment—the employee needs to have the relevant skills.

When labor skills come up, politicians immediately start talking about education (particularly government-funded education), but our schools don't (and shouldn't) teach factory skills or office skills. In the past, job skills were learned on the job. But someone who is learning a job is probably not very productive compared to experienced employees—and he may be taking up the time of the more senior workers training him.

On-the-job training often only makes sense at low wages—or even zero wages. Put another way, a young worker provides labor, and most of his compensation comes in the skills he acquires rather than in cash or benefits. Minimum wage laws severely restrict this sort of arrangement at the lower end. The result: fewer young American workers possess basic work skills. People in Mexico and China are allowed to work for low wages, and so more American jobs get shipped overseas. Also, there's no minimum wage for machines, and so more jobs get automated.

To make matters worse, the Department of Labor in August 2010 issued new regulations cracking down on unpaid internships. A businessman can run afoul of the law if the intern could be considered to "displace regular employees" or if the intern works under insufficiently "close supervision of existing staff." Even worse, the regulation requires that "the employer that provides the training derives no immediate advantage from the activities of the intern."

Crashproof Yourself: Look Out for That Union Label

The auto bailouts taught us an important lesson: Be wary of buying bonds in unionized companies, because if the company goes under while a Democrat is in the White House, creditors will get shoved to the back of the line. After George W. Bush bailed out the automakers, Barack Obama managed their bankruptcy. Obama threw aside bankruptcy precedent, and put senior creditors in line behind the United Auto Workers (UAW). Obama even used the bully pulpit to attack those senior creditors who wanted their due. The UAW, which had spent millions to aid in Obama's election, took ownership of Chrysler, while senior creditors took a bath. Not only are unions likely to push a company toward bankruptcy, they're also likely to cut in line when bankruptcy hits.

Predictably, internship organizations started reporting in early 2011 that they had difficulty placing interns, because employers feared running afoul of Uncle Sam. The inevitable result: employers needing interns and young people needing internships. This is just a variation on minimum wage laws, which keep willing workers from willing employers.

The argument usually given in support of the minimum wage is that no one can support a family on four dollars an hour. But entry-level jobs are not supposed to provide enough income to support a family. By the time individuals are old enough to marry and have children, they should have acquired the skills necessary to command much higher pay. They acquire those skills working for low wages while still in their teens and prior to marriage. If the minimum wage law prevents them from getting those jobs, they will never acquire the skills necessary to support a family. In other words, the minimum wage knocks the bottom rung off the job ladder, making it impossible for many to ever climb up.

For those still looking for a real-world example of how a minimum wage destroys jobs, there is no better example than American Samoa. In 2007 the U.S. Congress applied the federal minimum wage to Samoa, a U.S. territory. The increases walloped the Samoan economy, with the unemployed rate soaring to 30 percent and inflation hitting double digits. Its largest employer, Chicken of the Sea, shut down its Samoan canning operation completely in 2009, laying off 2,041 employees. The island's second largest employer, StarKist, laid off 400 workers the following year with plans to lay off 400 more.

Making matters worse, since the island's canned-tuna exports collapsed, fewer ships left Samoan ports. As a result, it became much more expensive to import, as tuna exports no longer defrayed shipping costs for imports. The island was hit by a double whammy of unemployment and inflation. Congress had succeeded in destroying the Samoan economy, not by an act of war, but simply by imposing a higher minimum wage.

Unemployment Insurance

Another government policy keeping wages and unemployment high: indefinite unemployment insurance. Why go back to work for a pay cut when you can take a government check indefinitely?

If you simply compare a paycheck to an unemployment check, you might find it hard to believe that anyone would tolerate being unemployed if there is an alternative—an unemployment check averages only about $260 per week (though in Massachusetts, they can go over $700 per week).[3] But when you step back and look at the whole picture, you begin to see how this isn't such a bad deal.

Total family income in a dual-earner family falls by an average of 26 percent when one worker loses his job and goes on unemployment, according to the Congressional Budget Office (CBO). Imagine that couple was earning a combined $70,000. According to CBO averages, they would now be earning $51,800. At first glance that looks like a loss of $18,200 per year, but here's the question to ask: how does that $18,200 compare to the *costs* of working and the *benefits* of not having to go to work?

What are the *costs* of working? It depends on the individual, but they could be many. Commuting costs can be huge. If you ride the train or the bus, you're spending somewhere from $3 to $10 per day, or $750 to $2,500 per year. If you drive, you're paying for gasoline, maybe tolls, maybe parking (which alone is easily $2,000 per year in a big city). Driving to work wears down your tires and puts wear and tear on your car—the Internal Revenue Service (IRS) estimates about fifty cents per mile.

So, you could easily be paying a few thousand dollars a year just to get to work. If you're unemployed, you save that money. Even better, you may be able to sell your second car, pocket the cash, and save on insurance and registration.

Depending on your occupation, the costs of working might include dry-cleaning bills, shoe shines, and the cost of replacing suits, dress shirts, and dress shoes.

Working people also pay more to eat: you're more likely to shell out $9 for a sandwich near your office, as opposed to making your own at home for a total cost of less than $2, probably. If you and your spouse both work, when do you have time to make dinner or go shopping? You'll order out more, adding to the cost of working.

And most significant, if you have young children, when both parents are working there are huge costs of day care. When one parent is unemployed, you can save that money.

Other domestic tasks for which you might normally pay someone—mowing the lawn, cleaning the house, walking the dogs—you can now do yourself, saving even more. Flexible hours and more free time also provide opportunities for savings: search for coupons, rush out to a sale, travel off-peak, catch the matinee.

For some people, all these costs of working could make up for the shortfall between a paycheck and an unemployment check, meaning that working simply isn't worth it. And we haven't even counted the nonmonetary benefits.

Most people don't live to work, they work to live. With a few exceptions, most people have jobs only because they need a job in order to afford the stuff they really want and need. When you're unemployed you can relax more, catch up on reading, visit family, exercise more, and go sightseeing. Also, you don't have to worry about annoying colleagues, stressful deadlines, and aggravating commutes. Government unemployment insurance (UI) is one more benefit of not working—obviously, you don't get unemployment payments if you're working.

So add up all the benefits of not working and all the costs of working, and it might be more than your pay (especially after taxes). This dynamic obviously increases unemployment by making it more desirable. It also drives up wages in a couple of ways.

First, unemployment insurance decreases the actual labor pool by decreasing the incentive to work. By decreasing the supply of labor, UI increases the price of labor. In other words, people who have jobs can ask for more money, because as long as some people are content to live on unemployment, current workers have less competition.

Second, unemployment insurance raises the marginal costs of working, meaning an employer needs to pay more to get someone to work. Think about it this way: if your take-home pay is $750 per week, but that involves giving up $250 per week in unemployment benefits, the marginal gain of your job is only $500 per week—before you even count all the costs of working that I discussed above.

For many of the unemployed, the marginal tax on getting a job is so high (the tax being the taxes paid on earned income plus the unemployment compensation forgone) that the only jobs many on unemployment will take are those that pay cash under the table. That way, the unemployed can earn extra tax-free income without giving up their unemployment benefits. From an economic perspective, society gains more when someone works under-the-table rather than staying home watching TV. But government loses tax revenue, pays unnecessary unemployment benefits, and unemployment statistics are exaggerated.

Abolishing government unemployment insurance would be a huge boost to employment. It would allow wages to fall and reduce the hiring tax by eliminating the required unemployment tax. As we discussed above, a free market could develop in unemployment insurance, but probably the best alternative would be self-insuring by workers.

Without unemployment insurance premiums, workers' wages would be higher, and they could save that money as a rainy day fund—effectively unemployment insurance. Savings would compound with interest, and society would benefit as those savings were invested to grow the economy and create other jobs until the employee needed the funds.

Now think about what happens when that self-insured person becomes unemployed. He can still get by, because he has his savings, but he has an incentive to find a job as quickly as possible, because the longer he's unemployed, the more his savings shrink.

Under the current system, there is no pool of savings—the government simply pays you as long as you're unemployed, up to some upper limit (which Congress keeps extending, and is now nearly two years). So finding a job in four weeks as opposed to four months might not save you any money. A self-insured person will rush back to work as quickly as he can find a good job. To the extent that we continue government-run unemployment insurance, it should pay off in one lump sum. That way there is no incentive to delay working. It might end up costing more money if every claim were to max out, but the government would recoup the losses by collecting payroll taxes from workers who otherwise would have delayed their return to the workforce until they had exhausted their unemployment benefits. In addition, the economy would be more productive due to all the additional effort of workers who otherwise would have been idle.

All of my policy proposals—not inflating the currency, ending minimum wage, and ending federal unemployment insurance—would result in lower wages. I know that sounds like a bad thing (if you're a wage earner reading this section, you're probably thinking "why would I ever want wages to fall?") but the overall effect will be beneficial.

What would broadly lower wages mean for the average American? For unemployed people, it would be easier to find a job, even if at a lower wage. For those of us with jobs, it would probably mean lower pay, but, in addition, prices would go down on many things. Your quality of life could increase even in the short term if prices fell faster than your wages.

It's also possible, though, that you're one of the people currently benefiting from artificially inflated wages. Maybe unemployment insurance is deterring a would-be competitor from going for your job. Maybe, without minimum wage laws and mandatory benefits, your employer would hire two low-skilled workers to replace you. But every time the government skews the economy somebody benefits and somebody loses. Removing those distortions will, of course, harm those who were previously benefiting.

But in the long run, we'd have a stronger economy with a manufacturing base and more flexibility for entrepreneurs to create value.

All Regulations Kill Jobs

It's not only workplace regulations that kill jobs. It's almost all regulations. While politicians and the media portray regulations as a way to keep "big business" in check, the real effect of regulation is often to crush their smaller competitors and to keep others from even entering the fray to begin with.

Now, I'm not one of those "small business" fetishists you always see in Washington and the media. I don't think government policy should favor small business over big, and even though I am a small businessman, I don't share the romantic view of Mom & Pop that most Americans do. But this much is clear: crushing small business is a great way to crush job creation.

Start-up businesses are easily the largest source of new jobs in the United States, according to a 2010 study by the nonpartisan, centrist Kauffman Foundation. According to this study, 64 percent of all net job creation came from companies that were less than five years old.

Even if we don't count new firms, the politicians' cliché is true: small business is the engine of job creation. In 2007, for instance, 53 percent of all net job creation (not counting new firms) came from firms with nineteen or fewer employees.

A 2010 Kauffman study makes it clear that there's nothing magical about small firms or new firms that makes them special job creators. In fact, a new company is more likely to fold than an established firm, thus shedding its new jobs. So, the answer is not to favor or subsidize small businesses, but to stop killing them. After all, regulations that prevent new businesses from entering the economy don't stop other small businesses from dying—they probably accelerate that process.

According to economist Mark Crain, the cost of complying with federal regulations is $1.187 trillion per year.[4] Repealing most of these regulations would stimulate job growth, but some regulations are more destructive of jobs than others. It's hard enough for a small business to succeed without government raising the bar with the high cost of regulations. Not only must a business succeed in satisfying some consumer demand at a profit, but it also must do so in a way that allows it to overcome the extra costs imposed by government regulation. As a direct result many business ventures that otherwise might have succeeded end in failure.

For pure stifling of entrepreneurship, nothing beats licensing laws. In Louisiana, you can't be a florist without getting a license. In order to get a floristry license, you need to spend a few thousand dollars and many hours studying. And who judges the test? Currently licensed florists. Guess what their incentives are.

The Institute for Justice regularly challenges unnecessary state-level licensing laws (tour guides in D.C., for instance, break the law if they describe historical sites without a license). The point of these laws is to protect existing businesses from competition. They kill jobs. Of course, the official justification is to protect the public from bad floral arrangements. But are bad floral arrangements really such an ominous threat as to merit costly government regulation to guard against them? The worst-case scenario is someone gets a bad arrangement and takes his future business to a different florist. The best protection consumers have is a highly competitive market. Ironically, licensing laws limit competition, thereby weakening that protection.

States should repeal all unnecessary licensing laws. They'll see more entrepreneurs if they do, and thus more new jobs, particularly among poorer minorities disproportionately harmed by such laws.

There are literally hundreds of federal and state regulations that deter entrepreneurs from starting new businesses. If Congress and state legislatures repealed these regulations—from forced unionization rules to environmental and safety rules—we would see thousands of new businesses bloom and hiring pick up. Of course politicians will claim those jobs will come at the expense of greater injury to workers in the unsafe working conditions that would exist absent government safety regulations. This is sheer nonsense, as in a competitive market workers will consider working conditions when evaluating jobs and employers will seek to provide safe working environments to attract employees. Complying with most safety related rules does little to improve safety but adds significantly to employment costs, resulting in fewer job opportunities and fewer competitive businesses.

So there's something the government *can* do to help job growth: get out of the way.

Jobs 2.0: More Thoughts on How to Bring Them Back

In 2013, government stepped up its war on jobs. It wasn't just the federal Obamacare program, which is encouraging not only businesses but also states, government-run universities, and municipalities to convert their workforces to part-time wherever possible. State control of the economy was on the march all over America.

Fittingly, the municipal government in Washington, D.C., was leading the charge. In 2013, Walmart had planned to open six new stores in Washington, and it had already broken ground on some of them. It was expected to be a boon for the city's residents, who often have to travel well outside the District's limits to shop. Unlike many of Walmart's previous ventures, this one was undertaken without corporate welfare incentives. They weren't getting any goodies in return from the District—they just wanted to expand and make a few more bucks by servicing an underserved customer base. By bringing fresh produce and meats into the district with their grocery sections, the new Walmart stores were additionally poised to end the so-called "food desert" status of several neighborhoods in D.C.

Naturally, the District's government tried as hard as it could to screw this up. Unions and incumbent local businesses held such enormous sway over the City Council that they got it to pass a law requiring Walmart to pay a minimum wage—a "living wage"—50 percent higher than the one that all other businesses must pay employees in the District of Columbia.

Unionized businesses were specifically exempted from this law, as were stores below a certain number of square feet. The fact that only Walmart would have been affected by the law is proof enough that its true purpose was simply to keep a competitor out of the market.

When the law passed the District's council, Walmart announced that it might not be opening three of its planned stores as a result. This would have cost the District—which had lost 4,000 jobs in May—another 900 new jobs. Mayor Vince Gray vetoed the bill, but that only put pressure on local lawmakers to chase away more low-skilled jobs by passing an across-the board minimum wage hike.

The Obama administration has also aggressively moved to expand the universe of lawsuits against businesses. One good example: The move to require wheelchair lifts (in many cases, multiple ones) for all public-access swimming pools, including public pools, under the Americans with Disabilities Act. At first, the Justice Department tried to force all pools to install fixed lifts before summer 2012. After pool operators simply threatened a mass shutdown, the deadlines were moved and the Justice Department "clarified" that lifts would not be required where owners could show the accommodation was "unachievable." Even so, that exception doesn't stop the nuisance lawsuits. In summer 2013, dozens of lawsuits were filed right away. One plaintiff filed twenty-two of them against Indianapolis-area hotels that had failed to comply, and received out-of-court settlements in several of the cases for his trouble. This sort of "legal extortion" is expensive for business owners, and obviously affects the number of people they can afford to hire.

Small pool operators have this in common with the National Football League, which was forced in 2013 to settle a case with 18,000 former football players who might have been harmed by concussions while playing the game. The NFL is paying out $765 million over the next twenty years. It's true that a growing body of science supports the idea that football is a dangerous game that causes more concussions than previously believed. But what's important to note here is the default assumption that the league, the employer, is responsible for players engaging in a risky game.

The NFL is Mr. Deep Pockets here. Those not being sued include the players themselves (who chose to play for a living and in most cases made millions doing so), players' parents (who may have encouraged them to play), their high school coaches, and their colleges. The litigators automatically latch on to employers—to those who create society's wealth—as the cash cows to whom all responsibility can be conveniently attributed in a courtroom.

Also in 2013, activists began a new push to forbid unpaid internships—the educational stints that young people go through in order to obtain job skills. It was a well-coordinated push, with a legal and social media presence as well as significant coverage in the traditional media.

The destruction of all internships or a war on unskilled workers wasn't the stated purpose of this crusade, of course. Rather, it was framed as an attempt by unpaid workers to get something they justly deserved. Interns began suing employers and winning judgments because they wanted pay for unpaid internships to which they had agreed. Two interns at Fox Searchlight's movie studios actually sued over the unpaid internships they had agreed to do, and won summary judgment in June 2013. So you can now accept a temporary job, knowing it's unpaid, and then turn around later and sue.

If this catches on, then the result is quite predictable—no more internships. As most professionals who have had to deal with interns can tell you, they are barely worth the trouble when they're free. But internships have traditionally existed so that young people can develop job skills and put something on their résumé before they apply for their first job. A lot of businesses take on interns because they're screening them as potential future employees, or perhaps just because they are generous enough to share their seasoned workers' experience with the young. That will soon end.

The Obama Labor Department has cooperated in this ill-conceived venture by cracking down on unpaid internships. The Labor Department's guiding principle is that unpaid internships are illegal if the interns involved do anything of use to the companies where they work—which, of course, completely defeats the purpose, if an internship is supposed to help someone gain job experience and skill.

Young people will, as a result, be forced to pay to work, instead of just working for free. Thanks to the government's intervention in this area, the only safe way for an employer to find interns now is to bring on people who get their internships through universities for college credit—after borrowing thousands of dollars and paying through the nose.

Politicians—including President Obama—frequently complain that

Americans lack job skills, and they propose a hundred different ways to confer those skills by spending billions of taxpayers' dollars. Yet private internships were providing such skills at no cost whatsoever to taxpayers, and government has found a way to step in and ruin it.

The ultimate irony is that were it not for the minimum wage and other government mandated employment related costs, most internships would come with some type of stipend. It might not be much, perhaps amounting to just a few dollars per hour, but most would consider low pay preferable to no pay. I said most, because the government actually prefers the latter. Up until these recent court cases, it was illegal to work for less then the minimum wage, but it was not illegal to work for free. So thanks to government, the only way many young people could gain the experience they needed was to work for free. The courts have now effectively closed that legal loophole, too.

In these and other ways, government is going to great lengths to end employment as we know it. Sure, it's true that many businesses can't avoid hiring people. But for any business that has a choice, the worst thing you can do today is become an employer. Fewer and fewer of them are making that mistake.

Every time government thinks it is doing something to help employees— forcing businesses to pay a minimum wage, "living wages," employee health coverage, workers' compensation, unemployment insurance, payroll taxes, et cetera—it is incrementally increasing the incentive not to hire anyone. For every job that once made sense for businesses to keep in-house, government keeps making it more cost competitive to automate, outsource to contractors, or send the work overseas. And incredibly, after voting for politicians who promise to put such new burdens on hiring, people still wonder why it's so hard for high-school dropouts to find work today!

Americans who lack skills can't find jobs anymore unless their employers are willing to overpay—and it's not necessarily even the workers' fault. They're not demanding outrageous compensation. But nowadays, an employer who simply wants to meet a worker's financial needs in exchange for his labor cannot do so without paying tribute into multiple government funds and then, on top of that, paying a premium for the opportunity costs of working—to make up for the fact that government rewards the choice not to work.

Let me illustrate what I mean by "the opportunity costs of working." I was recently in the market for domestic help, and a young woman I wanted to hire as a housekeeper refused the job because I wouldn't pay her under the table. No, she wasn't an illegal alien—she just wanted me to treat her as one.

The reason she made this unusual demand was that if she had income to report, she would suddenly have to start making student loan payments and paying taxes. To work for me would have cost her hundreds of dollars every month, creating a big enough hit to her bottom line that it wasn't worth working anymore. (Perhaps she wasn't savvy enough to apply for all of the available government programs, but she could have just as well pointed out that my hiring her would have cost her thousands annually in food stamps and other welfare payments.) Just imagine—there are so many unemployed people today, and yet government is making it too expensive for anyone to come and clean your floors for a fair wage. (By the way, the job I offered paid close to $40,000 per year.)

Here was someone who admitted that reality quite bluntly—and I still regret the fact that I couldn't hire her legally.

Wouldn't this young lady be better off if government wasn't giving her so many disincentives to work? And wouldn't most people in my position and yours—who have a severe shortage of time—enjoy a better quality of life and greater productivity if government didn't add so much to the cost of hiring unskilled people to help? There was a win-win proposition on the table for both of us and the government was preventing either of us from taking it.

When it comes to jobs, big government is creating a lose-lose situation for everyone.

In fact, domestic help is one area where government has had a major impact. At one time in America, it was quite common for middle class families to have full-time live-in help. All of the prewar apartments on New York's Upper West Side were built for middle-class families, and they all have servants' quarters and servants' entrances. (Today, of course, those quarters serve as home offices or even family bedrooms.) Just take a look at any prewar newspaper and they are filled with help-wanted ads for domestic help.

What happened? After all, back then, few women worked outside the home, yet they still had help. One would think that with today's working moms, there would be even more need for an extra pair of hands to help with the housework.

The answer is that government happened. First, income tax obligations reduced disposable income so that fewer middle-class families could afford to pay for housekeepers. Second, minimum wage laws and the requirement to pay payroll taxes and withhold income taxes on domestic salaries made offering such jobs more expensive as well.

But the real problem is that the government has made it so lucrative for young single women, who used to fill these jobs, to earn more money living on welfare instead. Why scrub someone else's floors when you can "earn" more money without doing anything? Can you blame a single parent for making this rational choice not to work?

According to a 2013 Cato study, a Connecticut unwed mother of two participating in seven welfare programs (Temporary Assistance for Needy Families, Medicaid, food stamps, WIC, housing assistance, utility assistance and free commodities) can receive an annual benefits package worth $38,761. Since these benefits are untaxed, and wages and salaries are taxed, she would have to earn $44,366 per year to be better off working.

But in fact, it's much worse than that. If this hypothetical welfare mom were to take a job paying $44,366 per year, by the time she paid for childcare expenses for her two children, transportation to and from work, clothing, hair, makeup, and other work-related expenses, her net earnings would be well below the $38,761 she would receive staying on welfare. And of course, factor in the natural preference for leisure over work. Sleeping late, spending time with the kids, hanging out with friends, walks in the park or on the beach, watching game shows and soap operas—these are much more appealing than a day doing laundry and scrubbing floors.

My guess is that when taxes, work-related expenses, and lifestyle preferences are taken into effect, the typical welfare mom might require at least $80,000 a year before taking a job becomes more advantageous than welfare. If she files her taxes as head of household, with two children and taking advantage of all available credits, state and federal income tax liability would be $11,270 and payroll taxes would add another $6,120. So her net after-tax income would be $62,680. If you assume childcare and all work-related expenses of $250 per week, her real net income would be $49,680. That is only $10,919 more then she receives in welfare without even having to work. Is that enough to persuade a mother of two to leave her children for the daily drudgery of manual labor?

Put another way, the effective marginal tax rate on this hypothetical woman's $80,000 paycheck is 86.5 percent, because taxes, work-related expenses, and the loss of welfare benefits cost her $69,151.

I am not saying that welfare moms are lazy. I am just pointing out that they're not stupid. There is no way I would work for 13.5 cents on the dollar.

Of course, there is also no way I would pay a housekeeper $80,000 per year. And since the typical welfare mom lacks the skills to land an $80,000-per-year job, the whole discussion is moot. The welfare state renders such an individual permanently unemployable.

Before welfare benefits were so lucrative and easy to come by, poorer women with few skills and no place to live could take jobs as housekeepers. The jobs were low paying, but they came with room and board. With tax-free incomes and few living expenses, these jobs allowed housekeepers to save money, take classes at night (secretarial and nursing schools were quite common) and eventually get better-paying jobs. (That is much better than borrowing a bunch of money to get an overpriced liberal arts degree, then moving back in with your parents because you are broke with no job prospects.)

Of course, in those days, many housekeepers eventually married, and no longer needed jobs, as their husbands were able to support them.

Today, it's a completely different story. If you are young, female, and poor, the government offers a much better deal. All you need to do is have a child out of wedlock and the government will set you up in your own apartment, and provide you with food, health care, and other cash and in-kind benefits. To most poor young women, life as a welfare mom is not only more appealing than being a maid, but more socially acceptable. In a world where welfare is seen as an entitlement, actually working as a maid is considered demeaning.

Back in 1932, when the average American salary was just under $1,400 per year (of course taxes were so low back then that take-home pay and pre-tax income were almost the same), the average live-in housekeeper earned just $260 per year. So the average American earned just over five times the average housekeeper. Today the average annual salary in America is about $40,000 per year. By the 1932 metric, a live-in housekeeper would make about $8,000 per year. But there is no way that any American will work for such low wages. I pay my current housekeeper about $40,000 per year. She lives out, so she does not get room and board, but when I spoke with local domestic staffing agencies I was told that few housekeepers nowadays want to live in, and those who do demand as much pay as those who do not. That is certainly true with my housekeeper, who is in her early thirties, and married with two young children. She is working to provide the second income that her family requires to make ends meet. I was actually told that $40K was the low end of the market—more experienced housekeepers would want $50 to $60K per year.

Because my housekeeper is married to her children's father, who also earns an income, her family is not eligible for the $38,761 tax-free welfare package a single mother of two would qualify for, and therefore does not have the same incentive not to work. But since so many potential housekeepers do lack the incentive to work, the labor pool of housekeepers is greatly diminished, and wages have risen sharply as a result.

I also contacted a few domestic service companies that provide services by the hour. The rates varied, but were generally between $30 and $40 per hour, with about half of that paid in salaries to the workers. You would think that with all the unemployment in Connecticut, it would not nearly be this expensive to hire someone to help with the housework.

Putting this all in perspective, someone in 1932 who earned $4,200 per year, or roughly three times the average salary, could afford to hire a live-in housekeeper for just over 6 percent of his annual income. With housekeepers now running $40,000 per year, a middle-class household earning $120,000 would have to spend a third of their pretax annual income to hire full-time, live-in help. This is not even remotely possible. You'd have to earn $670,000 per year to hire a full-time housekeeper for just 6 percent of your income. And when taxes are taken into consideration, that figure would be much higher.

For example, in 1932, a married couple earning $4,200 and claiming the standard deduction only paid $68 dollars per year in income tax, or just 1.6 percent of total earnings. There were no state income taxes to speak of, and payroll taxes did not exist yet. My guess is that a household would have to earn over $1.1 million per year—or 27 times the average income—to afford what a middle-class households in 1932 could easily afford earning just 3 times the average.

So one result of the welfare state and high taxes was basically to destroy the domestic help industry for all but the most affluent American families. These jobs not only provided employment opportunities for low-skilled, poorer Americans, at no cost to taxpayers, but they allowed middle-class families to live more graciously. The only exceptions today are those families willing to break the law by hiring illegal immigrants, who will often perform these services at more affordable rates.

5

How to Fix the Financial Industry: Deregulate

IN FINANCE, EVERYTHING IS UNCERTAIN. The best that you can do is play the odds.

In politics, though, there are some sure bets. One thing that's inevitable: in the wake of every crisis caused by government, politicians of all stripes will prescribe a cure consisting of more government.

In late September 2008, Americans were nearly at the height of financial panic when Barack Obama and John McCain met for their first presidential debate. That month, the Fed had bailed out Fannie Mae, Freddie Mac, and AIG. Treasury Secretary Hank Paulson and Fed Chairman Ben Bernanke were working tirelessly on Capitol Hill to rally support for the Mother of All Bailouts, the Troubled Asset Relief Program (TARP).

On September 25, when McCain and Obama met on the stage at the University of Mississippi, Americans were scared. Stocks were falling and banks were closing. It was clear that something in the financial world had gone seriously wrong, that the whole country was suffering—and that things could get far worse.

In this light, Obama offered the utterly predictable analysis:

> We also have to recognize that this is a final verdict on eight years of failed economic policies promoted by George Bush, supported by Senator McCain—a theory that basically says that we can shred regulations and consumer protections and give more and more to the most, and somehow prosperity will trickle down.[1]

Obama wasn't wrong to criticize Bush's policies, but he was wrong to put the blame on "shred[ding] regulations." More important, Obama didn't mention the Fed's culpability in the crisis, nor the way government guarantees of banks—explicit and implicit—drove banks to engage in the massively risky behavior that created the crisis. Of course, Obama wasn't in a position to critique government guarantees of banks—he was supporting Bush's TARP. I pick on Obama only as one example of the conventional wisdom that blames all economic problems on insufficient regulation. Hundreds of commentators and politicians said the free market was the cause, and that government would be the solution.

The problem with our banking system has not been too little regulation, but too much. To curb excessive risk taking, we do need more "adult supervision," as Obama put it, but that supervision should come not from government officials, but from creditors and customers.

So, the big-government types are correct that our financial system is dysfunctional, and that this dysfunction is the key destabilizing factor in our economy. But the solution isn't more regulation, or even "smarter regulation." To fix our financial sector and make our economy more stable, we need something far more drastic: an actual free market. Government needs to stop telling banks what to do and stop bailing them out when they fail. No regulator will ever be as effective as the threat of failure.

The New Deal Is to Blame

Paul Krugman and other economists and pundits of his ilk will tell you that Ronald Reagan and George W. Bush brought about the 2008 financial panic by dismantling the New Deal.

Roosevelt used regulation to curb excessive risk taking, this story goes, and conservatives beholden to bankers stripped these rules, letting unbridled capitalism run its destructive course.

But in the true story, Roosevelt's New Deal bears much of the blame. It created much of the moral hazard that spurred the excessive risk taking that caused the 2008–2009 crash. Chapter 2 discussed the large role of Fannie Mae, a New Deal creation, in the housing crisis, but another FDR institution has played an even more central role in destabilizing our banking system: deposit insurance.

The Federal Deposit Insurance Corporation (FDIC) is the longest-running bailout of American banks. In short, the FDIC insures the first $250,000 of your savings account at any bank and an unlimited amount of money in your checking account. If your bank goes under and can't redeem your deposits, the FDIC will cover the difference.

While some politicians will pretend that the FDIC is about protecting bank customers from the misbehavior of banks, the agency really was created to protect banks from the free market.

High school history books and most cable news pundits will tell you that the FDIC was a prudent response to the disastrous bank runs of the Great Depression. It's true that thousands of banks failed. Bank runs were a scary reality. And some depositors did lose their money in failed banks.

But if you look more closely, you'll see that the risk of lost deposits is overstated. Economist Paul Kasriel provides the numbers from the bank failures of the Great Depression:

> Starting in 1930 and continuing through 1933, almost 9,100 commercial banks failed with deposits of $6.8 billion. The deposits of these failed banks represented 13.3 percent of total commercial bank deposits as of 1929. Net losses to depositors of these failed banks were about $1.3 billion, or approximately 19 percent of the deposits of failed commercial banks.

Sounds bad, right? But do the math. If 19 percent of deposits were lost at those 9,100 banks, and those 9,100 banks held 13.3 percent of all deposits, then the total loss of deposits at failed banks in those years was 19 percent of 13.3 percent—or 2.5 percent.

So, in the worst period of bank failures our country has ever experienced (by far), 2.5 percent of all bank deposits were lost because of bank failures. I'm not saying that's nothing, but most years that much value is erased in Americans' checking accounts by inflation alone.

Prior to deposit insurance and the money printing that makes it possible, we had over one hundred years of deflation, where bank deposits actually gained value each year. In fact, from the summer of 1929 through the first quarter of 1933 consumer prices declined by a staggering 24.4 percent. That means that even though 2.5 percent of bank deposits were lost, the 97.5 percent that remained bought approximately 20 percent more goods and services than did 100 percent of deposits prior to the crash!

But those $1.3 billion in losses took on oversized importance. The vision of long bank lines was burned into the American imagination. As it's told today, you would think huge swaths of the American population lost their entire life savings thanks to Great Depression bank failures.

Instead, what happened was that much of the population lost faith in banks. Deposits went down by 30 percent, but most of that was due to people pulling their money out.

So there you see the real threat the FDIC was created to battle: banks were losing business because customers didn't trust them. The real effect of government deposit insurance is not to protect depositors, but to protect banks.

Deposit Insurance as Moral Hazard

Federal deposit insurance creates moral hazard and promotes risky bank behavior.

Consider the difference between a world with government deposit insurance and one without it. Without deposit insurance, bank customers run the risk of losing their deposits.

You're probably aware that when you put money in a savings or checking account, the bank doesn't just lock the cash in a vault with your name on it. The bank lends your money out, or invests it. If those investments or loans lose some money, the bank is fine, as long as people don't come calling for their money right away. But if your bank loses a lot of money, you might lose everything.

So, if it were important to you that your bank take care of your money—that is, if your money were actually on the line—you would conduct some due diligence. You would try to figure out which banks are the safest stewards of your money. You would value how transparent a bank is with its investments and loans. You would also value how conservative its portfolio was.

If a bank's soundness matters to you, you'll weigh that against the generosity of its benefits. A riskier bank might be able to pay a higher interest rate on your savings account or offer more free services like free checking and free online banking, or reimbursement of other banks' ATM fees, because they might be getting better returns on their investments. But banks will have to balance these risks against the pressure to be reliable.

However, thanks to the FDIC, depositors do more market research before buying a $500 flat-screen TV than they do before depositing their life savings into a bank. Banks realize that their customers only care about low fees and high rates, and could not care less about how much risk a bank takes to provide these things. They have no incentive to be safe, and lots of incentive to be reckless.

Perhaps more important than how these safety and soundness considerations affect a bank's potential customers is how these considerations affect a bank's potential creditors. Investors don't want to buy bonds from a bank that can't attract customers.

So without government deposit insurance, banks would have plenty of incentive to be safe. Those that took too much risk would have a hard time attracting customers and borrowing in capital markets.

Mission Creep

Originally, the FDIC was sold as a way to protect the average person from losing his life savings to a rapacious bank. When FDIC insurance began in 1934, only a customer's first $2,500 was insured. In 2010 dollars, that's $40,000. If you were putting more than that in the bank, you were assumed to be sophisticated enough to conduct your own due diligence.

But immediately, the government began expanding the insurance. By 1935, taxpayers were insuring deposits up to $5,000 ($80,000 in 2010 dollars). Eventually it became $100,000, and during the 2008 panic, it bumped up to $250,000.

In constant dollars, the limit on insured deposits rose sixfold. The FDIC went from being a tool protecting the average depositor from poverty to a way of ensuring that depositors never have to worry about their banks' behavior.

This evolution was important, because it undermined one of the original defenses of the FDIC. A standing bailout like the FDIC creates a moral hazard, divorcing depositors and banks from some of the consequences of the banks' risky behavior. But with low limits on insurance, that moral hazard was small, because ordinary investors might not care what the bank was doing, but the customers with actual clout were the big depositors. Because they still had most of their deposits on the line—and because they were the kind of people the banks would listen to—these big depositors could "regulate the banks," making sure they weren't being too wild.

Relieved of the fear of bank runs and from pressure to make sound investments, the market forces pushed only in one direction: toward risk. A bank can pay higher interest rates on savings accounts only if it is making bigger investment gains, and it can only make bigger gains if it takes more risk. Play it safe, and you're left in the dust.

Big depositors don't even lose their deposits that exceed the FDIC limit. For instance, when Washington Mutual (WaMu) collapsed in 2008, the FDIC came in, took ownership of the bank, and sold it at a huge discount to JP Morgan Chase, so that all WaMu depositors would be made whole. That discount amounted to a backdoor FDIC subsidy of WaMu's large depositors, beyond the alleged limits of FDIC insurance. So, WaMu's risky behavior—huge investments in subprime mortgages—didn't deter anyone from depositing money there, and its extraordinary save by the FDIC ensures that future large depositors won't care about their bank's soundness.

Overly risky behavior became the norm. Remember the savings and loan (S&L) crisis of the 1980s and 1990s? That was caused by excess risk taking spurred by the FDIC's twin, the Federal Savings and Loan Insurance Corporation (FSLIC), also a New Deal creation. The moral hazard encouraged excessive risk taking, and the result was the failure of 747 S&L institutions, $88 billion in losses to the sector, followed by congressional scandals ensnaring five U.S. senators and the Speaker of the House.

In addition, because banks no longer feared the possibility of a run, they no longer needed to hold adequate reserves. This allowed banks to make more loans than they otherwise would have done, had they needed to balance the risks and rewards of making more loans and maintaining too low a reserve cushion. More loans helped the banks make more profits, but with the trade-off being a less sound banking system more prone to failure. In the absence of the FDIC, banks are under competitive pressure to keep adequate reserves. Any loss of confidence in the safety of deposits could cause panic and ruin a bank's most important asset, its reputation. (Recall the bank scene in *Mary Poppins*.) With the FDIC, banks no longer have this concern, and the banking system suffers as a result.

Replacing Market Checks with Government Checks

Having wiped out the market forces that would regulate banks, the government decided it would step in. The FDIC, together with the Fed, became active regulators of commercial banks. But government agencies will never be as effective watchdogs as the market.

Market actors have their money on the line—as customers, investors, or creditors. Bureaucrats have little to nothing on the line. We saw this clearly after the 2008 financial crisis.

In 2008, it was universally agreed that bank regulators were "asleep at the switch." The Office of Thrift Supervision "did not react in a timely and forceful manner to certain repeated indications of problems" at the failed NetBank, concluded the Treasury Department's inspector general.[2]

The Office of the Comptroller of the Currency "did not issue a formal enforcement action in a timely manner" regarding the failed ANB Financial National Association, "and was not aggressive enough in the supervision of ANB in light of the bank's rapid growth," the IG found.

The FDIC decided, after New Frontier Bank failed, "In retrospect, a stronger supervisory response at earlier examinations may have been prudent."

How many of these failed bank regulators lost their jobs? Zero. None of the brass at the SEC were fired. Federal Reserve Chairman Ben Bernanke was given a second term. Tim Geithner, president of the New York Fed, was promoted to Treasury Secretary.

None of the front-line regulators were fired. In fact, many of them were rewarded with bonuses—funded by taxpayers. "During the 2003–06 boom," the Associated Press (AP) reported in March 2010, "the three agencies that supervise most U.S. banks—the Federal Deposit Insurance Corp. [FDIC], the Office of Thrift Supervision [OTS] and the Office of the Comptroller of the Currency [OCC]—gave out at least $19 million in bonuses, records show."

Here's the bitter icing on that cake, as reported by the AP:

> Nearly all that money was spent recognizing "superior" perfor-
> mance. The largest share, more than $8.4 million, went to finan-
> cial examiners, those employees and managers who scrutinize
> internal bank documents and sound the first alarms. Analysts,
> auditors, economists and criminal investigators also got awards.[3]

OTS spokesman William Ruberry had a telling excuse about the
bonuses:

> These are meant to motivate employees, have them work hard.
> The economy has taken a downturn in recent years. I'm not sure
> that negates the hard work or good ideas of our employees.

In other words, government bank regulators' financial incentives are
linked to how hard they worked, or whether their boss thought they had
come up with "good ideas."

"Regulators" in the private sector—for example, creditors—have their
financial incentives more intimately tied to the actual performance of the
banks. If a creditor or large depositor is too lax in supervising the banks
he's loaning to or depositing in, he loses his money.

If a hedge fund or investment firm made the sort of mistakes the Fed,
the FDIC, the OTS, and OCC made, the fund would go under. Government works the opposite way—failure is rewarded. Congress reacted
to the failure of bank regulators by giving them more money and more
power.

The OCC's budget rose from $638 million in 2007 to an estimated
$901 million in 2012.[4] The Dodd-Frank bill gave the FDIC added power
and permanently increased FDIC insurance to $250,000. During the bail-
outs and through Dodd-Frank, the Fed got more power.

A Dangerous Mix: Subsidize but Deregulate

One of the problems when talking about the banking industry is that
the government distortions are baked so deeply into the cake that many

discussions of "deregulation" or "subsidy" get hopelessly confused. A good example of confused "deregulation" was the Gramm-Leach-Bliley Act of 1999, removing some barriers to what banks could do.

It was heralded by conservatives at the time as free-market reform, and then blamed by liberals in 2008 as reckless deregulation. But both critics and defenders tried to explain Gramm-Leach-Bliley outside of its context.

Here's the context:

The 1933 law that created the FDIC was sponsored by Senators Carter Glass and Henry Steagall. It was known as the "Banking Act." The bill was also known by its sponsors' names. In addition to creating the FDIC, Glass-Steagall also prohibited bank holding companies from owning other sorts of financial institutions. Basically, commercial banks couldn't also be investment banks.

In the event of the financial crisis of 2008, when liberals were blaming "deregulation" for our problems, most of the blame was placed on "the repeal of Glass-Steagall." This was a reference to Gramm-Leach-Bliley, signed by President Clinton in 1999.

But Gramm-Leach-Bliley did not "repeal Glass-Steagall." If it had, it would have abolished the implicit bailout provided by the FDIC. But instead, it just removed the regulation that had tried to contain some of the moral hazard created by the FDIC.

In other words, the market used to regulate banks. Glass-Steagall killed the market regulation and replaced it with government regulation. Gramm-Leach-Bliley killed the government regulation, but didn't replace it with anything.

Had I been in Congress when Gramm-Leach-Bliley was debated, I would have proposed an amendment abolishing the FDIC and the rest of Glass-Steagall. Had my amendment failed, I would have voted against the bill.

The way I see it, as long as the federal government is cosigning all of a bank's debt, the government has the right to give some marching orders to the bank. If I asked you to cosign my loans, you might place some conditions on me, such as, *no taking this money and going to Vegas*. In theory, government shouldn't be telling anyone what to do with their money, but once government becomes the insurer, it gains that right.

So if you don't want government telling banks what to do, get the banks off the government dole.

Solution: Abolish the FDIC

The first step, then, in creating financial stability is to abolish the FDIC entirely. (This is, of course, the opposite of what Congress did—the Dodd-Frank bill of 2010 expanded FDIC insurance to cover $250,000 of deposits.)

Without the FDIC, bank deposit insurance would not disappear, but risk would still bear a cost. Private deposit insurers would arise, and risk would become more accurately priced.

To be fair, the FDIC does charge different fees based on its assessment of bank risk, but there are only a few tiers, and—more important—there's no market check. I'm sure the FDIC has a fine team of economists trying to find the appropriate risk premiums to charge banks, but this being government, nobody in charge of the risk-calculation operation has his own money on the line.

Private deposit insurance would have a few crucial differences. First, it would be optional. A bank could decide to eschew deposit insurance, and that bank's customers would receive the same disclaimer people receive when they invest in stocks: your investment could go down to zero.

A bank with no deposit insurance could be a risky bank—making a deposit account something like a stock investment, with high returns as long as they don't lose your money. Or a bank's eschewing of deposit insurance could be a sign of complete confidence in its soundness. You only invest in the safest things, and you have such trust from your clientele that you don't need to throw away the monthly premiums.

The other crucial difference between today's mandatory FDIC and an optional, private, competing deposit insurance industry: private insurers would have their own money on the line, guaranteeing that they would be better at making accurate estimates of risk. These private insurers, like a bank's major lenders, would be far better regulators than what we've had.

Also, customers would become regulators. Just as consumers do research before buying a flat-screen TV, they would also do research before choosing a bank. Some might argue that average Americans are just not smart enough to read a bank's balance sheet or understand its risk exposure. As a result, they cannot shop for a bank the way they shop for a TV. Our great-grandparents, however, were able to choose banks without deposit insurance or high school diplomas; it should be that much easier for the highly educated society we have today. Consumers in other countries manage to bank without deposit insurance. Are New Zealanders that much smarter than Americans? I would argue that it's much easier to comprehend a balance sheet than the schematics of a flat-screen TV. Accounting is much easier to grasp than engineering. Fortunately, most shoppers will not have to master either discipline. Advertising and brand reputation allow customers to decide which brand of TV to buy without ever having to understand how they work. The same market forces would educate consumers on which banks were the safest. Without mandatory deposit insurance, you could imagine a Consumer Reports for banks, studying the safety of their deposits, and weighing that against the perks like free checking.

This all sounds a bit odd to today's banking customer, and maybe it sounds undesirably burdensome. After all, right now, you don't have to spend any time examining the soundness of your bank. You don't care where they invest your deposits, because, heck, they could lose it all, and the FDIC would still pay you out in full. Instead, the only thing you shop for is the number of ATMs, free checking, the convenience of their online banking, and maybe the interest you can get on your savings account.

But consider the consequences of our current banking system, rife with moral hazard and thin on responsibility. Consider the costs of our bailout economy. Then the costs of an unsubsidized bank industry don't sound too bad.

Wall Street: Overregulated

Every time I hear someone complaining about lack of regulation in finance, I wonder if those people have ever worked a day in finance.

Finance may be the most heavily regulated industry in America. If not, it's certainly in the top tier. The problem with investing and banking companies is not that there is too little government regulation. It's that there is way too much.

I run an investment company. The number of regulations and the nature of regulations that cover me are absurd. From my perspective, many of these regulations haven't protected anyone. There is no doubt that these regulations hurt my firm and my clients, as well as investors in general. Along the way, they protect the big firms by keeping small firms from growing and new competitors from forming. In the end, all investors lose out, as they end up paying higher prices for a poorer quality of service.

Consider some examples from my own personal experience. For about three years, my firm was prohibited by regulation from hiring new brokers or opening additional branch offices. In addition, for a similar length of time, although I was sitting on some insightful research on individual stocks, which I was free to use privately, I was prohibited by law from showing any of it to my clients or prospects.

How did all this happen? The story starts in 2008.

In that year, as the housing market imploded, the big banks collapsed, and government rode to the rescue, people who had been paying attention began to realize that maybe I was onto something. Perhaps they picked up a copy of *Crash Proof* or perhaps they watched some clips of me talking on CNBC or Fox News, but plenty of new customers started coming my way.

To meet the new demand, I expanded rapidly. My firm went from about ten brokers to about seventy. At the time I assumed we had regulatory permission for these new hires. Unbeknownst to me, we did not. In fact, the Financial Industry Regulatory Authority (FINRA) became aware that we had hired beyond our safe-harbor regulator limit (we inform FINRA of each new hire with regulatory filings) and had sent a letter to my firm instructing us to stop hiring until we had proper regulatory permission to do so. The problem was that my then-chief compliance officer failed to bring this letter to my attention. As a result, I kept hiring brokers even though regulators had told me to stop. When this finally came to my attention as a result of my failure to get regulatory approval to publish research (I will get to that nugget in a moment) I immediately ordered a hiring freeze that remained in effect until summer 2011, about one week after I mentioned this fact in testimony before a Congressional subcommittee on job creation.

A lengthy FINRA investigation ultimately left the firm with a $15,000 fine for hiring too many brokers and over $500,000 in extra legal bills. However, other procedural compliance issues came up in a subsequent routine audit that needed to be resolved before I could formally request permission to increase the number of brokers my firm was legally allowed to employ.

The irony here could not be more obvious or more frustrating. As large firms that bet big on mortgages and got bailed out with government money were firing people, the firm that warned that the crisis was coming was being fined by regulators for hiring them.

As I mentioned earlier, I only learned that I hired too many brokers when I tried to find out why my application to gain regulatory permission to publish stock research was taking so long to be approved. As larger investment firms were losing credibility and shedding workers, my credibility was on the rise. I wanted to parlay that credibility and take advantage of an abundance of newly unemployed talented analysts by starting up a research team and cultivating what I hoped would be a lucrative institutional sales business. Not only would an in-house research department improve the investment advice I could give my own clients, it would pay for itself in that I could share my research with other institutions in exchange for their brokerage business. Up until that point, my firm was purely a retail shop. My media exposure and industry-wide layoffs were an ideal combination for me to build an institutional business.

This, by the way, is the beauty of the free market. When companies fail or contract, any useful services or assets they dump will be picked up. In this case, the service was research for institutions, and the assets were these skilled researchers.

I hired a very experienced guy to head the research department, and initially hired four top-quality analysts who began covering about sixty different foreign stocks. I assumed that regulatory approval for this new line of business would be a breeze. My assumption proved very costly. Because I had already expanded my retail business beyond its approved boundaries, FINRA would not allow me to expand any further until this prior issue was resolved. Then as other regulatory issues arose, they too blocked my desire to expand into research.

In the end, my head of research left to join another firm, while two other analysts focused their efforts on investment banking instead, also a new business line for me, but one for which I did not need any additional regulatory approval. (Actually, I didn't need approval for private placements or secondary offerings, but at the time I published the first edition of this book, I had still not been approved for IPOs—that has since changed. Of course, investment banking would have been much more effective had I been able to combine it with research and institutional sales as had been my plan, but regulators forced me to make a new plan. Unable to publish my research, I had to let the other two analysts go.

So, thanks to securities regulations, some people lost their jobs, others were never hired, and many investors lost the insights that my analysts might otherwise have been able to provide.

Had it not been for the existence of these regulations, my brokerage firm would be considerably larger than it is today. It would be more profitable, employ more people, and pay more taxes.

Does anyone really believe that preventing my firm from growing serves any useful purpose whatsoever? It may benefit my competitors, but does it benefit my clients, potential employees, or investors in general? Absolutely not! Sadly, this example is no exception. It's the norm.

For example, for many years I employed brokers who worked from their homes. Because of improvements in telecommunications and the Internet, it's now easier than ever for stockbrokers to telecommute. This is particularly convenient for brokers taking care of young children or elderly parents, or for those with physical disabilities. Not only were such arrangements mutually beneficial, but they also cut down on traffic, thereby reducing emissions and gasoline consumption. Everyone wins. Too bad securities regulators put an end to it.

Because of all the new supervisory requirements it is no longer possible for brokers to work from home. All the new rules and regulations make it impossible for brokerage firms to adequately supervise brokers working from home-based offices. Even though as a business owner I feel confident in my ability to supervise brokers working from home, security regulators feel otherwise.

For example, if a client loses money based on an investment recommendation he claims was made by a registered stockbroker, the firm he is registered with can be held liable for the losses even if it had no idea the investment was made, and in no way profited from the transaction. To defend itself in a lawsuit, the firm would have to show it provided adequate supervision. Letting brokers work from home invites lawsuits against the firm, and can make it look to a jury like brokers are running around unsupervised.

As a result, all of my brokers who worked from home were forced to resign, as they were not able to work from one of my established offices.

E-mail's benefits have also been destroyed by regulations. One would think the ability to communicate with clients via e-mail would improve efficiencies and lower costs. However, the regulatory costs of monitoring and storing all e-mails far outweigh the benefits of sending and receiving them. As a result, e-mail has actually made the brokerage industry less efficient.

In addition, regulations regarding customer complaints only pertained to written complaints. The idea was that written complaints were more serious. So when clients used to call their brokers to complain about something, brokerage firms only had to address the complaint itself. There was no extra regulatory burden imposed. However, since e-mails are written, any complaint, no matter how trivial, triggers extensive reporting requirements. Since it is very easy for clients to fire off e-mails, this process now absorbs considerable resources.

Complaints need not be investment-related to trigger compliance requirements. Any trivial customer service issue, such as an unreturned phone call or a statement that arrives late, creates hours of additional compliance work. Usually the clients themselves are surprised when my compliance department contacts them regarding complaints they had no idea they made. Ironically, many of the complaints relate directly to all of the compliance-related hoops we require clients to jump through to open and maintain their accounts. These "compliance-related complaints" only add to client frustration and add to my compliance costs.

What bothers me the most is that even though I own my firm, it often feels like I'm simply managing it for the government. Apart from the fact that taxes result in the government earning a lot more from my business than I do, regulators basically call the shots on how my business is run. Why do I need permission to hire people? Why do I need permission to publish my research? Isn't this a free country? That last question is rhetorical, as the unfortunate answer should now be obvious.

Regulatory Ridiculousness

FINRA rules don't protect investors from unscrupulous or incompetent advisors as much as they mandate a brain-dead formula for advising clients.

I won't deny there's plenty of dishonesty and shadiness in the financial world. Big banks, particularly, were famous for boosting their clients or for using their analysis to pump the stocks the firm was holding. At the other end of the spectrum, "boiler-room" pump-and-dump operations bilked unsophisticated investors.

But the rules put forward by regulators punish the innocent. If I recommend a stock or an investment strategy to a client, I can always be sued if the investment loses money. It doesn't matter how well informed and well intentioned my advice was. My client could sue me, and win, on the grounds that I suggested an "unsuitable" investment.

From a client's perspective, an investment becomes unsuitable as soon as it loses value. The problem is that this crazy concept often finds a lot of sympathy among arbitrators. And in an arbitration, I don't get to judge what's "suitable."

Say my client is sixty, and she plans to retire in five years. It's clear to me that we should be very conservative with her money. But what's conservative in these crazy times? The standard choice for a conservative investment is a U.S. Treasury bond—low risk, low reward, backed by the full faith and credit of the U.S. government.

But are Treasuries really conservative?

From my perspective the answer is definitely not. Assuming the U.S. government does not default, which we know from recent debt-ceiling posturing is not impossible, an investor in Treasuries will likely conserve his dollars. However, what if the dollars themselves conserve little in terms of their purchasing power? Would a portfolio of Treasuries really be suitable for such a conservative investor?

To regulators the answer is yes, but to me, or a client struggling to cope with a rising cost of living, the answer is no. I have different ideas about how to conserve purchasing power. But based on industry rules, I must present my ideas as speculative for them to hold up to regulatory scrutiny.

Swiss government bonds or gold bullion may look like safe havens to me, but regulators view such assets from a different perspective. If such investment recommendations lose value (which can often happen in the short run, even for those investments that produce solid long-term returns), and my client decides to sue me, FINRA is fairly likely to see the portfolio I picked as being very risky.

This isn't a regulator setting guidelines. This is a regulator substituting his judgment for my own. So an investment advisor now has two conflict-ing interests: (a) do what he believes is best for his client, or (b) do what he believes will insulate him from a lawsuit. If he tells his client U.S. Trea-suries are safe, and she loses money, he's protected, because that's the con-ventional wisdom. However, if he thinks outside the box and recommends foreign government bonds instead, he risks being on the losing end of suitability-based arbitration.

For now, I can still recommend foreign stocks and bonds to clients whose investment objectives are speculative. For those who describe their objectives as being conservative I have no choice but to turn their business down, or recommend investments that I personally believe to be highly speculative. However, if the industry moves from suitability standard to a fiduciary standard, I would be prohibited from recommending foreign stocks or bonds to many clients, even those who understand the risks and are willing to assume them.

The SEC Won't Let Me Be

The Securities and Exchange Commission is another New Deal creation that makes things worse. It obviously doesn't stop financial wrongdoing. Instead, it "protects" many investors from making money, and gives people a false sense of confidence in the market.

Here's another story of my own encounters with regulatory ridiculous-ness that cost ordinary investors money. In 2006, I helped set up a hedge fund specifically designed to short subprime mortgages. You can guess how well that did. I wanted to bring lots of investors into this fund, which I believed was the opportunity of a lifetime. But due to the security regula-tions governing private placements I was not allowed to offer it to new customers, but only to those with whom I had a "preexisting relationship." So I had to jump through hoops. I sent notes to those in my database whom I thought might be interested in profiting from a collapse in the housing market (see Appendix I, "Letter to Investors"), as a way of creating a pro-fessional "relationship." Those who responded were asked to fill out a questionnaire where their status as accredited investors could be verified. Once I had this information, I needed to wait six months for the relation-ship to qualify as preexisting. This lengthened and complicated the sales process, which severely limited the number of investors that came on board. Since there was only a short time window to put this trade on, many who might otherwise have invested before it shut were prevented from doing so.

SEC rules also forced me to cap the number of investors I could include in this fund. This cap made it impractical for me to allow smaller investors to participate. Every small investor I allowed in—say someone wanting to put up $5,000 to hedge on his new home losing value—meant one larger investor I would have to exclude.

Finally, SEC rules forced me to include plenty of warnings and disclaimers that I thought were misleading. Regulators required me to offer this investment as if it were incredibly risky. In reality, I thought this was the easiest bet I had ever made. I was betting against the weakest parts of the largest asset bubble in American history. By requiring me to treat this as some unorthodox long-shot bet, the SEC was basically forcing me to mislead potential clients.

Although some of my "private label" investments have lost money, in this case fewer than 5 percent of those who originally expressed interest in the fund invested any money. Many who were interested could not meet the $100,000 minimum. In the end, the SEC "protected" plenty of would-be investors from participating in what Greg Zuckerman later referred to in his 2009 bestseller as being "The Greatest Trade Ever."[5]

The JOBS Act 2.0

It's rare, but since the publication of the first edition of this book, the government actually did something right. Before I give them too much credit, I must point out that what they did right was to dismantle some of the regulations they never should have implemented in the first place.

The JOBS (Jumpstart Our Business Startups) Act was signed into law on April 5, 2012, and Title II of the JOBS Act became effective when SEC rules for its implementation went into effect on September 23, 2013. Title II of the JOBS Act removed many of the government-imposed barriers that previously made it more difficult for small companies to raise the capital they need to grow.

Title II of the JOBS Act removes the eighty-year-old ban on the use of general solicitation and general advertising in private placements. It allows issuers and the broker dealers that they engage to advertise private placements and to offer these private placements to accredited investors that they had no previous relationship with prior to the offering. As I note, above, we were raising money for the hedge fund that shorted subprime, we could only offer the opportunity on a confidential basis to accredited investors that we had personally known for at least six months. If Title II of the JOBS Act had been law back then, we could have advertised the opportunity in newspapers, magazines, e-mail blasts, or on the Internet. I could have even spoken openly about the fund during television interviews.

Of course, more investors in a hedge fund would not create many jobs, but when applied to real companies that actually produce products or provide services, the job-related aspects of the Act are clear. By making it easier for companies to raise money, it will be easier for them to grow, make capital investments, and hire workers.

Not only does this Act make it easier for small business to grow and create jobs, it levels the playing field for accredited investors, giving them access to more ground-floor investment opportunities. Prior to the implementation of Title II of the JOBS Act, the only way an accredited investor would know about an investment opportunity would be to have a brokerage account with the firm underwriting that offering. Since the rules were so cumbersome, many entrepreneurs did not even go this route, but instead relied on venture capital firms for their seed money. The result was that the first time most individual investors had the opportunity to invest in an emerging company was when successful start-ups went public. However, by that time, the big profits had already been made. It's ironic that by the time the SEC considers an investment appropriate for ordinary investors, the sophisticated investors are cashing out with huge profits. Thanks to government protection, individual investors pay maximum valuations for their shares, which means they assume lots of downside risk for limited upside potential.

Consider the Facebook IPO. Facebook went public on May 18, 2012 at $38 per share, valuing the eight-year-old company at just over $100 billion. However, after opening at just over $42 per share, the stock dropped sharply, hitting a low of $17.55 by early September. Investors who held on did well, as the shares eventually rose well above their IPO price by the summer of 2013, but many shell-shocked investors did not hang on long enough to enjoy the rebound. In fact, the fiasco surrounding the IPO has sparked dozens of investor lawsuits, and tarnished the reputation of the NASDAQ itself.

However, for earlier investors, who did not receive any government protection, the Facebook IPO was anything but a fiasco. Consider Peter Thiel, the PayPal cofounder, who invested $500,000 dollars in Facebook back in August 2004 (he was portrayed by actor Wallace Langham in the film *The Social Network*). When Facebook went public, Thiel sold 16.8 million shares, netting him $640 million. During the ensuing months, as various lockup periods expired, Thiel sold another 20 million shares, netting an additional $395.8 million. In total, Thiel cashed out over 1 billion dollars' worth of Facebook shares, representing almost 90 percent of his total holdings. For Thiel, the Facebook IPO was an opportunity to harvest huge gains on an investment he made eight years earlier. The government made sure there was an ample supply of average investors waiting to provide early investors like Thiel with a lucrative exit strategy.

To help position ordinary accredited investors to participate in the next Facebook (though most likely on a much smaller scale) at the start-up level rather than at the IPO level, and to take full advantage of Title II of the JOBS Act, I funded the launch of a brand-new broker dealer called Digital Offering. My goal is for this technology-driven broker dealer to act as a platform for issuers, placement agents, and accredited investors to come together to facilitate the efficient private offering of securities. Through Digital Offering investors will be made aware of a wide range of investment opportunities, and companies and placement agents will gain access to a large group of accredited investors seeking opportunities. The offerings distributed through the Digital Offering platform will be thoroughly vetted from a due diligence perspective and the entire due diligence data room will be available online. In addition, in many cases investors will have access to proprietary research reports and analytics on the companies that raise capital through the platform and the industries that they operate in. (To learn more about this company, and to join the community, visit our Web site at www.DigitalOffering.com.)

The main problem with the JOBS Act is that it did not go far enough in removing previously erected barriers to capital formation. Non-accredited investors are still not permitted to invest. It should not be up to the government to decide what risks investors should be allowed to assume. A highly educated, well informed young investor should not be told by regulators that he cannot invest his money where he wants to, just because he is not already rich. The JOBS Act does try to provide some relief to non-accredited investors in that it allows non-accredited investors to participate in crowdfunding, which the SEC has yet to implement. However, companies raising money through crowdfunding will be limited to just $1 million offerings in a calendar year. Given the restrictions on the amount of money that can be raised, more established private companies will likely not utilize crowdfunding and instead rely on Title II of the JOBS Act to raise capital without limits.

So it turns out that the government is helping the little guys invest in the more risky investment opportunities and preventing them from investing in the less risky ones. As of this writing, the SEC had yet to finalize the regulations governing crowdfunding. As a result, the most promising opportunities will be limited to wealthy investors, and for their own protection, less affluent investors will only be able to invest in riskier deals that are less likely to succeed, or pay top dollar in traditional IPOs for companies that have already succeeded.

The JOBS Act does have its critics. Some believe that advertising private placements will result in more fraud and more investor losses. However, by allowing a freer flow of information, I believe the opposite will be true. By preventing good deals from being advertised, the government creates an environment that is riper for fraud. Fraudulent promoters will not call attention to their scams by advertising. Instead, they rely on under-the-radar private conversations to entice their victims. However, since their prospective victims will now be aware of far superior offerings though legitimate advertising, they will be far less likely to fall for the scams.

Deregulate 2.0: Needless Requirements

I have already shared several of the frustrating experiences I've had with pedantic financial regulations that don't actually improve consumers' experience or financial security. But it's just as bad to see such nickel-and-dime requirements used by regulators to harass, intimidate, and cause added expense for bigger firms working in this sector.

In August 2013, UBS AG was forced to pay $4.6 million to settle an investigation by New Jersey state financial regulators. The question involved its "client services associates"—essentially stock brokers' assistants—who had been taking clients' buy and sell orders over the phone. This is a time-saving device for busy brokers, who in the current era of consumer Internet brokerages and the nightmarish regulations against prospecting for new clients, need to spend more of their limited time cultivating relationships.

Despite the fact that these assistants already hold hard-to-obtain Series 7 licenses and are perfectly capable of taking down a client's unsolicited order, the New Jersey regulators faulted UBS because its assistants were not always licensed in each and every state from which a client might call in to place an order.

As you can imagine, the process of licensing an assistant in all fifty states is an expensive and time-consuming hassle. In fact, the annual fees alone exceed $3,300 per individual, to say nothing of the man-hours required to file all of the paperwork. Yet the regulators found it profitable to extort a settlement by harping on this requirement—which ultimately diminishes the compensation for sales assistants (since they now cost their employers more) and does nothing positive for financial services clients, aside from making it increasingly difficult for brokerages to serve them.

In the final analysis, my small brokerage firm now has a rather sizable compliance department. Had all the rules and regulations that exist today been in place in the mid-1990s when I started my firm, I simply would not have had the financial resources to start it up. Instead, I would have either remained a broker at a larger firm, or looked for a different occupation.

The sad truth is that many of the regulations we enforce today have more to do with spying on clients than with protecting them. Thanks to the anti–money laundering provisions of the Patriot Act, every banker and broker is now an unpaid IRS and FBI agent. At great expense to myself, I am continuingly monitoring my customers' accounts for suspicious activity that might indicate tax evasion or some other type of illegal activity. If I find evidence of any, I am legally required to turn the information over to regulators and am legally barred from even alerting my customers regarding my suspicion (this is to prevent them from trying to cover up their crimes). Failure to do so could result in up to a two-million-dollar fine and twenty years in prison. One of the many ironies of this process is that industry regulators make a big deal about protecting customer privacy. Yet as a result of regulation my customers have absolutely no privacy at all in the situation where it matters most. The government knows more about my customers than the Politburo ever knew about a typical Soviet citizen.

Too bad the Truth in Lending Act does not apply to legislation. If so, this legislation never would have made it out of committee. Not only is the PATRIOT Act one of the most unpatriotic pieces of legislation ever passed, it's also one of the most costly to comply with, costing the financial industry over a billion dollars a year. It costs my small firm alone hundreds of thousands of dollars per year and now acts as the greatest barrier to entry in the brokerage industry. Had this act been in place when I launched my brokerage firm, I would have lacked the financial resources to start it up. My total compliance cost since these anti–money laundering rules went into effect in 2003 has been well in excess of $1 million. Despite this great expense, I have yet to uncover a single act of money laundering, or identified a single terrorist among my clients.

Ironically, the political rationale for passing the PATRIOT Act was to deny terrorists access to U.S. financial institutions. By limiting their investment options, the terrorists would have less money available to finance their activities. However, just like most legislation, it backfired, likely producing the opposite of its intended objective. Had we made it easier for terrorists to send their money to major U.S. brokerage houses, they likely would have lost most of their money. Maybe they would have invested in subprime mortgages, or bought shares in General Motors (GM), Freddie or Fannie, Washington Mutual, AIG, Lehman Brothers, MF Global, American Airlines, or a host of other brokerage industry favorites that either went bankrupt or lost better than 80 percent of their market values. Instead, we made it so hard for the terrorists to invest in our stock market that they likely ended up buying gold by default. As a result they now have a lot more money to terrorize us with!

Another casualty of the PATRIOT Act is that my U.S.-based brokerage firm, Euro Pacific Capital, no longer accepts foreign customers. That is because anti–money laundering rules have dramatically increased the compliance costs associated with servicing foreign-owned accounts. To overcome this competitive disadvantage I established a new offshore brokerage firm, which I named Euro Pacific International. I now direct all non-U.S. prospects desiring to do business with me to my Caribbean-based brokerage firm instead of to my American company. Revenue that otherwise would have been earned here in America, and the additional jobs that would have been created to service those accounts, are instead redirected to Anguilla. So with unemployment at a generational high and politicians in both parties crying jobs, jobs, jobs, regulations are forcing me to create jobs overseas that I would otherwise prefer to create here in America. With budget deficits running out of control, profits that would have been taxable here are instead earned untaxed offshore.

In addition, to secure a more business-favorable tax and regulatory environment, I am currently scouting overseas jurisdictions in which to locate my asset-management business.

False Confidence

The worst thing about the SEC may not be the burden of the regulations, but the misplaced confidence it generates.

At the founding of the SEC and FDIC, lawmakers and journalists praised these New Deal creations for "restoring confidence" in the stock market and in banks. I've always assumed it was up to my employees and me to boost confidence in my firm. Why should it be the government's job to instill confidence in anybody else's business?

Often, that confidence is misplaced. Investing in the stock market is always risky. Any stock can go down to zero. It's impossible to know all the potential risk factors for any stock or industry. It's impossible to guarantee that company managers aren't incompetent. Nobody can time the market. Obviously, I have a bias here, but amateurs picking stocks on their own are playing with fire.

That doesn't mean nobody should invest. It means that nobody should take investing lightly. Nobody should assume it's easy. Nobody should ever assume investing is "safe."

But half the purpose of the SEC is to make investors feel safe. These regulations create an illusion of safety, and politicians, whenever they increase regulations, promise the public that they are making it safe to invest.

Our tax code also creates artificial incentives for people to invest. Once an individual is making more than $40,000, income tax eats up 25 percent of his paycheck. Add on state income taxes (in Connecticut, it's 5 percent for a person making $40k, which is lower than neighboring Massachusetts or New York), and you're likely losing about 30 percent to income taxes.

Roth IRAs and 401(k)s allow you to shield some of that income on one condition—if you invest it in an approved fund or security. Absent income taxes, almost all of that money would be invested or spent in some other way, but government has decided to favor this one economic activity. Because employers get a tax deduction for matching part of your 401(k), that tax break is even more subsidized.

These subsidies and this false confidence are great for publicly traded companies and for stockbrokers. But it's not great for the country. First, people blindly throwing their money into the market does not yield an efficient allocation of resources. It creates bubbles, because uninformed investors follow fads and trends. I don't want to suggest that anyone should be kept from investing, but the government shouldn't be in the business of shouting, "Come on in, the water's fine."

Much worse than the inefficiency brought about by unsavvy investing is the government's reaction when ordinary people lose their money. Think back to Enron's 2001 collapse, when people lost their life savings because of misdeeds of corporate executives—cable television trotted out a parade of ordinary Americans who fell victim to ruthless capitalism, and Congress predictably rushed ahead with a slew of new regulations.

The same thing happened during the financial crisis. The bailout was justified, in part, as a way to save the portfolios of the millions of Americans invested in the stock market. Maybe you could let a Big Bank fail, but only a heartless person would stand by while grandpa's retirement evaporated.

Then the Dodd-Frank regulations were also sold in part on the grounds of protecting those ordinary Americans invested in the market.

So Republicans, talking up an "ownership society," and Democrats, singing of equality, push policies that induce more people to invest, thinking it's safe. Then when it proves not safe, purportedly free-market Republicans use this as an excuse for more government intervention, and purportedly populist Democrats use it as cover for handing billions to rich bankers.

In addition, the existence of government regulation creates a moral hazard among investors. Believing the government is protecting them, brokerage customers often do far less due diligence on their own. Had Bernie Madoff not had the blessing of regulators, I'm confident his Ponzi scheme would have been uncovered much sooner.

In a more recent example, MF Global allegedly used customer funds to collateralize leveraged bets that ultimately bankrupted the firm. That has produced calls for even more regulation to protect investors. However, commingling customer funds is already prohibited by existing regulation. Does anyone think that Jon Corzine—the former CEO and chairman of MF Global, former CEO of Goldman Sachs, former U.S. senator, and former governor of the state of New Jersey—did not know this? Would new regulations requiring firms to comply with existing regulations really make a difference? The reality is that some people will simply ignore the new regulations too, while honest businessmen, who represent no real threat to investors, will be forced to waste even more money complying with them.

Solution: Abolish the Wall Street Regulators

We don't need "smarter" regulations or better regulators. We need to get rid of the regulatory bodies—or at least make them optional.

FINRA is technically a private organization, but it is effectively a government agency, because government requires brokers to be members and thus abide by FINRA's rules.

Congress should abolish the SEC and make FINRA membership voluntary.

Eliminating the SEC will remove the government stamp of approval from the stock market. Just as you know you could lose all your money when you invest in your brother-in-law's new Irish pub, people putting money in the stock market would be more likely to study and understand the risks. Of course, abolishing the SEC would not mean stock fraud would run rampant. Fraud would still be a crime—only it would be prosecuted on a state level, or by the Justice Department directly if the fraud involved interstate commerce.

Insider trading, on the other hand, is not nearly as bad a problem as the regulators pretend it is. Ironically, while rigorously enforcing overly broad insider trading laws on the general public, Congress has exempted its own members from those same laws. As *60 Minutes* reported in 2011, it is perfectly legal for elected officials to profit by trading nonpublic information, even if their votes directly determine the extent of that influence. So if a congressman has firsthand knowledge that the FDA is going to turn down a promising drug, it's perfectly legal for that congressman to buy puts or short the shares of the biotech company whose prospects depend on that approval. On the other hand, if someone overhears a conversation in an elevator about a tip a barber claimed to have received from his friend's cousin about a stock merger, and he takes a flyer and buys some call options, he risks civil fines of triple his profits. More serious offenders risk criminal penalties of up to five million dollars in fines and twenty years in prison.

If you recall, Martha Stewart paid a $137,019 fine for avoiding a $58,062 loss by selling 3,928 shares of ImClone Systems on the advice of her stock broker, who was allegedly in possession of nonpublic information that he allegedly passed on to Stewart. She also agreed to a five-year ban on being a director, CEO, or CFO of a publicly traded company. In addition, Stewart served five months in federal prison and two years of home confinement with electronic monitoring for obstruction of justice charges related to the insider trading investigation. Yet the members of Congress investigating her were exempt from the laws they accused her of breaking, and routinely made far greater sums trading on nonpublic information.

My guess is that far more money is lost trading on stock tips than is made. More often than not, the tips turn out to be false, or the market does not react to the news the way an insider trader expects. On the other hand, congressmen have firsthand knowledge of information that can severely impact corporate earnings and have been able to use that information to reap handsome profits over the years. A 2004 study by the *Journal of Financial and Quantitative Analysis* showed that not only did U.S. senators' stock performance substantially beat the market and retail investors, but they outperformed investment professionals and corporate insiders as well. Now either these senators are selflessly giving up multimillion-dollar jobs running hedge funds, or they have access to inside information they would no longer be privy to once they left the Senate. My idea is not to remove all laws against insider trading, but I think at most the remedies should be civil. However, if anyone should be banned from trading on non-public information, especially involving their own legislation, it is members of Congress.

How would publicly traded corporations react to the deregulation? If you believe the media or politicians, corporations would all become utterly secretive. But those shielding their books from the public's eyes would have a pretty hard time getting investors. Different companies would provide different types of disclosure, and the market would help set a value on these different methods. Private exchanges would still impose listing requirements, and companies would have to meet them as a condition of listing their shares.

Maybe some investors would want to see week-by-week financials. Others would see that quarterly filing spurs companies to short-term profit taking at the expense of long-term business soundness. These investors might want less disclosure of revenue and profit figures, and more disclosure of management strategies.

Independent research and auditing firms—operating without the imprimatur of government, but trading entirely on their reputation—would do much of the legwork.

It's a similar story with FINRA. If I could opt out of FINRA, I would. If the government was worried about me lulling unsuspecting investors into an unregulated free-for-all, I would go along with a rule requiring me to declare NOT REGULATED BY FINRA. CAVEAT EMPTOR.

While such a disclosure would turn away some potential customers, I'm pretty sure I would gain many more. After all, it was FINRA rules that forced me to mislead my customers about the subprime mortgage bet and to keep out smaller investors.

Would my clients be "unprotected" if there were no FINRA or SEC over my shoulder? Let me ask you this: who do you think cares more about my clients—SEC and FINRA regulators or me? Who actually stands to lose money if I screw over a client—SEC and FINRA regulators or me?

I do not have the power to force people to invest with me. My ability to attract customers depends on my ability to convince them that I can take care of their money better than my competitors. I can't do that without a reputation for competence, honesty, and fair play.

There would be costs to a deregulated financial world, with the costs of individuals' performing real due diligence being the biggest. But those costs would far be outweighed by the growth of profits and jobs.

Investors would educate themselves better without government regulators constantly swearing they have everything under control. Smaller investors would also have better options. Right now, many investors get shunted off to mutual funds or online discount brokers, because no investment professionals will help them, thanks to regulations.

A deregulated world of investment and finance would spawn small investment firms that would pay more attention to customers.

The deadweight loss of regulation would be lifted from the economy. We'd be richer as an economy.

There are always unscrupulous operators in any profession, and brokerage is no exception. However, the amount of money that would be lost by some investors due to scams would pale in comparison to the losses imposed on all investors through the higher costs and lower quality that are the by-products of regulations meant to guard against those losses.

It's not as if all this regulation has kept fraudsters out of the investment business. In fact, I would argue that by causing investors to drop their guard, we actually have more fraud with the regulation than we would without it.

Further, in a free market, the fraudsters would go out of business long before their clientele grew to a significant size. In a true free market, only those firms pursuing an honest approach would gain the needed reputation to achieve national prominence. So fraud would be rare, and occur on a small scale, while reputable firms would flourish and the vast majority of investors would not be ripped off.

However, in today's highly regulated environment, larger firms are protected from potential competition from start-ups that lack the resources to overcome the regulatory barriers to entry. This is particularly helpful in preventing individual brokers from quitting their jobs and forming their own brokerages to compete with their former employers. In addition, smaller competitors are more likely to fail as they lack the economies of scale to afford the ever-rising costs of regulatory compliance. In the past few years more than a third of small brokerage firms have disappeared.

One of the biggest ironies of the system is that each time a major firm rips off its clients, FINRA responds with sweeping regulations that especially hurt smaller competitors that did no wrong—more than the large firm whose bad conduct prompted the regulation. The result is that despite a fine, the offending firm actually benefits from its malfeasance in that more of its competitors are forced out of the industry.

In the end, instead of a thriving competitive market that forces out bad players and allows the most innovative and effective firms to gain market share, we have a contracting industry dominated by a few too-big-to-fail firms that offer limited service and cookie-cutter advice.

Solution: Tort Reform

Bubbles happen in part because of groupthink. One major cause of groupthink is the government regulations I've written about above; a second cause is the threat of lawsuits.

Very often, there's a divergence between where an investment professional steers his clients' money, and what he thinks is best for his clients. The reason: the threat of lawsuit.

During the health-care debate in 2009 and 2010, you might have heard people speaking about "defensive medicine." That's the idea that a doctor will sometimes treat their patient with an eye more on insulating himself from a lawsuit than on serving the patient's best interest.

Well, "defensive investing" happens, too, and like "defensive medicine," it's not the customer who's being "defended." There's an old saying, "no one ever got fired for investing in IBM." Self-preservation for brokers and advisors often means making a bet traditionally understood as safe, regardless of what you think is best. If you put your clients' money where everyone else is putting it, you've got a good defense if things go badly ("hey, *nobody* saw this coming"). If you put your clients' money somewhere else and you lose money, you're exposed.

You could lose your job if you work at a big firm, but worse, you could lose your shirt, thanks to lawsuits.

The net effect: defensive investing pumps up bubbles and destabilizes our economy.

Of course, we need a good tort system to protect investors from fraud, but we don't need a whole class of torts for securities law. Defrauding an investor or investment client should be treated the same as defrauding someone whose deck you're building or whose car you're buying.

Lawsuits are a far better regulator than actual regulations—unless they're abused. One form of abuse is suing someone just because your account lost money. Some of that problem can be fixed by folding all securities law into standard tort law. But we also need tort reform.

The most important reform is Loser Pays. Right now, there are lawyers whose business model seems to be filing knowingly frivolous lawsuits in order to garner midsized settlements. Say a client of mine sues me to recover the $20,000 she lost. I know I did nothing wrong, and I'm confident that I would win in arbitration. I also know that "winning" an arbitration could cost me $40,000 in legal fees, plus take up my time and cause me unnecessary aggravation. Her lawyer offers to settle for $10,000. What do I do? Do I make the right financial decision and settle, or do I pay $40,000 to stand on principle? Sometimes a principled stance may seem like a good business discussion, if it discourages future frivolous lawsuits, but more often than not, most firms settle merely as a necessary cost of doing business. But what if the plaintiff had to cover the defendant's attorney fees whenever the defendant won? Frivolous lawsuits would dry up overnight.

The standard objection to this sort of policy is that poor people who have been wronged won't be able to afford lawsuits if they run the risk of paying the defendant's legal fees. But there's no reason that has to be true. Plaintiffs' lawyers regularly take cases on contingency, meaning they only get paid if they win something. Similarly, they could promise to cover the defendant's legal fees in case they lose. There are insurance products that cover this sort of circumstance.

That way, you'll still have lawyers willing to take up cases for the indigent—but only cases they think they have a reasonable chance of winning, not merely those where they feel they can extort a quick settlement from plaintiffs that did nothing wrong.

With good tort reform, investment advisors, corporate executives, and brokers would still have to worry about lawsuits, but only if they did something unethical or criminal. Such reform would curtail defensive investing, which would lead to smarter investing and less fuel for bubbles.

The ultimate irony of our current tort system is that many full-service brokerage firms now refuse to deal with small investors.

In industry terms, all small brokerage accounts come with put options, whereby clients can literally put any losses back to the broker, because the legal costs of defending against frivolous arbitrations typically exceed the alleged damages. As a result, most firms have imposed account minimums that preclude the little guys from opening accounts. After years of resisting this trend, I finally imposed account minimums at my firm as well. This was done not merely to mitigate frivolous lawsuits, but because even without lawsuits, small accounts are simply unprofitable to service. The fees and commission they generate do not cover the regulatory costs necessary to maintain them.

As a result, the little guy is left out in the cold. I believe that no legitimate full-service broker will touch him, as the costs and risks of accepting him as a customer far outweigh the modest fees or commission his account would generate. This leaves him vulnerable to unscrupulous investment scam artists who rip off their customers with huge fees on shady deals. Often such losses are hard to recoup with lawsuits, as the operators do not stay in business long enough to satisfy judgments.

Many of these small investors end up picking their own stocks using online discount brokers, or subscribing to investment newsletters written by nonprofessionals exercising their First Amendment rights to freedom of speech. So, regulators' attempts to make sure that small investors get sound professional advice instead guarantee that small investors get no professional advice at all.

Tort Reform 2.0

Bloomberg reported in August 2013 that since the financial crisis, the largest six banks have racked up $103 billion in litigation costs—that's more than they have paid in dividends over the same period. That is to say, lawyers, not shareholders, effectively owned Bank of America, JP Morgan, Wells Fargo, Goldman Sachs, Morgan Stanley, and Citigroup during that period.

That's not to say there wasn't actual wrongdoing for which people might deserve some recompense. But a "loser pays" system would separate the wheat from the chaff among all the lawsuits. It's absurd to have taxpayers bailing out banks with one hand and then passing the same money to lawyers with the other.

Solution: End Bailouts

The single most destabilizing factor in our financial sector is the "too big to fail" mind-set.

The FDIC's moral hazard is a minor problem compared to the belief that the Fed and Congress will come swooping in to save big banks—or at least their creditors—if anything bad happens.

There's no doubt today that Wall Street and big banks, high on cheap money from the Fed, were taking extra risks during the last decade on the assumption of bailouts, including the FDIC, Fannie Mae, and the sort of extraordinary saves by the Fed we saw at Bear Stearns, AIG, and, eventually, the TARP. The bank executives taking the risks saw all the signs: politicians' rhetoric and government policy made it clear that the government was in the business of propping up housing. If banks bet big on housing, would Washington really let them fail?

Washington is sending the same message today, with President Obama still using the TARP in order to bail out underwater mortgages, and the FHA underwriting 3.5 percent down as payment mortgages. In fact, the FHA has basically taken over the subprime market now that the private sector will no longer touch it. In 2006 FHA insured only 3.3 percent of total mortgages. During 2010, the Federal Housing Authority (FHA) insured 40 percent of all new mortgage originations. By the end of that year, 20 percent of the entire mortgage market was FHA guaranteed. The private sector lost so much money making subprime loans that it abandoned the practice completely. The government then saw an opportunity to corner a market no private firm wanted any part of—making risky loans to people unlikely to repay them. When I wrote the first edition of this book in 2011, I predicted the FHA would need a federal bailout as early as 2012. As it turns out, it got one in October 2013. Unfortunately, this bailout is merely a down-payment on a much larger bailout to come. At least the private sector learned from its mistake. The government adopts such mistakes into official public policy.

And the Big Banks also have brand-new reasons to suspect Washington won't let them fail. Think of Bank of America. At the request of Ben Bernanke, B of A bit two bullets: eating up Merrill Lynch and taking on subprime-riddled Countrywide. Bank of America has a couple of favors to call in from the Fed.

Crashproof Yourself: If You Can't Stop Bailouts, Profit from Them

If I had my way, the government wouldn't be in the business of propping up big banks. But just because I don't like the rules doesn't mean I can't profit from them.

If the government is willing to backstop the losses of big banks, I want in on some of that guarantee action, too. That's why I keep my deposits with Bank of America. This megabank isn't terribly sound financially, but I'm pretty confident Washington has its back. After all, B of A, at Washington's request, took on the failed financial firms Countrywide and Merrill Lynch—the Fed and the Treasury now owe B of A a favor. I figure any bank can fail in the future, but not all of them will be saved. Bank of America is as likely as any other to be bailed out.

Moody's agrees, giving the bank a significantly higher rating because it finds the likelihood of a bailout, if needed, to be "very high." I'm not saying you should buy stock in these too-big-to-fail banks, but they're as safe a place as any to keep your deposits. Of course, I only keep my working capital on deposit. As any bank bailout will be financed with a printing press, you want to keep your real savings out of U.S. banks and out of dollars.

In fact, that's why I keep lots of my money at Bank of America—I don't think Washington will let it fail. I am, literally, banking on a bailout. Think about that for a moment. Money that I might otherwise have deposited into a sound financial institution that I think is less likely to fail but unlikely to get bailed out, ends up being deposited into an institution that I think has serious financial problems but is sure to be bailed out if it fails. This is the exactly the opposite of what would happen in a free market. But the big banks get much more lucrative benefits from this implicit bailout than just my deposits. Most important, they get much cheaper credit. In June 2011, credit-rater Moody's commented in a research paper that it gives Bank of America debt "five notches of uplift" due to "government support assumptions."

In other words, B of A debt would be considered barely "investment grade" except that Moody's assumes the bank's senior creditors will get bailed out by Washington. As a result, the bank has the third-highest credit rating possible. This gives B of A a competitive edge in capital markets against smaller banks that might actually be more creditworthy. Instead of these smaller banks gaining market share, they might fail or be forced to merge with larger ones to stay afloat. More perversely, B of A ends up attracting more capital despite its problems. This simply exacerbates the losses, or the size of the future bailout needed to offset them. It's a reverse Darwinism where the unfit survive and the fit die off.

Don't Let Them Get Too Big to Fail

So how do you abolish bailouts? You start by abolishing the FDIC and dissolving Fannie and Freddie. But what about implicit bailouts? You can't pass a law blocking them because there is no law promising them. It's just how Congress or the Fed reacts when an actual crisis arises.

The first step would be to stop propping up the giant banks and investment banks. People often assume big banks are a creation of capitalism. Instead, they are the creation of government.

First, regulation always acts as a barrier to entry by adding to overhead. This punishes smaller banks and keeps out new entrants, allowing the bigger guys to proceed with less competition. Dallas Fed president Richard Fisher aptly voiced this concern about the effects of Dodd-Frank:

> Imposition of the new requirements and restrictions risks creating new economies of scale in banking generated by the costs of regulatory compliance, many of which could be fixed costs not fully proportional to bank size.
>
> To the extent that a large scale becomes necessary to absorb the regulatory cost associateed with reform, Dodd-Frank could intensify the tendency toward bank consolidation, re sulting in a more concentrated industry, with the largest institutions predominating even more than in the past.[6]

Some academic studies have found that, past a certain threshold, size provides only one sort of benefit for big banks: political favor.

This is why Bank of America can borrow much more cheaply than a smaller, sounder bank. This is one reason Goldman Sachs is able to draw institutional clients.

In other words, through implicit bailouts and regulations, government creates this class of superbanks. Without bailouts and with less regulation, banks wouldn't get so big that they pose "systemic risk."

How to End Bailouts

Keeping the banks small enough to fail would be an important first step to preventing future bailouts and removing the "too big to fail" mind-set.

Politicians can also make bailouts less likely by stopping the practice of picking winners and losers. If government isn't busy saying "build more houses, hand out more mortgages," or "build more electric cars," industries, investors, and creditors won't proceed on the assumption that the taxpayer has their back.

Maybe we need to amend the Constitution. In truth, nothing should be needed to prevent bailouts, because the Constitution doesn't give the government authority to do them. But it might help to pass an amendment prohibiting the government from owning, guaranteeing, or lending to any private company.

If you look back at the TARP, Bear Stearns, Fannie Mae, and Freddie Mac, you begin to see the same culprit at the scene of every crime. It's the Federal Reserve Bank of the United States.

The only way to create a stable financial system is to force banks, investors, and creditors to bear their own risk. The only way to make them bear their own risk is to end bailouts once and for all. And the only way to end bailouts once and for all may be to dissolve—or at least permanently weaken—the Fed.

6

Sound Money: Return to the Gold Standard

IF A PATIENT CAME INTO a hospital with bad symptoms in his hands, feet, eyes, chest, and other parts of his body, the doctors would first look for a single cause: *is there something common to all these symptoms in these different parts of the body*. Rather than trying to fix the patient's hands, then his feet, then his eyes, and so on, the doctor would do well to check the patient's blood, because the blood courses through the whole body.

Today our economy shows maladies in manufacturing, employment, savings, housing, banking, and nearly every other sector. So it's a good idea to ask what the common cause might be. What courses through the economy and touches everything?

Money. The common cause is money.

Our dollar is sick, so the entire economy is sick.

If we're going to reduce unemployment, revive manufacturing, restore personal savings, foster a sane housing market, keep banks in line, and generally get the economy back to creating value and increasing prosperity, we need to make the dollar healthy.

In short, that means giving our dollar real value: ending our system of fiat money, in which the Federal Reserve can endlessly inflate and fix interest rates, and returning to a Gold Standard. Talk about a Gold Standard and people get pretty worked up—whether you're talking to a rabid liberal Keynesian or a disciple of Milton Friedman, there's a good chance he'll react to the Gold Standard with disdain.

We'll go through the economic arguments for commodity money like a

Gold Standard in this chapter, but just as important is the political argument for gold: the only reliable way to stop burgeoning federal deficits,
end the moral hazard of bailouts, and pare government back to its appropriate size is by fixing the value of the dollar.

Economist Joseph Schumpeter put it well. "Quite irrespective of" all
purely economic arguments, he wrote:

> There is one point about the gold standard that would redeem it
> from the charge of foolishness; even in the absence of any purely
> economic advantage. An automatic gold currency is part and
> parcel of laissez-faire and free trade economy. *This* is the reason
> why gold is so unpopular now and also why it was so popular in
> the bourgeois era. It imposes restrictions upon governments or
> bureaucracies that are much more powerful than is parliamen-
> tary criticism.

Government is our new bubble. Saving the economy requires deflating this bubble before it gets bigger. The only way to do that is to instill
politicians with discipline. Sound money is the only way to impose that
discipline.

What Is Money?

Today, we're accustomed to thinking of small greenish paper rectangles as
the definition of money, and we think of the U.S. government as the only
source of money. To honestly discuss sound money, we need to realize where
our current money customs came from.

At first, it was every man for himself. You ate or wore what you could
pick or catch.

Barter was the first advance. If you had some extra meat, and your
neighbor had an extra fur, you might make a direct exchange. If food,
water, clothing, and basic tools are the only goods on the market, barter is
fine—you can always find someone who has what you want and wants what
you have.

But as soon as there's basic manufacturing and prosperity begins increasing, barter becomes inadequate. Say you're a hunter and you want a

bed, but the only bedmaker in town is a vegetarian. What do you do then? You would have to figure out what the bedmaker wanted (maybe tofu), and then find someone who had tofu and wanted meat. If you couldn't find that person, you would have to find a fourth person (someone who wanted meat, and had the hats that the tofumaker wanted), or try to convince the vegetarian bedmaker to take the meat and trade it for something else.

Meat, however, spoils, and so the bedmaker would have to unload it pretty quickly. So, unable to get your hands on anything the bedmaker wants to consume, you trade your meat for some salt and approach the bedmaker. "Look, I know you don't want salt, but think of all the people who do. They use it to preserve their meat and flavor their soup. And this stuff is nonperishable, so you can hold it as long as you want. And if, when the tofu dealer comes through town, he doesn't want salt, you can explain to him what I've explained to you—*he* can use it to buy something *he* wants."

If you and the bedmaker agree, you've just created money. Organically, more people in your community begin taking salt for payment, even if they have no intention to use it, because they know others will accept it. But—and this is important—the value of salt money is not entirely dependent on other people accepting it as payment. If, for some reason, folks stopped taking salt as payment, you could use it as, well, salt.

Salt was a pretty good currency, especially before refrigeration, because it was widely demanded, divisible down to the grain, very portable, easy to weigh, and could easily be tested for counterfeit by tasting it. Romans used salt for money.

But just because salt served as money didn't mean there would be no other form of money in circulation. Tobacco leaves might be widely accepted as payment. So might gold or silver.

The Greatest Invention Ever?

The point is that money arises naturally in society, as a way of aiding in voluntary economic transactions. It was one of the greatest inventions ever. Money not only made it easier for people to buy what they want, it also made saving much more possible—you could accumulate excess money to spend at a later point.

While saving is frowned upon by the elites today, it's an essential element in economic progress. By making it easier for people to save, money did two crucial things. First, it inspired more industriousness: there was now incentive to work harder to earn more in a day than you could spend in a day. Second, savings enabled ambitious entrepreneurs to make big capital investments: labor-saving machines, big houses, transportation.

If the saver didn't have any big plans in mind for his money, he could still make it productive by lending it out. Finance was nearly impossible without money. Sure, you could give your neighbor a pig this year in exchange for a pig and a chicken next year, but there would be a lot more opportunity for squabbling (*this pig isn't as healthy as the pig I gave you last year*).

With a commodity money, where there is little or no deviation in quality, and using universal, objective measures, like weight, you can lend with the confidence that what you get back will be of the same quality as what you loaned out.

Money also made specialization more practical. If you were really good at one thing—manufacturing nails (to borrow Adam Smith's famous example)—you could make a living just by making nails. Without money, someone who spent his whole day making nails would have to find (a) someone with excess food who wanted nails, (b) someone with excess shelter who wanted nails, (c) someone with clothes to spare who also wanted nails at that moment, and so on.

Once money is introduced, the nail seller only needs to find (a) people with money who want nails, and (b) different people with everything the nail seller needs who want money. Facilitating specialization creates efficiencies, as folks get to divide up labor according to skill and interest.

In countless ways, money improves society.

Competing Currencies

In the past, different types of commodity money competed. Salt had its advantages, but also disadvantages—you had to keep it dry, it was easy to spill. In Rome, rising sea levels made it much harder to get salt over the years.

Gold had a lot going for it. It's fairly easy to store. Like salt, it's easy to divide, but also easy to combine: you can make blocks, or coins of different weights or denominations, which can be standardized. It doesn't rust. It doesn't tarnish or undergo other unpleasant reactions with chemicals.

Like any money, gold has underlying value. Mostly, we think of its decorative value—across nearly every culture, gold is considered beautiful. Women love it, and pleasing women's fancies is universally considered a good thing. It has industrial uses due to its resistance to corrosion and how thin it can be hammered.

Gold is also rare enough to be valuable, but plentiful enough that it can be widely circulated. Its supply grows, but never very quickly.

No authority had to declare gold to be money. It arose as a good medium of exchange, and in many cases it won out in competition against other moneys. It didn't always win out to the exclusion of other types of money, but it was probably the most successful money ever, thanks not to some order from above, but thanks to gold's own attributes.

Gold, in many cases, won in the competition among moneys.

This is very important: money doesn't come from government; it comes from civil society.

Government Gets in the Money Game

But as with anything good, government eventually got its hands on money, too.

Government coins made some sense, at first. Creating uniform, convenient denominations of gold or silver was a good idea, and governments could certify that the metal was pure and the weight was correct—not every merchant needed to carry a gold scale and try to sniff out impurities.

But this wasn't what government coinage was about. In fact, governments typically use a monopoly on coinage as a way to steal from their citizens.

Say a ruler wants to build a new road, and he needs new government revenue. Maybe he could borrow. Certainly, he could tax. But an even easier way is to debase the coinage.

Here's how it works: the government melts 10 ounces of gold. Then it mixes in 2 ounces of molten copper, which is cheaper. Now you've got a mixture that weighs 12 ounces. The Mint turns out 120 coins that weigh 1/10 of an ounce each, and the government uses it to pay its road-pavers' wages worth 120 ounces in gold.

A private business could get away with this only by outright fraud—and the culprit, if caught, would go to jail. Government doesn't even need to lie about it, though—it just requires the vendor to take the watered-down money. Many governments create "legal tender laws," which require everyone to accept the nation's official currency for all payments. In other words, you're legally required to pretend that this copper-gold slurry is really gold.

Because government typically requires that taxes be paid in official currency, the rulers can convince the paving crew to take this money. The crew knows someone else will take the payment, because, at the end of the day, the government will accept this money as payment of tax liabilities.

So, government has made a nearly 20 percent profit (the copper isn't free, but it's a fraction of the value of gold), simply by debasing its coins, and now people are told to accept this debased coin as the real thing, not because it's actually worth an ounce of gold, but because someone (the government) will pretend it's worth an ounce of gold.

Worth the Paper It's Printed On

Paper money was the next step in the evolution of money, and like coinage, paper money comes from a good idea, but it provided government with an opportunity for theft.

As scholar Tom Woods explains it, you can think of paper money originally evolving as a warehouse receipt at a gold storage facility. In other words, wealthy people probably wouldn't want to keep gold lying around their houses, and so gold-storage vaults came to be demanded. Since gold is a commodity, and Mr. Smith's one hundred-oz bar is identical in value to Mr. Jones's one hundred-oz bar, the gold vault doesn't need to put Mr. Smith's name on his gold bar. Instead, the vault—or bank—gives him a certified receipt for 100 ounces of gold.

Any time he wants, Mr. Smith can go to the bank, hand in his receipt, and pick up his gold. Maybe he only wants a bit of his gold, so he walks in with a 100-oz certificate, and walks out with 10 ounces of gold and a certificate for 90 ounces.

Alternatively, he can give his gold certificates to the tailor in exchange for a new suit, and the tailor can go get some gold, or he can use it to buy something else. Soon, the banks start issuing standard smaller-denomination notes (put in 100 ounces, and get ten 10-oz gold notes). Now these warehouse receipts—or bank notes—have become a money substitute, called *currency*. However, *currency* must not be confused with *money* itself.

The introduction of money substitutes represented another advance in money. Paper money, backed by gold or any other commodity, is much more convenient. Paper money is much lighter, and uniform, convenient denominations are much easier to divide. But with the added convenience comes new opportunities for fraud.

When people begin getting used to paper money, they can easily confuse it with a store of wealth in itself. At that point, governments can get away with removing any backing from the currency, and can print as much as they want. It's called fiat currency, and it gives government unlimited power to pilfer. It's a total fraud. (For anyone who wants to read in more detail about how we arrived to this sorry state, turn to the Appendix II, where I have included "A Brief History of Money in America.")

Sound Money 2.0: Stay Away from Bitcoin

Lately, it's become fashionable for tech geeks to create electronic currencies. Bitcoin is by far the most famous. People think of it as an alternative to gold because it supposedly liberates its users from the whims of governments and central banks. Its purveyors try to frame it as some kind of modern day gold standard, or "gold 2.0."

Don't be fooled. Bitcoin is really just a sort of modern day alchemy. It's the tulip-mania of cash.

Bitcoins have most of the flaws of paper money and few of the advantages. Like paper money, they lack intrinsic value. Unlike paper money, they are not legal tender and cannot be used in payment of taxes.

A major problem with fiat money is its lack of intrinsic value and

bitcoin is not much of an improvement. The only reason people use fiat
money in the first place is because some government declares it legal tender, and compels its citizens to use it to pay their taxes. Without this legal
status, fiat currency would not work, and a loss of confidence would soon
cause its market value to equal its intrinsic value, zero

Of course the same can be said for dollars, as there is no real difference
between a ten- and a twenty-dollar bill, other than the number written on
the paper. When paper money was backed by gold that was not the case.
There was actually twice as much gold backing a twenty-dollar bill as a
ten-dollar bill.

Copying the flaws of fiat money does not represent a substantial improvement. Just because bitcoin is not a government creation does not
mean the scheme will work any better. There is no substitute for real
money. Bitcoin enthusiasts will argue that scarcity represents a significant
improvement. There is no limit to the number of dollars the Fed can create, whereas the supply of bitcoins that can be mined is limited to just 21
million. But competing digital currencies have no such limits. And limited
supply still means nothing if there is no demand.

But for now there are plenty of buyers of bitcoins, and the price keeps
rising. However this is because only a small fraction are actually used in
commerce, with the vast majority being hoarded by speculators who are
confident that prices will keep rising. So far they have been correct. The
problem starts when the price stops rising and really begins to fall. When
all the bitcoin speculators want out, who will take the other side of their
trades?

Another part of bitcoin's appeal is the ease with which they can be
transferred. However, as governments begin imposing more stringent
reporting requirements on banks, financial institutions, or even retail
establishment that transact in them (particularly with regard to anti-
money-laundering measures), many institutions may refuse to accept
them. Even if they do accept them, the costs of transacting in them may
rise considerably.

In addition, the more valuable bitcoins become, the greater the incentive for theft or counterfeiting. For now, bitcoin users are confident
that the code is unbreakable and that their stashes are secure. I'm no
computer programmer, so I'm not really qualified to dispute this, but

people also said the Titanic was unsinkable. We all know how well that worked out.

Bitcoin defenders also argue that its ease of use and lack of government oversight itself confer some intrinsic value. This is a mistaken idea. Currencies backed by gold were also easier to use than the gold itself. But had the gold not been there, no one would have accepted the currencies.

The idea behind bitcoins was to digitally replicate gold: take all of the attributes that made gold so desirable as money, and replicate, or better yet improve upon them digitally. The problem is that bitcoin's designer replicated every characteristic of gold except the most important one—its intrinsic value. Without that, none of the other characteristics matter.

Of course, for now, the wild daily price fluctuations make actual commerce in bitcoins quite impractical. Also, given the rapidity with which prices can rise and fall, it's hard for an actual saver to trust his savings to bitcoins, and loans or long-term contracts payable in bitcoins are impossible. Besides, no one knows for sure whether anyone will value bitcoins in the future. Maybe it's just a fad. Maybe digital currency really will catch on, but maybe it will be some other digital currency.

Perhaps someone will launch a digital currency backed by gold. In fact, there may be many gold-backed digital currencies in circulation.

But given all the unknowns, bitcoins can hardly be seen as a store of value, and therefore cannot really function as money. It is possible circumstances will change in the future, which is what bitcoin speculators are betting on. For now, if you are looking for a safe place to store your wealth, don't bother with Bitcoin.

The Fed and the End of the Gold Standard

The ultimate destroyer of the U.S. dollar was the Federal Reserve System, which was supposed to be the guardian of the currency. As I discussed in chapter 2, the original idea of the Fed was a good one: providing a uniform currency backed by gold.

But once again, government officials, given the power to manipulate money, couldn't resist it. They cheapened the dollar badly. Within a few years of the Fed's birth, it began injecting fiat money into the economy. Woodrow Wilson increased the monetary supply to help pay for World War I, and soon afterward, the Fed inflated again, in an effort to help Europe's recovery. The 1920s' inflation (which pumped up the real estate and stock market bubbles that sparked the Great Depression) was fueled by "credit reserves." In other words, the Fed loaned out money backed by absolutely nothing—it was money created out of thin air.

After decades of doing this sort of thing, the U.S. government eventually went all-in: President Richard Nixon on August 15, 1971, unilaterally abolished the gold standard. He declared that the Fed would no longer redeem dollars with gold. Officially, now, the dollar was backed by nothing.

It's important to repeat the real way in which the Fed makes money. Big U.S. banks all keep their money at the various Federal Reserve Banks—they are the banks' banks. So, Bank of America, Chase, Citibank, and so on all have accounts at the Fed.

If the Fed wants to buy something from Bank of America—say a U.S. Treasury, or some mortgage-backed securities—the Fed simply credits B of A with the new money. This doesn't lower the amount of money the Fed has. New dollars have simply come into existence. The Fed isn't *spending* money. It's *creating* money.

Under this system, the dollar is now worth only whatever the dollar will buy. Whereas paper currency backed by gold or some other commodity always had an intrinsic value, the only value the U.S. dollar has is whatever value others attach to the U.S. dollar at a particular moment in time. And there is no fixed supply of dollars, meaning the supply is whatever government says it is. This is called fiat money.

Fed Chairman Alan Greenspan knew the dangers of fiat money. He said in 1973:

> In the absence of the gold standard, there is no way to protect savings from confiscation through inflation. There is no safe store of value. If there were, the government would have to make its holding illegal, as was done in the case of gold. If everyone decided, for example, to convert all his bank deposits to silver or copper or any other good, and thereafter declined to accept checks as payment for goods, bank deposits would lose their pur-

chasing power and government-created bank credit would be worthless as a claim on goods. The financial policy of the welfare state requires that there be no way for the owners of wealth to protect themselves. This is the shabby secret of the welfare statists' tirades against gold. Deficit spending is simply a scheme for the confiscation of wealth. Gold stands in the way of this insidious process. It stands as a protector of property rights. If one grasps this, one has no difficulty in understanding the statists' antagonism toward the gold standard.

Yet when he was in charge, these worries seemed to fade away. Greenspan said in 2002:

> Central bankers' success, however, in containing inflation during the past two decades raises hopes that fiat money can be managed in a responsible way. This has been the case in the United States, and the dollar, despite many challenges to its status, remains the principal international currency.[1]

In other words, fiat money was dangerous when *bad* central bankers were in charge, but now that we have enlightened and restrained men and women in charge, there's nothing to fear.

Of course, there was plenty to fear, as Greenspan's record made clear. Chapter 2 discussed Greenspan's record: S&L bubble, tech and stock bubble, and housing bubble, which Ben Bernanke followed with a government bubble. Greenspan's Fed fueled all of these bubbles by injecting excess money into the system—money created out of thin air.

It's hardly a record of managing fiat money "in a responsible way."

Yes, the dollar is still the "principal international currency," but Greenspan's tenure went a long way toward ending that.

Politicians Love Free Money

Don't be misled into thinking this abuse of fiat money is an Alan Greenspan problem. Fiat money is problematic as long as human beings—fallible, corruptible creatures—are in charge.

Think about it. Politicians love spending money. They love giving free health care to people, they love building train stations that will be named after them, they love giving contracts to their friends and campaign contributors. There are three ways to get this money:

First, government can get the money through taxing. While some politicians seem to like taxes, especially taxes on the rich, most lawmakers with any political ambition shy away from tax hikes whenever possible The reason is simple: voters don't like paying higher taxes.

Second, government can get the money through borrowing. The U.S. Treasury sells bonds and bills and other types of debt. The buyer is now walking around with an IOU, and the Treasury now has cash. This is much easier politically, but it still has downsides: Interest and principal payments cost money, and down the line they reduce the portion of federal money politicians can spend on bridges to nowhere. High debt can raise interest rates. A high national debt displeases voters, too, who don't like their country being in hock to the Chinese. And given the recent trouble Obama had getting a hike in the debt ceiling, borrowing has its own political constraints. Any money borrowed today needs to be repaid plus interest. Deficits today mean even higher taxes tomorrow.

But there's also a third option: inflation. Simply print the money or make it out of thin air. The Fed can create money and give it to the U.S. Treasury. Then the Treasury can spend it on whatever it pleases. This is not a cost-free way of financing government spending—not by any means. Inflating the supply of money makes every dollar worth less, bringing along all the evils of excessive inflation (more on this in a moment). While taxes deprive taxpayers of their money, inflation deprives money of its purchasing power. No matter which method of finance the government chooses, taxpayers pick up the tab. The more a government relies on option two, borrowing, the higher the propensity to inflate the debt away rather than raise taxes to pay it off legitimately.

But the key, for politicians, is that inflation's costs are obscured. Nobody really notices that there's more money floating around. It's not as if anyone can count how many dollars there are. When inflation's effects show up in the form of rising prices, consumers don't typically blame politicians, they blame the merchants. In fact, politicians—the ones who caused the higher prices—are often the first ones to scapegoat merchants or manufacturers when prices start rising.

Many gold-standard opponents used the 2008 bailouts as proof positive of the virtue of fiat money. Had the Fed not been able to create money out of thin air, it couldn't have bought AIG and loaned all the money to the Treasury that the Treasury used during TARP. If you believe that TARP and the AIG bailouts saved the economy, this sounds like a good thing. If you see how destructive these bailouts were in terms of moral hazard, economic inefficiency, and corruption, this merely strengthens the argument for a gold standard.

Inflation Is Not a Force of Nature

For any American alive today, slow inflation can seem as natural as aging. Every year, on average, everything gets a little bit more expensive, but wages also climb. *It's just the way things are.*

But this is a misperception. The dollar, unlike the human body, doesn't naturally degrade over time.

For one thing, this steady devaluation of the dollar is a new practice, relatively speaking. For most of our country's history, the dollar gained value. The dollar was worth 75 percent more in 1912 than it was worth in 1800. You know those stories your parents or grandparents tell about how they used to buy a sandwich and a fountain soda for a dime? How everything was so much cheaper back in the day?

If you were around in 1900, for instance, the old folk didn't tell those sorts of stories. What cost a dime in 1900 probably had cost fifteen cents in 1875, and twenty cents in 1800.

Of course, since 1912, the dollar has lost more than 95 percent of its value. What cost a nickel in 1912 costs a dollar today. What cost $50 in 1912 costs $1,000 today. You will recall what happened in 1913: the Fed was created. The 1971 abolition of the gold standard just accelerated things. It took fifty-eight years after the Fed's creation for the dollar to lose 75 percent of its value, but it only took twenty-six years after killing the gold standard for the dollar to lose another 75 percent. The scary part is that the next 75 percent decline could happen in just five years, or even less!

It's not hard, from this little history, to see that money doesn't naturally lose value unless it's manipulated by central bankers.

What's So Bad About Inflation

If the money supply is growing fast, prices go up, but wages also go up. Your first reaction might be, "Well, what's wrong with that? Higher prices and higher wages mean steady purchasing power, right?"

It turns out, though, that there are plenty of problems with constant inflation.

In cases of hyperinflation, there are all sorts of logistical problems, like denominations being so large they're confusing (schoolteachers in Zimbabwe earn many million Zimbabwe dollars per month), and until the printing presses can catch up, the wads of cash are unwieldy.

The fiat currency issued by the colonies during the American Revolution lost so much value that George Washington once complained, "A wagonload of Continentals will hardly purchase a wagonload of provisions."[2]

Things don't need to be as bad as Zimbabwe for inflation to cause economic harm. Inflation discourages savings and encourages consumption. If you save your money for later, you know it won't be worth as much later. That means you may as well spend it today before it loses its value.

This sounds great to a lot of economists, but it's actually bad. Savings are the only way an economy can progress. Only with savings does anyone have the capital or the leisure time to make machines, invent something new, or launch companies. So by discouraging saving, steady inflation stultifies economic progress.

This dynamic particularly hurts regular working-class people. In the 1800s, if you wanted your savings to grow, you could often just put your money in the attic, and wait a few years. It was pretty easy to grow your wealth. But today, even if you put your money in an interest-bearing savings account, there's a good chance your money is losing value.

So the only way to make your money grow is to invest it. Investing money involves either expending your own expertise and time researching potential investments, or paying a fee to someone like me who does it for a living. In any event, protecting the value of your money carries greater costs, thanks to constant inflation.

Another cost is the moral hazard for politicians. Congressman Ron Paul likes to talk about the "inflation tax." It's an apt term because inflation is government taking wealth away from citizens. But again, it's not overtly a tax, which makes it more insidious.

Crashproof Yourself: Some TIPS on How Not to Protect Yourself from Inflation

Treasury Inflation-Protected Securities (TIPS) are a popular hedge against inflation. These are Treasury bonds where the principal grows with inflation, supposedly protecting you from losing purchasing power as the dollar falls. But asking the government to protect your money from inflation is like asking the fox to protect your hens. The Treasury uses the Consumer Price Index to measure inflation, and so your principal rises or falls proportionally to the CPI. But CPI is a bogus way of measuring inflation. The Bureau of Labor Statistics tweaks the formula for CPI to make inflation appear lower. Government has a vested interest in disguising the true magnitude of inflation, because inflation is a hidden tax on the people. One last strike against TIPS: the semiannual interest payments are taxed when they are credited to your account, even though you don't get that money until the bond matures—so government is taxing you on money it hasn't even given you yet.

Also, inflation expands the tax base. Say you buy a certificate of deposit from a bank in order to protect your money from losing value. Maybe you'll make 2.5 percent in a year, equal to inflation. That 2.5 percent gets taxed. So government gets to tax you for income, even though you didn't actually gain any wealth. This is particularly problematic for capital gains taxes, where inflation results in phantom gains that generate real liabilities.

The Deflation Boogey Monster

"Deflationary spiral."

Those are the scariest words in the English language for many economists. It's also the threat central bankers use to coerce skeptics into accepting their inflation.

It was deflation fears in 2010 that drove Fed chairman Bernanke to declare that inflation was too low, and so he was going to undertake a second round of "quantitative easing," or inflation. Bernanke, as the media constantly inform us, is a student of the Great Depression (though if he were my student I would have flunked him), and he sees that period's deflation as being the central cause of economic misery.

Deflation is when the dollar gains in value, and so prices and wages fall. The standard economic argument about deflation is that when prices start falling, people postpone purchases in order to get lower prices, which slows economic activity to a crawl, which further depresses prices—thus, the "deflationary spiral."

These deflation fears provide an excuse for intentionally causing inflation, which government likes, because it acts as a hidden tax. Also, the U.S. government is the world's largest debtor, and debtors benefit from inflation because it allows them to pay off their loans with dollars that are cheaper than the ones they borrowed.

So, fears about the Great Depression have combined with political ulterior motives to turn deflation into this looming monster in the imagination of many economists, politicians, and writers.

Deflation Is Natural

Slow, steady deflation, though, is the natural state of things in an economy with sound, stable money.

Think about it this way: does creating a particular product or performing a particular service generally become easier or harder over time? In most cases, it becomes easier: your computer becomes faster and the software gets better. Manufacturing equipment improves. Through practice, people figure out more efficient ways of doing the same thing.

So as widgets get easier to make, the cost of production goes down. In a competitive market, this will bring the price of the widget down. In other words, what we see with electronics would be the case with everything.

But this also has an effect on wages.

If, despite efficiency gains in the widget-production industry, you are still producing the same number of widgets per day as you were producing last year, guess what? You're not producing as much value. So, in a competitive labor market, your wages will fall unless your efficiency improves at the same rate as that of your competitors and colleagues.

So, as long as you keep pace with the market, you can keep your pay steady, but prices will fall. That way, you're getting richer.

If Prices Fall, Will Anyone Buy Anything?

The scare story about deflation is that no one will buy anything because they will wait for it to become cheaper. But if that were the case, nobody today would own a flat-screen TV, a DVD player, or a cell phone.

Most electronics fit the pattern I described above because the efficiency gains in productivity bring down the price even faster than the dollar loses value. So why does anyone ever buy a cell phone or a TV if we know it will be cheaper in three months?

It's because consumers attach a value to having something now, rather than waiting to have it later. It's also because some consumers value it more than others.

Remember the movie *Wall Street*, where billionaire Gordon Gekko was talking on a cell phone on the beach in 1987? It was a giant clunky thing, bigger than any landline handset you'll see today. The reception on mobile phones back then was spotty, they didn't send e-mails, and you couldn't play "Angry Birds" on them. The phone cost about $2,500 and was very expensive to use.

So why did anyone get one? Well, almost nobody did—but for a few people, it was worth it.

At first, in 1984, when Motorola began selling the first mobile phone, it cost $4,000.[3] Who bought it? First of all, people whose time really was so valuable that paying a ton for a phone paid off in terms of efficiency. Second, rich people who attached a high value to being early adopters— guys who liked to be the first to have something, or to show off to their friends.

With the money Motorola made off of these few phones, the company looked for new efficiencies—less expensive materials, more efficient manufacturing processes. And with each new phone to roll off the assembly line, the average cost of a phone went down. That is, the marginal cost of each unit went down thanks to efficiencies, and the overhead (R&D, building the factory, et cetera) was spread over more units.

By 1987, the cost of a cell phone had fallen to $2,500. *The New York Times* ran an article that year that began, "When cellular mobile telephones were introduced four years ago, they were gadgets only of the rich and powerful. Now everyone from drug dealers in Miami to the taco vendor in Rockefeller Plaza has one."

Again, it was a tiny minority that owned them. In 1987, the *Times* reported, 800,000 mobile phones roamed the U.S. That was three cell phones for every one hundred people. You still needed a good reason, and probably a lot of money to get a phone. The fact that these phones found a market inspired investors to inject cash into mobile companies, thus enabling the companies to seek more efficiencies.

Today, the most basic phone—many times better than Gordon Gekko's phone—basically sells for free and calls cost almost nothing to make. Even if you don't have much need for a phone, why not get one?

There's just about one cell phone for every person in the world. But if the deflation scare stories were correct, nobody would have a phone.

What happened? Early adopters effectively subsidized the purchases of later adopters. The early adopters do so willingly, because it's worth it, either economically or psychically.

This happens with flat-screen televisions, too. The first buyers are sports bars, which see them as investments, because they draw in customers. Then come the early adopters who want to be able to show it off to their friends. Then, rich people and big sports fans or movie buffs. Then, anyone with an extra $800 whose old TV broke picks one up.

How is it a bad thing that everyone can now afford a cell phone, and that every American household has at least one TV? According to the logic of the deflation scaremongers, this is simply awful.

General Electric introduced the first television set in 1928. It had a three-inch screen. There was only one channel that broadcast Tuesday, Thursday, and Friday from 1:30 PM to 3:30 PM. It retailed for $60, or three ounces of gold. In today's terms that's almost five grand. By 1942, a ten-inch black and white set cost $375 (about 10.7 ounces of gold or about $17,000 in today's money). Of course there was a much better picture and far more programming available by that time. RCA introduced the first color TV set in 1954. It sold for $1,000, or 28.5 ounces of gold, which equals about $45,000 in today's inflated dollars. For the same $1,000 one could have purchased a brand-new Chevrolet.

How many color TVs do you think RCA sold to millionaires back in 1954? Today, even the poorest American families have at least one color TV, and most have several. Not only are they color, they are high definition, some are 3D, they come with flat screens, remote controls, and 150 channels broadcasting 24/7. The reason so many Americans now enjoy television, and that the sets and the service are now so much better, is falling prices. It was falling prices that created demand and drove the profitability of the industry.

Going back to cell phones: imagine what would have happened if handset prices had gone up instead of down. According to conventional wisdom the industry would be in much better shape, as rising prices would have motivated buyers, who would want a phone before the next price jump. But how many people would have cell phones today if they sold for over $4,000 a piece?

In fact, not only would they still be obscure toys for the superrich, they would not be much better than the Gekko original. That is because the industry never would have earned the profits to invest in the research and development that resulted in the vastly improved models of today. The truth is, falling prices do not discourage people from buying; they entice people to buy. The lower prices fall, the more people can afford to buy!

When confronted with real-world examples of consumer electronics, economists often dismiss them as the exceptions that prove the rule. However, apply the same logic to other prices.

What if someone made an invention that could create a mansion for ten dollars? Think about that: 99.999 percent deflation in housing prices. Would that be disastrous? No. It would be the greatest advance in human prosperity ever. But it would be vastly deflationary.

Would it really be so bad if gas prices fell? How about health care—would it really be so bad if insurance premiums fell each year instead of rising? What about food? Would it be such a disaster if food became less expensive? How about education? Would parents really consider it a tragedy if college tuitions went down instead of up? You get the point. For all the talk about the horrors of deflation, I do not know anyone who would not benefit were it actually allowed to happen.

It is just plain common sense. Of course, getting an economics degree means your common sense goes out the window. If a merchant wants to sell more stuff, he has a sale. The bigger the discounts, the more stuff he is likely to sell. Putting stuff on sale means falling prices, which is what most economists have in mind when they warn about the dangers of deflation. Imagine if a merchant, who also had an economics degree, decided to promote sales using a different marketing strategy—advertise big price increases coming soon as a way to encourage customers to buy before the markups kick in. That is probably why economists rarely run successful businesses.

Massive, persistent deflation would be disruptive in many of the same ways hyperinflation is disruptive. But the effort to scare us about any deflation is misguided at best, and at worst, a dishonest cover story for those who benefit from inflation.

Gold and the Fed 2.0

In her confirmation hearing, when asked if she paid attention to the price of gold, the new Fed chairman, Janet Yellen, answered by admitting that she really had no idea why it rises or falls. It is merely, she said, "an asset that people want to hold when they're very fearful about potential financial market catastrophe or economic troubles."

She seems oblivious to the fact the "fear" relates directly to the monetary policy she herself has committed to continue. This is really a lot like a coal miner not understanding why there is a canary in the mine, and assuming that all of the other miners are similarly bewildered.

Even when he served as Fed chairman, Alan Greenspan acknowledged the importance of gold. A rising gold price indicates that monetary policy is too loose, interest rates are too low, and too much inflation is being created.

Yellen should be checking the gold price each morning even before she gets out of bed. Somehow, it seems unlikely she will do so as she continues the destructive program of quantitative easing.

Return to Sound Money

So far, we've discussed the nature of money, walked through how and why governments debase currency, and picked apart the phony scare stories told by those who cheapen our money.

The next question is what we should do to stop the constant devaluation of the dollar. How do we return to sound money?

Many of my friends and ideological fellow travelers have a simple answer: End the Fed. That's the title of a Ron Paul book, and it's a rallying cry for many libertarians and believers in the Austrian School of economics.

I agree with the sentiment to this extent: the Fed, as it currently exists, is the chief cause of our economic problems. The Fed serves mostly to cause inflation, facilitate the growth of government, and create moral hazard through bailouts.

But ultimately, I wouldn't abolish the Fed, at least not right away. In an ideal world, there would be no Fed, and I think the nation would be better off if the Fed had never been created. However, this is not an ideal world. The Fed is already here, and abolishing it completely is fraught with risk. The most important reason to have an independent central bank is that the alternative is puting monetary policy in the hands of politicians. Yes, the Fed is overly politicized as it is, but this is a case where you should prefer the devil you know to the devil you don't know.

Imagine if the treasury secretary controlled the money supply. Or even worse, if Congress did. Cheap politics, cronyism, and corruption would explode, and inflation would run rampant because there would be even less separation between the big spenders in government and the guys who control the printing press.

For practical reasons, we should preserve an independent central bank that provides a single currency. But in order to prevent the sort of bailout gamesmanship we've seen, we should bar the Fed from owning U.S. Treasuries, as the original Federal Reserve Act did.

Most importantly, the Fed shouldn't be allowed to create money out of thin air.

We need to return to the gold standard. Every dollar the Fed issues should be backed by a fixed amount of gold. Everyone holding a dollar should be able to redeem it for gold on demand. And the Fed should be barred from issuing "credit reserves"—or money backed by nothing. In other words, we need to restore the original Federal Reserve Act as it existed prior to 1917. If we do that, we may one day be able to abolish it completely, but I do not think we go should cold turkey on the Fed. If you recall, in theory the Fed was a good idea. It's just that in practice it did not work, because politicians quickly abused it. Perhaps now that we know all the problems based on a disastrous test run, we can redesign the system with better safeguards.

A gold standard would keep the money supply stable, and would shackle the ability of the Fed to inflate.

I admit it will be a bit tricky to convert back to gold. Where would the Fed set the price? My guess is the Fed would not even have to, as the market could set it. All the government would have to do is announce in advance its intention to return to a gold standard, and let the market set the new equilibrium price of gold. Once a steady price was established, the government could fix the dollar to that new price. Of course, the new price would mark a significant devaluation of the dollar from the obsolete official gold price of $42 per ounce, but it would put a real price tag on years of government excess.

The new official gold price would be a function of the supply of gold, the total number of dollars in circulation, the demand for gold, and the demand for dollars. Once fixed, the money supply could grow no faster than the increase in the supply of gold.

If this sounds like a difficult political transition to make, think about the reverse. When we went from a gold standard to fiat money, Nixon had to convince the public that a dollar backed by nothing was better than a dollar backed by something. If the government was able to pull that off, convincing the public that a dollar backed by gold is better than one backed by nothing should be a piece of cake.

Regardless of any problems associated with the transition, the long-term benefits will be well worth the short-term cost.

The Benefits of a Gold Standard and Sound Money

The first and most obvious benefit would be that your dollars would stop losing value. The stability and predictability of sound money would make our economy more efficient, and thus make us wealthier.

But also, without the Fed buying up Treasuries and printing money, government spending would be under actual constraints. Government wouldn't be able to borrow as easily and wouldn't be able to make money out of thin air. Every dollar spent would have to be taxed or borrowed from an actual taxpayer or investor.

With no fiat money, we wouldn't have bailouts like AIG, where the Fed bought the company by creating dollars out of thin air to pay for it. A constrained Fed also would make it harder for Congress to do things like TARP. This might be the only effective way to prevent bailouts and thus reduce moral hazard.

Shoring up our money by backing it with gold may also be the only way to retain our position as the reserve currency of the world. If we keep diluting the dollar, we'll definitely lose that privileged role.

And if you want to help U.S. manufacturing, a gold standard is the best way to do it. If the amount of dollars is fairly fixed, then a trade deficit leads to a lower supply of dollars in the United States. A lower supply of dollars in the U.S. means prices have to come down. When U.S. prices come down, that boosts demand for our goods, thus driving exports. It's self-regulating.

A restoration of manufacturing would help restore an American middle class. A prospering middle class is the key to a prosperous nation.

Listen to what politicians say they want: stronger economic growth, more American manufacturing, an end to bailouts, a stronger middle class. They could get all these things with a return to sound money. But, of course, politicians would lose power without the ability to manipulate currency at will.

The money issue—like many issues—clearly puts the politicians' interests on one side and the people's interests on another.

In fact, up until recently, promoting price stability was part of the Fed's dual mandate, the other part being maximum employment. However, without any congressional action, the Fed changed its mandate. According to Ben Bernanke, the Fed's new mandate is to ensure that consumer prices, as measured by the CPI, rise by at least 2 percent per annum. Anything less risks the possibility that prices might fall, which according to Bernanke would be a disaster.

However, for prices to remain stable over time, prices must fall during some years to offset rises in other years. Prior to the Fed we did not have stable prices, we had prices that gradually declined over time. The government told us that falling prices were bad, and that price stability would better promote economic growth. Now they are telling us that stable prices are bad, and that rising prices are more desirable. Think about this. When the Fed's goal was price stability we experienced steadily rising prices instead. Now that the Fed is pursuing rising prices as its official policy objective, imagine how much higher they will soar.

To make matters worse, the 2 percent annual consumer price increases the Fed considers a must are based on the CPI. However, thanks to the Boskin Commission, the CPI no longer accurately measures price increases. Instead, a complex methodology using geometric weighing, substitution, and hedonics results in a CPI that rises more slowly than the general price level. So a 2 percent CPI might actually equate to annual price increases of 6 percent or more. The people running the Fed may be completely inept at most things, but the one thing they do well is create inflation.

Sound Money 2.0: Talk to the Hamburger

Leading up to President Obama's re-election, a FOX News poll of Oct 7-9, 2012 asked voters, "Which one of the following is the biggest economic problem facing people like you?" You might think it was unemployment, but that was only a distant second. Their top concern? *Rising prices*.

We have a central bank saying we need more inflation—higher prices—and yet the biggest problem people are worrying about is inflation. Maybe everyone is crazy. Or maybe they're on to something.

We've already seen how sick our economy is—a reduced labor force, a decline in full-time jobs, and all of the available lending capital being absorbed by government, speculation and consumption. Unemployment remains high and malinvestments in housing continue to grow. Real wage growth fell off a cliff in late 2012, and real wages actually declined by 0.1 percent year-over-year in May 2013.

These are all signs of an economy that's getting smaller, yet we're told it continues to grow. There's another disturbing problem that is being ignored—flaws in the government's calculation of inflation are hiding our real economic situation from us. I am not alone in believing that the government's method for calculating the consumer price index (CPI) has become useless, and is now causing a substantial underestimation of inflation.

To test this idea, I conducted an experiment. I looked at several of the items whose prices the government measures when calculating the rate of inflation. I studied the prices of several components: Eggs, new cars, milk, coffee, dental services, potatoes, electricity, butter, airline tickets, apples, public transportation, cereal, beef, store-bought beer, tires, sugar, prescription drugs, gasoline, rent for a primary residence, and bread.

From 1970 to 1980—a period of significant inflation—the numbers stacked up pretty well. The CPI rose by 112 percent, and the the prices I tracked rose by 117 percent. But for the period between 2002 and 2012, there was a sudden divergence. The official CPI rose by 27.5 percent, but the basket of goods I was studying rose by 44.3 percent—61 percent faster.

Likewise, the government claims that newspaper and magazine prices between 1999 and 2012 rose by 37 percent—and that figure goes into the official CPI calculation. But my team and I looked at the beginning and end prices for that period and found that the actual average increase was 131.5 percent. In fact, we didn't find a single magazine or newspaper that had gone up by only 37 percent.

The government underestimates inflation. And I don't want you to take my word for it. Take a hamburger's word for it instead, because hamburgers never lie.

The "Big Mac Index" is a tool invented by the British magazine *The Economist* to compare purchasing power between various countries. But if you look at its data in the U.S. over time, it tells another shocking story.

Between 1986 and 2003, both CPI and the price of a Big Mac rose in sync, by about 4 percent annually. The Big Mac Index was fairly representative of the CPI in general. But beginning in April 2003, the CPI rose 2.5 percent annually, whereas the Big Mac started rising in price by about 6.1 percent annually. Between April 2003 and December 2012, the CPI rose about 25 percent, but the Big Mac rose by 61 percent in price.

None of the ingredients in the Big Mac have changed. It's the same two all-beef patties, special sauce, lettuce, cheese, pickles, and onions. It's the same sesame seed bun. So that leaves us two explanations. Did McDonald's suddenly become so inefficient that its prices shot up? Or is the CPI no longer reflective of the prices consumers actually pay?

If inflation is actually two to three times the CPI, as the Big Mac index suggests, then that implies the economy has been contracting in real terms. It would mean that in March 2013, when 60 percent of Americans told an *Investors Business Daily* poll that they thought the economy was still in recession—as large majorities had in various polls throughout 2011, 2012 and 2013—*they were right*. It would explain why today, American consumers in the lower middle class (households making between about $35,000 and $50,000) have tremendously less confidence in the economy, according to the Conference Board's consumer confidence index, than their wealthier peers—a gap of 46 points in the index. As Bloomberg's Mark Gimein pointed out in September 2013, the two income groups shared nearly identical consumer confidence before the current recession began.

Mind you, I'm not asserting a conspiracy here—just bad methodology. Hamburgers don't miscalculate inflation, but bureaucrats do. And if their methodology is bad, then there's an enormous disincentive for anyone in the government to fix it. A sudden revelation of massive amounts of hidden inflation would really upset the apple cart. The government, as we've discussed in earlier chapters, obviously can't afford the rise in interest rates that would be necessary to fight inflation. In far more basic terms, it can't afford the rise in Social Security benefits that would result by law. It can't afford the reduction in Americans' income tax liability that would result, because tax brackets are also indexed to inflation.

When the Commerce Department calculates economic growth these days, it is assuming very low inflation based on the numbers from the Bureau of Labor Statistics. Yet if you look out at the statistical evidence in the economy—at how many people have left the labor force and gone on government disability, our energy use, the fact that the number of full-time employed in the U.S. is six million less than before the recession—there are signs that the economy has been getting smaller amid nominal (non-inflation-adjusted) growth. Another indicator: Workers are seeing not only their real wages decline, but also their vacation. The share of U.S. workers with paid vacation has actually declined since 1992, from 88 to 77 percent.

For a look at more recent data suggesting decline, have a look at this chart (based on data from the U.S. Energy Information Administration), which shows the amount of end-use energy consumption in the U.S. economy—the residential, commercial, industrial, and transportation sectors combined:

There are more people in America today than there were in March 2003, and according to the official numbers, our economy has grown since then by about 18 percent. Yet in March 2013, our economy was using less energy than it had ten years earlier, with industrial energy consumption

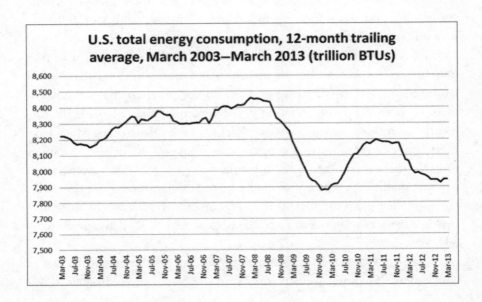

leading the decline (down more than 6 percent). In fact, you have to go all the way back to 1999 to find a time when we were using less.

Lower energy use is typically a symptom of economic contraction. If the economy is really 3 percent larger today than it was before the recession began in December 2007—as the government's numbers suggest— then how is it that we're consuming so much less energy now than we did then? Some of it is surely due to greater efficiency, but that explanation only goes so far. (It certainly doesn't explain the double-dip in the graph above).

Transportation and industry account for about half of the energy use plotted above, and for most of the decline (but not all of it). Both sectors have probably become more energy-efficient since 2007, but they're also producing less in absolute terms.

According to the Transportation Department, the growing U.S. population was actually driving fewer miles in 2013 than it had in 2008, probably in part because they enjoyed less purchasing power when it comes to gasoline. According to MIT, the number of passenger-trips on domestic flights, at 565 million, was lower in 2012 than it was in 2005, 2006, 2007, or 2008, despite a growing U.S. population. And with respect to industry, the Fed reports that industrial production in May 2013 was down 1.3 percent from 2007 levels.

In other words, we're using less energy because there's less economic activity. Has our economy shrunk—along with the number of full-time jobs it is sustaining?

The real problem, which I alluded to above, goes back to tinkering with the way the government measures inflation. In 1997, the Boskin Commission, referenced earlier in this chapter, asserted that the government was overestimating inflation by 1.1 percent annually. In order to correct this, it introduced controversial changes to the calculations, which have been applied ever since in a very opaque manner. One of these changes involves the use of "hedonic adjustments," by which improvements in product quality are now considered a form of deflation. So if a television cost $500 last year, and it costs the same amount this year with a slightly better screen, the Bureau of Labor Statistics treats it as if the price actually went down.

There are two major problems with this line of thinking. The first is conceptual: "Hedonic adjustments" turn the reality of technological advancement into a mere novelty rather than an inescapable reality of modern life. You couldn't buy an old box television set or a 1979 Dodge Dart even if you wanted to. But BLS still adjusts downward the price that you pay for your modern set or car in order to compensate for your psychic satisfaction with the era you live in.

The ideal BLS consumer is that cranky guy in your neighborhood who uses a mechanical, non-power lawn mower, clings bitterly to his collection of VHS cassettes, and curses Russian communists. Unless we all live as he does, we're introducing some kind of psychological deflation into the economy.

The second problem is one of consistency: Hedonic adjustments only go one way. The government doesn't adjust inflation upward for reductions in quality. For example, have you noticed that when you call customer service, you get an inferior experience because a computer system answers and it's impossible to get a real person on the phone? That's because companies have reduced costs (and kept prices down) by cutting corners on customer service. Have you noticed that, above and beyond any changes to ticket prices, airlines have added baggage fees and increased the cost of changing tickets? These things affect your standard of living the same way a better television set does, but they don't make it into the CPI.

Have you noticed how the items you use each day—umbrellas, can-openers, outdoor furniture—have declined in quality, so that you have to replace them more frequently? Have you ever purchased a product and then spent hours trying to put all the pieces together? To keep costs down, many products that were once manufactured in the U.S. and sold fully assembled are now imported from China, and sold in boxes with tools, various screws, and complex instruction manuals on how the pieces can be easily assembled. If you value your time, the hours spent putting all those pieces together increases the cost of the product. However, that significant cost is not factored into the CPI.

In some consumer sectors, it costs more to get the same quality of goods and services that were available in years past. If you have to purchase business class tickets to get the same amount of legroom and service once available in coach, then hasn't the cost of a coach ticket effectively increased? Many manufacturers routinely substitute lower quality ingredients or reduce quantity without rasing prices. The makers of Makers Mark were considering watering down their bourbon rather than raising prices, until a consumer uproar changed their plans. If Kimberly Clark reduces the sheet count in its toilet paper rolls by 10 percent but maintains the same price, you may not pay more per roll, but over a year you will buy 10 percent more rolls. If a dog food company substitutes beef by-products for whole beef, you may have to trade up to a premium brand to maintian the nutritional quality for your pet. None of these changes factor into the CPI.

As long as hedonic adjustments are made to account for high-quality goods replacing inferior ones, why doesn't the opposite logic apply when you're forced to replace that old metal blender that lasted you twenty years with a cheap plastic one that may last just two or three? Some writers have attempted to recreate the old methods of calculating inflation without "hedonic adjustments" and other dubious devices. They find that inflation is higher—perhaps significantly higher—and the Big Mac Index seems to corroborate their findings.

As the government's underestimation of inflation goes ignored and unrecognized, perhaps concealing the recession that labor and energy markets hint at, the Obama administration has now proposed making the problem even worse by shifting to something called "Chain Weighted CPI." Unlike the Boskin Commission, which was merely accused of cooking the books in order to reduce government liabilities, this even lower estimate of inflation is openly billed as a way of holding down Social Security benefits.

Chained CPI tries to account quickly for changes in spending patterns when consumers switch from products whose prices are rising to more affordable products. This is known as "substitution." You can't afford steak anymore because of inflation, so when you switch to eating pork, chicken, or dog food, the government takes that into account as proof that there's no inflation. Chained CPI measures the cost of survival rather than the cost of maintaining a constant standard of living. People admit openly that this is a manipulation, but no one really seems to care. It's a lot easier to shift to Chained CPI or otherwise manipulate economic numbers than it is to vote on cutting Social Security benefits.

The bottom line here is that we've found yet another way of fooling ourselves in order to sustain the government's massive liabilities, and it's all to the detriment of consumers and the broader economy.

7

Tax Reform: For Starters, End the Income Tax

TAXES IN THE UNITED STATES today are too high, too intrusive, too economically distorting, too arbitrary, and too politically determined.

We need to cut taxes, but we need to do more: we need to completely overhaul the tax code. Ideally, we should scrap the current system and start all over again. The federal income, payroll, estate and gift taxes should all be eliminated. On the state and local level, income and residential property taxes should also go. As much as possible, we should transition to user fees. Revenue should come from excise taxes, sales taxes, and flat tariffs. And government revenues, frankly, should be smaller, because government should be much smaller.

A guiding star in a true tax reform could be the Founding Fathers' view of taxation.

Getting Us into This Mess

The history of taxation in the United States, in brief, is this: steadily, all limits on Congress's ability to tax have been worn away, and Washington's ability to take our wealth and property and use taxes to steer the economy has become nearly absolute. And as the federal government's taxing power has grown, so has our deficit.

So we should look at the earliest ideas the Founding Fathers had about taxes—back before power started corrupting our government leaders so much.

Taxes weren't popular in the newly independent American states. Stamp taxes and tea taxes had been a central rallying point for the Revolution, after all. The widespread idea at the birth of the country was that federal taxes were to be avoided except as necessary for national defense.

The first constitution, the Articles of Confederation, didn't allow the federal government to collect taxes from individuals. In case of war, the federal government would collect from the states, which would pay proportionally to the value of their land.

The U.S. Constitution gave the central government more taxing power than did the Articles of Confederation, but the Constitution still seriously curtailed federal taxing power. The most important restriction was the limitation on federal *direct* taxes, such as income taxes or property taxes.

After the U.S. Supreme Court shot down the income tax in 1895, the progressives stepped in and passed the Sixteenth Amendment, legalizing an unapportioned income tax. This opened the door for massive increases in government spending, huge growth in federal power, and the use of the tax code to steer behavior. This has crippled our economy, and ironically, helped create our debt crisis. That's why it was appropriate for angry voters to invoke the Boston Tea Party in their anger about taxes and debt.

Abandoning our Founders' intense resistance to federal taxing power has helped get us into the bind we're in. Let's see if we can untangle this mess.

Direct and Indirect Taxes

The Constitution establishes two great classes of taxation, direct taxes that are governed by the rule of apportionment, and indirect taxes that are subject to the rule of uniformity.

In two different locations, the Constitution requires that "direct taxes" must be "apportioned"—that is, collected from each state proportionate to each state's population. In fact, this is the only provision the Constitution states twice! Since revenue bills must originate in the House, where representation is also proportionate to population, creating and raising direct taxes involved quite a hurdle. And that provision was for a reason.

To lay a direct tax, the government would first be required to determine how much money it needed to raise. Then it would have to collect from each state its share of that tax based on each state's percentage of the total U.S. population. So if California had 10 percent of the population, it would be responsible for paying 10 percent of the tax.

Apart from being very difficult to do, the requirement to apportion direct taxes had other benefits. First, it prevented poorer states from trying to loot the wealth of wealthier states, as apportionment effectively requires that tax rates in poorer states be higher than those in wealthier states.

Second, it kept states honest in reporting their populations. If a state exaggerated its population in order to secure more representation in the House of Representatives, it would also be required to pay a higher share of any direct tax that might be levied.

Again, the Founders saw direct taxes as something government should only implement in dire circumstances, such as war. So, what is a *direct* tax, and how does it differ from an *indirect* tax?

Think about it this way: if the taxpayer is directly sending a check to the government (or having it removed from his paycheck or insurance escrow) it's a *direct* tax. If instead, the tax is attached to some sort of transaction, and thus a merchant or provider acts as the middleman between the taxpayer (purchaser) and the government—that's an *indirect* tax.

Income tax, payroll tax, and property taxes are examples of direct taxes. Sales tax, tariffs, or value-added taxes are indirect taxes. You pay the sales tax, but you never get a sales tax bill. To levy an indirect tax, Congress need only apply the tax uniformly, that is equally, in all states.

There are a couple of reasons to prefer indirect taxes. First, they are less intrusive. Think of all the time wasted and all the privacy invaded through paying income taxes. Second, they are self-limiting.

Alexander Hamilton wrote in *Federalist Paper* #21:

> It is a signal advantage of taxes on articles of consumption, that they contain in their own nature a security against excess. They prescribe their own limit; which cannot be exceeded without defeating the end proposed, that is, an extension of the revenue.

Hamilton explained it clearly:

> If duties are too high, they lessen the consumption; the collection is eluded; and the product to the treasury is not so great as

when they are confined within proper and moderate bounds. This forms a complete barrier against any material oppression of the citizens by taxes of this class, and is itself a natural limitation of the power of imposing them.

In other words, indirect taxes were preferable, because government would have some incentive—maximizing revenue—to keep them from getting too high.

Of course, some direct taxes have the same character, to some extent. This is the idea behind the Laffer Curve: raise income tax rates too high or capital gains taxes rates too high, and you actually reduce revenue by discouraging labor and investment. But indirect taxes tend to have even more self-correction, in part because they tax consumption, which is more "optional" than earning a living. For some direct taxes, such as property taxes, there is no restraint at all. If you own property you are forced to pay the tax, no matter how high the rate.

If the whiskey excise tax is too high, people start drinking beer, or even water. Alternatively, as happened early in the Republic, people start making their own moonshine in their backyards. At some point, the cost of enforcement and the revenue lost to black markets is too high, and so the government is better off with a lower rate, removing incentives for a black market.

If a sales tax is too high, people consume less and start producing more for themselves. If tariffs are too high, people produce domestically. Sure, nobody can avoid consumption altogether, but consumption is easier to reduce or alter in response to taxes than income is.

So, a government based on indirect taxes is a government constrained in its revenue—and thus in its expenditures. This was the Founders' vision. That's why the history of taxation in the United States is a history of moving away from the Founders' vision.

History of Taxes in the United States

Early on, the federal government got by on a handful of excise taxes— basically, a sales tax—on a few goods, including sugar and whiskey. Also, many of the functions Washington was originally intended to perform could be funded through user fees rather than taxes.

Article I section 8 of the Constitution enumerates the powers of Congress. Most of these powers have particular beneficiaries that could be expected to finance the functions.

Congress is supposed to "regulate Commerce with foreign Nations," which could be paid for through tariffs. Immigration law and bankruptcy law are also among Congress's enumerated powers, and it would be easy to let the users—immigrants and bankruptcy-proceeding participants—fund these administrative activities.

Post offices and post roads can obviously be paid for by postage fees, and a patent and trademark office can be funded by fees. User fees are different from taxes. First, they are optional. If you don't want to pay a toll, you don't have to drive on the postal road. Second, they are tied to a service or a good. Your toll pays for a road, your stamp pays for postal service, and so on.

Government user fees are second-best to market prices. If a user-funded government service isn't worth the cost, it will wither away, because folks won't pay the associated fee. That applies some competitive pressure on quality and price. In this way, user fees mitigate some of the harmful inefficiencies government spending creates.

Besides the activities that could easily be covered by user fees, Article I's other enumerated powers mostly involve defense and prosecution of federal crimes.

In other words, in the Founders' idea of government, taxes were for defense and criminal law—and little else.

Even our early taxation, mostly through tariffs and excise taxes, was not trouble-free for the government. George Washington's first major headache as president was putting down the Whiskey Rebellion—an uprising by frontiersmen who refused to pay the tax on distilled spirits.

For the War of 1812, Congress created luxury taxes, but again they were indirect. These taxes included a sales tax on jewelry. This tax was created with an automatic expiration date, once the war ended.

Come the American Civil War, we got another expansion of federal taxes. Congress created an income tax for the first time. The top rate (what the wealthy paid) was 5 percent. By Reconstruction, Congress had repealed the income tax.

In 1894, led by populist William Jennings Bryan, Congress resurrected the income tax. With no Civil War to distract attention, this became a very contentious issue. It seemed clear to many people that an income tax was unconstitutional, because it was a direct tax that was not apportioned among the states.

In 1895, the court struck down the 1894 income tax in *Pollock v. Farmers' Loan & Trust Co.* (157 U.S. 429). In that case the Court said, "It is true that the power to tax is a very extensive power. It is given in the Constitution, with one exception and two qualifications. Congress cannot tax exports, and it must impose direct taxes by the rule of apportionment and indirect taxes by the rule of uniformity."

Congress soon set about to amend the Constitution to explicitly allow an income tax. The tax was sold to the American public as a means of soaking the rich, enabling the government to lower taxes on everyone else, principally tariffs. No one envisioned that average Americans would ever be subject to the income tax, and even the wealthy did not get soaked too badly. The top rate was just 7 percent on incomes over $500,000, which is well over 10 million in today's dollars.

In fact, the first $20,000 of annual income was not taxed at all, and incomes above $20,000 but below $50,000, taking into account all the deductions and exemptions that were far more generous than they are today, were taxed at just 1 percent. In today's dollars those brackets would be well in excess of $400,000 to $1 million. In terms of gold, which was $20 per ounce back then, one had to earn 1,000 ounces per year to hit the $20,000 minimum. Using $1,300 gold, the 1 percent bracket would only apply to annual incomes between $1.3 million and $3.25 million!

This shows the dangers of the type of class warfare that exists today in American politics. Prior to 1913, the only federal taxes most Americans paid were tariffs. In exchange for imposing a tiny income tax on the top 1 percent of Americas, the 99 percent were told they would basically pay no federal taxes at all—that the entire cost of government would be shouldered by those fortunate few most able to bear the burden. So the 99 percent made a deal with the devil, and now their incomes are taxed at levels far in excess of anything envisioned for the Rockefellers, Carnegies, or Vanderbilts. In 1913 gold dollars (with gold priced at $1,300), today's income tax on single filers would start at 10 percent on the first dollar earned (67 percent higher than then 1913 top bracket reserved for the superrich), and top out at 39.6 percent (not counting a Medicare tax of 3.8 percent that did not exist back then) on incomes above $6,150. Remember the 1913 income tax did not even apply to incomes below $20,000, which is more than three times the level at which today's maximum bracket kicks in! So the next time some politician promises you free stuff paid for by taxing the rich, think about how much you enjoy paying income taxes before taking the bait.

In 1913, as the first of four Progressive Era constitutional amendments, the Sixteenth Amendment allowed Congress to "lay and collect taxes on incomes, from whatever source derived, without apportionment among the several States, and without regard to any census or enumeration."

However, as my father pointed out in his book *The Great Income Tax Hoax,* contrary to popular belief, the Sixteenth Amendment did not overturn the *Pollock* decision, nor did it allow the government to levy an unapportioned direct tax on income. In 1916, the Supreme Court in *Brushaber v. Union Pacific Railroad* (240 U.S. 1), in upholding the constitutionality of an income tax imposed subsequent to the Sixteenth Amendment, ruled that the Sixteenth Amendment "contains nothing repudiating or challenging the ruling in the *Pollock* case."

And in *Pollock*, the court held that:

> taxes on real estate being indisputably direct taxes, taxes on the rents or income of real estate are equally direct taxes. Taxes on personal property, or on the income of personal property, are likewise direct taxes. The tax imposed by sections twenty-seven to thirty-seven, inclusive, of the act of 1894, so far as it falls on the income of real estate and of personal property, being a direct tax within the meaning of the Constitution, and therefore unconstitutional and void became not apportioned according to representation, all those sections, constituting one entire scheme of taxation, are necessarily invalid.

I would also point out that one's labor is also personal property. Therefore a tax on wages or salaries, the income derived from that property, is also a direct tax, and according to the Supreme Court in both *Pollock* and

Burshaber, still subject to the rule of apportionment, despite the ratification of the Sixteenth Amendment. These two cases prove conclusively that an unapportioned direct tax on rents, dividends, interest, wages, salaries, et cetera is still unconstitutional, void, and invalid.

Since the Sixteenth Amendment authorized Congress to levy an income tax without apportionment, the court ruled that it must be levied as excise taxes. The court was not prepared to authorize a tax that was limited neither by uniformity nor apportionment. The Supreme Court again recognized this fact in 1920 in *Mark Eisner v. Myrtle H. Macomber* (252 U.S. 189), when the court said, "The Sixteenth Amendment must be construed in connection with the taxing clauses of the original Constitution and the effect attributed to them before the Amendment was adopted."

To constitutionally tax income as an excise, the court held that income must be separated from its source. A tax on sources of income, such as fees, rents, dividends, commissions, and so on, would constitute a direct tax. But a tax on profits, which separated income from its sources, could be imposed as an excise. That is why the income tax is really a profits tax (more on that later).

However, when it comes to personal income, the scope of these decisions has been completely ignored by lower courts, and the government now levies an unapportioned direct tax on the sources of income, rather than an excise tax on income itself, in direct violation of the Constitution, the Sixteenth Amendment, and several Supreme Court decisions. As a result, the passage of the Sixteenth Amendment in 1913 allowed the federal government to usurp nearly unlimited taxing power.

If the year 1913 rings a bell, it may be because that's also the year Congress created the Federal Reserve. It's no wonder the size and scope of government has expanded immensely since that year.

Today, in contrast to what the framers wanted, a vast majority of federal revenue comes from direct taxes. The largest chunk of tax receipts, at more than 40 percent, is the individual income tax. Second place is the payroll tax (half of which, being paid by the employer, is an indirect tax). So 60 percent of all taxes are direct taxes on wages.

Twenty percent of all tax receipts are the employer portion of payroll taxes, and 9 percent are corporate income taxes. Customs, duties, excise taxes, and the like—the sort of taxes on which this government originally ran—make up less than 9 percent of all federal tax receipts.

Solution: We Need a New Tax System

If you were trying to create a tax system to destroy the economy, you would come up with one not too different from the one we have.

Our tax code discourages work, promotes consumption, induces wasteful behavior, imposes huge compliance costs, invades privacy, and tramples on individual rights.

We ought to scrap the entire tax system and start anew. We should return to what the Founding Fathers envisioned, and rely on indirect taxes and user fees. There is room for disagreement on the details, but the principles are these:

> *Low:* Government should tax only as much as it needs to carry out its essential and legitimate duties.
>
> *Neutral:* As much as possible, taxes should avoid picking winners and losers, or otherwise alter decision making, resource utilization, or capital allocation.
>
> *Tax consumption, not productivity:* To the extent our taxes are steering economic activity, they should not discourage labor, savings, or investment. Taxing consumption is least harmful, because consumption is the least productive economic activity.
>
> *Less intrusive:* Government shouldn't need to know all your personal details in order to collect taxes.
>
> *Simple:* Individuals and small businesses shouldn't need an accountant or a lawyer in order to figure out taxes (if they owe them at all). Big businesses shouldn't need armies of tax experts. Also, gaming the tax code shouldn't be as profitable as it is today.

With these principles in mind, this chapter will lay out a better tax code. Given the political difficulties in obtaining an ideal system, I'll also lay out second-best options—the sort of changes we should make to our existing system.

First, Make Government Fund Itself

Most things that government does today, it shouldn't do at all. Of those government functions that are productive, the private sector should take care of most (more on this in later chapters).

For those functions that are best done by government, or are traditionally performed by government, we should make them pay for themselves.

Most obvious is the highway system. There is no reason drivers in Mississippi should pay for drivers in Oregon. There's also no justification for funding a highway with the income taxes of someone who doesn't own a car or who drives only local roads. But that's what we do.

Currently, most of our highway money comes from the federal gasoline tax, which is a net transfer from those who drive on local roads to those who drive more on highways. But much of our highway money also comes from income-tax payers, which is a net transfer from nondrivers to drivers.

Highways can pay for themselves, through tolls. That way, the people who use a road are paying for the road. This has two positive economic effects.

First, it provides a price signal for what roads are worth building and worth improving. If a government doesn't think it can recoup its costs through tolls, then it can build or expand the road only if it gets subsidies from other taxes. But if drivers aren't willing to pay the price for a road, that's a signal that the road is not worth the cost.

Of course, all roads provide commercial value by making it easier to move labor and goods. Roads also have personal, noncommercial value: helping us visit friends, go to the pool, or take a road trip to Mt. Rushmore.

But sometimes that commercial or personal value doesn't equal the cost. If all roads had to pay for themselves—say, if the bonds used to build the roads could only be paid off by toll income from that road—then the only ones that would be built would be those that provide a higher value than the cost to construct them. Here's a second advantage, which liberals ought to like: if we stopped subsidizing driving, we would get less driving. As it is now, taxpayers pick up part of the tab for everyone who commutes by car and for everything that is shipped by truck across the country. There's nothing wrong with commuting by car or shipping goods across the country—these are typically good things. But subsidizing driving, like subsidizing anything, creates a less-than-optimal allocation of wealth, and thus reduces our prosperity.

Many highways, especially in the Northeast, where I live, are already tolled. They all should be.

Anti-toll arguments have traditionally centered on the inefficiency of collecting them—traffic backups, the cost of labor and maintenance for the toll booths. But that inefficiency is greatly mitigated by E-ZPass or other automatic toll transponders. On many highways now, you need only slow down to fifty-five in order to pay the toll.

On local roads, you could use congestion fees. New York's Mayor Michael Bloomberg has pushed for tolling anyone who drives into midtown or downtown Manhattan. Of course, Bloomberg would use these fees for general purposes, but every municipality that can do it efficiently—those with limited entrances, mostly—should consider using these sort of fees, combined with market-priced street parking, to cover the costs of all their local roads.

Gasoline taxes are next best, because they don't provide as much price information, but they're still a better source of road funding than are property taxes, sales taxes, or income taxes.

Public transit should also pay for itself. Advocates of subways and light rails always tout the economic benefits of such transit infrastructure. Let riders, therefore, pay for the system. If it's mostly poor people riding the transit, then fine, defend the system as a form of welfare. But if a light rail system really is stimulative, the riders should be willing to pay the cost.

As I suggested above while discussing Article I section 8, of the Constitution, there are plenty of government functions that could be funded by fees on the users.

Think of international commerce. The U.S. Trade Representative and the Commerce Department travel around the world trying to open up avenues of trade. Much of this is good work but some exporters often are the prime beneficiaries of this work. To some extent, these businesses already pay for these sorts of missions. I think the entire Commerce Department could probably be funded by those businesses relying on it most. The parts that business doesn't want to fund should be abolished.

I don't need to run the whole gamut, you get the point: The Post Office should pay for itself. If government is going to run an air traffic control system, the airlines should pay for it. National parks should be covered by the visitors, or even vendors on park property. Why should some blue-collar guy working every day of his life in Bethlehem, Pennsylvania, be forced to pay for some rich hippies to camp at Yosemite?

Again, unless the government service is explicitly a service for the indigent, we should look for ways to have the users pay for it. Technology increasingly makes it easier to collect revenue in this manner. Sometimes, it's impossible to pinpoint and charge the direct beneficiaries, and so those services—most notably, defense—need to be covered by taxes.

Least Bad: Consumption Tax

There is an old economic adage that you get less of what you tax and more of what you subsidize. To paraphrase Chief Justice John Marshall, tax something high enough and you will actually destroy it. Politicians at times seem to understand this, which is why they create "sin taxes" to discourage the use of tobacco or alcohol. So why do we tax savings, investment, and productive labor?

Taxing any economic activity or asset ownership is bad. But when we need taxes, we should try to tax the least valuable economic activity. And that's consumption.

When you work, you create value. When you save, you provide the opportunity for future capital investment. When you invest, you provide capital for others to create new efficiencies. Consumption is the least economically productive activity. I'm not attacking consumption. Consumption is the ultimate goal of all economic activity. You work or invest so that later on, you can consume more. Consumption is not the means, it's the ends.

But the standard economics of our politicians and pundits is dead wrong when it holds that consumption is the root of economic activity. It's the fruit.

So, the least economically harmful tax is a consumption tax—precisely the type of tax the Founding Fathers envisioned would fund the peacetime activities of the federal government.

On the federal level, this could be a national sales tax. Government should never artificially discourage consumption when it doesn't have to, but along with the costs of doing so are some benefits. For one thing, it promotes savings. If work pays more (because there's no income tax), but shopping costs more, you'll see savings grow. This is the reverse of our current system, which discourages savings through taxes on interest (and, of course, through inflation). Liberals will object to replacing the income tax with a sales tax on the grounds that it is regressive. That's because poorer people dedicate a higher portion of their wealth to consumption. This is natural, because they are closer to subsistence. It's understandable that people would want the wealthy to pay more, but this argument against a consumption tax is misplaced.

Think about what wealthy people do with their money. Consider Paris Hilton. First of all, if she doesn't want to pay any income taxes, she doesn't have to. She already has more money than she can ever reasonably spend. Oh, but she tries—houses, cars, trips to resorts, nights on the town, limousines. Paris Hilton, rock stars, and professional athletes who live a flashy life of conspicuous and copious consumption would be the biggest payers under a national sales tax.

And those rich folks "avoiding" a national sales tax? What are they doing with their money? The prime example is probably Warren Buffett. He always drives a simple car, and he lives in a simple house in Omaha he bought decades ago. You don't spot him at fancy restaurants or exclusive resorts. Yes, he flies in a private jet, which is pretty nice, but that's mainly for business, not personal reasons (it pays for itself by saving him so much time). He has a beach house in California, but for his wealth—his net worth was $62 billion in 2008—he's incredibly frugal.

So, is it unfair that so much of Buffett's wealth should be untaxed under a national sales tax? Well, what's he doing with that money? He's not swimming in it. He's not really enjoying it all. Buffett's wealth that he's not consuming is mostly, for now, benefiting other people.

He gives tons of it away. He's one of the biggest givers to charity in the world. More important, he invests the rest of his wealth. If Buffett bought a $1,200 bottle of champagne to celebrate a big stock gain, he would provide a very small benefit to other people. The champagne maker would get some profit, and that money would circulate (and presumably, he would share the champagne with a couple of people).

Instead, he typically pours that money back into more investments.

He's not reaping the fruits of his wealth; he's growing the economy. Some-day, down the line, when he does use that wealth to consume, he will pay the national sales tax. The only way he could avoid taxes on that money forever is if he never spent it—either giving it away to charity or passing it to his heirs. But his heirs will spend it, or give it away.

So don't get too upset about rich people paying a smaller portion of their wealth under a sales tax system, because all the money they earn will someday be spent by someone, and thus be subject to the tax. In the mean-time, the only way to "evade" taxes is to use the money to grow the econ-omy, providing jobs and higher living standards to others, or to give the money to charity.

Warren Buffett pays a lot more of his income in taxes than he publicly admits. In fact, he has become the poster boy for the tax-the-rich crowd. President Obama has labeled his planned millionaires tax "the Buffett Rule" in reference to Buffett's false claim that he pays a lower rate of tax than his secretary. Buffett is able to perpetuate this myth because he only includes the income taxes he pays as an individual. Buffett earns 99 percent of his income as the largest shareholder of Berkshire Hathaway. However, he completely omits this income, and the billions he pays in taxes, from the public discussion.

In 2010, he paid a 17.4 percent rate on his $39.8 million of personal in-come. But Berkshire Hathaway earned $19 billion that year and paid $5.6 billion in income taxes, for an effective tax rate of 29.5 percent. Since War-ren owns 37 percent of the company, over $2 billion of that is Warren's money. Should he choose to pay it to himself in dividends, he would pay an extra 15 percent tax, for a total tax rate of 40 percent. That is a much higher rate than the 17.4 percent he pays of the tiny fraction of his income that he earns personally, and much more than what his secretary pays.

The reason that Buffett's personal rate is so low is that it consists mainly of capital gains, interest, and dividends, taxed at just 15 percent. Warren pays himself a nominal salary of $524,000 a year as CEO of Berk-shire Hathaway, which is taxed mainly at the 35 percent rate. I think he does this not only to avoid the income and payroll tax, but to maximize his net worth. Since Berkshire Hathaway trades at twenty times earnings estimates, every dollar Warren Buffett doesn't pay himself in salary adds twenty dollars to the Berkshire stock price, six dollars of which belongs to Warren himself.

Another way to look at it is that since most rich people only spend a small percentage of their incomes, the income tax mainly reduces the money they otherwise would have saved, invested, or donated. So in reality, taxes on the rich fall mainly on the poor and middle class, in that they diminish employment opportunities, raise prices, diminish the quantity and quality of goods and services offered for sale, and reduce charitable giving.

Of course, the political rhetoric is just the opposite and amounts to nothing more than class warfare. The argument for taxing the rich rests on the perverse logic that such taxes do not hurt the economy, as the rich will not reduce their spending to pay them. That is precisely the point. They will not reduce their spending; they will reduce their savings, investment, or charitable giving instead (though itemized deductions for charitable contributions in the current tax code are a mitigating factor).

Don't Freak Out About Tariffs

For so many free-market types, the worst insult in the world is "protectionist." For some reason, Republican politicians can get a free pass from conservatives for backing bailouts, or earmarking billions, but these same commentators will burn you in effigy if you mention a tariff.

I think I've got some credibility on the question of free markets, so please take a deep breath and listen to me when I say that we might want to place tariffs on imports.

I'm not talking about protective tariffs. I'm talking about revenue-raising tariffs, as a way of replacing the income tax. Yes, tariffs suck. But they suck less than an income tax. In fact, they might be preferable to a national sales tax.

Tariffs are less intrusive than income taxes. They are one of the least intrusive forms of taxation imaginable. We already have Customs. Our government already keeps track of what enters the country. So, there's almost no additional invasion of privacy involved in taxing imports.

The trouble with most tariffs is that they are designed not to raise revenue, but to keep goods out. These are called "protective tariffs." For instance, U.S. steelmakers and their labor unions pressed President Bush to impose protective tariffs on imported steel. These never raised much revenue, because they were so high that they discouraged U.S. manufacturers from buying foreign steel altogether—which was the point. The "revenue" from this tariff went mostly to domestic steelmakers who had effectively outlawed competition.

Our first source of government revenue should be low tariffs that don't target specific countries and that don't target specific goods. To the extent that this discourages imports, there are some upsides to offset the costs. It would spur domestic manufacturing, something which we need to do, especially after all these years of our monetary policy turning us into free riders who consume without making anything. Put it this way: It's not great to discourage imports, but that's better than discouraging work.

Most Important: Abolish the Income Tax

The income tax is one of the worst laws in America. It's hard to imagine a tax more destructive of productivity, more destructive of entrepreneurship, more destructive of our lives, more difficult and costly to comply with, more subject to gaming, or more absurd in its logical consequences. Congress should immediately, fully, and permanently abolish the income tax, and the Internal Revenue Service (IRS) along with it.

Begin with the premise of the individual income tax: that government should take a portion of your wages. This implicitly values all labor at nothing.

If you invest $100 of capital and get back $120, you're only taxed on the $20 gain—you get to deduct the cost. But if you spend all day working and get $120, you're taxed on the entire $120. Your cost—your day of labor—is worth $0 in the eyes of the government, which is absurd.

You would think that liberals, with all their paeans to the labor movement and their charges of exploitation of the working man, would be upset about a tax system calling labor worthless. After all, the most basic asset a man possesses is his own labor. If he wants to exchange it for wages, that exchange should not be taxed as if it were a pure gain. What is his leisure time worth? What about the time he gives up with his family? If a person wants to exchange $40,000 dollars of his labor for $40,000 of someone else's cash, there is no gain, and there should be no tax.

However, the IRS goes even further. If a dentist barters his services with a lawyer, the IRS claims both parties must pay taxes on the value of the services they received with no deduction for the value of the services they provide. Now here is where it really gets ridiculous. Suppose that dentist hires a part-time employee to handle his books and records. If he pays the employee cash he can deduct the payment from his income taxes. However, if instead of paying cash he barters his services as a dentist, not only can he not deduct the value of his labor, but he must pay income taxes on the value of the accounting services he receives!

Going backward from the ridiculous to the sublime, think about this situation—assuming it were legal, what if a man decided to sell his kidney for $50,000? The IRS would consider the $50K to be taxable income. But what is the value of the kidney he gives up? The IRS would say nothing. There are many who would say that their kidney is worth more than $50K, meaning the seller is actually taking a loss.

Despite all the claims that an income tax is progressive in that it falls most heavily on those that can afford to pay, the reality is that it taxes labor far more heavily than it does capital. Since it's generally the rich who have capital, while the poor have only their labor, the income tax is truly the most regressive tax we have.

Income Versus Profit

When corporations pay an income tax they do not pay a tax on their income (which is called revenue—after all that is what *comes in*) but on the gain derived from that income, which we call profit. Corporations therefore can deduct all of the costs associated with generating their income. Many large corporations have millions of dollars of income, yet pay no income tax. That is because while they have income, they have no profits. So from a corporate perspective, corporations pay a profits tax, not an income tax.

For individuals, however, it's an entirely different story. Individuals pay taxes on their incomes, regardless of the cost necessary to produce that income. Sure, there are some business expenses that the IRS will allow, but most are disallowed because they are personal expenses.

But are those "personal expenses" really personal, or are they necessary to have a job and earn a wage or salary? You cannot deduct the cost of a college degree, even though one is required for many jobs. You cannot go to work naked, yet the IRS will not let you deduct the cost of clothing. You cannot even go to work without a means to get there, but the IRS says transportation costs to and from work are not deductible (except for a limited amount of parking or public transit cost, if your employer participates in such a program).

It would be hard to perform a good day's labor if you did not eat; yet the IRS says food is a personal expense and not deductible. How about your house or apartment? Could you really prepare yourself for work if you lived on the street? Where would you shower, change your clothes, or rest up for the following day's work? In fact, try telling potential employers that you live in a cardboard box on the street and see how many job offers you get. You see my point here. All of these so-called personal expenses are completely necessary to earn a paycheck, yet the IRS will not allow them to be deducted. Yet corporations can deduct every expense necessary to generate income.

The awkward fact is that the federal government doesn't really have a working definition of "income."

The Supreme Court in *Stratton's Independence v. Howbert* (231 U.S. 406) defined income as it applied to the corporate excise tax of 1909 as "the gain derived from capital, from labor, or from both combined." Then in *Southern Pacific v. John Z. Lowe* (247 U.S. 330), the court ruled in 1918 that, "Certainly the term income has no broader meaning in the 1913 Act than in that of 1909, and for the present purpose we assume there is no difference in its meaning as used in the two acts." Finally in 1921, in *Merchants' Loan & Trust Company v. Smietanka* (255 U.S. 509), the Supreme Court held "there would seem to be no room to doubt that the word income must be given the same meaning in all of the Income tax acts of Congress that was given to it in the Corporation Excise Tax Act and that what that meaning is has now become definitely settled by decisions of this court."

Legally, therefore, *income* has been defined as a corporate profit, and since individuals do not earn profits, they have no income subject to an income tax. Congress has no legal authority to alter this definition, as observed by the Supreme Court in *Eisner v. Macomber*, when it said with respect to the definition of income that "Congress cannot by any definition it may adopt conclude the matter, since it cannot by legislation alter the Constitution." That is why the Internal Revenue Code does not even define the word "income." Section 61 defines "Gross Income" but not income itself, as the definition of income is a legal one that has been determined by the Supreme Court. However, since "gross income" is defined in the Internal Revenue Code as "income from whatever source derived," the code does not even define "gross income," as you cannot define a word using the very word you are attempting to define in the definition!

The failure of the Internal Revenue Code to define income was verified by the Court in *U.S. v. Ballard* (535 F2d 400, 404), which noted, "The general term 'income' is not defined in the Internal Revenue Code." In fact, according to the Congressional record of the 63rd Congress, 1st Session, page 3844, Senator Albert B. Cummins of Iowa not only admitted that the term income was not defined in the Income Tax Act itself, but that any attempt by Congress to do so would not only be useless, but dangerous.

None of these Supreme Court decisions, the Constitution, the Sixteenth Amendment, or the Internal Revenue Code itself, are followed today. When it comes to individuals, the IRS considers *income* to mean anything that *comes in,* and levies the tax in complete violation of law, the taxing provisions of the Constitution, the Sixteenth Amendment, numerous Supreme Court decisions, and with full support of federal judges.

In addition, there are many absurd implications of an income tax. The income tax doesn't simply apply to cash income—if it did, your boss would just pay you with housing, food, a car, gasoline, cable, and baseball tickets in order to reduce everyone's tax burden. But most employee benefits are taxable. If, as a bonus, or just because your boss is nice, the company sends you and your wife to a fancy resort for the weekend, guess what? That's taxed.

What if you like to grab a cup of office coffee on the way out of work? Well, that's for personal consumption, and that should be taxed under the logic of the income tax. How about using the company phone to check in on your wife or fight with your cable company over the bill? Since the company is providing you with a phone connection and a phone for your personal use, that should be taxable. Same with the paper and toner you use to print off your boarding pass before you hop on a plane to visit Grandma.

But don't think this is limited to your boss. Say you promised to cover your roommate's rent for three months until his new job started, and then for the next three months, he would pay the entire rent. Well, guess what? You're providing him an interest-free loan, which is taxable.

If you have a beat-up old car, and you let your neighbor borrow it regularly, as long as he fills up the gas tank, that's probably taxable, too.

Because these logical consequences of the income tax are so absurd, the IRS often has had to issue rules exempting certain transactions from the tax. An extra cup of coffee or even employer-bought muffins in the break room are considered "de minimis" payments from employer to employee. In other words, they should be taxed, but the IRS doesn't want to keep track of them.

So, in order to make the income tax work, the IRS needs to pretend the law means something else. Following the law to its logical consequences would highlight how tyrannical a law it is.

It's a logically absurd law that discourages labor. But there are still more reasons to hate the income tax.

Compliance Cost: Six Billion Hours and $430 Billion

The compliance costs, in time and money, of our tax system are horrible, mostly because of the income tax.

The IRS's taxpayer advocate found in 2011 that "taxpayers and businesses spend 6.1 billion hours a year complying with tax-filing requirements."[1] Think about it this way: If we created a government agency to do all of the tax compliance work for businesses and individuals—keeping receipts, filling out 1040s and W-2s, fighting with the IRS—that agency would have to employ three million people working full time. And that doesn't even include more than 100,000 IRS employees working on tax compliance from the other side.

Or think of it the other way: if we didn't have to worry about complying with this tax code, our country's economic output could grow as if we'd gained three million more workers.

Complying with the income tax is so difficult that 60 percent of filers hire a professional tax preparer. Another 29 percent of individual filers pay for tax-prep software. That means only one in nine American taxpayers even tries to do his taxes on his own.

And it's no wonder. If you make an honest mistake, you can get hit with a big fine and huge interest charges. In 2010, the IRS filed tax liens against 1.1 million Americans. These people all had their credit rating harmed for seven years, at least.

What is the total price tag of compliance by taxpayers plus administration of the IRS? More than $430 billion, according to a study by the Laffer Center. That means that for every dollar the IRS collects, another thirty cents is spent to collect it. Put another way, for every dollar spent complying with the tax code, twenty-three cents is simply dead-weight loss, going to activities that provide no value to anyone.

No value, that is, except for accountants and tax specialists. There is an entire industry dedicated to helping people pay their income tax. If we replaced income tax with a national sales tax, there would still be compliance costs but they would be a tiny fraction of current compliance costs, and they would all be borne by business owners, who are more sophisticated with money than the average American.

"Forgive Me Father, for I Have Earned"

You may think of confession as something that's mostly for gray-haired church ladies, but thanks to the income tax, we're all required to confess annually, laying our lives bare to the taxman.

Think about which personal matters you might not even discuss with your friends. How much money you make, your monthly mortgage payment, your doctor bills, details about your marriage. You might have to tell all those things to the IRS.

If you're a reporter having a business lunch with a whistle-blower leaking you information on the condition of anonymity, you're still required to name that source if you want to deduct that meal.

What percentage of your computer's use is for business? The IRS wants to know. You'd better ask your wife how many hours she spent in the last year sending pictures of the kids to her mom.

In order to legally pay your taxes and get the deductions or exemptions to which you're entitled, you need to expose intimate details to the IRS. And if they're not satisfied with what you tell them, you might get audited, which is even more intrusive. They'll ask for proof of how you spend your time, including receipts for everything. The fact is, because of the income tax, the federal government now knows more about American citizens than the Supreme Soviet ever knew about citizens of the USSR.

And, thanks to the income tax, you don't really have rights anymore. As currently enforced, the income tax effectively overturned a big chunk of the Bill of Rights.

The Fourth Amendment is gone. "The right of the people to be secure in their persons, houses, papers, and effects, against unreasonable searches and seizures, shall not be violated. . . ." The income tax declares the opposite: the government inherently has the right to see your house, papers, and effects, because any search and seizure is a "reasonable" way to enforce the income tax.

The Fifth Amendment protects Americans against having to provide information to the government that might be used against them in a court of law. All the information provided on a tax return can be used against the preparer by the government in all manner of criminal and civil prosecutions. It also protects Americans from having their property seized without due process of law (meaning a court order). Today, IRS agents routinely seize property simply by signing a notice of levy. Taxpayers are then required to sue to get their property back.

The Seventh Amendment is supposed to guarantee a trial by jury, but that doesn't apply to the income tax. You get tried instead in the U.S. Tax Court, with no jury, but with a judge providing the verdict and the sentence. If you want your trial by jury, you need to first pay whatever the IRS says you owe, and then sue.

And the First Amendment's freedom of speech and right to petition the government is curbed, too. If a pastor gets too political in the pulpit, the IRS could revoke his church's tax-exempt status. Many nonprofit organizations are severely restricted in their ability to speak on political matters for fear of being severely taxed.

The presumption of innocence is an important element of American jurisprudence. In tax court, however, taxpayers are presumed guilty and have the burden of proving otherwise.

Throughout history, the United States government has frequently trampled on the life, liberty, and property of its citizens. Black slavery and internment of the Japanese during World War II were the worst examples. The draft was pretty bad. The income tax, however, is the broadest assault on basic rights, because it hits every adult in America.

For the sake of the economy, for the sake of fairness, and for the sake of domestic peace, Congress should immediately, completely, and permanently end the income tax.

Some say that the best way to do that would be to repeal the Sixteenth Amendment. While I would be in favor of its repeal, it would be very difficult to do and take way too long to achieve. Of course, the federal government ignores the Sixteenth Amendment anyway, as it currently collects income taxes in complete violation of that amendment. In fact, since most of what the federal government currently does is unconstitutional, why should taxing income be an exception? Back in 1913 we still had respect for the Constitution, and therefore Congress had to amend it to levy an income tax. However, given the way the Constitution is currently ignored, Congress would simply impose an income tax anyway if the Sixteenth Amendment did not exist. The key to getting rid of the tax now lies in electing representatives who understand its destructive nature and are willing to permanently abolish it.

By now, you should realize just how far we have strayed from the original intent of the income tax. Had an income tax with a top rate of 35 percent been proposed back in 1913, which would also apply to middle-class Americans, the Sixteenth Amendment would have been defeated in a landslide. No one would have had the nerve even to propose such a tax, let alone vote to amend the Constitution to enable one.

There's a similar plan called the "Fair Tax," which has many passionate backers. The Fair Tax plan would abolish all federal payroll, income, inheritance, and gift taxes and replace them with a single 30 percent sales tax (it has to be that high only if we want to maintain current revenue levels).

Of course, sales taxes are more "regressive" than income taxes, because poorer people dedicate a greater portion of their income to consumption, and because our income tax code is so graduated. The Fair Tax plan mitigates this concern with a "prebate": the IRS cuts a check to every family to offset the first portion of their national sales tax. Bigger families get bigger prebates. The idea of the prebate is that all spending up to the poverty level should be effectively tax free.

This plan has many virtues. It wouldn't discourage work, and it wouldn't encourage debt or overconsumption. Also, it would be transparent. Income taxes are disguised, thanks to withholding. With a Fair Tax, in order to raise revenue, government would have to raise the tax rate everyone pays on every purchase. Finally, a Fair Tax doesn't cause all the distortions our jury-rigged income tax does.

Second-Best Options

For all the reasons discussed above, it's hard to stomach the income tax's continued existence. But for political reasons, it might be impossible to kill the tax. In that case, it needs some severe reforms.

Here are some changes that would dramatically reduce the evil effects of the income tax:

Flat tax, no exemptions

A good chunk of the stuff that brokers do for clients, such as setting up special accounts like Keoughs, IRAs, college savings plans, and so on, are activities nobody would undertake if not for the income tax.

Any time a business or an individual does something for tax purposes, that makes the economy poorer. Typically, in a free economy, the most profitable course of action is finding an efficient way to deliver to people what they want. Profit is correlated with usefulness.

But a high tax rate riddled with loopholes creates a very different landscape. Profit is now highly correlated with gaming IRS rules and the tax law. This leads to a suboptimal allocation of resources around the economy. And the distortions are huge.

Do you remember the big hubbub when it came out in 2011 that General Electric, the largest industrial conglomerate in the United States, had paid zero U.S. corporate income taxes for 2010? I'll address the corporate income tax below (hint: abolish it), but the most interesting thing was how GE used a 57,000-page tax return to get its income tax bill down to zero despite profits of $14.2 billion worldwide and $5.1 billion in the U.S.[2]

The New York Times article on this impressive feat of tax avoidance mentioned that GE's tax department employed 975 people, and that the company "has placed tax strategists in decision-making positions in many major manufacturing facilities and businesses around the globe."

Think about what that means. Those 975 people added no value to the economy, yet they were paid handsomely by GE to help the company reduce its tax burden. All their skills, knowledge, and labor was profitable to the company, but unlike the guys who devise better refrigerators or microwaves at GE, these guys didn't make anything useful.

Worse is how they may have influenced GE's behavior. How many activities were moved to certain countries or islands in order to minimize taxes? How many solar panels were built in order to get tax credits? How many useless financial tricks did GE play just for tax avoidance?

These unproductive business and investment activities by corporations and individuals are more dead-weight economic loss, on top of all the compliance costs.

A flat tax with no exemptions would minimize these distortions. People wouldn't own a home anymore just for tax benefits. They would only own a home if they actually thought it was best for them. This would bring down the price of houses, thus freeing up more money for other things.

Industries dependent on tax breaks, such as green energy, much of financial consulting, and some portion of the mortgage and real estate businesses, would dry up (the National Association of Homebuilders, dependent on the home mortgage interest deduction, came out against Herman Cain's plan in 2011 to slash the income tax), and that labor and money would go somewhere else—somewhere determined by consumer demand rather than by what's politically favored.

There's another reason tax credits and deductions are so harmful—they are insidious subsidies, protected from the budget knife. Republicans like cutting spending, but tax credits aren't technically spending, so Republicans often leave them alone. During a 2011 debate over eliminating a tax credit for ethanol, many Republicans hesitated, even though the "tax credit" really comes in the form of a check from the U.S. Treasury, and you can get the "credit" even if you owe no tax. Conservative Republicans didn't want to eliminate the credit because it would count as a tax hike.

We need a clean tax code.

A consumption-based income tax

One idea that fits my criteria for tax reform is called a "consumption-based income tax."

Here's how to think about it: under current law, you can shield a few thousand dollars of your salary from the income tax by putting it in a traditional IRA. Of course, you can basically only do one thing with an IRA, and that is spend it in retirement.

Crashproof Yourself: The Tax Hikes Are Coming! The Tax Hikes Are Coming!

Think about this as you invest: tax rates in the future will be higher than they are today. Think of the austerity measures in bankrupt countries like Greece—that's where we're headed. So tax-deferred investments, like 401(k)s and traditional IRAs, aren't as good a deal as you might think. When you pay taxes on this money down the line, you'll be paying higher rates. A Roth IRA makes more sense, because you pay the taxes on the income today, but your earnings are tax free when you cash them out. Be careful when you invest for future tax hikes, though, as some people might advise you to invest in tax-privileged industries. There are two pitfalls here: (1) some tax-privileged industries, like housing and government bonds, are already bubbles; (2) those tax deductions might be taken away from higher-income individuals.

What if you could use your IRA money on education, too? So, you combine college savings and retirement savings, and increase the annual limit. Then let's say you can also save for a new home, and we expand the limit again. If you want to save for a rainy day, or future health-care expenses, fine, throw those in, too. Also, if you think stocks or bonds are undervalued, and you want to invest in them for ten years, but pull the money out before retirement age, let's allow that.

Now let's say there's no annual limit on how much you put in this "All-Purpose IRA." And you can split up this "IRA" into as many different actual accounts as you want—your stocks with a broker, your emergency buffer at a bank, your college money in gold, and even the $10,000 you invested in your daughter-in-law's start-up clothing company.

In short, you could deduct every penny of investment and savings. The only income on which you would be taxed would be the money you spent, and that money you left in your checking account. In other words, it's a consumption tax, but through the income tax code.

Kill the corporate income tax

While the individual income tax is the most harmful tax, the corporate income tax is the dumbest, because the truth of the matter is that corporations don't pay taxes, they collect taxes.

Corporations can do three things with their earnings: (1) pay bonuses to their employees, (2) pay dividends to shareholders, or (3) retain the earnings for future expenditures, make capital investments and grow the business.

When a corporation pays bonuses (of course this applies to all forms of employee compensation), those expenses are deducted, but the recipients pay personal taxes on whatever they receive. So in that respect corporate earnings paid to employees would be taxed even if no corporate income tax existed. Similarly, when a corporation pays dividends, shareholders pay income taxes at the personal level on their dividend income. Of course, since dividends are not deductible, the corporation also pays the tax at the corporate level as well. To avoid double taxation, many corporations pay no or very low dividends (though this has changed somewhat due to the Bush tax cuts, which temporarily lowered the tax on dividends to 15 percent). Instead they use their earnings to buy back stock. The point is that if we abolished the corporate income tax, corporate income would still be taxed to the extent it was paid out to their employees or shareholders.

The one exception would be retained earnings. But why would we want to tax retained earnings? Earnings are retained for one purpose, and that is to facilitate the growth of the company. They are used to make capital investments, fund acquisitions, and hire more employees. To the extent that taxation diminishes corporate earnings, it diminishes a company's ability to grow.

If we simply abolish the corporate income tax, corporations will be better positioned to grow their earnings, which the government could later tax when those higher earnings are paid out to employees and stockholders. In the meantime, the economy would grow and jobs would be created.

The corporate tax code is another reason why businesses finance so much of their expansion through debt. If a company saves up to buy equipment, it pays taxes on those savings. If it instead borrows to buy equipment, there are no savings to be taxed, and the interest is deductible. Expanding through debt is as legitimate as expanding through savings, but why should our tax code prefer the former? It's not as if we have too little debt in our country.

There's an emotional appeal to the corporate income tax, though. Corporations aren't popular. They are the embodiment of evil for many people. It's nice to think that these evil corporations are paying taxes.

But corporations don't pay taxes. Corporate taxes are paid by consumers, employees, or shareholders. All of these are people. So, if you work for a corporation, own stock, or buy anything from a corporation, you are paying a hidden tax. If we abolished corporate income taxes, it's not as if this would simply benefit corporate profit.

Some eighty-year-old retired widow collecting dividends is the one paying the corporate income tax, and so she's paying a 35 percent rate despite living on a cat-food diet and a fixed income. That's hardly the picture people have of corporate income tax, but that's the truth.

Other tax reforms

Whether or not we abolish, cut, or flatten the individual and corporate income tax, there are plenty of other tax reforms we can institute to help the economy.

First, we should make the cost of taxation more apparent to people. Income tax withholding, by which the federal government takes a big chunk out of your paycheck before you ever see it, is evil in a few ways. One thing it does is to obscure how much folks are paying in taxes.

Especially now, in the age of direct deposit, many people don't look at their pay stubs. So when April 15 arrives, folks enter a bunch of numbers into TurboTax or give their papers to their tax accountant and, wow, look, you get a refund! In truth, this is the payoff of an interest-free loan you extended to Uncle Sam, but it causes many people to think that they're making a profit off of the IRS.

We should end withholding. If people knew their true tax burden, they'd be a lot angrier. If we did this, and moved tax day to a week before Election Day, I think we'd see some good tax cutting by politicians. In fact, the withholding tax itself did not even start until 1942, as part of the Victory Tax to win the Second World War. Up until then anyone who paid income taxes had until April 15 of the following year to send the money in.

The estate and gift taxes need to be abolished as well. The idea that you shouldn't be free to give your money to your kids is one of the most tyrannical things I can think of. Teddy Roosevelt's administration, however, decided that giving money to your kids is a privilege, and the estate and gift taxes are an excise tax on that privilege. In reality this is a phony privilege. The government is merely trying to get around the constitutional requirement to apportion direct taxes. The courts have held that excise taxes may be levied on privileges, so Congress created a phony privilege out of a right. If someone owns property, he has a fundamental right to do with it what he wants, including gifting it during life or bequeathing it at death.

The biggest beneficiary of the estate tax is not the federal government, but the estate-planning industry. Businessmen waste billions every year trying to figure out how to minimize the estate tax. Again, this is deadweight loss, because that money could be spent doing productive things.

Estate-tax proponents employ class-warfare populist talk, arguing on principle against inherited wealth. But think about the effects of the bill—it helps corporations while killing family-owned businesses.

If a successful businessman dies, and his business is worth $10 million, his son will have to pay taxes on $10 million in order to inherit it. With a $5 million exemption and a 35 percent rate, the son would owe $1.75 million. But the business might not have that much in liquid assets. The result: he has to fold the business, or sell out. If he folds the business, his workers are out of a job. If he sells, this just helps the corporation that buys it up, and the corporation—not being a human—doesn't ever have to pay the death tax. Great work, populists.

One of the truly remarkable features about capitalism is that it allows a business owner to think beyond his own lifetime—to make investments that he may well not live long enough to profit from himself. He makes the investments anyway to benefit his children and grandchildren who will ultimately inherit the business. But if he knows the business will be liquidated on his death to pay the taxes, his time horizon is significantly shorter. As a result it's the economy that suffers most.

For that reason, the estate tax is one of the dumbest on the books. Sure there are some wealthy proponents of this tax, like Warren Buffett. But think about what Buffett does for a living: he buys companies. Many of the companies he buys would not even be for sale but for the existence of the estate taxes. I'm sure Warren knows where his bread is buttered, and he wants to make sure there is plenty of it.

Local and state governments need to employ these tax reforms, too. Local and state income tax should be abolished, and so should property taxes—another direct tax.

Property taxes are harmful because they break up communities. A couple that raises its kids in a small town and pays off its mortgage often can't stick around, because they can't afford to pay the property tax. It's as if the government charges you rent to live in your own home. Property taxes should be reserved for rental or business property, where the property itself generates the income necessary to pay the tax.

The guiding principle on tax reform should be to make taxes lower and simpler, and to replace direct taxes with indirect taxes. Of course, in order to have a bearable tax code, we need to shrink government to the appropriate size.

Tax Reform 2.0: The IRS Scandal

It's good to see politicians from both parties acknowledging the need for tax reform, but there's little point if it leaves a thoroughly corrupt system in place. The Supreme Court has ruled that there's a right to privacy if you want to have an abortion, but our income tax system is living proof that this privacy doesn't extend to your economic life. There, you have no privacy at all.

The income tax is repugnant to everything the Constitution stands for.

It means that the government now owns you. You have to report everything you make to the government. You have to confess everything to the
government, especially if you want to get the deductions you're entitled
to. You sign forms under penalty of perjury—and heaven help you if you
make an honest mistake.

If we want to restore freedom to America, it begins with the replacement of the income tax with a national sales tax that ends the confes-
sions, the surveillance, the civil and criminal penalties.

The various Internal Revenue Service scandals of 2013 (and there were
more than just the one) show just how badly power corrupts. The IRS is
an agency gone wild.

It's the least of their vices, but IRS employees have proven they enjoy
living at your expense. As this second edition of *The Real Crash* was being
written, the House Oversight Committee was investigating an IRS conference from 2008 that had cost $2.4 million, in which IRS workers spent
taxpayers' money on $140-per-person dinners, bottles of wine, baseball
tickets, and even Internet pornography.

But the IRS, whose staff is now larger than the Canadian army, can do
an amazing amount of damage without firing a single shot. It has been
and can be used to destroy lives and punish political enemies.

In June 2010, a documentary called *Please Remove Your Shoes* was
released in theaters. The film featured whistle-blowers from the Federal
Aviation Administration and the Transportation Security Administration,
who had at various times revealed to Congress the total incompetence of
the federal airport security apparatus. Many of them suffered retaliation
on the job. But at least one of them was also targeted by the IRS after he
retired.

Jeffrey Black, a former Air Marshal, appeared in the film. Years earlier,
he had revealed to Congress how TSA bureaucrats had watered down the
marshals' training. He described how the bureaucrats in his agency insisted on dopey practices that made them easy for terrorists to spot and
identify the marshals on every flight.

The very day this film came out, Black would later tell CNN, the IRS
showed up at his door to announce an audit and placed a $24,000 lien on
his home. In the end, the audit actually found that Black was owed money
by the IRS—which it refused to pay. Only in 2013, with the emergence of
the larger IRS scandal, was the Treasury Department Inspector General

able to initiate an investigation, which is why Black's story came to light. The IRS is a tool powerful enough that it can be used to settle bureaucratic and political scores.

Our corporate tax system, with its series of special exemptions for nonprofits, creates the opportunity for even more such abuses—and that's the locus of the main IRS scandal, which received so many hearings before various congressional committees during the spring and summer of 2013. Our tax laws require that corporate entities either pay taxes on their income or claim a nonprofit status that exempts them. This is what 501 c(4) designation is all about.

The groups that fall under the 501 c(4) umbrella are not getting a subsidy from the government. They're not the ones that can actually give you a tax deduction for your donation—that's a different class of nonprofits. Rather, the 501 c(4) designation applies to any group of citizens that merely wants to pool money to advocate for some social cause. Unless they get 501 c(4) status, the money they collect to advance their cause gets double-taxed—once when it's earned by the donors, and a second time when it's donated.

You need permission to operate under a nonprofit status for any length of time—and that's where the bureaucrats come in. In early 2010, just as Tea Partiers were starting to raise hell over the ObamaCare law then under consideration in Congress, the IRS began targeting conservative groups that applied for that status—rounding up and stalling their applications and harassing applicants who perhaps had anti-IRS views.

The bureaucrats managed to make many of these groups wait for years just to get an answer on their status, whereas traditionally the process takes just a couple of months at most. The IRS served applicants with lengthy, intrusive, and in many cases illegal questionnaires filled with inappropriate questions. They asked groups that mentioned some kind of Christian affiliation what prayers they said at meetings. They asked pro-life groups whether they would be fairly portraying both sides of the abortion debate. They asked whether people involved in these groups had any plans to run for office. Applicants were asked to sign promises that the IRS is in no way permitted to require.

In at least one case, an applicant from Texas even saw her family business and personal finances suddenly and coincidentally scrutinized by multiple government agencies (OSHA, ATF, and the state environmental agency) after she filed a nonprofit application with the IRS—which also made her answer "hundreds and hundreds" of questions. Even the FBI came around, asking questions about a person who had once attended one of her group's meetings.

Also bear in mind that the groups targeted in this scandal were small potatoes—precisely the kind that lack the power to fight back. The Associated Press found that the groups given the third degree by the IRS had income and expenditures, on average, of less than $20,000 per year. These weren't the massive "secret money" groups that Team Obama had whined about so much during the 2010 election cycle (and offered later as an excuse for their defeat).

The effect of all this IRS malfeasance was to hinder citizens from raising money for various legitimate causes. Many groups, learning from the experience of others, disbanded or chose not to form.

In short, our tax code empowers some really awful people to do really dangerous things to citizens who just want to live their lives or (God forbid) exercise their constitutional rights and become involved in public issues.

This only adds urgency to the push for tax reform.

8

Tear Up the "Third Rails": End Social Security and Medicare

AMERICANS INCREASINGLY REALIZE WE ARE facing a debt time bomb. The impending explosion of the national debt helped spur the 2009 and 2010 Tea Parties, and it set the political stage for the mid-2011 debt-ceiling spectacle.

But even the politicians who claim to be serious about addressing our fiscal solvency avoid the real drivers of our long-term debt. Foreign aid isn't the problem. Earmarks aren't the reason we're headed over an economic cliff into a sea of debt. It's not even Defense spending, though excessive spending here is certainly one of the major contributors to our problem.

Social Security and Medicare are the real causes of our long-term debt crisis. We call them "entitlements" and "mandatory spending," because payments from these programs are set not by congressional appropriators or even executive-branch bureaucrats. Instead, benefits are determined by a formula and paid out automatically.

If we don't take care of these programs, there is simply no way to make ours a functioning, solvent government. Most "reforms" of Social Security and Medicare are too modest.

In short, we need to end these programs.

The Price Tag

Take every appropriated federal dollar that goes to education, social work, energy, or anything else not related to defense or security, and you've got $491 billion in 2010. That's less than what we paid out in Social Security benefits: $701 billion.

Add together all appropriated spending for security and non-security for fiscal year 2010, and you get a whopping $1.31 trillion. But that's less than the $1.42 trillion we spent on Social Security, Medicare, and Medicaid last year.

Between the three of them, they take up 41 percent of the federal budget.

And it's set to get much worse. Just by 2021, the federal budget estimates an 81 percent increase in Social Security spending, and a 78 percent jump in Medicare spending. However, these estimates are way too low, as the economic assumptions that underlie them are far too optimistic. Even by the government's own ridiculously optimistic assumptions, within twenty years, these three entitlements could cost $3 trillion a year and take up half the federal budget.

In reality, in far less time than that, entitlement spending plus interest on the national debt will consume 100 percent of all federal tax receipts. The cost of everything else will have to be borrowed. Of course it may never get that far, because before then, the whole system will have collapsed beneath its own weight.

Our politicians tell us that these programs are funded by dedicated payroll taxes. That's always been a fiction, and it's even more imaginary today. As of the last couple of years, both programs pay out more in benefits than these "dedicated" taxes collect. So Medicare and Social Security are now funded by general revenue, and thus by borrowing.

Some defenders of these programs claim that they're drawing down on trust funds that had run surpluses, but the trust funds are insolvent—they are filled with IOUs from the federal Treasury (more on this below).

If we want to fix our debt problem, we need to fix these programs. And, again, that means winding them down.

What Is Social Security?

What is Social Security?

That's not as easy a question as you might think.

We can agree it's a federal program created by Franklin Roosevelt as part of the New Deal. In the name of Social Security, the federal government cuts checks to the elderly, disabled, and widows. In the name of Social Security, the federal government also takes a chunk out of paychecks.

But that still doesn't answer the question. What kind of program is this?

Sometimes, you'll hear it described like a savings account. The government sets aside your money for you, and then sends it to you in checks when you retire. This is not what happens. There is no account with "your money" sitting in it. Everything you've paid in has already been spent.

Social Security was originally sold to the American public as if it were an insurance program. Franklin Roosevelt deliberately used deceptive language to persuade the public to believe that Social Security was something it was not. The program was described as "social insurance," meaning that it was a sort of safety net. Social Security taxes were labeled as "premiums." Payments were described as being "benefits," and there was supposedly a giant trust fund out of which future benefits would be paid.

To maintain the illusion that a trust fund was actually being accumulated, the first benefit check was not mailed out until after taxes had been collected for five years. The whole thing was a lie designed to fool Americans into believing that their "premiums" entitled them to a legally guaranteed benefit just like private insurance. There is no such guarantee with Social Security.

Many Americans who pay attention to Social Security consider it a transfer payment. Today's workers pay their Social Security tax, which fund the benefits of today's retirees. It's like you're cutting a check to your mom, grandmother, or even your elderly boss. This is closer to the truth, but even this misses the mark, because Social Security isn't really funded by Social Security taxes, at least not on the margins. It's funded by general revenue, borrowing, and Federal Reserve printing, just like everything else.

An Insurance Program?

Much of the early discussion of Social Security described it as if it were an insurance program.

The first signal was the word "benefits" to describe Social Security checks. People don't talk this way about other government handouts. Subsidized farmers get "farm *payments*." Welfare recipients get "welfare checks." For Social Security, we've adopted the same language used by insurance companies: "*benefits*."

On the Social Security Administration's (SSA) Web site today, you can look at early documents issued by the SSA.

One SSA form describes "The Federal old-age benefits systems" as bringing "increased assurance of an independent old age." Franklin Roosevelt pitched Social Security to Congress in the context of providing "safeguard against misfortunes." It's called "Social *Security*," because, as FDR said, it was supposed to provide "security against the hazards and vicissitudes of life."

In a June 1934 address pushing Congress to pass the bill creating Social Security, Roosevelt repeatedly described it as "social insurance," charging the federal government with the job of "investing, maintaining and safeguarding the funds constituting the necessary insurance reserves."[1]

He stated that a strong old-age social security program "is possible only on insurance principles."

Pitching it as an insurance product was politically important. For one thing, it played into Depression-era fears. Also, it made the program seem sounder. This was no pay-as-you-go wealth transfer. You were paying in now and then, if you fell victim to the "hazards and vicissitudes of life," as FDR put it, you would collect later.

Whether it was presented as an insurance plan or as a savings account, the idea was that many Americans were not savvy enough to save for their own retirement. Working-class Americans, especially, were thought unlikely to have the time or training to invest wisely. Look at the language the government used: "Its purpose is to bring to those persons employed in the broad fields of commerce and industry increased assurance of an independent old age." Uncle Sam was going to make sure the workingman had a nest egg.

That's part of why there has always been a Social Security "cap," where your benefit went up as your income went up. The thinking was that your lifestyle in retirement should be comparable to your lifestyle while working. As a result, higher income folks get larger benefits upon retirement—up to a point.

Individuals making enough money didn't need to be taken care of so much—they could handle their own savings. So, after a certain amount of income, you stopped paying the payroll tax, and your future benefit stopped growing.

For similar reasons, the self-employed were originally exempted. If you could run your own business, you could arrange your own retirement savings. (Today, the self-employed pay the tax.)

Smoke and Mirrors

This sounded like a great deal. The government takes a small portion of your paycheck, your employer is forced to match the contribution, and in exchange, you get retirement security.

Consider the famous Ida May Fuller. She paid a total of $24.75 in Social Security taxes just before she retired at age sixty-four in 1939 and became the first person to receive Social Security benefits. Thirty-six years later, she died at age 100, collecting $22,888.92 over her life—not a big amount, until you realize that it was a 1,000-to-1 return on her investment.

But for most American workers, Social Security has not been a great deal.

First, Congress has repeatedly hiked the tax. It was 1 percent until 1950, when it went up to 1.5 percent. They raised it eleven times in the next thirteen years, until it was 5.85 percent in 1973. A couple of hikes later, it was 7.65 percent in 1990—the current level (though it was "temporarily" reduced to 5.65 in 2010).

But that number is misleading. The Social Security tax (Federal Insurance Contributions Act, or FICA, on your pay stub) has always been higher than government pretends it is. When Congress created the law, the Social Security tax was, supposedly, 1 percent. But that 1 percent was the amount taken out of the employee's paycheck. The employer was also forced to contribute one percent.

Most young workers don't realize that their employer is paying an equal amount. If the FICA on your paycheck is $100, your employer also has to pay $100 for you. Even if you already knew about this "employer contribution," you might believe that this costs your employer and not you.

But the employee basically pays every penny of that "employer contribution." Think about the economics. When an employer tries to figure if you're worth the salary, he doesn't consider what you get paid, he considers what he has to pay in order to get you. So, if you're worth $1,000 a week, the most your employer can afford to pay you is $929, because at that rate, his FICA tax of $71 brings your cost up to $1,000. (In truth, there are plenty of other costs to employing someone, as I discussed in chapter 3, but you get the idea.)

Maybe you're thinking, "Well, tough. I don't care what a company has to pay the government, I know how much I need to get paid." But unless you're willing to work outside the United States or on the black market, you don't have anywhere else to go. Every employer has to pay this tax. Any time a cost is imposed across an industry, it moves prices. In other words, almost all of the "employer contribution" is a pay cut for you.

You Are Not "Entitled" to Anything

The biggest fraud regarding Social Security may be that it's an "entitlement." Remember how FDR pitched it as an "insurance" program?

Well, here's a big difference: If you pay your insurance premiums, you are legally entitled to the benefits. But you're not legally entitled to Social Security benefits.

Congress, at any time, could change the benefits formula. A majority of both chambers, together with the president could simply slash benefits, or change the cost-of-living formula, or raise the retirement age, or tell you you're too rich to get benefits. Repeatedly, Congress has hiked taxes on Social Security benefits, which is effectively a benefits cut.

In fact, Congress *has to* cut benefits in some way in order to avoid fiscal disaster (more on this below), but this just underlines the ways in which Social Security, although called an "entitlement," doesn't entitle you to anything. The terms on which Social Security was sold to the people—as a savings or insurance program—were bogus.

The Roosevelt administration stated as much in court.

Many people do not realize that Social Security was actually declared unconstitutional by the First Circuit Court of Appeals back in 1937. In two related cases, *Davis v. Boston & Mane R. Co.* (89 F.2d 368) and *Davis v. Edison Electric Illuminating Co. of Boston et al.* (89 F.2d 393), the court ruled the Social Security Act unconstitutional. According to the court, the act, which contained numerous titles establishing benefits for the aged, unemployed, and dependent children, and imposed two new taxes, an excise tax on employers and a special income tax on employees, was unconstitutional on a variety of grounds.

One in particular was that the Social Security Act violated the "general welfare" clause of the Constitution, in that Social Security taxes were paid by some for the specific benefit of others. In so doing, the Act did not promote the general welfare of all, but the specific welfare of some.

To counter this claim, the government argued that the tax and benefit provisions of the Social Security Act were in no way related. The taxes were true taxes, paid unrestricted into the U.S. Treasury for the general support of government. The government claimed that Social Security taxes were enacted for the sole purpose of raising revenue and were not earmarked for any particular purpose.

Actually, if you look carefully at the formula used to calculate Social Security benefits, you'll see that benefits are determined not by the amount you pay in taxes—as an insurance plan would—but by how much you earn in wages. So in truth, Social Security was two separate programs—one a defined-benefit pension and the other a payroll tax (excise tax on employers, income tax on employees)—that coincidentally just happened to be passed at the same time and share the same name.

This was the exact opposite of what the government was telling the public, and the First Circuit Court saw right through the ploy. It correctly observed, "Congress has not an unlimited power of taxation; but it is limited to specific objects—the payment of the public debts, and the providing for common defense and general welfare. A tax, therefore, laid by Congress for neither of these objects, would be unconstitutional, as an excess of its legitimate authority."

The court went on to state:

> A tax, in the general understanding of the term, and as used in the Constitution, signifies an exaction for the support of government. The word has never been thought to connote the expropriation of money from one group for the benefit of another. The exaction cannot be wrested out of its setting, denominated an excise for raising revenue and legalized by ignoring its pur-

pose as a mere instrument for bringing about a desired end. To do this would be to shut our eyes to what all others than we can see and understand.

It further observed:

> If the act is carried out as planned by Congress . . . it amounts, in effect, to taking the property of every employer for the benefit of a certain class of employees. The entire plan, viewed as a whole, is an attempt to do indirectly what Congress cannot do directly, and to assume national control over a subject clearly within the jurisdiction of the states.

The court also remarked:

> The Constitution, in all its provisions, looks to an indestructible Union, composed of indestructible states. Every journey to a forbidden end begins with a first step; and the danger of such a step by the federal government in the direction of taking over the powers of the states is that the end of the journey may find the states so despoiled of their powers, or what may amount to the same thing—so relieved of the responsibilities which possession of the powers necessarily enjoins, as to reduce them to little more than geographical subdivisions of the national domain. It is safe to say that if, when the Constitution was under consideration, it had been thought that any such danger lurked behind its plain words, it never would have been ratified.

The ruling looked prophetic in this section:

> That this amounts to coercion of the states and control by Congress of a matter clearly within the province of the states cannot be denied. If valid, it marks the end of responsible state government in any field in which the United States chooses to take control by the use of its taxing power. If the United States can take control of unemployment insurance and old age assistance by the coercive use of taxation, it can equally take control of education

and local health conditions by levying a heavy tax and remitting it in the states which conform their educational system or their health laws to the dictates of the federal board.

It's amazing just how right they were.

The court concluded by stating, "It is plainly the duty of the courts to uphold and support the present Constitution until it has been changed in the legal way."

This decision has to be one the best ever rendered. If only we had judges of similar integrity and understanding presiding today. The government appealed and on May 24, 1937—in hindsight one of the darkest days in American history—in two concurrent cases, *Helvering v. Davis* (301 U.S. 619) and *Stewart Machine Co. v. Davis* (301 U.S. 548) the Supreme Court reversed the First Circuit Court, and held the Social Security Act constitutional. Even though the First Circuit Court had ruled the Social Security Act unconstitutional on several grounds, only two issues were raised by the plaintiff before the Supreme Court, one being the fact that the act sought to raise revenue for a particular purpose, not merely to raise revenue for the United States as claimed by the government.

The government, of course, repeated its claim that Social Security taxes were not enacted to finance Social Security benefits. Such tax revenue was not earmarked for any particular purpose, but paid unrestricted into the Treasury to use for the general support of government.

The most amazing aspect about this decision is that the Supreme Court did not even address this issue. Instead it merely summed up the arguments by stating, "The argument for the respondent is that the provisions of the two titles dovetail in such a way as to justify the conclusion that Congress would have been unwilling to pass one without the other. The argument for petitioner is that the tax monies are not earmarked, and that Congress is at liberty to spend them as it will. The usual severability clause is embodied in the act. We find it unnecessary to make a choice between the arguments, and so leave the question open."

One might wonder why the Supreme Court felt that it was not even necessary to decide such a contentious issue, lying at the very foundation of the case. I think it was obvious to the court that the government's position was absurd. After all, there is no way the public would have accepted the imposition of Social Security taxes without the simultaneous promise of secured Social Security benefits. How else would the promised trust fund have been financed without the earmarked revenue from a dedicated payroll tax?

So rather than making the obvious choice and affirm the First Circuit, the Roosevelt-stacked Supreme Court found a way to overturn the decision without addressing this key issue at all. Remember that the argument regarding the relationship of the tax and the benefits centered on the general welfare clause of the Constitution. So in order to find Social Security constitutional without having to accept the government's absurd position, the court decided to render the issue moot by rewriting the Constitution instead! While the First Circuit Court rightly refused to amend the Constitution by judicial decree, the Supreme Court had no problem doing exactly that.

Writing for the majority, Justice Benjamin Nathan Cardozo ruled "the concept of the general welfare (is not) static. Needs that were narrow or parochial a century ago may be interwoven in our day with the well-being of the nation. What is critical or urgent changes with the times."

In other words, the Supreme Court basically repealed the Tenth Amendment. It claimed the government had the ability to redefine the meaning of "general welfare" to suit its fancy. Anything the government felt would improve the well-being of the nation could now be justified under the General Welfare clause. This was something even the government itself lacked the chutzpa to argue, yet the court concocted this idiotic interpretation on its own to avoid affirming the government's even more obviously idiotic argument.

So in one sentence the Supreme Court threw the concept of limited government out the window. This decision gave the federal government unlimited power to do whatever it wanted. As the First Circuit pointed out, had the framers envisioned such a possibility, the Constitution never would have been ratified.

The fact is that the meaning of the Constitution cannot "change with the times." Such a condition would render it meaningless. Two justices, James Clark McReynolds and Pierce Butler, had the integrity to dissent, and they agreed with the First Circuit that Social Security was unconstitutional.

So in enacting and litigating Social Security, the government argued one thing to the courts and said the exact opposite to the public. In other words, it was a complete fraud.

I once asked Charles Blahous, a trustee for Social Security and guest on my radio talk show, if he could tell me the difference between Social Security and a Ponzi scheme. After a pregnant pause, he could identify just one—that a Ponzi scheme is based on fraud. As you just discovered, so is Social Security, so there really is no difference at all.

A Ponzi Scheme

It's sometimes difficult to argue with Social Security defenders, because they keep sliding in their defense of the program: it's self-funding, it's savings, it's a pension, it's insurance . . .

Social Security's defenders will rely on whatever characterization of the program they need in order to win an argument. But probably the most accurate description of Social Security is that it's a Ponzi scheme.

Texas governor Rick Perry stated this clearly in a 2011 presidential debate. For this bit of honesty, he was derided as a simpleton and attacked as an enemy of seniors—not only by the liberal media, but also by Republican front-runner, Mitt Romney.

Romney and others don't like anybody denigrating Social Security, but if you look at what a Ponzi scheme actually is, it's impossible to disagree with Perry.

Charles Ponzi was an Italian immigrant who couldn't hold down a job. Then he came across a clever way to make money—arbitrage in postal-return coupons. If you were mailing your little brother who was studying in France, you might stick in the envelope a coupon that he could redeem for the postage necessary to write back to you.

These coupons often sold for less than the cost of postage, and so Ponzi could have agents buy, for instance, French coupons in bulk when they were cheap relative to postage, and then sell them in France for a markup. This was guaranteed profit, on a small scale. But this wasn't the *scheme*.

Ponzi lined up investors in his business. If he was making 50 percent returns on his money, he promised, he could do it with your money, too! Millions of dollars poured into Ponzi's fail-safe investment plan. But Ponzi wasn't investing that money in postal coupons. He couldn't have: there were only a few thousand postal coupons in existence, and his "investment" portfolio far exceeded the value of every postal coupon on the planet.

Ponzi, of course, was simply taking investors' money and not investing it. When it came time to pay off the early investors, he tried to convince them to reinvest. If they didn't want to reinvest, but demanded their payout, he paid them—not from any investment earnings, but simply from the money he had taken from later investors.

You can see how the scheme works: If you need to pay the second wave of investors, you just find a third, bigger wave, roping them in by pointing out how well the first wave did. In order to provide a decent rate of return, each wave of investors needs to be bigger—dollarwise, at least—than the previous.

Ponzi got filthy rich off the scheme, making millions simply by convincing people to give him money. But eventually, all Ponzi schemes fall apart. The original one fell apart after *Barron's* carried a report raising serious questions about his investments, forcing Ponzi to scramble in order to maintain investor confidence.

As more people (including the public relations man he hired) started raising alarms about Ponzi, the scheme began unraveling. Soon, the government got on the case, and Ponzi went to jail.

Bernie Madoff ran the most successful Ponzi scheme ever, raking in $50 billion in "investment capital" that was never invested. He paid the early investors with money from the later investors, keeping everyone happy with doctored financial statements.

He could have kept on doing this, except that the stock market collapse of 2008 caused many of the investors to come asking him for their cash—which, of course, he didn't have. That's when he confessed to his sons, who subsequently turned him in.

So, what are the characteristics of a Ponzi scheme? All investors are promised a healthy return, but there are no appreciating or income-generating assets. The only way any investors get paid off is when the schemer takes money from new investors and gives it to the original investors.

The Securities and Exchange Commission has a definition of a Ponzi scheme:

> A Ponzi scheme is an investment fraud that involves the payment of purported returns to existing investors from funds

contributed by new investors. Ponzi scheme organizers often so-
licit new investors by promising to invest funds in opportunities
claimed to generate high returns with little or no risk. In many
Ponzi schemes, the fraudsters focus on attracting new money to
make promised payments to earlier-stage investors and to use for
personal expenses, instead of engaging in any legitimate investment activity.[2]

Social Security fits this description. But if you say this, the program's
defenders just change their defense again, sliding right along any time you
pin it down.

> *It's a savings plan!*
> But I don't own the money.
> *That's because it's an insurance plan!*
> But I'm not legally entitled to the benefits.
> *Well, it's a standard pension plan.*
> But Congress doesn't have the authority to create that.
> *Actually, the tax and the benefits have nothing to do with each
> other.*
> So, it's just a tax on me?
> *No, it's an entitlement!*

Any time someone changes their argument that much, you can be sure
of one thing: they're speaking falsely at some point. In other words, Social
Security is a fraud.

However, there is one real difference between Social Security and a
Ponzi scheme that even Blahous failed to point out. With the schemes run
by Charles Ponzi and Bernie Madoff, victims *chose* to invest with them.
With Social Security, there is no choice. If you're an American and you
have income, you have to take part in the scheme.

Here's the real difference: You don't get to stop paying into Social Security once you realize it's a Ponzi scheme. In that respect the Ponzi and
Madoff schemes were actually far more honest!

Social Security defenders use this as a point in favor of the program.
Nobody can opt out of Social Security, so confidence in it is not essential

to its strength. By that logic, the only real problem with Ponzi and Madoff was that they stopped attracting new investors.

But the problem with a Ponzi scheme is not that investors lose faith, it's that it's an "investment" that doesn't have any appreciating or income-generating assets. A Ponzi scheme tries to create payouts without creating wealth. This is what Social Security does. The government cannot make a Ponzi scheme viable simply by mandating participation. It's precisely because such schemes can never work that they are illegal in the first place.

The Scheme Is Crumbling

What made Ponzi's scheme fall apart? The public figuring out that there was nothing *there*.

And when did Madoff's house of cards collapse? It was when investors started calling on their money.

The point at which Ponzi and Madoff and dozens like them finally were exposed, and thus crumbled—that's where Social Security is now.

The idea of Social Security as a self-funding, reliable source of retirement security is a joke. Social Security taxes no longer cover Social Security benefits. In 2011, benefits were expected to be $733 billion, while taxes were estimated at $637 billion.[3] How did Congress react to this imbalance? By reducing Social Security taxes, and thus widening the deficit.

As part of the late 2010 tax-extenders deal, Congress passed a temporary cut in the Social Security tax. Republicans liked it because it was a tax cut. Democrats liked it because it was a rare tax cut that could benefit the lower middle class (many of whom don't pay income taxes).

This tipped the scale, sending Social Security into a deficit from which it will never emerge. For every year from now until the end of time, Social Security is projected to pay out more than it takes in—even if the temporary tax cut is ended.

Things are just going to get worse for this program.

As unemployment continues to grow (and it will), there are fewer workers paying in. With jobs hard to find and wages stagnant, people are retiring earlier than they otherwise would.

Demographics are also driving Social Security toward insolvency. After

World War II, America enjoyed a Baby Boom, but those Baby Boomers didn't have as many kids. The result, as the Social Security Administration puts it: "After 2014, cash deficits are expected to grow rapidly as the number of beneficiaries continues to grow at a substantially faster rate than the number of covered workers."

In 1950, there were 35 million workers paying Social Security taxes and 222,000 retirees collecting it—a 159.4 to 1 ratio.[4] That eventually stabilized by 1975, at about 3.2 workers to every retiree. Now, with Baby Boomers retiring and job growth near zero, that ratio has begun plummeting.

In 2010, the number of beneficiaries (roughly equal to new retirees minus deaths) grew by 1.5 million, while the number of workers grew by 700,000. From 2000 to 2010, the number of recipients grew by 18.2 percent, while the number of payers grew by less than one percent.

This trend is only going to accelerate. By 2031, SSA forecasts there will be one Social Security retiree for every 2.1 workers.

This is unsustainable.

The "Trust Fund"

If you listen to politicians talk about Social Security's soundness, you might hear them mention the year 2036. That's supposedly when the program goes broke.

But this year, and every future year, Social Security pays out more than it takes in. So why isn't it "broke" now? What happens in 2036?

These claims rest on the idea of the Social Security "trust fund."

Almost every year since 1935, Social Security has run a surplus: Social Security taxes have exceeded benefits paid. Those surpluses—about $2.5 trillion at the end of 2010—constitute the "trust fund." But as you can probably guess, there is no checking account with $2.5 trillion sitting in it from which Social Security can cut checks to today's beneficiaries. Every single penny of Social Security surpluses for the past sixty-six years has already been spent by Congress.

With its annual surpluses, Social Security bought Treasuries. That is, it loaned every spare dime it had to the U.S. Government. But these aren't normal Treasuries, they are "Special Issue" securities. Social Security can sell them only to the U.S. Treasury. How does the Treasury pay for them? By borrowing or taxing.

So, the trust fund doesn't have any money in it. It's filled with IOUs. But who owes whom? The federal government owes itself.

And these IOUs are supposedly assets. If I wrote myself a check for a million dollars, I wouldn't have created a million-dollar asset. The reason is obvious, in that the asset—"the check"—is also my own liability. I owe the money to myself. This is exactly what the government does when it effectively writes itself a check and deposits it into the Social Security trust fund.

For some reason this fact is lost on most economists, who regard government bonds as assets. Of course they are assets, just not assets to the government. My million-dollar check would be an asset if I gave it to a third party (assuming it would clear), but that does not mean the same check is an asset to me. Similarly, a government bond in a government trust fund is not an asset to the government.

So in other words, there is no Social Security trust fund. Every dime paid out of that trust fund will be financed by taxes or regular government debt. It's as if I told you that I had set aside $10,000 for you, but if you wanted it, you needed to either get a bank loan, or earn it. It's not really set aside for you, now is it?

Think about it this way. If the Social Security trust fund did not exist, how would the government make up the current shortfall in Social Security? It could raise taxes, borrow money (either legitimately or from the Fed, which would print it), or reduce other spending. Well, these are the exact choices that exist today. When the trust fund presents its bonds to the Treasury for redemption, the government can raise taxes, borrow money, or cut other spending to make good the IOUs.

So Social Security, just after its sixty-fifth birthday, has gone broke.

Political Clout

The thing is, there was no catastrophe, no great depression, no great event that brought Social Security to its current point of insolvency. It's just the way it was built.

We've known for decades that the program was headed to this point. Why didn't we fix this before now, when we had a surplus?

Politics is the answer, and this is particularly insidious politics. By handing checks directly to people, Social Security turns all Americans into welfare recipients and dependents. Because today's dependents spent decades "paying in," they feel particularly entitled.

So, any time someone mentions changing the program, it provides an easy line of attack for political opponents. If you're willing to rob Peter to pay Paul, you can count on the political support of Paul—especially when he was robbed twenty years ago to pay Patrick.

Other welfare programs have been reformed and modified, but that's partly due to the fact that they benefited politically weak groups. The poor don't carry much clout. They are less likely to vote, and they don't contribute to campaigns.

The elderly, on the other hand, vote like no other group. Americans between the ages of sixty and seventy-five are nearly twice as likely to vote as Americans in their mid-twenties. Current Social Security recipients are by far the most likely people to vote. They have more time to follow politics, they're less likely to have to work on Election Day, and, of course, they depend on politicians for some of their money.

Compounding this clout for the elderly, the largest nonprofit lobbying organization in the country is the American Association of Retired Persons (AARP). From 1998 through 2011, AARP spent $207 million on lobbying, more than any company in the United States besides General Electric. This pays for sixty in-house lobbyists and three outside lobbying firms.

With all this political power wielded by its beneficiaries, it's no wonder that Social Security is safe. We know it hasn't survived on its own merits.

Destroys Savings

Social Security has added to the tax burden of Americans, added to the national debt, and is, in many cases, the biggest part of the hiring tax I discussed in chapter 3. But the economic and moral harm of Social Security goes beyond that.

Social Security destroys savings. Savings are the root of economic growth, because savings are the root of all investment (when you borrow, you're borrowing someone else's savings).

A tax taking 15.3 percent out of everyone's pay undoubtedly erases savings. People only save after they've earned enough to cover necessities. Taking a huge chunk of someone's paycheck mostly harms their ability to save.

But government also discourages savings when it tells people they don't need to save—that Uncle Sam is taking care of everything. This is the whole message of Social Security: don't worry about building a nest egg; Washington will just take your money while you're working, and then take care of your retirement.

This leaves people without savings, and thus exposed if their benefits are too small (or if Social Security eventually collapses), but it also hurts the broader economy. Remember, all investment comes from someone's savings. By constricting the national savings rate, Social Security has reduced the pool of available savings. This reduces our ability to make capital investments and grow businesses.

As is the case with all government programs, Social Security achieved the exact opposite of its intended purpose. The rationale behind Social Security was that average Americans were too irresponsible to be trusted to save for their own retirement.

So the government created Social Security as a form of forced savings. If Americans wouldn't save on their own, Congress would tax their wages and save for them. The problem is that every penny taken from taxpayers to fund Social Security was spent. So the government took money from taxpayers on the premise that they were not smart enough to save for their own retirement, then recklessly spent every dime it took. No matter how irresponsible taxpayers might have been, had the government left them alone, it's clear that they would have done a better job of saving than the government did. After all, the government saved nothing. It's safe to say that even in a worst-case scenario, most taxpayers would have at least saved some portion of what was taken from them in Social Security taxes.

Not only did Social Security undermine the retirements of generations of Americans, but it deprived the American economy of all the economic growth retirement savings would have enabled.

Hurting the Vulnerable

Think about the way Social Security pays out benefits: once you retire, SSA determines your monthly benefit, and then pays that to you every year (adjusted for inflation) until you die.

This amounts to a net transfer of wealth from those who die younger to those who die older. There's nothing inherently wrong with old-age insurance. It is a real problem that people outlive their savings. But there are perverse consequences to forcing everyone to buy into such a plan.

For instance, black men have a life expectancy six years shorter than white men. As of 2006, the average white man lives to 75.7 years and the average black man dies at 69.7. Full Social Security retirement age is sixty-seven years. That means that a black man can expect to take in 2.7 years of benefits, while a white man can expect to get 8.7 years. In other words, a white guy gets three times as much bang for his buck on Social Security. Suddenly, this program sounds less "progressive."

This is true regarding wealth, too. Richer people live longer. They have better doctors, easier jobs, more time for exercise, and are more likely to make healthy lifestyle choices. This life-expectancy gap makes Social Security benefits regressive.

Of course, those retirees currently collecting benefits are far wealthier than those currently working to pay the taxes. Sure, current recipients paid taxes when they were younger, but the rates were far lower than they are today. So Social Security really amounts to reverse welfare whereby money is transferred from the young and poor to the rich and old.

Also, on the micro level, you can see plenty of moral problems. What if you're a forty-year-old who can still work, but has a terminal illness and you have near-zero chance of reaching sixty-seven? Of your own volition, you would stop paying into a retirement plan that only pays out when you reach sixty-seven. But Social Security is not of your own volition. I remember during the 1980s several young men suffering from AIDS tried to get out of paying Social Security taxes on the grounds that they would not live long enough to receive the benefits. Instead they wanted to use the money for medicine that might extend their lives. For their own good, their requests were denied.

Further, unlike actual retirement savings, you can't leave any leftover money to your children. Rich people can still afford to leave something to their kids. It's the middle class that gets robbed.

Like many aspects of the New Deal, Social Security was a raw deal.

Saving Social Security?

Politicians are usually pretty good at pretending there is no problem with Social Security, but every once in a while, you hear Washington talk about how to "save Social Security." These plans all have serious problems.

The Left's favorite idea today is to lift the cap on the Social Security tax. Currently only your first $108,000 or so of income is subject to FICA. Again, this is because your benefits are supposed to vary with your contributions, and the wealthy don't need big Social Security checks.

This upsets liberals for obvious reasons—poor people are paying a tax on their marginal dollar that rich people aren't paying. So, liberals want to lift the cap. Make people pay FICA on every dollar they earn. This is what Congress did on Medicare.

But think about what that would mean. Currently, the top tax rate is 39.6 percent. A couple earning enough to pay that (over $400,000 per year) pays Medicare tax, and so they pay 41.05 percent on their marginal dollar. If this couple lives in New York and is earning over $500,000, they're paying 8.97 percent in state income tax, meaning taxes already eat up 50.02 percent of their marginal dollar.

If you do tack on the 6.2 percent "employee contribution" of Social Security, then the marginal tax rate is 56.22 percent. The most successful workers would be keeping less than half of the money they earn. And if you count the employer contributions, then over 60 percent of every additional dollar this couple makes would be going straight to government.*

---

* When the first edition of *The Real Crash* was published, the numbers were somewhat different because the top tax rate was increased as of January 1, 2013. In 2012, our hypothetical couple would have had a 55 percent marginal tax rate under this scenario, provided they exceeded $380,000 in wage income.

I've got bad news for any liberal class warriors drooling over this prospect: this sort of tax hike doesn't really hurt the rich. If you start penalizing high earners like that, the truly rich (as opposed to people just having a good year or two) stop expanding their businesses (it's much harder to justify further risk when you're keeping less than 40 percent of what you earn), let a few employees go to cover the lost income, or even just stop working. Sure, that means they might have to sacrifice the dream of a private jet or a new beach house, but for the benefit of not having to work, deal with employees or regulators anymore, it's worth it.

So guess who suffers? The employees of the rich person. When they lose their jobs because their boss couldn't eke out a meaningful profit, they give up more than a few luxuries. Soaking the rich doesn't hurt the rich as much as it hurts those who depend on the rich. That also includes their customers. If a rich person shuts down his business, many of his middle-class customers must then choose another merchant, whose prices might be higher or whose quality of service might be lower. Of course, with reduced competition, those remaining merchants will be better positioned to raise their prices even higher.

The most straightforward way of "saving Social Security," and what Congress has done in the past, is simply to raise the tax rate from its 6.2 percent to whatever it needs to be in order to support benefits. Considering what we're talking about—going from 3.2 workers per retiree to 2.1—that's roughly a 50 percent hike. Make FICA 9.3 percent from the employee and 9.3 percent from the employer, and you're basically telling young people it's not worth working.

You'd see plenty of young people opt out of the job market, that is, mooch off Mom and Dad. You'd see an explosion of a black market labor. You'd also see American youth pack up and get jobs in Australia.

If our politicians follow the same path on Social Security it looks like they'll follow regarding our national debt, then they'll just try to print the entitlement program into solvency. The catch here is that Social Security benefits are indexed to inflation. In order to really make due on Social Security through inflation, Congress would have to game the rules covering the cost-of-living adjustments. And this fix is effectively the same as cutting benefits, but with less political risk.

Crashproof Yourself: Don't Count on Social Security

If you have a typical financial advisor, his plan for your retirement probably includes Social Security as a substantial factor. But if you're more than a couple of years from retirement, you shouldn't count on meaningful Social Security benefits. The only way government could realistically make due on its long-term Social Security obligations is by inflating, and then gaming, the CPI so that Cost-of-Living Adjustments don't keep pace. Another likely alternative is means-testing of benefits, so that wealthier people get smaller benefits. For six decades, people have counted on Social Security to bolster their retirement. Those days are over. You're on your own now.

In fact, this scenario is already taking place, as current Social Security cost-of-living adjustments, like the CPI, fail to adequately measure the inflation the government is creating. This stealth reduction in Social Security benefits will continue, but it's unlikely to "solve" the problem.

The cynic in me believes that the government's secret plan to "save" Social Security is to bankrupt all those hoping to retire on it. Since most people look to Social Security merely to supplement their retirement, if enough money is lost in stock and real estate markets, if interest rates remain near zero, and the cost of living continues to rise faster than Social Security cost-of-living adjustments, most Americans will not be able to afford to retire, and will therefore never draw their full Social Security benefits. Even though they will be collecting benefits, they will be paying more taxes on those benefits, and since they are still working, they will continue paying Social Security taxes until the day they die.

The Solution: Give Social Security a Slow Death

The truth is that you can't really fix Social Security. It's a machine whose self-destruction was in the design. Like Charles Ponzi's and Bernie Madoff's schemes, it was only a matter of time before it all collapsed.

You can tell the whole thing was a scam by the way the government kept shifting its story. *It's insurance! It's savings! It's a pension! It's pay-as-you-go!*

So now that we're face-to-face with Social Security's inherently dysfunctional nature, what do we do about it? Again, let's return to Bernie Madoff. Dozens of his investors were left in the cold, but there simply wasn't money to pay them all back. They could take all his money and sell all his property, and the amount would still be far short of what people thought they were owed.

There is no "fair" answer. Just as Madoff destroyed the possibility of fair, Congress destroyed the possibility of fair. Everybody will have to suffer. Some will suffer more. What is the *least unfair* way to settle the score and retire Social Security?

Here's the plan in brief:

First, abolish the Social Security tax completely, and finance the program through general tax receipts, my favorite being a national sales tax that replaces not only the Social Security tax, but also the personal and corporate income taxes, and the estate and gift taxes.

Second, slowly phase out Social Security benefits, beginning by removing the least needy from the rolls. Eventually shrink it down to nothing.

When Republicans do talk about Social Security, they always begin with the promise that current retirees and those on the brink of retirement will not see any changes. This is pointless and cowardly. The program is already broke, and the longer we wait to fix it, the more painful it will be. Waiting ten or fifteen years before adjusting benefits, as Paul Ryan advocates, just makes things worse, especially because the Baby Boom armies are now hitting the retirement-age beach.

Beginning today, we cut benefits for every recipient who is not *dependent* on Social Security. The general idea is to convert Social Security from an entitlement that you get for being old to a welfare program for being old and needy.

If you did decently well over forty-five years of working, there's a good chance that at age sixty-seven you're much better off financially than the twenty-something kid who graduated in the midst of this recession and is burdened under huge college debt. Transferring wealth from the worse-off to the better-off is senseless.

First, the wealthy shouldn't get anything. Second, the comfortable should get reduced benefits. If reducing Social Security benefits means you'll have to sell your house and move into a smaller one, that's no fun, but sorry. That's fairer than the alternatives. It's also a lot fairer than taxing a poor worker who can barely afford to pay his rent to send money to a wealthy retiree so he does not have to downsize his McMansion.

This is called "means testing." If you have greater means, you get less in benefits. Your benefit reduction would be calculated from your assets and your current income.

Assets should be weighted most heavily in the means test, so that work and income aren't punished as much. Under current law, retirees with high incomes are subject to a tax on their Social Security benefits, which are tax-free for most people. But this is basically a penalty for working. That's why I look more at *assets*—net worth—than at *income* when judging whose Social Security benefits we should reduce.

One reason we acquire assets is because they have value and can be sold later, when we need money. Again, if you have a huge house, you can sell it (empty nesters no longer need such large nests anyway) and begin renting or buy a condo. If you have two cars, you might not need both if you're not working. Sell one. Retirement, and the end of life generally, is a great time to unwind your possessions. You can't take them with you, as they say. Live by selling off the stuff you don't need.

Ending Social Security also means that you would be expected to spend down your life's savings. But what do you think life's savings are for? There's no scoreboard whereby we judge everyone by how much money they have when the final buzzer rings.

If you think about it, Social Security benefits for the well-off don't really subsidize the well-off as much as they subsidize their heirs. By freeing the wealthy of the need to unload assets, you're increasing the size of their kids' inheritances. So, you can see Social Security as a transfer from the working youth to the youth about to inherit a bundle. In other words, the children of poor parents, who will likely inherit nothing, pay high taxes, so the children of affluent parents can inherit larger fortunes. As you peel the onion, Social Security just keeps looking worse and worse.

Income will count in the means test, too, but it won't be weighted as heavily, because we want to minimize the cost of working. (Reducing benefits proportionately to a senior's income has the same economic effect as raising their taxes, I understand, but remember, we're trying to find the least bad solution to a really bad problem).

More people can work into their late sixties and their seventies than ever could before. We're healthier longer, and more people have desk jobs that allow them to work. Technology eases the workload, and telecommuting helps as well. For this reason, the retirement age can steadily be raised—it *has* to be raised because life expectancy is getting longer.

Speaking of living longer, the means test will take this into account. If you keep working until you can't, you sell your house and live off that, spend down your savings, then sell more assets, but live long enough that you've run out of assets, your Social Security benefits could kick in then.

After we raise the retirement age today, knock the rich off the rolls, and reduce benefits for the comfortable, we begin tightening. We keep pushing the retirement age back a few months every year. We also set stricter standards on the means test every year.

Eventually, Social Security will be benefiting only the elderly poor. Some of these will be people who retired poor. Some will be people who retired comfortably but lived long enough to become poor. But it will be a relief program, not a subsidy program.

At some point, even this relief program can be phased out. Those who still need it could simply apply for regular welfare, or better still, seek the help of their own families or private charities.

Of course, once the government ends Social Security, and the punitive taxes that finance it, Americans will be able to save comfortably for their own retirements. In addition, the economy will benefit from the extra productivity created by the capital investments financed by those savings. The extra growth and jobs created by millions of Americans who are once again saving for their retirements will do much more to eliminate poverty than any government antipoverty program ever could. In the process, perhaps we can restore respect in our judicial system for the Constitution to prevent Congress from resurrecting a similar program in the future.

Short of the best solution, there are alternatives that would improve our current situation. I am of the opinion that the government should not be involved in the retirement process at all. However, if going cold turkey is too much for the public to stomach, one compromise would be the Chilean approach.

Chile privatized its Social Security, which is a vast improvement on what we have now. It's forced savings, though, which is still paternalistic. How does the government know what portion of your income is appropriate to save? If you own your income, it should be your right to decide for yourself how to use it.

Of course, any privatization plan cannot be adopted with substantial cuts in current benefits. That is because young people cannot simultaneously save for their own retirements and finance the retirement of the Baby Boomers. That is why these plans never go anywhere in Congress, as no one wants to open that can of worms.

The U.S. plans for privatization floated last decade would have required you to put your money in stocks and bonds. What do you think would have happened when the stock market dropped? There would have been massive demand, from people who invested without understanding the risk, for bailouts of everyone's Social Security accounts.

Social Security should not be transformed. It should be withered down to nothing.

Politicians will always try to win elections by pandering to Social Security recipients, and those about to join their ranks. They will resist any cuts in benefits, and jump on any opponent who even hints at cutting benefits. Of course, by refusing to cut benefits, Congress assures that the real value of those benefits will plunge. The inflation that would have to be created to pay these benefits would render them practically worthless to recipients.

As a matter of fact, the inevitability of Social Security benefits eventually becoming worthless was discussed in a Congressional hearing way back in May 1976. In a two-day hearing commencing on May 27, Senator William Proxmire questioned James B. Cardwell, the commissioner of Social Security, regarding concerns raised by Senator Charles Percy about the possibility of a Social Security default. Proxmire pointed out that between 32 and 34 million Americans were drawing Social Security benefits and then added the following:

> Almost all of them, or many of them, are voters. In my state, I figure there are 600,000 voters that receive Social Security. Can you imagine a Senator or Congressman under those circumstances saying, we are going to repudiate that high a percentage of the electorate? No.

Furthermore, we have the capacity under the Constitution, the Congress does, to coin money, as well as to regulate the value thereof. And therefore we have the power to provide that money. And we are going to do it. It may not be worth anything when the recipient gets it, but he is going to get his benefits paid.[5]

To which Commissioner Cardwell replied, "I tend to agree."

While technically Proxmire was wrong as to the government's Constitutional authority (while Congress has the power to coin money—that is, produce gold and silver coins—it does not have the power to print paper money), he hit the nail right on the head. Rather than risk their reelections, politicians would instead render U.S. currency completely worthless. For if Social Security checks become worthless, so would the U.S dollar itself and all dollar-denominated assets.

In contrast, if my plan were adopted, benefits would be cut for those who do not need them, but at least be preserved for those who do. However, if no cuts are made, all Social Security recipients will see the purchasing power of their benefits collapse, even those who depend on the benefits the most.

So while politicians will accuse anyone advocating cutting Social Security benefits of hurting the elderly, it's those resisting the cuts that will inflict the most pain on retirees. It's the elderly, retired, and those living on fixed incomes that are hurt the most by inflation. As Senator Proxmire pointed out, because creating massive inflation is the only way to preserve nominal Social Security benefits (the Fed will have to print the money to buy all the bonds the government will have to sell to keep Social Security checks from bouncing), those who are hurt the most are the very people receiving the checks.

Just like all government programs, Social Security will most hurt the very people it is designed to help!

Medicare

The sad thing is that Social Security isn't the most insolvent of our federal entitlements. Medicare is in far worse shape.

This chapter has focused on Social Security because we'll treat Medicare in chapter 9, on reforming health care. But here, let me talk about the fiscal situation. As with Social Security, the ratio of workers to Medicare recipients is dropping rapidly. Currently about 3.4 Americans work for every Medicare recipient. By 2040, that ratio will be more like 2.2 to 1.

Medicare outlays are expected to grow from $526 billion in 2010 to $980 billion in 2021—nearly doubling in a decade. The driver here has been and will be increased medical costs. We'll discuss that further in chapter 10.

Similar to Social Security, we need to end Medicare, but the process will be easier. Once you abolish Medicare, poor seniors will be rolled into Medicaid, the federal program that helps the poor pay for health care. Those seniors who can afford it will need to buy their own insurance. This will bring down the cost of health care, because private insurers and actual patients will be far more price-sensitive than Medicare is.

Ending Entitlements

Social Security and Medicare are great examples of what happens when government ventures into territory it should avoid. The nature of these government programs made it nearly inevitable that they would become massive drags on America's fiscal condition. Had we simply heeded the wisdom of our Founding Fathers and followed the Constitution, we would have avoided these problems. It is amazing just how wise our Founders were.

These are called the third rails of politics, because supposedly touching them is instant political death. But if we don't touch them, we're dead all the same.

Entitlement Reform 2.0

Not much has changed with regard to Social Security and Medicare since the first edition of this book was published, but the condition of both programs remains dire. Social Security's disability insurance benefit program is already teetering on insolvency as Americans, unable to find work, are falling back on it. By law, the so-called "trust fund" bolstering the program runs out in 2016. Automatic benefit cuts may take effect, by law, before the next presidential election.

According to the latest Social Security trustees report, the main program that Americans deal with—the retirement program—can continue paying out full benefits until 2033, at which point the "trust fund" runs out. (Which is to say, that's the point at which Congress has already taken all of the debt it owes Social Security and sold it to the public instead, increasing our nation's indebtedness.) At that point, the benefits are cut back to about 75 percent of what's expected. And Medicare's trust fund runs out in 2026.

But even these grim estimates are based on a robust economic recovery later this decade that I believe will never come. Another major economic catastrophe would dramatically darken the programs' revenue picture.

And even setting aside the real crash for the moment, there are no signs right now that the labor market will be able to sustain the growth that monetary manipulation has given us so far. With ObamaCare adding to all of the other drags on hiring that exist today, it's quite likely that payroll taxes will fall short of estimates, causing the program to run out of gas years earlier than expected.

Of course, long before the so-called trust fund is exhausted, rising interest rates will make it impossible for the government to sell enough new bonds to the public to redeem those held by the trust fund. Sure, the Federal Reserve could buy the bonds, but then the payments would be practically worthless to those receiving their benefits.

9

Fixing Higher Ed:
Time to Drop Out of College?

POLITICIANS ARE ALLOWED TO BE pro-war or antiwar, pro-taxes or antitaxes, pro-life or pro-choice. But everyone has to be "pro-education," and more specifically, pro–public education. In addition, being pro-education always means being pro–spending-more-money-on-education.

We hear debates about how to improve public education and higher education. But you never hear politicians arguing that we are spending too much on public education, or that too many kids spend too much time in classrooms.

That would be like opposing Mom and Apple Pie.

As a result, there's no upward boundary to the amount of money the educational establishment can demand. K-12 education takes up about a third of all state and local spending,[1] yet the public is led to believe that schools are getting shortchanged. California has a law setting minimum levels of education spending, even while the state is so deeply in debt. Politically, you cannot spare any expense on education. Does any politician ever say, "Okay, that's enough education spending"? Have you ever heard a public figure declare a desire to reduce the number of people attending college?

But an honest accounting of the situation, outside of the pressures of politics, destroys our standard nostrums. We need to admit to some unpopular facts about education.

Governments spend too much, not too little, money on K-12 education. Ideally, government would simply exit the educational sector completely.

And Americans spend way too much time and money on college.

Fewer kids should go to college, and Washington should end all subsidies for college tuition.

Is Our Education Spending Worth It?

Amid the call for more and more school spending, we don't often stop to ask what good that money will do. The evidence shows clearly that more money doesn't equal smarter or more skilled kids.

On a national level, over time, you see a stark pattern: huge spending increases, huge increases in staff-per-student, and little or no increases in test scores. One Cato Institute study found that, adjusted for inflation, school spending increased 140 percent between 1970 and 2007, and staff per student increased by more than 75 percent. Meanwhile, looking at the National Assessment of Educational Progress tests, reading and math scores were flat, while science scores were down.[2]

From locality to locality, it's hard to find any correlation between spending and success. Take the District of Columbia. D.C. taxpayers, according to a 2010 study,[3] shell out $16,353 per pupil. Only two states spend more. But D.C. has the second-lowest graduation rate, 56 percent. New York, with the second-highest per-pupil spending at $16,784, is in the bottom third of states in graduation rate. The number one state in graduation rate is Wisconsin, but there are fifteen states that spend more.

All of these per-pupil-spending figures understate the cost to taxpayers, too. Sometimes, the real per-pupil cost is nearly twice the "official" number. Adam Schaeffer, an education expert at the libertarian Cato Institute, in a 2010 study, found that:

> Real spending per pupil ranges from a low of nearly $12,000 in the Phoenix area schools to a high of nearly $27,000 in the New York metro area. The gap between real and reported per-pupil spending ranges from a low of 23 percent in the Chicago area to a high of 90 percent in the Los Angeles metro region.[4]

Official data tend to rely on old or incomplete numbers, and they often omit large investments, like new buildings or capital improvements.

It's not much different in higher education. College tuition is skyrocketing, but does anyone really think the quality of education is skyrocketing? Mostly, campuses are getting fancier gyms and student centers.

Doubts are spreading about the value of a college education. As students graduate with crippling debt and curricula get watered down, more and more commentators and parents are wondering aloud if it's all worth it.

That's why academia is furiously turning out studies purporting to show that going to college—and especially to an elite college—is a *great* investment. Georgetown University recently put out a study proclaiming "Obtaining a postsecondary credential is almost always worth it, as evidenced by higher earnings over a lifetime."

The RAND Corporation did a study along with Brigham Young University and Cornell University, concluding: "strong evidence emerges of a significant economic return to attending an elite private institution, and some evidence suggests this premium has increased over time."

Of course elite college graduates and Ivy League graduates make more money. But that doesn't prove anything about the value of college. Maybe college doesn't help you earn more; maybe it's just that the traits that help you get into and finish college help you earn more.

Think about it: Who is more able to get into college, go to college, and graduate from college? What traits do these kids have that are absent among their cohorts who don't go to college?

First, kids who go to college are probably smarter. Smarter kids are more likely to get good SATs and thus get into good colleges or get scholarships that make college more affordable. Smarter kids are also more likely to be able to finish college.

Harder-working kids, for similar reasons, are more likely to get into college. They get better grades in high school. They too are more likely to finish college.

Children of wealthier parents are also more likely to apply to college—they will have higher aspirations, are more able to afford college, and are better connected to get jobs once they graduate. These kids are also more likely to attend private schools or good public schools, and an SAT prep course, thus improving their chances of getting into a good college. And they are less likely to drop out for lack of funds.

Students whose parents attended college are in the same boat: more likely to consider, get into, and finish college.

Now here's another question: Who is more likely to make higher-than-normal incomes? Smarter people make more money. Of course many smart people are dumb about money, or they take jobs that are more intellectually than financially rewarding, but in general, studies find that income correlates with IQ.

If you're a hard worker, you're likely to earn more than someone with an inferior work ethic because you will get more done and you'll impress your bosses.

It's also true that coming from wealth is itself a boon to your income. Wealthier parents are more likely to get you good connections, open doors for you, and make good internships more affordable.

Private schools and good public schools are also cleaner pipelines to college and especially good colleges. Teachers and parents at these schools convey an expectation that students will go to college. These schools have counselors pushing kids to apply to college and helping them with their applications.

Finally, if your parents went to college, the expectations are also there, and your parents' alma mater is more likely to accept you.

In other words, all the factors that make someone more likely to go to college and finish college are also the same factors that, in and of themselves, raise one's likely income. This fact takes much of the steam out of studies showing a correlation between a college degree and income. The correlation only proves that high earners and college graduates have similar traits—it doesn't show that a college degree contributes to higher income.

Correlation does not equal causation, but that notion seems lost on the schools pushing these numbers. A real statistician would adjust these results for SATs and high school grades. If you did that, you would find a very small premium for kids with degrees.

Sure enough, *The New York Times* reported in 2011 on the data that went into that RAND report-Brigham Young-Cornell study:

> In 1999, economists from Princeton and the Andrew W. Mellon Foundation looked at some of the same data Professor Eide and his colleagues had used, but crunched them in a different way: they compared students at more selective colleges to others of "seemingly comparable ability," based on their SAT scores and

class rank, who had attended less selective schools, either by choice or because a top college rejected them. The earnings of graduates in the two groups were about the same—perhaps shifting the ledger in favor of the less expensive, less prestigious route.[5]

I suspect you'd find similar results on the question of whether or not it pays to go to any college. If we compare the lifetime earnings (netting out the cost of the degree) of high school graduates to college graduates (excluding those with more advanced degrees), who have similar high school GPAs, SAT scores, and demographics, my guess would be those who skip college earn more than those who finish. Other than the costs of the degree itself (plus interest), and the lost income and work experience that result from studying and not working, competent dropouts may in fact be more driven to achieve than those who finish. They are likely to be more entrepreneurial, have greater self-confidence, and are more willing to swim against the tide.

Employer Bias

If you look at all the data and adjust for all sorts of factors, there is probably some economic value in a college degree. But even that fact doesn't prove that college provides knowledge or skill that's of actual value. Much of the economic value of a degree, I believe, is employer bias.

Many employers still think college is valuable. However wrong they are, that still matters. Sadly, this is one reason many parents give for sending their kids off to college: even if the education is worthless, employers, especially big companies, demand one. Many of the executives or managers who do the actual hiring are older. They have outdated ideas of college as being something providing real education and skills.

Think of all the inefficiencies created in the economy when millions of families go through a worthless but highly expensive certification process.

As an employer, even if you think college has no value, you might count on colleges to perform a screening function. Getting into college and finishing college indicates some level of competence and ability to follow instructions. It may not impart any important skills, but it reflects basic competency.

Having a college degree can be valuable for landing your first job, no doubt. For a second job, though, your first job matters much more than your schooling. Every year, the screening functions and the irrational pro-college bias are fading. Big companies devise more accurate screening methods. Smaller businesses become more flexible, especially as the products of our sclerotic higher education system become hiring managers and business owners.

It's a bubble. Right now, much of a college degree's value comes from the perception that it has value—like condos in Las Vegas in 2006. As the societal bias fades, a college degree will come to be worth only as much as the value of the actual education—and that's not very high.

A Waste of Time and Money

How many college graduates today feel they acquired great skills or knowledge in college? Do you really think that today's college education is stellar?

What we know about college—how much drinking there is, how much cramming, dozing off, and corner-cutting by students, how tenure deflates the incentive to perform well—also indicates we shouldn't put too much stock in a degree.

Specifically, we shouldn't push everyone to get a degree. To put it more bluntly: not everyone is college material. The world is not Lake Wobegon, where all the kids are above average. By definition, half of American eighteen-year-olds are below average.

Above-average intelligence does not automatically make one college material. It sounds like a mean thing to say, but most of the population isn't well equipped mentally to attend college. If your attention span is short, your study habits incurably bad, or—to be blunt—your IQ is just a bit too low, college probably doesn't promise some great intellectual awakening. Frankly, it means years of struggling and frustration, or alternatively, a college education so simplified that it's nearly worthless.

This wastes everyone's time and money. Instead of banging his head against the wall or taking useless courses, the student could be making money and acquiring skills. Colleges waste money and time on the misguided idea that everyone should get a college education. The resources that go to remedial courses or to less fit students could be spent on making curricula more thorough. It certainly wastes the parents' money.

The opportunity cost to the student is the most damaging. During those years, the eighteen- to twenty-two-year-old kid who isn't college material could be acquiring marketable skills, learning how to handle himself in a workplace, and learning something about dealing with money. It's much easier to take a low-paying job when you're young, still living at home, and have few financial responsibilities. Once skills are acquired, earnings will rise, enabling kids to leave the nest, perhaps share an apartment with a roommate, and take on more responsibilities. Eventually they will acquire enough skills to be able to support a family of their own.

Crashproof Yourself: The Case Against Saving for College

Every responsible parent saves for college, right? It's the best thing you can buy your kids, right? Wrong. College might be a huge waste of your kids' time and your money. Maybe college will be right for your child—she'll study hard, learn a lot, and bolster her career. But many kids get sent off to college just because that's what parents and students think they're *supposed* to do. Don't insist on your kid going to college, and don't tie your hands financially. If you're going to save for your kids' post–high school adventures, do it in an open-ended account. Maybe your son will want to travel instead of going to college, or maybe your daughter will need some living expenses while she does an internship. If your cash is in a dedicated education savings account, you'll take a penalty for spending it on non-college activities. And given the sad state of American colleges, there's a good chance you'll want to do that.

Maybe he or she goes to work for a tailor, or gets a job at an auto body shop. If he or she works under skilled experts in these fields, pretty soon he'll be proficient. Many of these skilled manual jobs pay well. Suits and cars are expensive and valuable. People with money need their suits and cars to be in good shape.

A college degree won't help you in these fields. Comparative literature classes or women's studies won't make you a better plumber, general contractor, or electrician.

For some fields—for example, computer programming—you would need some classes, which you could find at a technical school or a community college. For many fields, the best training is an entry-level hands-on job. As I wrote in chapter 3, an apprenticeship could be incredibly valuable for an eighteen year-old kid taking a pass on college. But, of course, state and federal labor laws get in the way of apprenticeships.

Plenty of kids do enter the workforce like this straight out of college, but too many kids who would benefit from a real job instead pick college. They don't leave four years later with an executive-track job. They often graduate to a bad job market and go into a job they could have had right out of high school.

Next time you're at a supermarket checkout line, ask the cashier what her major was. She'll probably tell you. Perhaps it was English or history.

Given how intellectually barren college education has become, and how economically worthless a degree is, "higher education" often amounts to a four-year party. You get drunk on cheap beer, hang out with your friends, and skate on cheap financing and Daddy's money.

Costs—and Benefits

The problem is not simply that kids come out of college no better off than when they went in. The problem is that many come out worse off than if they had never enrolled.

First, students accumulate huge amounts of debt. The typical college graduate is sitting on $24,000 in student loans.[6] Because they had to go four years without a full-time job (some kids actually opt for a five-year plan), it's not uncommon for new graduates to have significant credit card debt, too. This debt can hobble someone's career prospects. Often, the best long-term career move is not the most lucrative move in the short term. An internship at the best firm might provide invaluable contacts and irreplaceable experience. It might also pay little or nothing. Someone facing huge debt payments won't have the luxury of taking the lower-paying job or internship that provides the best experience, training, and contacts. He'll have to take whatever job pays more. In the long run, this could mean lower pay and less enjoyable work.

Then there's the simple math of the matter: those who went to college enter the workforce four years (often five) behind their peers who didn't. The kid who didn't go to college could easily be the boss of his old high school classmate just emerging from the ivory tower.

When so much of the population goes to college, it also cheapens a college degree. In today's job market, a college degree likely confers less relative value than a high school degree did prior to World War II. Having graduated from college used to reflect something meaningful. A minority of people went to college, and the coursework was harder. If you hired a college graduate, you could have some confidence in his intelligence and work ethic. Back then; a bachelor's degree was a valuable asset for a job applicant.

These days, someone looking for a leg up in the job market might feel the need to get a master's or Ph.D. It's a fine analogy to compare our currency devaluation to grade inflation—it's the debasement of academic degrees. It makes everyone's degree worth less, and it makes it harder for employers to judge the competency of applicants.

With all the harm that results from expanding college enrollment, you have to ask: who's benefiting?

Sure, there's the rare diamond in the rough that never shined in high school, but goes to college and flourishes intellectually. But that's probably a rarity. Who is the real beneficiary from policies and cultural biases that push more and more eighteen-year-olds to go to college? The answer, of course, is the educational establishment itself.

Universities get more students, and thus more money. Administrators, specifically, are able to demand higher pay and nicer digs. Sometimes I think the biggest beneficiaries of our government and cultural obsession with college are the construction companies that build the new dorms and campus buildings. Look at any college campus today, and you're likely to see a building boom: cutting-edge student centers, shiny new gyms, state-of-the-art dorms.

For a long time, of course, the biggest beneficiary of our college mania has been the student lenders—the big banks that have made bank off of societal attitudes and governmental policies creating inelastic demand for college.

And thinking about those lenders helps point us to the root of this problem.

College Should Be Getting Cheaper

From 1978 through 2008, the dollar lost a bit more than a third of its value. That means the cost of living slightly more than tripled. The cost of college increased about tenfold. Put another way, college costs have increased three times faster than the cost of living. That's faster than health care, where cost increases spurred Congress and President Obama to rush to a big-government "reform."

At a time when the value of a degree is falling, how is college getting more expensive? It's certainly not worth more. More to the point, the cost of providing an education is falling, so why is the cost of a degree rising?

Think about what's involved in educating someone today compared to twenty years ago. Automation and computers should be making things cheaper. Being a college professor is less labor-intensive than it used to be. Professors don't need to put all their notes on note cards, copy everything by mimeograph, and meticulously file documents in file cabinets. Computers make this all much quicker and easier. A basic desktop costs about $500 and lasts a couple of years. E-mail, the Internet, and a wealth of other computer programs make many administrative positions less necessary.

Also, the costs of materials have gone down. Things like lightbulbs, chairs, and beds aren't as expensive. Books are cheaper to print, and colleges can increasingly use e-books, or at least use the Internet to access the required books to print off.

The very fact that so many more students are going to college should introduce economies of scale that drive down the per-pupil cost. Bigger population and higher enrollment rates create these economies of scale. The ease with which most people can travel facilitates students attending larger schools.

Finally, competitive pressures should be bringing down the cost of college. Colleges used to brag about their huge libraries—and some still do—because so many books at, say, Harvard's library, were hard to find. If your town library and neighborhood bookstore didn't carry Balzac's oeuvres completes, how were you supposed to get one of his more obscure works? Amazon and eBay have solved much of that problem, as has the growing digitization of great works that are out of print. So there goes that whole idea of colleges providing valuable aggregations of important scholarship.

Online education further lowers the barriers to an education. I'm not just talking about bare-bones "correspondence courses." These days, you can watch lectures online, and ask questions real time. Putting tests online is easy, too. These aren't community college 100-level courses.

In 2011, Stanford began offering engineering classes free online to everyone. The school's Web site describes the program called "Stanford Engineering Everywhere":

> A computer and an Internet connection are all you need. View lecture videos, access reading lists and other course handouts, take quizzes and tests, and communicate with other SEE students, all at your convenience.

SEE programming includes one of Stanford's most popular sequences: the three-course Introduction to Computer Science taken by the majority of Stanford's undergraduates and seven more advanced courses in artificial intelligence and electrical engineering.[7]

Yale has a similar program called "Yale Open University." MIT offers something called "Open Courseware." Observing these developments, liberal writer Matthew Yglesias made an acute observation: "one way or another, the current paradigm, where it's cheaper and easier than ever to learn something but harder and more expensive than ever to get a degree, isn't going to persist."

In other words, all factors suggest college prices can't stay high. But they do.

Why Does College Cost So Much?

Supply is up, cost is down, and quality is down, so what's driving the price up? The heart of the matter is bottomless demand. Parents and students are seemingly willing to pay any price for a college education.

Subsidized student loans are the main reason behind this bottomless demand. When anyone can borrow cheaply, then nobody is price-sensitive. If a college raises the price, that doesn't greatly diminish demand. In fact, higher prices can add an air of prestige to a university, thus actually boosting demand.

So, student loan subsidies, pitched as a way to make college more affordable, have the opposite effect.

Sputnik launched the federal student loan program. The Soviet satellite, sent into orbit in October 1957, left Congress afraid that schooling was better in the USSR than in the U.S.A. Eleven months after Sputnik, President Dwight Eisenhower signed the National Defense Education Act, aimed at getting more kids into college. The law created direct government loans to students at low interest rates, with ten-year repayment periods. These became Perkins Loans.

In 1964, Congress created a work-study program, whereby the federal government would reimburse schools for wages they pay students for on-campus jobs.

Then, as part of his "Great Society," Lyndon Johnson (LBJ) signed the Higher Education Act of 1965. This created direct federal grants and loan guarantees. Congress chose loan guarantees over direct loans largely for budgetary reasons. Guarantees were scored as less costly than direct loans, because Uncle Sam was only on the hook in the case of default.

After 1965, Congress started piling more and more subsidies onto private student loans. While students were in college and for the first six months, the taxpayers paid the interest to the banks. If the student defaulted, the taxpayers picked up the tab. If the student borrower went bankrupt, he still couldn't discharge his debt. Later, Congress fixed the interest rate, promising to pay the lender the difference between the students' rate and the market rate.

You can probably guess that a driving force behind all these subsidies was the banks, who got to earn a profit while off-loading the risk to taxpayers. This backfired in the end, though. Under President Obama and a Democratic Congress, the guarantees and protections that LBJ and President Clinton had heralded as student aid were deemed "unnecessary taxpayer-subsidies that go to financial intermediaries for student loans."

Obama, in a provision buried within his health-care bill, took the logical next step: he cut out the middleman, ended the subsidies to banks, and made the Department of Education the financier for all college educations.

Since taking over the student-loan industry, Obama, through executive order—without even asking Congress first—has increased the taxpayer subsidies for student debt. First, graduates will never be forced to pay more than 10 percent of their discretionary income in loan repayments. Discretionary income is how much your income exceeds 150 percent of the poverty level. For single individuals, that's about $16,000.

So, even if your loan terms dictate you would owe $200 a month (or $2,400 a year) if your disposable income is only $14,000 (that would be for a total income of $30,000), your maximum annual payment is $1,400 or $116.77 a month.

Obama accompanied this with a new rule forgiving any remaining balance on student loans after twenty years of payments. Combine these two rules, and all of a sudden, it doesn't matter how big your debt is because your repayment is determined by your income. So why not borrow even more? Why care what the tuition is?

Think about it. If students were willing to borrow so much money when they believed they would have to pay the money back, imagine how much more they will be willing to borrow when they know that much of the debt will be forgiven. As highly indebted students become an even larger voting constituency, political pressure for even greater loan forgiveness will intensify. In fact, it's not illogical for students to believe that all student loans will eventually be forgiven in a total bailout.

We are effectively creating a third-party payer system for college education, where the one paying most of the bill is not even involved in the negotiation (we'll explore how "well" the system is working in health care in the next chapter). Universities want high tuitions and students want degrees with as many bells and whistles as someone else's money can buy. As a result of this new moral hazard, universities will be free to raise tuitions faster now than ever before. All sorts of perks will be thrown into tuition packages. Who knows, perhaps colleges will even include free sports cars.

My guess is that before it gets that bad, complete nationalization will be proposed as the only viable solution to contain runaway costs. College education will then become a birthright, provided free of charge by taxpayers. That is when it really gets expensive. This is typical government action. Wreck an industry with subsidies and regulation; blame the ensuing failure on capitalism; then "solve" the problem with a complete government takeover.

From 1958 until today, then, Congress and the White House have steadily increased the subsidy for student loans. Over that period, tuition also rose, steadily at first, and then astronomically: again, increasing tenfold from 1978 until today.

This is no coincidence. When you subsidize something, you don't necessarily make it more affordable, you often make it more expensive, because you increase the price the buyer is able to pay. Parents and students may get some financial benefit from tuition subsidies, but the colleges (and previously the private lenders) likely get most of the subsidy.

In fact, if you look at college tuitions prior to guaranteed student loans, they were remarkably stable. For example, the annual tuition at Yale University from 1810 to 1852 was just $33. It did not rise at all for forty-two years! From 1874 to 1918, annual tuition rose by only 14 percent to end that forty-four-year period at $160. That is an average annual increase of less than one third of a percent per year.

For the 2011–2012 academic year, annual tuition at Yale was $40,500, up 55 percent in the last ten years! What is even more remarkable is that this staggering increase occurred despite the financial crisis of 2008 and the deepest recession since the Great Depression. Such factors should have forced prices down, or at least held increases in check. But the upward influence of government subsidies was so strong that it overpowered the downward pressure exerted by a collapsing economy.

To put these numbers into perspective, in terms of gold, tuition from 1810 to 1852 equated to 1.65 ounces (the price of gold was fixed at $20 per ounce until 1934 when Roosevelt devalued the dollar to one thirty-fifth of an ounce). Gold began the 2011 academic year at about $1,750 per ounce, putting Yale's tuition at twenty-three ounces of gold, or fourteen times its 1810–1852 price.

Another way to think about it would be to relate college tuition to wages. It was in 1914 that Henry Ford first started paying his factory workers five dollars a day. At that rate, a factory worker would have to devote thirty-two days' labor to send one kid to Yale for a year. Today the factory workers at Ford Motor Company earn about $250 dollars per day, which equates to 162 days of work for one year at Yale. However, today's Ford workers have to pay payroll and income taxes that did not exist in 1914. So if you reduce gross income by 25 percent (a conservative estimate) to get a modern day take-home equivalent of five dollars a day, Ford workers now must devote 216 days' labor to buy one year at Yale. That's seven times more work than was required in 1914.

Contrast that to other goods, such as the cost of making a telephone call from a pay phone. It cost a nickel to make a call from a pay phone in 1914. Today it costs fifty cents. That meant a Ford worker's daily wage equaled one hundred phone calls. Today's Ford worker can afford to make five hundred calls (after tax the number would be reduced to 375) with a day's wages. Of course, modern Ford workers don't need to pay the fifty cents, as they likely carry their own cell phones. But the point is that even as the free market has brought down the real price of a phone call to a fraction of what it once was, government has prevented the same forces from bringing down the price of a college education.

Costs of Borrowing

There are also economic costs to policies that drive more kids to borrow for college.

Most obviously, you end up with a bunch of twenty-two-year-olds deep in debt. This is not healthy for the economy. As we mentioned above, weighing kids down with debt as they enter the workforce limits risk-taking and opportunity. Also it directs much of their wages to simply paying down debt, rather than saving, investing, or spending—all of which are more stimulative.

And morally, it's hypocritical for Congress to push eighteen-year-olds to take on $20,000 or more in debt. Our federal government is always trying to say who shouldn't be borrowing, and which loans are "predatory," claiming that lenders are exploiting people who don't know better. Is there any clearer example of someone who doesn't understand debt than a high school senior who has never handled his own finances on a meaningful level?

For the federal government to push debt on people who don't understand what they're getting into is a clear example of bad policymaking.

I had a young lady on my radio show who graduated from Northwestern University with a sociology degree and $200,000 in debt. It's hard to believe someone could borrow so much money in so short a time period. Perhaps her year studying abroad helped. Clearly, she would have been better off living at home and going to a less expensive college, or simply skipping college altogether. In fact, if she had it to do all over again that is exactly what she claimed she would do. But at age seventeen, she simply followed the advice of her guidance counselor to get the most expensive education student loans could finance.

There are more negative distortions of student loan subsidies. When Congress was subsidizing private undergraduate loans, it was pushing banks to lend to students instead of other would-be borrowers. This takes capital away from more economically promising activities and directs it to more politically favored activities.

Direct government loans distort in a different way. The loans are backed by federal money. That means that every dollar loaned out is either taken from a taxpayer or borrowed by the government. In either case, money is taken from one sector of the economy and moved to another. Again, the money could have been invested in something judged to be more economically promising.

On net, this hurts business. Why should banks risk money lending to small businesses when they can lend, risk free, to students? Ironically, student-loan subsidies hurt job creators, thus making it harder for the indebted students to find jobs after they graduate.

The ease of student lending surely opens the door for more kids to go to college (for better or worse), but it also changes things for people who would have gone to college anyway. For one thing, it drives up tuition and the long-term cost of college. It also encourages more kids to borrow and fewer kids to work their way through college.

My father was from a lower-middle-class family, but he was able to pay for college himself, largely because he had a job. He worked full time waiting tables over the summer and graduated in four years, debt-free. Most of his friends did the same thing. Back then, it was very common for students to "work their way through college," either by working full time during the summers or part-time during the school year. It was only the rich kids who spent their summers lying on the beach.

You could say that students with jobs would have been better off had they been able to fully dedicate themselves to their studies (although the amount of alcohol consumed on college campuses suggests students have more than enough time on their hands). But it's certainly less harmful to work a job during college than to graduate with debt. Debt that's more easily acquired and pushed on the financially unsavvy leads more kids to borrow rather than work. I think it's far better for a student to spend four years working his way through college than to spend a lifetime working to pay off student loans.

What If We Didn't Have Subsidized Student Loans?

Whenever I speak to college audiences, I ask how many of the students have student loans. Most of the crowd raises their hands.

Then I ask a few of them what they would do if student loans weren't available. Most of these students say they simply couldn't afford college. Then I make a point:

Look, just about everyone in this room couldn't pay for college without loans. What do you think would happen if you could not get those loans? Would you just skip college? If so, this room would be practically empty right now. In fact, with so few customers, wouldn't this college simply shut down, fire everyone, sell the buildings?

Of course not. Just like any other business, universities would find ways to cut costs. Maybe they would pay teachers less and cut down on administrative staff. Schools might skip the fancy new gym (or, sorry, "athletic center"). As with any business that faced price pressures, colleges would try to find new efficiencies so that they could lower prices and be affordable and price-competitive. Plenty of kids went to college before student loans existed, and plenty of people will go after they are eliminated. The main difference: tuitions will be a lot lower, and those who do graduate will do so with little or no debt.

However, it is also true that without student loans, fewer kids would go to college. But that would be a good thing.

Don't Go to College

For many young people, college is a great blessing and a good investment. For a talented youth from an underprivileged background, college can be the gateway to success. For a budding engineer who takes his study seriously, college can be an invaluable first step on a promising career path. For the intellectually curious kid, college can be incredibly rewarding.

But for many Americans, enrolling in college is the biggest mistake of their lives. They take on tens of thousands of dollars in debt with no idea what it means or what they expect from college. Often they don't get a good education, and they delay the day when they start acquiring real skills in the workplace. Even if they do increase their earning potential, very likely, the benefit isn't worth the cost.

Once we lose the idea that all kids must go to college regardless of their aptitude, parents can focus their resources on those children most likely to benefit from a degree. This will substantially reduce the financial burden paying for college places on families. And because tuitions will be much lower absent loan guarantees, the burden will be that much lighter.

Some might view this as unfair. Some kids get to go to college, while others are left without degrees. However, I would argue it's a lot fairer not to waste a kid's time in college if the benefits are marginal or nonexistent. Some kids excel at sports, while others are gifted in the arts; is that fair? Would a parent of a tone-deaf child encourage him to pursue a career as an opera singer? How about encouraging a kid with two left feet to take up ballet? You get the point. Life is not fair. The key is to recognize your strengths and limitations and to pursue vocations accordingly.

Not all kids are equal, and parents are in the best position to evaluate their kids and help them make the best decision. For a kid with a high IQ, good grades, and high-test scores, college makes sense. However, not all kids excel academically, and for them college would be a waste of their time and their parents' money. It would be far better for parents to encourage a more appropriate career path. If later in life circumstances change, a better-prepared, more motivated individual can always go to college at a time when he is more likely to benefit from the experience. We have to come to grips with an uncomfortable fact: too many Americans go to college.

We have trouble accepting this fact because we see college as the key to opportunity. But that's a narrow view. College is the key to many sorts of opportunities, but certainly not all. Majoring in engineering will send you on a career path. If you want to be a college English professor, you need to first get an advanced English degree.

But not everyone in America is going to be a "knowledge worker." We need someone to repair broken plumbing. We need someone to tailor suits. Someone needs to mow the high school soccer field, and someone needs to do the landscaping homeowners want. All of these jobs involve skills, and all of them can be very rewarding personally and financially.

In fact, it's often easier for a skilled manual laborer to start a small business than it is for college grad with a desk job. Your Bachelor of Arts from Vassar might send you down a smooth road toward a decent-paying office job, but it probably won't help you pick up the skills needed to strike out on your own. If you get good at planting trees, building retaining walls, and designing gardens, on the other hand, you're pretty well equipped to launch your own business. Once you own something, that's when opportunities really open up.

A motivated gardener can become the owner of his own gardening company. He may eventually employ other gardeners to do all the dirty work, and may even employ some college graduates to perform accounting or similar functions. Such employees may have degrees, but will likely take home smaller paychecks than their bosses.

Some people will read this and say it's offensive. *Peter, why are you saying some kids are only good enough to mow lawns? That's elitist!* No, what's elitist is the mind-set that the only dignified work involves wearing a jacket and tie or sitting in an office. What's elitist is looking down on manual labor and even on small businessmen.

Cornelius Vanderbilt quit school at age eleven to work on his dad's ferry. At sixteen, he launched his own ferry business. A few decades later, he was a fabulously wealthy shipping magnate. Bill Gates dropped out of college. So did Facebook founder Mark Zuckerberg.

It's clear that in America, where hard work and ingenuity pay off, you don't need to go to college to be successful. We should stop pretending college is a necessary condition for business success.

Higher-Ed Solutions

Let's stop pushing all kids to go to college.

We start by abolishing all tuition subsidies. End the federal direct loan program. Scrap any remaining loan guarantee programs. End the federal subsidy for college work-study programs. None of these subsidies are available for learning a trade, and it's increasingly clear that our policies shouldn't favor college over work.

Much of the work to be done is on the cultural front. Teachers and counselors should stop broadcasting expectations that everyone should go to college. Counselors ought to be working to identify whom they think would actually benefit from college, and help those kids get into college. If high schools want to help the rest of their graduates, they could connect them with local businessmen.

Parents need to come to grips with the fact that not every kid is above average, and even for the above-average kids, college may not be the right choice. In middle-class and upper-class America today, there's a level of shame if your kid isn't going to college. That needs to end.

Many of these destructive cultural prejudices are driven by politicians' pronouncements and the clear implications of their policies. But these biases will begin to crumble once the bubble bursts. As college costs keep going up and a degree looks like a bad deal, savvy parents and students will start skipping it. As those kids turn out to be successful, the illusion will be punctured. The bubble will pop.

Back on the policy front, we need to make sure that high school graduates can work. This involves scrapping minimum-wage laws—at least for those under twenty-five. In other words, we should legalize apprenticeships again. This is where it will be particularly helpful to scrap all those federal policies encouraging lavish benefits: an eighteen-year-old kid can use his parents' health care.

To make our economy friendlier to high school graduates, we need more domestic manufacturing. Back in the first part of the book, we talked about our trade deficit and the dearth of manufacturing in the United States. Protectionism is not the answer, but reducing the "hiring penalty" is—get rid of the regulations, taxes, and mandates that add to the cost of hiring. Most important, though, is to fix our monetary policy so that we're not constantly cheapening the dollar. Sound money will bring back manufacturing jobs.

I know this sounds backward to many people—saying that we should have fewer people in college and more in factories. But the push to get everyone going to college and working in "knowledge jobs" was never grounded in reality.

Even today, my advice for most eighteen-years-olds would be to give college a pass. Instead of going to college, why not just go directly into the job market? They could look for the same entry level jobs most college grads would be applying for. However, since they have no student loans to pay off and likely still live with their parents, they could offer their services for a fraction of the price that a college grad would require.

They could even offer their services free for a while. After all, working for free is better than paying to work, which is effectively what college students do. My guess is that during these hard economic times, businesses are more interested in reducing labor costs than in hiring college grads. Some businesses might even lay off newly hired twenty-two-year-old college grads if they can replace them with eighteen-year-olds willing to work for a lot less money. With four or five years of real work experience under their belts, high school grads would be positioned to earn more money than college grads with none. Even if high school grads still earned less, they would likely take home more cash, as none of their paychecks would go toward paying off student loans. In today's job market, being able to work cheap gives one a real advantage. Recent college grads living on their own, making rent and loan payments, are in no position to compete with eighteen-year-olds living at home willing to work for beer and gas money.

Higher Ed 2.0: Are You Smarter Than a College Borrower?

In July 2013, the interest rate on a particular type of federally subsidized student loan doubled, from 3.4 to 6.8 percent. It caused a tempest in a teapot on Capitol Hill, and it spawned a great deal of lazy political journalism and demagoguery by officeholders in both parties. Hardly anyone pointed out that this ridiculous "controversy" meant a difference of a mere $7 per month in the payments of the average student borrower with that kind of loan.

Yes, just seven bucks. That's not a typo.

But that same month, a far more meaningful number was released. That was when annual college borrowing finally topped $100 billion, and total outstanding student loan debt topped the $1 trillion mark. In other words, on top of the $18 trillion that the younger generation is saddled with—a mess they might still be cleaning up years after we're dead—they're also saddled with an extra trillion dollars in personal debt that can't even be discharged if they declare bankruptcy.

The Wall Street Journal reported a few even more depressing numbers the following month, in August 2013. Of the 28 million student loan borrowers, only 10 million were current payers. Setting aside the 7.9 million still in school, another 10 million were either in default, deferment, or some form of forbearance.

At the very least, we can conclude that the brightest college grads today, who are lucky enough to find satisfying jobs commensurate with their intelligence and their student loan bills, are being cut off at the knees. They have enough debt that they can't afford to invest or save for retirement—and at the very moment in their lives when their early contributions have the most time to grow and serve them best in their old age. And let's be brutally honest, here: It's not exactly like the Class of 2014 can count on a robust and well-funded Social Security system.

But what about the college grads who can't find good jobs—or can't find jobs at all? It's true that the unemployment rate for college grads is lower, but that's no consolation for graduates who are entering the workforce today at the margin. BLS reported over the summer that between March and July 2013, Americans over age twenty-five with college degrees lost 90,000 jobs on net. Meanwhile, high school graduates without college degrees gained 600,000 jobs.

For all that debt, what are young Americans getting? Wells Fargo (which services a lot of student loans) conducted a survey of more than 1,400 college graduates between the ages of twenty-two and thirty-four, and found that one-third wished they'd just gone to work after high school instead of going to college. As I noted above, I think they're on to something.

Rolling Stone's doctrinaire liberal journalist Matt Taibbi was so shocked by what he found when reporting on student loan debt that he upbraided conservative politicians for departing from their principles on this issue and allowing easy government-subsidized borrowing for college:

> [C]onservatives most of all should hate the current system for any number of reasons—for being a massive hidden tax, for being a market-defying subsidy artificially keeping ineffective and poor-performing institutions in business, and for being an example of arbitrary government power seizing not just money borrowed plus interest, but billions in additional fees and penalties from ordinary people.

Former Obama White House budget director Peter Orszag also raised questions with a June 2013 *Bloomberg News* column suggesting that college might be a bad deal. Orszag pointed to new research showing that the ranks of low-skill professions—taxi drivers, chauffeurs, bartenders, and firefighters—are now swelling with much larger numbers of college graduates than in years past. In fact, back in October 2012, while in New Orleans participating in an investment conference, I decided to conduct an experiment of my own. Microphone in hand and cameraman in tow, I walked Bourbon street in search of bartenders, bouncers, cabdrivers, strippers, and anyone else working that night to ask them four questions:

1. Did you go to college?
2. When did you graduate?
3. What was your major?
4. How much do you owe?

The resulting footage was posted on YouTube and should be required viewing for anyone considering borrowing money to attend college. (You can watch this highly entertaining video, "Is a College Degree Worth the Cost, You Decide," either by going to my YouTube channel, "The Schiff Report," or by searching for the title on YouTube.)

The reason that so many college grads now work in occupations that do not even require high school diplomas is actually simple: The "cognitive" high-end jobs that college graduates seek were not materializing in

the U.S. economy of 2013. There was far less demand for the skills that a
college credential supposedly signifies. Given that the reason most kids
attend college—and the reason most parents want them to—is to find a
good job afterward, this should give everyone a reason to think.

Orszag cited the work of two Canadian researchers—Paul Beaudry
and David Green—who found that the demand for cognitive skill in the
labor market peaked around 2000. Since then, they argued, "the demand
for cognitive tasks that are often associated with high educational skill
underwent a reversal, and that this reversal can help in understanding
poor labor market outcomes after 2000 more generally."

Why are cognitive jobs disappearing? There are many possible explanations. In many cases, such jobs can be offshored or automated. And with
the extra burdens that government has been imposing, it is already providing companies with extra incentives to automate or offshore wherever re-
motely feasible. Computers and foreign workers don't require health
coverage (see the next chapter on ObamaCare) or payroll tax contributions. They can't sue you for wrongful termination or sexual harassment.

Why hire an employee to transcribe your conversations from tape—
with all the red tape and expense that entails—when you can go online,
find a firm in India, and pay a low flat rate for the same job? Or better still,
how about buying software (a one-time purchase) that can transcribe your
voice automatically?

Orszag's essay concluded that "college may still be worthwhile—if not
to be sure of qualifying for skilled jobs, then at least to avoid the even
worse prospects of those who don't get a degree." But he fails to account
for the other side of the ledger—the enormous costs paid by those who go
through college, only to end up in jobs that really don't require a college
degree in the first place. There's nothing dishonorable about tending
bar—you can actually make some good money that way, and a lot of experienced bartenders end up starting or buying a stake in bars of their
own. Nor is it degrading to drive a taxi. In fact, a driver who saves up
enough to buy his own cab can make pretty good money. And if the choice
is between spending tens of thousands on college or spending it on a taxi
cab, the latter might be a much better deal, depending on what city you
plan to drive it in.

Who knows? You might eventually buy more cabs and rent them to
other drivers. You might set up a dispatch service and charge other cabbies

for the privilege of using it. And once you've made your fortune, if you want to go back and study the ethics of Aristotle or fourteenth-century French literature—well, why not do it then?

In the meantime record numbers of college graduates are moving back in with their parents. After years of borrowing money to live in college dorms, fancy off-campus housing, or apartments, grads with worthless liberal arts degrees, mountains of debt, and few good job prospects, are returning to their high school rooms in droves.

According to a 2012 Pew Center Research analysis of census data, 36 percent of young adults aged eighteen to thirty-one lived with their parents. This is the highest percentage in over four decades, and 4 percentage points higher than it was prior to the beginning of the great recession in 2007. Among those aged 18–24 years the picture is even bleaker, with 56 percent now living with their parents compared with just 16 percent in 2007.

Clearly many high school grads would be better off skipping college, living rent-free at home for a few years while they develop skills working low-wage jobs. As their skills increase, so too will their earnings, the majority of which can be saved. Then, instead of returning to the nest in their early twenties with mountains of debt and no marketable skills, they could venture into the world to build their own nests, with real work-related experience and wads of cash under their wings.

Fix K-12 Education, Too

Getting the federal government out of higher education is not hard to imagine, considering this was the norm before 1960. It's a harder climb, however, to argue that we need to get government out of K-12 education.

Public education is widely considered to be the bedrock of our country. But there's nothing in the Constitution requiring states to provide education. In fact, the word "education" does not appear anywhere in the Constitution or the Declaration of Independence. It's not as if there were no schools back then. If the Founding Fathers had wanted government to be involved in education, they would have provided for it. One could hardly attribute the omission to an oversight. On the contrary, education was intentionally left out because the Founding Fathers did not want the federal government to be involved in it at all.

Just because something is necessary doesn't mean that government should provide it. In fact, education is far *too* important to be left to government.

Our public schools are broken. There are countless studies that show how little our children are learning in public schools. The U.S. Department of Education uses the National Assessment of Education Progress to judge how well kids are learning what they're supposed to learn. Across the various disciplines, the scores are depressing.

In the latest study of long-term trends, reading and math scores were up from 1973, but if you use 1992 as the baseline, scores tend to be flat for thirteen-year-olds and seventeen-year-olds, and up a bit for nine-year-olds.[8]

Less than 40 percent of students scored at or above "proficient" in mathematics in a 2009 NAEP report.[9] In reading, it's a similar situation, and average scores are not increasing for older students.[10] Only about one quarter of U.S. students are proficient in geography.[11]

Many inner-city public schools are a national embarrassment. If teachers and administrators can prevent bloodshed, they've done their job. Kids are graduated not because they've demonstrated knowledge or skills, but because no high school wants twenty-year-olds roaming the hallways.

So, what's the problem?

Accountability

Public schools are the institutions most insulated from competitive pressures. That means there are few rewards for success and few punishments for failure. This lack of accountability persists at all levels.

Bad teachers don't lose their jobs, and good teachers don't get raises and promotions. This isn't a coincidence; this is deliberate policy. Teachers unions demand, and school districts embrace, compensation rules that allow only two factors in determining pay: length of time served and what degrees the teacher has. An awful teacher with a masters and twenty years under his or her belt will be paid multiples of an excellent teacher four years out of college.

The National Education Association has officially resolved that "performance pay schedules, such as merit pay . . . are inappropriate." What do you think happens when teachers know that their performance can't get them either gains or losses? Yes, the most motivated teachers might continue to strive for improvement. Many others will lose the fire in their heart and start coasting. Those desiring a truly competitive atmosphere where achievement is rewarded will leave teaching.

(A quick side note: government employees shouldn't be allowed to unionize. Teachers unions are particularly unacceptable because they are actively working against students.)

It's a common refrain that teachers are underpaid. I agree that many teachers are underpaid: the smart and hardworking ones. And again, those are the ones who usually exit the profession. If you have a workplace openly antagonistic to meritocracy, you will (a) attract the unmotivated, (b) drive out the motivated, and (c) suck the motivation out of those who remain.

Wealthy families have a way around this problem: they pay for private schools that don't have these absurd rules. Middle-class families who want a better education for their kids, however, are forced to pay for school twice. They pay private school tuition, and they finance public schools through their property taxes.

As a result, most middle-class families' children remain in public schools, though they generally strive to live in public school districts known for better schools. Ironically, it's the children of the poor who are the most damaged by public education, as their parents can neither afford to pay twice for private schools nor can they move into more expensive neighborhoods with better public schools.

In other words, inner-city public schools skate by with little or no pressure to improve. The worse they do, the more money they get. It's a machine made to work poorly. However, there is at least some competitive pressure in schools in more affluent communities, as good schools attract families, increase property values, and grow a tax base. And if the schools are bad enough, parents are better able to bite the bullet and pay double for private alternatives.

What If We Ended Government Schools?

Imagine if we didn't have any public schools. Would parents just let their kids go uneducated? Would we all walk around unable to read, write, or do arithmetic?

No. There is always demand for education. If government wasn't providing "free" education, parents would pay for it, using the huge tax savings from not having to pay for bloated public schools. Poor people wouldn't be left out. In the United States, poor people aren't starving. Almost all poor people have housing. The market has solutions, and private charity helps, too.

But government doesn't set up public schools as a way to help those whose parents can't afford private schools. If that were the case, public schools would be means-tested, like welfare benefits. Government creates public schools because politicians don't trust parents to provide for their own children's educations.

This is demeaning and silly. Who cares more about a kid's education than her parents? Sure, not all parents are perfect, but do you really trust government more?

Absent government schools, then, we wouldn't lack a school system. We would just have a very different school system. Most notably, we would have a school system where competition was a central feature. Schools would need students in order to stay open. To attract better students, they would have to attract better teachers. Schools would find new efficiencies and new methods.

We don't know what schools would look like in a competitive K-12 economy, because the ultimate shape of schools would be determined not by some grand plan, but by the clash and testing of a million different plans.

In other words, if government wasn't setting most of the rules in education, we could have a flourishing of educational entrepreneurship. Think about it: you get the best and brightest business minds going into finance, industry, health care, engineering, and marketing. Why not education?

Risk takers and creative thinkers have revolutionized transportation, computing, communications, and most other industries. But in education, we're still using the methods developed by John Dewey over a century ago.

Some schools would simply become more efficient at the current model. Administrative budgets might be cut. Schools probably wouldn't place such a big premium on credentialing. They would cut extraneous costs like any other business, and focus on the things that matter most to parents. Parents could then use the money saved to pay for the greatly reduced college tuitions that would result from the absence of government subsidies.

But many schools would try something completely different. Maybe someone would launch a school where kids spend most of the day outdoors. Other schools would spring up that only meet three days a week. We might see more boarding schools. Online education could work for high school kids, especially if some entrepreneur figured out the right way to do it.

In some schools, teachers might become superfluous for particularly motivated students. On the flip side, maybe someone would start offering $150,000 salaries for the smartest, hardest working, most able teachers.

There wouldn't be just one model. Different types of schools would appeal to different parental tastes, ideology, or geography. Many schools would tailor their curriculum to students with particular strengths or weaknesses. Maybe you create a school for boys with attention deficit disorder. Maybe you create a school for particularly science-inclined kids, or musical kids.

Many different models will work, and many will not. Some will work spectacularly for a narrow niche. Someone might invent a great school that works for all sorts of kids. He or she will open a second school. Soon, he or she will open franchises across the country. (If you don't like the sound of "chain schools" ask yourself what public schools are.) Such an education entrepreneur may become a K-12 billionaire—a Bill Gates of schools, who grows filthy rich because he invented a better way to help kids learn.

Some of this innovation is already going on. We have Montessori schools, creative private and charter schools, and "schools" that are essentially hubs for homeschoolers. But if we cleared public education out of the picture, we'd have a much more robust market for educational innovation, because more money—all the money Americans spend on education—would be at stake, rather than simply the sliver that is spent today outside of public schools.

A Compromise: Vouchers

Ending public schools is probably too radical for most people. The best alternative is to end public schools' near educational monopoly. Let's end their ability to suck up so much money and force them to compete with private schools for taxpayer dollars.

Here's my plan: If a school district spends $10,000 per pupil, choose some portion of that—say 50 percent or 75 percent—and allow parents who withdraw their kids from public schools to claim a (taxpayer-funded) voucher for that much money. It would be a win-win. Taxpayers would save money, because they now pay only half or three-fourths of what they were previously paying for that student's education. And the parent and student win because they now have educational choice. The public school has the same amount of money per pupil as it had before.

A huge voucher program available to all parents would create a massive pool of money seeking a good education. This would spur much of the competition and innovation I described above. It would also pressure public schools to improve.

To spur even more price competition among private schools, let parents use any leftover voucher money to fund special savings accounts for their kids. Money in such accounts could be used to supplement future vouchers, to pay for college—or simply be made available to kids after they graduate or reach some predetermined age, such as twenty-one. In the meantime the money could earn interest, or even be invested by the parents for the benefit of their kids. This money could be used to start a business, or maybe just begin adult life with some cash in the bank instead of accumulating credit card debt. This concept would really put pressure on schools to deliver the best education at the lowest cost. As costs came down, so too could the amount of the vouchers, producing even more savings for taxpayers, including of course those taxpayers who received the vouchers.

Public schools would be forced to dramatically improve quality and lower costs to force down the value of those vouchers. Otherwise they would simply lose all their "customers" to private sector alternatives that offer kids not only better educations, but also fat bank accounts once they graduate.

Education Reform

The similarities between health care and education are striking. In these two fields government hasn't allowed markets to work, and prices have skyrocketed as a result. Government involvement and rising prices are not mere coincidence, but the predictable consequence of basic economic laws.

In the 1990s, Congress passed welfare reform. States measured their success by counting how many people the state removed from the welfare rolls. Maybe we should measure education reform by the number of students removed from public schools and graduating debt-free from colleges and universities.

Waste of scarce resources in the name of education makes our entire nation poorer. The insistence that every kid go through college regardless of aptitude, cost, or benefit is helping to bankrupt our nation. More strategic education spending will produce a more effective workforce, made even more productive by the additional capital investment that less education spending will make possible. The result will be a substantial rise in America's standard of living.

Health Care: Repealing ObamaCare Is Just the Beginning

"HEALTH CARE IS DIFFERENT."

When Americans discuss health care, one fallback line is that health care is not like any other part of the economy. Of course it is different—every industry is different from every other industry.

But "health care is different" is meant to convey something more. Often, politicians and journalists say it in order to justify government interference. *We can't just leave this up to the market, because the market doesn't work here. Health care is too different.*

Or people say "health care is different" as a way of explaining away all the problems regarding health care in our economy. It's easier than trying to root out the causes.

But no, health care isn't that different. The laws of supply and demand still apply. If health care seems to operate outside the normal laws of economics, it's because our government treats it so differently.

But *health care is different*, politicians often say, because "health care is a right." It's hard to know exactly what that means, but we can begin refuting it by pointing to the Constitution and the Bill of Rights. Speech, property, freedom of worship, and gun ownership are all protected in the Bill of Rights. Health care is not.

When they wrote the Constitution, we had doctors. We had people getting sick. It's not as if health care was omitted from the Constitution because it didn't exist. It was very different, but it existed.

The Constitution's silence on health care suggests we shouldn't treat it as a "right." It also means that the federal government has no legal authority over health care.

Health care is different, they sometimes respond, *because a free market doesn't work in health care.* And so we need the federal government involved.

What did we do before a federal role in health care? Before Medicare, was the United States similar to that Monty Python skit, with dead bodies piling up? ("Bring out your dead!") Were people dying left and right?

No, we were getting healthier. From 1850 until 1960, life expectancy at birth increased dramatically—rising by more than 80 percent. The polio vaccine and penicillin made us all much healthier. So, even before Washington got into health care, people survived, and were getting healthier.

So, again, we return to the question: Why should health care be treated differently? It's not because it's so important. Other things are more important than health care, like food and housing. Government doesn't dictate how everyone gets those things.

Many liberals object that if it were left up to the market, only the rich would get health care. But that's not true. Emergency care and basic care have long been provided as a charity to the poor. Would the rich get *better* health care in a freer market? Yes. But the rich get better versions of lots of things.

They drive fancier cars, eat better food, live in more luxurious homes, and wear nicer clothes. That's why we all want to be rich. But that does not mean the poor or middle class go without all these things. In fact, under free markets, the poor fare far better than they do under centrally planned economies theoretically designed to create equality.

Since we don't feel the need to make sure that nobody has a nicer car than anyone else, why do we feel differently about health care? Inequality in health care is no more a crime than inequality in transportation, shelter, food, or clothing.

As far as helping the poor—look around the world and you'll notice that the freer an economy is, the richer it is. The richer a country is, in general, the better health care the poor have. The poor in the United States get better health care than most people in the world—and this was true before Medicaid.

The rich here can also get much better health care. There are clinics where you shell out a big wad of cash, and they give you an incredibly thorough checkup with more tests than you can imagine. If Bill Gates lost his arm, he could probably get a bionic arm for $10 million. Should everyone be entitled to these things just because the very rich can get them?

These are extreme examples, but it is almost what we have today: more people getting more health care with no sensitivity to price. Everyone wants everything. Nobody wants to pay for it. These desires are understandable, but the more our government tries to bring this about, the worse the health-care system gets.

We need to fix our health-care system. Barack Obama understood that, but his plan takes us in the wrong direction.

Health-Care Costs

Health-care costs are exploding as a portion of our economy and our national debt. In 1960, health-care spending accounted for 5.2 percent of our Gross Domestic Product (GDP). By 2007, that number had more than tripled to 17.4 percent, and it is rising every year.

In September 2010, six months after President Obama signed his health-care bill, the Washington insider magazine *National Journal* (NatJo) hosted a conference, sponsored by drugmaker Eli Lilly, titled "Prescription for Growth." The central question of the conference, according to an e-mail NatJo sent out, was "will the new law accelerate growth in health-related jobs and industries, and are the right jobs being created?"

It's as if creating jobs in health care is a good thing.

But it's not good. Is it good if we spend more on alcoholism treatment than ever before? How about some kind of plague, would that be a good thing? Was it a good thing that we spent so much money fighting AIDS? Sure, if people got really sick we would create all sorts of jobs in caring for the ill. But wouldn't we be better off if no one got sick?

All else being equal, health-care spending is a bad thing. In an ideal world, we would not need any health care at all. Think about it, what would you want your personal health-care budget to be? Ideally zero, just like your car-repair budget. We all want to be healthy, we just want to spend as little as possible to be that way. So progress in health care should be measured by how little, not how much, a society is forced to spend on it. But our health-care spending keeps climbing.

Why?

Don't Blame Technology

Hospitals have all sorts of equipment, and laboratories can perform all sorts of tests that weren't possible in the past. Many commentators assert that we pay more because we have much more technology.

This is not completely wrong. For instance, MRIs (magnetic resonance imaging) weren't available before. These are expensive machines, far more expensive to build and use than X-ray machines. So, people today pay for MRIs, while nobody in 1970 paid for MRIs. The same is true with other expensive technologies and surgeries.

So as we've gotten more technology, health care has gotten more expensive. The correlation seems to make sense.

But it shouldn't work that way. In other sectors of the economy, technology brings costs down. Usually technology means getting more bang for your buck.

Today, cars have many more options and features than they used to—surround sound, antilock brakes, computers that manage all the car's systems, and side air bags—but they are more affordable than they used to be. In 2010, it took 23.6 weeks of the average family's salary to buy the average new car. That's 30 percent less than it cost in 1997. And that's only for new cars. The used-car market is constantly growing because cars are built to last longer.

Computers, cameras, cell phones—all of these are much more advanced than they used to be. As we discussed in chapter 5, your phone today can do infinitely more than a mobile phone could do twenty years ago, and it costs a fraction of the price.

To some extent, this could happen in health care.

As new drugs are invented, pills could accomplish what used to take an operation or other hospital treatments. This does happen, but it could happen more with the right reforms.

More tests and more precise tests should reduce the guess-and-check treatments that doctors often have to do. Better testing should reduce the need for invasive surgeries.

Surgery technology has improved, and surgeries are more precise and less invasive. Combine this with more precise diagnosis, and you get lower recovery times and less need for post-op treatment. This reduces costs.

And computers and the Internet can exert a huge downward influence on health-care costs. Computers should mean less time filling out forms, which means less staff. Health-care information should also flow more freely. On a macro level, more information can provide us with better data on what works and what doesn't. On an individual level, more information should mean fewer errors. In similar ways, computers have created new efficiencies in other industries.

In fact, we *do* see costs coming down in some rare corners of medicine. LASIK eye surgeries get cheaper every year. The reason, again, is technology and simple maturity of the industry—businesses come up with more efficient models. The difference: insurance doesn't cover LASIK, so customers are aware of the price. John Goodman of the National Center for Policy Analysis, told John Stossel in 2009 "the price of LASIK surgery, on average, has gone down by 30 percent."

The same dynamics can be seen in cosmetic surgery, which like other forms of surgery involves doctors, nurses, radiologists, complications, and malpractice lawsuits. Even so, liposuction cost slightly less on average in 2011 ($2,884)[1] than it did in 1995 ($2,000)[2] if you adjust for inflation. Compare that to other health-care prices.

The difference: cosmetic surgery lacks a third-party payer, as insurance does not cover elective procedures. This means that doctors are forced to compete for patients on price as well as quality. As a result, while the cost of non-cosmetic procedures has far outpaced the general rise in consumer prices, the real cost of most cosmetic procedures is flat. At the same time the quality has improved, recovery times are shorter, and far more people are having the procedures.

What was once strictly a perk reserved for the rich, cosmetic surgery is now routinely performed on middle-class patients. This is precisely how capitalism works. However, if cosmetic surgery were paid for through employer-provided insurance, prices would instead be spiraling out of control. No doubt rising prices would then be attributed to improved quality and a rising demand for the procedures.

The irony is that the goal of government policy is to get more Americans insured. However, the evidence is clear. The more we encourage Americans to pay for their health care with insurance, the more expensive health care will be.

Why Did Government Show Up?

If government hasn't proven able to make health care cheaper or better, why is government so involved? What brought government into the sector?

Were the poor all getting sick and dying? Not really. Not here at least. In poor countries, and in the poorest parts of the United States, there is and has been a shortage of available health care. But in most of the United States, including the cities, health-care services have long been available for the poor.

Often, doctors simply took care of the indigent, as a matter of charity. It was expected of them. This happens less today, in part, because Medicaid now pays for poor patients. Why treat patients without charge if you can get paid for it? (Lawsuits also make it increasingly unwise for doctors to provide free care.)

Government has increasingly inserted itself into the sector for the same reasons it often does: cheap politics.

Politicians are very aware of the point I was making above: people don't like paying medical bills any more than they like paying auto repair bills. Other spending—buying food, investing, buying clothes, or even paying for school—provide real benefits for the money you spend, as you end up having something you didn't have before. We all want a shiny new car and are happy to pay to purchase one. However, once we buy it, we do not want it to break down. Health-care spending is mostly about maintenance. You don't walk out with anything new.

It's a real drag to spend money fixing something that you expected to work fine on its own. This makes it popular for politicians to offer to cover some people's health-care bills.

Government also had more legitimate reasons to get involved. For instance, some people were being devastated by the costs of treating cancer. Helping those randomly and undeservedly hit with financial devastation seems to many people like a fine role for government to play.

Another important factor drawing government so deeply into health care has been the difficulty in putting a value on health care. When you're dealing with your life and your health, it's tempting to think that no cost is too high. This idea spurred many politicians to think that markets couldn't work in health care.

Whatever the cause of government's entry into this sector, we know that the consequences have been disastrous.

The Third-Party-Payer Problem

Government's negative impact on health care can be summed up in the phrase "third-party payer."

Increasingly, people don't pay for each marginal unit of health care they consume. If you go to the doctor or don't go to the doctor, it doesn't make much of an impact on your pocketbook. Your insurer or the government picks up most of the tab.

The average person has little price-sensitivity when it comes to health care. On an aggregate level this means people consume more health care than they normally would. More health-care consumption means increased demand for health care. Increased demand for health care means increased prices for health care. Multiply higher prices by higher use, and you've got the explanation for the growing share of our economy that goes to health care.

Medicare is the most obvious example of a third-party payer reducing price-sensitivity in health care. The stereotypical story is a comatose woman with one month to live getting a costly hip transplant. In a market economy for health care, this wouldn't happen. But the family sees no cost in doing this because Medicare covers it.

Even short of that sort of absurdity, you can count on plenty of Medicare recipients receiving medical care because it's costless to the patient and lucrative to the provider. It's basically a conspiracy to steal from taxpayers.

Medicare is obvious. But the third-party problem extends to private insurance. Or, maybe I should say "insurance," with quotation marks.

Think about the concept of insurance. What is it? What do we use it for?

There are certain things that we know happen to people, but we consider them unlikely to happen to a particular person in a given time frame, or maybe at all. If these things do happen, they are very expensive.

Maybe this costly event happens to only one in every 1,000 people. You could imagine 1,000 people getting together and pooling their money. If one guy gets unlucky, the insurance pool covers his cost.

So what sort of things do you insure against?

You don't insure against risks that are predictable and expected. Nobody buys insurance to cover the rent on their apartments. Your auto insurance doesn't cover oil changes. You don't buy insurance for something you know you'll have to pay. When the probability of an event is near 100 percent, insuring against it makes no sense. The insurer knows it will have to pay, and so premiums will always cost more than the expense.

Auto insurance also doesn't cover flat tires, just as homeowner insurance doesn't cover unclogging a bathtub drain. These are unexpected, but they aren't that expensive, and they're not extremely unlikely.

Instead, your car insurance covers a big accident, and your home insurance covers your house burning down. Shouldn't health insurance be the same?

It makes little sense to insure against small sprains, colds, or even against routine procedures like tonsillectomies or childbirth. Everyone knows these sorts of things happen. People who can afford insurance can afford to pay for these events out of savings.

Health insurance, in a sensible world, would cover the equivalent of your house burning down or your car getting badly wrecked. It would cover your getting hit by a bus or getting a brain tumor. If health insurance functioned normally, it would cover only unlikely and large health-care costs.

But the standard health "insurance" plan today is really a prepaid health-care plan. It's *like* insurance because you pay monthly "premiums," but it's unlike insurance because it covers standard expenses like checkups.

Americans are so unaccustomed to paying out of pocket for health care that they actually complain about $25 co-pays for doctor visits that probably cost $400. Politicians feed this odd sense of injustice by demagoguing about the very existence of co-pays. Obama's health-care bill actually outlawed co-pays in many cases.

Once people become accustomed to not paying medical bills, or to paying only a small fraction of their true cost, it becomes hard to convince them that they should pay for medical visits. Health care begins to feel like an entitlement.

Where did this idea come from, that the proper health-care market involves huge monthly premiums and no cost for the marginal visit? It came from government.

The Tax Deduction

Imagine you worked for me. Every dollar I pay you in salary counts toward your taxable income. If I were to go further and pay for your auto insurance, guess what? That would be taxable, too. If I were to cut a monthly check to your landlord to cover your rent, you would pay taxes on that money, just as if I had cut that check directly to you.

But if I pay part of your health insurance, that's not taxed. There's no good reason for this, it's a historical quirk of Franklin Roosevelt's World War II–era wage and price controls. Further, the portion of your health-insurance premiums that come out of your paycheck counts as a tax deduction and reduces your taxable income. You don't get to deduct auto insurance premiums from your taxes, but health insurance is deductible. This is also why auto insurance premiums, or other forms of property or life insurance, do not rise nearly as fast. We pay for these policies on our own, with after-tax dollars. However, if all forms of insurance were provided tax free from employers, we would have not just a health insurance crisis, but an overall insurance crisis.

The result of this special tax treatment for health insurance: you and I both get an advantage if, instead of giving you more money and letting you cover your own health care, I pay you in the form of health care.

This gives rise to huge distortions. In a normal health-insurance market, you would shop for the plan that leads to the lowest overall expected cost, taking into account premiums and your likely out-of-pocket costs. In short, you would pick as low a premium as possible with as high a deductible as you could afford.

But premium subsidies distort things. If you get your health insurance through your employer, your share of health insurance premiums is tax deductible—while out-of-pocket health-care expenses are not deductible. The tax provisions encouraging employers to provide health care also make it more likely that your employer will subsidize your premiums, but he won't pay your doctor bills. And there's a subconscious effect, too: premiums come out of payroll deductions, and they feel less costly than cutting a check to your doctor.

So your incentives get tilted, and you end up buying more coverage, at higher premiums than you would without the distortions in the tax code.

As a result, people end up being overinsured. With more thorough insurance, you're less price-sensitive. Enter the third-party-payer problem. Nearly three fourths of insured Americans are on Medicare, Medicaid, or an employer-sponsored plan. This means that almost nobody is really paying for his own health care.

If you're not paying for your health care, why not get more and get the most expensive kind? If your doctor orders a test, why not get it? An ultrasound for your baby just to find out if it's a boy or a girl? Why not? It's not like you're paying for it.

To consider how bad the third-party-payer problem is in health care, think about this: when was the last time you saw prices displayed at a doctor's office? Go into a barbershop, and the prices for different services are on the wall. They might even advertise prices on the street. But throughout your entire doctor or hospital visit, you might never see a price.

Recently I was in the hospital for some tests. Almost as a joke, I asked the people caring for me how much some of these particular tests cost. Nobody could tell me. They thought it was a very odd question. When I persisted, the only answer I got was "Why do you care? You're not paying. Your insurer is."

I wish I could do that with my clients. *Why do you care what fees I'm charging you? Someone else is picking up the tab!*

Again, the effect of this is obvious: less price-sensitivity means higher demand and higher prices.

Imagine if government gave the same tax treatment and subsidies to grocery shopping as to health insurance. Your boss would reduce your salary, but buy you an all-you-can-eat prepaid pass to redeem at various grocery stores. The grocery stores wouldn't show prices, because it wouldn't matter to you. You would pick the fanciest food and more of it than you actually needed. And all food would cost more, but nobody would care because nobody would be paying for their shopping choices. As prices spiraled out of control, the government would declare a national food crisis, offering more government as the solution.

It doesn't make sense in food shopping. It doesn't make sense in health care.

Regulating the Insurers

The tax treatment of health insurance is a subsidy for insurers that drives up costs. But regulations on insurers also drive up costs.

Under state and federal laws, insurers are extremely restricted in what they're allowed to do and what they are forced to do.

Most states have an entire list of procedures and types of care which insurers are required to cover. These laws are always presented as patient-protection laws: *Your insurer cannot deny you coverage for mental illness.* But they actually take away consumer choice.

Here's another way of phrasing these regulations: You are prohibited from buying health insurance that doesn't cover mental illness. If you want insurance to cover getting hit by a car, you need to buy insurance that also covers fertility treatment.

It's as if everyone who wants to buy a car was forced to buy one with power windows and surround sound. Congress would declare, "Car dealers can no longer deny people the right to power windows and surround sound." As for everyone who wants to pay simply for the ability to get around town in passable comfort—their "rights" aren't worth anything.

Again, these regulations are born of special pleading. Some class of people with specific health-care needs—say, people undergoing in-vitro fertilization (IVF), and very upset about the costs—lobbies for mandatory coverage. (Of course, the provider of this treatment joins in the lobbying effort, too.)

The result is folks being forced to pay for things they don't want. What if you have six kids, and have no need for IVF? You're still paying for insurance to cover it. What if you don't want any kids, ever? Same thing. What if you want more kids? You're probably paying for insurance to cover birth control.

There are two wasteful results of these insurance mandates. First, people are forced to pay for insurance they don't want. Second, and more importantly, people end up even more overinsured. Once you're insured for something, there's little or no cost to consume it. These mandates, then, drive up health-care consumption, and thus health-care costs.

While state governments set the rules for individual health-insurance plans, ObamaCare has expanded the number of rules covering all insurance plans.

Another mandate that will narrow choices and increase insurance premiums is the requirement that insurance plans that cover prescription drugs also provide free birth control (no co-pay, no deductible), as well as other family planning benefits. While the political firestorm this generated was largely limited to separation of church and state—specifically Catholic churches being subject to the requirement—the larger issue is that the government has no authority to require anyone to provide free birth control, and that the requirement itself will lead to higher insurance premiums as more women opt for more expensive birth control than they would if they paid for it out of pocket. With price no longer a consideration, women will choose the most expensive option available. In fact, even woman that do not need birth control will get in anyway, maybe selling the unneeded products overseas on eBay or finding other creative, non–birth control uses for them.

President Obama claims this requirement gives all women access to birth control. The truth is that women with jobs that include employer-provided health insurance already have access to birth control. As a result of Obama, now that it's "free" they will end up paying much more money for that access, in the form of higher premiums or lower wages.

ObamaCare: Because a Little Government Wasn't Messing Things Up Enough

Whenever government really messes up the economy, you can always count on it to inject itself even more. ObamaCare is one of the best examples in recent memory.

The government's interventions in the health-care system had screwed up health care, and so Obama decided that what we needed was even more government intervention in the health-care system.

ObamaCare imposes even more costly mandates on the insurance industry than existed previously. Most important, the bill prohibits insurers from discriminating against customers due to age, health, or preexisting conditions. In other words, an insurer must take all applicants, may not charge the old or infirm too much more than it charges the young and healthy, and may not refuse coverage for preexisting conditions.

Sure, it sounds terrible when a sick person can't get insurance for the very thing making her sick, but if you consider the logic of insurance, you might see it differently. If we imposed the same regulations on property insurers, you could call Allstate while your house was burning and get insured for fire damage. Imagine if you could get insured for auto repairs after you got into an accident. No one would bother to buy the insurance.

However, if no one buys the insurance, where would the money come from to pay the claims? Fire insurance only works because most people's houses do not burn down, yet they buy coverage anyway just in case. If you remove the "just in case," there is nothing to insure against. Of course, if fire insurance were tied to employment, this might be a problem if you lose your job on the same day your house happens to catch fire.

For medical care, this is a real problem only because people are regularly bounced from insurer to insurer, thanks to government. The laws favoring employer-based health insurance lead you to switch insurers when you switch jobs, or when your boss switches insurers. If you get insurance outside of your work, you are prohibited from shopping across state lines. This means that if you move from Greenwich, Connecticut, to Rye, New York, you probably have to switch insurers.

So government is the main reason preexisting conditions are such a problem. But if government makes it illegal for insurance companies to discriminate against preexisting conditions, no healthy people would buy insurance and the industry would collapse. So how does government attempt to solve the problem it created? Does it reform the tax code or repeal the offending regulations? Not a chance. Those solutions involve less government and would actually work. No, Obama's solution is to require everyone to carry insurance.

The individual mandate is an unprecedented government overreach that clearly exceeds the constitutional powers of Congress. The Obama administration's defense in court rested on the interstate commerce clause of Article I. But the individual mandate doesn't regulate interstate commerce, because someone not buying health insurance is by definition not participating in commerce. If the power to "regulate" interstate commerce means Congress can force people to engage in commerce, then there is simply no limit to what Congress can do under this clause. If Congress can force us to buy health insurance, it can force us to buy anything. If it can force us to buy anything, it can prohibit us from buying anything. In other words, if the federal government can get away with this, it will have succeeded in usurping absolute power that will most assuredly corrupt absolutely.

The broader problem related to the commerce clause is that the courts have completely ignored its meaning in order to grant the federal government powers not delegated to it by the Constitution. The conventional wisdom is that the Supreme Court interprets the Constitution. But the Constitution does not have to be interpreted. It's not written in Chinese. The Constitution is clear. It means precisely what it says. The problem is that liberal judges do not like what the Constitution says so they change its meaning and call it interpretation. The Supreme Court is supposed to enforce the Constitution. The only things that need interpretation are the facts as they apply to the Constitution, not the Constitution itself. If the meaning of the Constitution were open to interpretation, if it simply meant whatever the Supreme Court decided it meant, then the whole document would be meaningless. This concept taught in civics classes—that the Constitution is a living, breathing document—is absurd. There is a legal concept called "void for vagueness," meaning that if the language of a statute is not clear, it's void. If the meaning of the Constitution were not clear, it would be void.

Under the pretense of interpretation, the Supreme Court changed the meaning of the commerce clause. Originally written to enable Congress to regulate commerce, it now enables Congress to regulate anyone engaged in commerce. There is a huge difference between the two.

The plain language of the commerce clause is clear. It reads: "Congress shall have the power . . . to regulate commerce with foreign nations, among the several states and with the Indian tribes."

In *Federalist Paper* #42, James Madison, the "father of the Constitution," makes it clear that the intent of the commerce clause was for Congress to regulate trade to assure the free flow of goods across state borders.

According to Madison, the sole purpose of the clause was to prevent the states from laying tolls or customs on goods shipped across state lines.

However, since everyone engages in some form of commerce, the Supreme Court has given the federal government immense powers far beyond what the framers intended. One example is the minimum wage law. Clearly the Constitution does not give Congress the authority to set wages, yet since businesses engage in commerce, the Supreme Court has ruled that Federal Government has the power to regulate anything a business does. Does that sound like the limited government, with few and defined powers that the framers intended to establish?

The key question in early 2012 was, will the Supreme Court expand the commerce clause even further, to allow the federal government to regulate even those not engaged in commerce? There is already some precedent for this, in that the Supreme Court has ruled that actions that merely affect commerce count as activities that may be regulated under the clause. So by that "reasoning" the court could argue that by not buying health insurance, individuals affect commerce. If so, the new meaning of the commerce clause would be "the federal government can do whatever it wants. It can regulate anyone, doing anything, for any reason."

ObamaCare 2.0: It's Constitutional Because It Won't Work

When the first edition of Crash Proof was published, the Supreme Court had yet to issue its ObamaCare decision. To nearly everyone's surprise, the court skirted the fundamental Commerce Clause issue and instead rewrote ObamaCare's individual mandate as if it were a tax, so that it could pass constitutional muster under Congress's separate power to impose taxes.

Of course, even if the penalty is a tax, it's an unconstitutional tax. As discussed, the power to tax is not absolute. Indirect taxes must be geographically uniform, and direct taxes must be apportioned by state according to each state's population. Justice Roberts wrote that the "tax"

> does not fall within any recognized category of direct tax. It is not a capitation. Capitations are taxes paid by every person, "without regard to property, profession, or any other circum-

stance." The whole point of the shared responsibility payment is
that it is triggered by specific circumstances—earning a certain
amount of income but not obtaining health insurance. The payment is also plainly not a tax on the ownership of land or personal property. The shared responsibility payment is thus not a
direct tax that must be apportioned among the several States.

This argument fails on several fronts. First, a tax need not be a capitation to fall within the category of a direct tax. A capitation is but one
form of a direct tax. Sometimes direct taxes are not imposed on everyone,
but only on people who meet specific criteria upon which the direct tax is
based. Generally that criterion is the ownership of property or on the
income derived from that ownership. But the fact that such taxes are
generally imposed on the ownership of property, and not on the lack of
ownership thereof, is a legal distinction without a difference. If Congress
decided to tax all citizens who *did* own health insurance, such a tax would
clearly be a direct tax on people based on their ownership of something. If
Congress imposed the tax not on people who own health insurance, but on
people who *do not* own health insurance, that doesn't change the nature of
the tax. It is still a direct tax. One is imposed based on the ownership of a
health insurance policy, and the other is imposed based on the lack thereof.
  Since the penalty tax amounts to a direct tax on individuals who chose
not to purchase health insurance, it falls under the category of a direct
tax, subject to the Constitutional requirement that it be apportioned.
Since the tax is not apportioned, it is unconstitutional.
  The dissent did not address this issue directly, but it did note that "the
meaning of the Direct Tax Clause is famously unclear, and its application
here is a question of first impression that deserves more thoughtful consideration than the lick-and-a-promise accorded by the Government and
its supporters." The conservative dissenters went on to castigate Roberts
for failing "to demand more than fly-by-night briefing and argument before deciding a difficult constitutional question of first impression."
  Still the very idea that ObamaCare's mandate is a tax is itself questionable.
  Some conservatives have taken solace in the fact that the Court rejected
sweeping Commerce Clause powers. But in many ways, the hair-splitting
result that Chief Justice John Roberts produced is the worst of all worlds.

It affirms that limits on federal power do exist, but then renders them al-most meaningless. It's all the more tragic because Roberts was apparently prepared to strike down the law (or at least its key component) and then had a change of heart.

In his majority opinion, Roberts writes this of Congress's claimed power to force all Americans to purchase health insurance under penalty of law:

> The proposition that Congress may dictate the conduct of an individual today because of prophesied future [economic] ac-tivity finds no support in our precedent. We have said that Con-gress can anticipate the *effects* on commerce of an economic activity . . . .But we have never permitted Congress to anticipate that activity itself in order to regulate individuals not currently engaged in commerce . . . .
>
> Everyone will likely participate in the markets for food, cloth-ing, transportation, shelter, or energy; that does not authorize Congress to direct them to purchase particular products in those or other markets today. The Commerce Clause is not a general license to regulate an individual from cradle to grave, simply be-cause he will predictably engage in particular transactions. Any police power to regulate individuals as such, as opposed to their activities, remains vested in the States.

So far, so good. This knocks down the government's main argument for the health-care law—that such all-encompassing economic regulation is somehow justified by centrally planned health care scheme.

But Roberts then throws in the ugly "but"—one of the biggest sur-prises of 2012. He begins by noting that "The text of a statute can some-times have more than one possible meaning." This statement, while perhaps plausible on its own, is the beginning of a contorted attempt to save ObamaCare by "re-construing" it. Having rejected the government's main argument, he goes on to accept its argument in the alternative—that the individual mandate is not a mandate at all, but a tax.

> The Government asks us to interpret the mandate as imposing a tax, if it would otherwise violate the Constitution. Granting the

Act the full measure of deference owed to federal statutes, it can
be so read . . .

Roberts goes on to impute to Congress and President Obama intentions they clearly never had—intentions which Obama had, in fact, specifically rejected. George Stephanopoulos famously confronted him on
this issue in 2009, asserting that the mandate was a tax increase, even pulling out the Merriam-Webster dictionary definition of a tax in order to
prove his point. Obama replied thus:

> That's not true, George. For us to say you've got to take respon-
> sibility to get health insurance is absolutely not a tax increase. . . .
> You can't just make up that language and decide that that's
> called a tax increase. . . . George, the fact that you've looked up
> Merriam's dictionary, the definition of tax increase, indicates to
> me that you're stretching it a little bit right now.

As it turns out, that "stretch" was the thin reed upon which Roberts
somehow upheld the law. The Supreme Court could, in fact, "just make
up that language and decide that's called a tax increase." If it hadn't,
ObamaCare would be no more.

In 1936, the Supreme Court in *U.S. v. Butler* (297 U.S. 1), defined a tax as
"an exaction for the support of the Government." So for an exaction to be
a tax, its true purpose must be to raise revenue for the general support of
government. However, the penalty for not buying health insurance is not
imposed to raise revenue but merely to encourage a particular behavior.
Its purpose is purely regulatory and cannot be called a tax.

If Congress can simply label any regulation a tax, then all Constitutional limits to its regulatory powers go out the window. In fact, in 1922,
the Supreme Court recognized this problem in *Baily v. Drexel Furniture
Co.* (259 U.S. 20), when it held the Child Labor Tax Law of 1919 unconstitutional because it was a penalty disguised as a tax. Writing for the majority, Chief Justice Taft wrote:

> A court must be blind not to see that the so-called tax is imposed
> to stop the employment of children within the age limits pre-
> scribed. Its prohibitory and regulatory effect and purpose are

palpable. All others can see and understand this. How can we properly shut our minds to it?

But with respect to the ObamaCare tax, not only did the court not refuse to see through the government's obvious attempt to disguise a penalty as a tax—it dressed the penalty in the clothing of a tax itself!

Now some might argue that sin taxes, such as those on tobacco, also affect behavior, in that by raising the cost of tobacco, they discourage people from smoking. However, this is but an ancillary effect of the tax, the true purpose of which is to raise revenue. With respect to the Obama-Care penalty, the real purpose is to compel behavior, with the revenue feature being ancillary.

The most perplexing part of the Roberts decision is the fact that the individual mandate was allowed to stand precisely because it can't work. In distinguishing the mandate from a tax, Roberts writes that

> for most Americans the amount due will be far less than the price of insurance, and, by statute, it can never be more. It may often be a reasonable financial decision to make the payment rather than purchase insurance.

He then goes on, in a footnote, to describe how consumers can game the system by paying low fines (excuse me, taxes) instead of high insurance premiums. In other words, because the penalty for lacking insurance isn't large enough to be "prohibitory"—to *force* anyone to purchase insurance—this is only a tax and not a true mandate. So even in saving the law, Roberts puts his finger on the whole problem with ObamaCare—the main reason it won't work.

Sick people do not need health insurance—they need health care. Insurance is for healthy people who want to make sure they can afford that care if they get sick. But by prohibiting insurance companies from denying coverage based on preexisting conditions, the government has made insurance obsolete—a fact that the Supreme Court clearly understood. Individuals no longer need worry about unanticipated health-care expenses as they can simply cover the cost by buying "insurance" after they get sick. Meanwhile, if they're smart, they will pocket the savings for all the years they stay healthy (less the small "tax" they pay for not buying insurance).

Consider this scenario for a moment: you're faced with a choice between paying thousands of dollars this year for an insurance policy for yourself and your family, or else paying a modest fine for lacking that insurance. Now remember: Under the law, even if you do get hurt or sick, you can't be turned down for coverage due to your condition at that point. So which choice seems more rational to you?

And it gets worse, because the people with the greatest incentive to go without coverage will be the ones the system relies on most. ObamaCare prevents insurers from charging the old and the sick more than three times what it charges the young and the healthy. For that reason, the law's success depends on healthy young people who lack insurance behaving like suckers—contributing their money to the risk pool at an age when they are unlikely to reap any of its benefits. It should come as no surprise, then, that a study conducted in 2013 by the National Center for Public Policy Research found that even after the ObamaCare subsidies they stand to receive, about 3.7 million childless young people (age 18 to 34) would save more than $500 by paying the tax instead of getting insurance, and that 3 million of them would save more than $1,000 apiece. As long as they can't be turned down for insurance when they actually get sick, they'd have to be suckers to pay the extra cost of buying insurance when they're healthy.

It became clear throughout 2013 that ObamaCare plans would cost more than insurance once did.

Young people who don't get insurance coverage through work—something that will become more common now that ObamaCare's employer mandate has been delayed until 2015—will be deciding whether to purchase insurance at these new and higher rates. If they hold down even average jobs, they will not get a large enough subsidy to make it worth carrying insurance policies whose premiums looks like rent payments.

And if a significant share of the young responds by opting out, then the pool will skew older and unhealthier. This will force rates up for everyone else, causing even more healthy people to opt out, which in turn will cause rates to rise yet again—the dreaded "death spiral" of the health insurance industry.

This could lead to a collapse of health insurance as we know it—which is going to cause a lot of short-term pain. It might not be all bad, depending on how we react. As ObamaCare makes insurance increasingly scarce and expensive, it could cause a large cash market for health care to emerge. And who knows? That might even be the beginning of a real solution. Then again, depending on who's in power when it happens, it could create an excuse for a single-payer system like the ones failing patients in Canada and all over Europe.

In any event, Obama was smart to make sure the worst parts of Obama-Care didn't kick in before his re-election. In fact, by mid-2013, as many employers were transforming their workforces from full to part-time to avoid the employer mandate, Obama extended the deadline from January 2014 to January 2015, to contain the damage until after the 2014 midterm elections. As of September 2013, *Investors Business Daily* had already documented more than 300 cases (their list was not exhaustive, they warned) of employers publicly announcing or admitting that they were cutting back on hours specifically because of ObamaCare. It was not clear how many jobs were affected, but the lower bound for the number is greater than 19,000—perhaps several times greater, since many employers did not clarify.

Despite ample evidence that this was happening, the president still denied that his signature legislation was creating any problems. In fact, in August 2013, the Federal Reserve Bank of San Francisco published a study in which it claimed it could find no evidence to support the theory that the rise in part time employment was in any way related to ObamaCare. Since no legitmate study could possibly arrive at such a perverse conclusion, it's clear the bank was politically motivated to provide cover for the president in the face of overwhelming evidence that ObamaCare was directly responsible for converting jobs from full to part-time.

A longer-lasting consequence of the Roberts decision is that the court has placed nearly unenforceable limits on federal power over the economy. Sure, Congress cannot get away with doing just any old thing under the guise of regulating interstate and foreign commerce—but only if it cannot somehow rationalize that "any old thing" as being tax-related.

In the last several decades, Congress has demonstrated almost limitless creativity in abusing the tax code in this way. And the Roberts decision will only make matters worse. Want to create millions of gallons of useless ethanol? There's a tax for that. Want government to spur people who can't afford houses to buy them anyway? There's a tax for that. Want to make companies waste good money on bad investments like windmills and solar panels? There's a tax for that, too.

When creative minds in Congress get together, there can be a tax for anything.

This can only result in further government-generated distortions in an already over-complicated tax code (as discussed in another chapter), so that private resources are further misallocated. Congress will be emboldened to create incentives for malinvestments, further stunting the productive potential of American businesses and individuals.

The irony of course is that over time, assuming the ACA is not repealed, Congress will be forced to raise the penalty for lacking health insurance high enough to actually force healthy people to buy it. Since such an inevitable outcome should have been obvious to the court, given its understanding of the effect of the penalty being too low, the court should have stuck it down when it had the opportunity.

Getting a case up to the Supreme Court is no easy task. If a higher tax results in a future constitutional challenge, the court may refuse to rehear the case on the premise that it had previously ruled the act constitutional—conveniently forgetting the basis upon which that ruling was initially made. The unfortunate result will be that ACA will ultimately be enforced in the precise manner the court had already ruled to be unconstitutional.

As we have already seen with paper money, the income tax, and a host of other unconstitutional federal activities, this is par for the course in American jurisprudence.

Socialized Medicine

As the Obama administration began implementing ObamaCare, new problems kept popping up that threatened to crash the whole system.

The utter failure of the government's Web portal prompted many to call for a delay of the mandate, but if you eliminated the mandate, but kept the regulations on insurers, the whole thing would fall apart, as discussed above. Insurance premiums began to increase. Millions lost their insurance as the bill came into effect, raising the specter that the bill would merely raise prices without significantly expanding the number of insured.

Sometimes it's hard to shake the suspicion that ObamaCare was an intentional sabotage of the health-care system by people who want to move us to a more thoroughly socialized model, like in Europe or Canada. Canada has a "single-payer" system, in which the national government is the health insurer for everyone. The United Kingdom has a total government-run system, where even the doctors work for the Crown.

U.S. liberals love to point to Europe and Canada as superior models. People live longer there, they argue, and health-care costs take up smaller portions of those countries' GDP. Canadians spend only 11.4 percent of their GDP on health, while the British are below 10 percent, compared to 17.4 percent in the United States.[3]

It may be true that the UK's model or Canada's model is better than our screwed-up, hodgepodge system. It might be that our government-controlled but industry-run health-care system is the worst of all possible worlds. But that doesn't mean we should move toward Canada's or the UK's models.

Even before ObamaCare, we were in this valley of half-socialized health care. Instead of climbing out to the slightly higher land of fully socialized medicine, let's go for the highest ground possible—an actual free market.

Solutions: "Shred the Employer-Based Health-Care System"

Barack Obama attacked John McCain's health-care plan in 2008, saying it would "shred" the employer-based health-care system.

That's exactly what we should aim to do. Shred it.

The simplest way to end the distortions that push people into employer-sponsored insurance would be to abolish the income tax. If you've got no income tax, then government can't use it to steer the economy in destructive ways.

Second best: end the tax exclusion for employer-based health-insurance premiums. If your boss pays part of your premium, that should be imputed as income. And, you would no longer get to exclude your premiums from your taxable income. Because this would represent a tax hike, we should pair this fix with across-the-board cuts in the income tax rate, to make sure that, on net, taxpayers are paying no more in taxes.

Third best: Allow individuals to deduct all health-care costs from their taxable incomes. By leveling the playing field between employer provided and individually purchased health insurance and health care, employees would shop for better-priced alternatives and policies would no longer be tied to a job, but follow employees from job to job, eliminating the pre-existing condition problem for most people.

The main problem with this option is that, like the home mortgage deduction, it still amounts to a government subsidy of health care and insurance, meaning prices will be higher than would be the case in a unsubsidized approach. Allowing the deductions to take place at the individual rather than the employer level lessens this distortion. From a political perspective, this option might be the easiest to pass, as it does not appear to be a tax hike.

Also, ObamaCare's employer mandate needs to be repealed. This provision requires large and midsized employers to offer health insurance. This needs to be killed. Other federal laws, such as the Employee Retirement Income Security Act (ERISA), favor employer-based health insurance. They all need to be ended.

Crashproof Yourself: Insure Yourself

Many people get health insurance through their job, partly because that seems the easiest—heck, the premiums just come out of your paycheck effortlessly. But employer-based health insurance is often not the best deal. The tax code (premiums are deductible but out-of-pocket expenses are not) pushes employers to offer high-premium plans that cover everything. If you're relatively healthy, buying into one of these plans is agreeing to subsidize your less healthy colleagues. Instead, consider buying a high-deductible, low-premium plan. You can't deduct the premiums, but if you use a health-savings account (HSA), you can deduct the money you pay into the HSA, which you can then use for out-of-pocket expenses. Even without an HSA, you can basically self-insure by setting aside a few bucks a month (say, the savings from switching from your high-premium plan to your low-premium plan) as a cushion to pay doctor bills. If you're already sitting on a good pile of cash, that's a great reason to switch to a lower premium, less-comprehensive plan.

So, what would happen if we killed all the government preferences for employer-based health insurance?

First, pay would go up. With no artificial incentive to pay people in health insurance, employers would start paying people with something more useful—cash.

With more money in their pockets, people would start shopping for insurance like actual consumers (it is also important that this reform be combined with a reduction in income tax rates so that it's a double win for taxpayers and not a windfall for the government). Instead of just taking what your human resources director chose for you, you would compare the costs and benefits of different plans offered by different insurers. You would call your friends to check on the quality of service, just like you ask your friends how good Verizon's cell phone signal is, or whether they have an auto mechanic they trust.

Once we have more health insurance consumers, magazines and nonprofits would begin offering reviews and evaluations of different health insurance plans. This would spur insurers to compete—which is something they don't really do. Insurers would have to behave like players in a market, rather than like government agencies, as they currently do.

And consumption patterns would change. On average, without the current tax incentives for high premiums and low deductibles, people would buy less comprehensive insurance. With higher deductibles, price-sensitivity would return for patients. You would shop more for health care. Doctors and other providers would have to start competing on price. In addition, because consumers would now be paying cash for office visits and routine procedures, doctors would no longer have to process so much insurance-related paper work. This would greatly reduce overhead, making it much easier to slash prices for cost-conscious consumers shopping around for the best deals.

Imagine that—competition! And whatever money taxpayers saved by purchasing lower-priced insurance would be available for other purposes, such as buying something else, or added to their savings or investment accounts.

Fix the Individual Market

Once we've stopped pushing people into the employer-based insurance market, we need to fix the problems with the individual insurance market. This means legalizing consumer choice.

State governments need to end all coverage mandates. Let consumers choose—and pay for—whatever coverage they want. I can buy a car without a sunroof, or with manual windows. Why can't I buy insurance that doesn't cover IVF or pregnancy? Maybe I don't want to cover dialysis, because if my kidneys fail, I'd rather just die.

Just as cars would be more expensive if government required they all come fully loaded, insurance prices are higher today than they would be if people could pick and choose what they want covered.

People need more options among insurers than they currently have. Repealing state regulations would help improve the marketplace, but Congress needs to allow people to buy health insurance across state lines. Amazingly, this is basically prohibited today in the individual market. Many smaller states have only one or two insurers, and so there is no functioning marketplace.

But why stop at state borders? Why not let Americans buy insurance across national borders as well? I can buy a Swiss watch, why can't I buy Swiss health insurance? Switzerland has some great insurance companies. I wish my government would let me use them for health insurance. International competition works well for automobiles and it will work just as well with health insurance. Many Americans choose to buy imported cars, and even those who buy domestic end up with better cars due to intense competition from foreign brands.

Malpractice Reform

One reason health-care costs are so high is that our legal system refuses to accept that doctors are people, too.

All human beings make mistakes. All doctors are human beings. Therefore, all doctors will make mistakes. Nobody is perfect. But doctors are expected to be perfect.

It's one thing if a professional in any industry harms someone through malice or negligence. That person should be legally liable. But if someone uses her best professional judgment and is careful, she can still mess up. If she's a doctor, she might be liable for malpractice. We hold doctors to standards of perfection.

Malpractice lawsuits run rampant. In any given year, one in fourteen doctors is hit with a malpractice suit, according to a study in the *New England Journal of Medicine*.[4]

This obviously imposes costs not only on doctors, but also on their patients.

One result: doctors are less likely to do small treatments inexpensively or (for the poor) free. The costs of any visit needs to cover the added legal risks. The economics of malpractice risk makes it much harder for doctors to work part-time. This means more doctors simply retire instead of doing what they used to do, which is go into semiretirement. This dynamic adds to the shortage of doctors.

The threat of malpractice also spurs a nasty phenomenon called "defensive medicine." What if there's a 100,000,000-to-1 shot that a patient has a specific illness? What if checking on this costs $10,000 and is incredibly time consuming and painful for the patient? Rationally, you would ignore this risk and address more likely risks.

But in our world of malpractice litigation run wild, the doctor's incentive is to run the test. Even though the odds of the patient having the illness is 0.000001 percent, you have to multiply those odds by the $10 million a malpractice suit could cost him if the patient had this illness and the doctor missed it. The smart play for the doctor is to order to test. The patient will not object to the cost, as he is not paying for it.

How many unnecessary tests and procedures do doctors run simply to protect themselves from liability? How much does it cost the economy? One insurance-industry-funded study revealed that as much as 10 percent of all health-care costs are linked to malpractice lawsuits and defensive medicine.[5]

We need to fix this problem, and we should start with standard tort reform, including making plaintiffs pay the legal costs for frivolous malpractice suits.

But more specific to medicine, we need to change the burden of proof regarding malpractice. If a basketball player misses a free throw is he guilty of malpractice? Not if he had been practicing, and he used proper form.

Regarding malpractice, the question should not be whether the doctor messed up. The question should be *did the doctor use her best judgment and make her best effort*. If the answer is yes, it's not malpractice. The biggest irony is that there is probably more legitimate malpractice in the legal profession than in any other. Lawyers blow cases all the time, yet trying to sue one for malpractice is nearly impossible.

Open up the Field

Reforming malpractice laws will expand the supply of doctors, but there are other ways to make medical care more accessible.

Non-doctors can safely do many routine treatments or procedures, and any laws getting in the way of this should be repealed. Do you really need an advanced medical degree to bandage a wound, put in a few stitches, or take blood pressure?

All too often, expensive and time-consuming doctor visits are overkill for the task at hand, and someone with far less training could have done the job just as safely and effectively. Think of all the lives saved by medics in combat situations where medical doctors are scarce. Paramedics, physician's assistants, midwives, nurses, and nurse practitioners must all be given greatly expanded roles if we are ever to begin controlling runaway health-care costs. Nurse practitioners have just recently been allowed to set up private practices and prescribe medication, a welcome innovation that was bitterly fought and won against a resistant medical establishment. And we need many more health clinics manned by non-doctors in the near future. As long as the health practitioner is upfront about his or her training and certification, why shouldn't we let him operate?

Clearly, medicine is serious business and professional training is needed. But we still overly restrict the practice. And we ought to give consumers more choice.

Fold Medicare into Medicaid

If people are made poor by health-care expenses, one could argue that the government should try to take care of them. Medicaid is the federally created and state-run health-care program for the poor. It could be reformed, but its existence is not a substantial part of our health-care problem.

But Medicare, the federal health insurance program for the elderly, is at the heart of the problem. Medicare spent a half trillion dollars on benefits in 2010. It is expected to explode in the future as the population ages.

As discussed in chapter 8, this is an unsustainable program. It needs to be drastically reformed. And, as with Social Security, there are some straightforward fixes we could do. First, we stop subsidizing the health care of rich seniors.

Anyone who can afford to pay their own medical expenses—even if that means selling off assets—should be expected to pay their own medical expenses. Again, this will increase price-sensitivity. It will also reduce fraud. The more people we take off Medicare, the more health-care costs will go down.

If we gradually lower the wealth ceiling for Medicare, we'll get down to the point where it's only covering the poor elderly—who are already eligible for Medicaid. Then we can let Medicare quietly pass away.

Abolish the Food and Drug Administration

When liberals try to make small government sound scary, they typically hold up the FDA as the shining example of a crucial government service. Without the FDA, we're told, we would all be taking poisonous medicine and eating contaminated food.

But the FDA actually imposes great harm on our health. Most of what it does is useless or harmful. We should abolish the agency, even if we keep some of its functions.

Of course it should be illegal to sell a drug that cripples or kills you. But short of that, as long as the seller discloses the negative side effects, the choice should be left to doctors and patients whether the side effects outweigh the benefits.

One particularly silly responsibility of the FDA is ensuring the efficacy of a drug. The biggest expense in bringing a new drug to market is proving how well it works. Even after you've proved your drug is safe, you need to spend years proving that it works really well.

In the meantime, people can't get the drug. This is absurd. You might have people dying of a disease, and someone has a drug that can treat it and is shown to be safe, but the FDA won't let the sick person buy the drug because the manufacturer hasn't proved how well it works yet.

Instead of the government keeping drugs off the market, let doctors and patients decide. Doctors and hospitals could all set their own standards. They have an incentive not to kill or cripple patients. If people are desperate or foolhardy, they should be allowed to take risks on unproven drugs—after all, it's their own life they are putting at risk.

The FDA's absurd advertising rules need to go, too. The FDA whacked General Mills for placing the true statement on Cheerios boxes that the cereal was "clinically proven to help lower cholesterol." This was a "serious violation" of the law, the FDA said. General Mills was making claims about Cheerios that were only allowable for a drug.

The upshot is this: if you want to sell a product that has known health benefits, the FDA prohibits you from advertising the benefits unless you send the product through the same testing regimen as a pharmaceutical product.

On the whole, then, the FDA makes drugs more expensive and less plentiful. The harm falls largely on those suffering from rare diseases. When fixed costs—like the FDA approval process—are so expensive, nobody can afford to make a drug that will only sell to a relatively small group of people. Instead, we get tons of baldness and impotence drugs.

That's government for you.

The Free Market Is the Answer

As with most things, government is the problem, and the market is the solution.

A market allocates resources where there's demand. That doesn't happen in health care—not because "health care is different," but because government won't let the market operate.

Politicians see how screwed up the health-care sector is, and so they think they need to fix it. It never even occurs to them that they are the ones who broke it in the first place. If only they would take a cue from the Hippocratic oath, by which doctors swear "to abstain from doing harm."

ObamaCare 2.0: Buyer's Remorse

"It's going to be very, very exciting. *But we have to pass the bill so that you can find out what is in it,* away from the fog of the controversy."

House Speaker Nancy Pelosi made this now-famous remark just before ObamaCare passed. In fact, ObamaCare has become exciting now that it's passed—but not in the way she intended.

It's probably not that exciting for the 15,000 or so spouses of UPS employees who as of August 2013 were being dumped from the company's health coverage as a result of the law. And don't blame UPS for being greedy—the nonprofit, state-run University of Virginia announced around the same time that it's doing the same thing.

ObamaCare is certainly not exciting in the way that the law's supporters in the organized labor movement expected. Unions were among the biggest backers of ObamaCare. They were very excited about the bill when it passed. They were even willing to swallow a tax on so-called "Cadillac" health plans—the kind that many unions had negotiated for their members over the years—as long as the Obama administration was willing to delay it for a few extra years.

But by 2013—just three years after ObamaCare became law—the unions were already suffering a major case of buyer's remorse. In fact, they began voicing the same objections to the bill that their political enemies, the Republicans, had been voicing for four years.

Three union presidents—the Teamsters' James Hoffa, the United Food and Commerical Workers' Joseph Hansen, and UNITE-HERE's Donald Taylor—sent a letter to Pelosi and to Senate majority leader Harry Reid in summer 2013 demanding they fix the law, fearing that it "will shatter not only our hard-earned health benefits, but destroy the foundation of the 40 hour work week that is the backbone of the American middle class." They wrote:

> The unintended consequences of the ACA are severe. Perverse incentives are already creating nightmare scenarios:
>
> First, the law creates an incentive for employers to keep employees' work hours below 30 hours a week. Numerous employers have begun to cut workers' hours to avoid this obligation, and many of them are doing so openly. The impact is two-fold: fewer hours means less pay while also losing our current health benefits.
>
> Second, millions of Americans are covered by non-profit health insurance plans like the ones in which most of our members participate. Unions and companies govern these plans jointly under the Taft-Hartley Act. Our health plans have been built over decades by working men and women. Under the ACA as interpreted by the Administration, our employees will treated differently and not be eligible for subsidies afforded other citizens. As such, many employees will be relegated to second-class status and shut out of the help the law offers to for-profit insurance plans.

Although this second objection is more proper to unions, it could apply just as well to generous health packages that some non-union employers had developed in order to attract the best talent. Those workers will soon get inferior plans as their employers scramble to avoid the tax.

So both of these objections raised by the union bosses had been brought up in one form or another before ObamaCare passed with these three unions' help. Both the unions and the Obama administration ignored them in their rush to pass something.

In 2013, the International Brotherhood of Electrical Workers and the Laborers' International Union of North America joined the rebellion against the law. Terry O'Sullivan, the president of the latter, pointed out among other things that union insurance plans were becoming more expensive because of ObamaCare's coverage mandates. Union workers, who hadn't been unhappy with their health care up to that point, were now legally required to be overinsured.

Kinsey Robinson, president of the United Union of Roofers, Waterproofers, and Allied Workers, made the same point and others when he called for the law's repeal in April 2013. By forbidding annual caps on coverage—which makes the average person's insurance much more affordable—ObamaCare was going to cause his members to lose the coverage they had. Other unions—especially locals—faced similar situations. Many unions had been able to secure temporary waivers protecting the health-care plans they had and liked from this provision, but those waivers were running out. Now, their premiums were going to skyrocket.

The fact that ObamaCare would cause employees to lose hours has always been obvious. And the unions should have realized that Obama-Care, which subsidizes employees who don't get health insurance at work but not those who do, will soon make unionized companies even less competitive than they are now in relation to their nonunion competitors. Non-union firms would soon be undercutting union ones in bids on jobs, saving money by dropping health care and having employees buy subsidized plans on ObamaCare's insurance exchanges.

After all, many unions owed their existence and the continued membership of millions of their workers to the health-care plans they once negotiated. Now, ObamaCare was on the point of rendering those plans worthless, and in fact making many of their members better off forgoing them. And why would anyone join a union in the future if, as it appeared already in 2013, ObamaCare had placed their health plans on the road to extinction as expensive dinosaurs?

This was quite a reversal indeed. But it goes to show that when they're faced with their own bottom-line problems, even union bosses suddenly start to recognize the power of economic incentives.

Perhaps the greatest irony of all is that the National Treasury Employees Union, which represents close to a million IRS workers, is applying political pressure to have its members exempted from ObamaCare. The IRS, if you recall, is the very agency charged with enforcing the individual mandate and collecting the penalty tax from the uninsured. In fact, 16,000 new IRS agents were to be added to accommodate the additional workload. It seems that IRS agents are happy to force taxpayers to comply with the law as long as they are exempted from complying themselves.

Another ObamaCare feature is that it doesn't allow health insurers to charge different rates for men and women. The way the Democrats like to put it is that "being a woman is no longer a pre-existing condition."

To some people, this probably sounds fair—but it isn't. Insurers aren't "discriminating" against women any more than nature does. Insurers underwrite them based on actuarial science. The reality is that at certain ages, women are more expensive to insure than men. Young women usually need to see the doctor more often than young men, and they also have this habit of giving birth.

Maybe it seems unfair that insurers should be allowed to place people in different categories because of their sex, and that's obviously the thinking behind the law. Think of it as an appeal to egalitarianism. But also think about this for a moment: If we can no longer adjust health insurance premiums for the risk of covering young women, should we make those same women pay more for auto and life insurance?

Auto insurers know that young men are far riskier to insure than young women. Being a young man is still a pre-existing condition, and they charge for it accordingly. If you have teenaged sons, you know what I'm talking about.

In the same way, older women often pay less for the same amount of life insurance as men pay at the same age. Why? Because women have a longer life expectancy. That's the way it should be.

You won't see anyone out there leading a crusade to stop auto and life insurance companies from discriminating against men. So why the irrational rush to make health insurers pretend all of their patients pose the same risk, regardless of sex, when clearly they don't?

Besides, the chief effect of imposing all this ideological egalitarianism on the health insurance market—whether based on gender or pre-existing medical condition—has been to make nearly every man and woman pay more for insurance that pays out less. We saw this in late 2013, as millions of Americans' individual market insurance policies were canceled. It was contrary to Obama's promise, but part of his plan's design.

When Washington, D.C., journalist David Frum had his high-deductible plan canceled, the District's ObamaCare exchange offered him an inferior plan that cost him $200 more per month. As he put it:

> My family was enrolled in a CareFirst high-deductible plan that
> cost $667.63 per month. In-network deductible, $5,400; out of
> network, $10,800 . . . . The most directly comparable plan on
> the D.C. health exchange will cost $865. The deductibles are
> somewhat higher: $6,000 and $12,000.

Likewise, Hadley Heath, a single female health-care researcher at the
Independent Women's Forum, had her plan canceled. ObamaCare offered
her a plan with a premium twice as high and a deductible $800 higher.

Such stories were typical and representative among those receiving
cancellation notices. Yes, ObamaCare treats men and women as equals—it
makes them both pay a lot more than they used to, and for less insurance
than they used to have.

The reason is that, as people who were already insured, ObamaCare's
"cancellation victims" are by definition not the uninsurable people with
pre-existing conditions that we keep hearing are supposed to benefit so
much from ObamaCare. Rather, the ones being canceled—excluding
those with very low incomes—are simply the cannon fodder who must be
sacrificed to make this unworkable law work.

The Obama administration designed the law's "grandfather" regulations to throw as many people as possible out of their plans because the
law's proper functioning requires more relatively healthy people to start
paying more into their insurance pools and getting less out of them. That's
the only way to generate the cash flow that insurers will need to take people with costly pre-existing conditions, no questions asked.

In a November 14, 2013, interview on MSNBC, MIT economics professor and ObamaCare architect Jonathan Gruber actually admitted that
the Obama administration knew all along that there would be losers under his plan. In an incredible admission, the significance of which was
perhaps lost on Gruber himself, he said:

> We currently have a highly discriminatory system where if you're
> sick, if you've been sick, or if you're going to get sick, you cannot
> get health insurance. The only way to end that discriminatory
> system is to bring everyone into the system and pay one fair
> price. That means that the genetic winners, the lottery winners

who've been paying an artificially low price because of this discrimination now will have to pay more in return.

So there you have it. It's not just the rich Obama distains, but the healthy as well. If you were born with good genes—or more likely, simply take good care of yourself, watch what you eat, exercise regularly—well, you're the enemy now. In Obama's opinion, you've been getting a free ride with artificially low insurance rates. It's time for you to pay your fair share so those who do not take care of themselves can finally get a break. In the District of Columbia, even nonsmokers don't get a break from subsidizing two-pack-a-day smokers. Personal responsibly and healthy lifestyle choices be damned—every American has a right to pay exactly the same health insurance rates.

I wonder how far ObamaCare would have gone legislatively, had this been part of the original marketing campaign. Had Obama told the truth about ObamaCare, and not lied about those who liked their plans being able to keep them, there is no way the law would have passed. Had the truth come out prior to the 2012 election Mitt Romney would be president.

The program, like most big government programs, was sold to the nation based on fraud. Had Obama been honest about ObamaCare, the nation never would have bought it.

Putting Government in Its Place

GOVERNMENT IS WAY TOO BIG. It spends too much, taxes too much, regulates too much, and meddles too much in the economy. This causes our debt problems, it drags down the economy, and it makes us all poorer. But big government isn't only destroying the U.S. economy. It's destroying the country.

We need to radically shrink government. Earlier chapters addressed the most pressing problems caused by government and how to fix them. This chapter goes through the other crucial areas where we need to get government out of the way.

For this project of shrinking government, one good guide is the Constitution. The Founders did not give the federal government the authority to do whatever it wanted to. Article I section 8, enumerated a few powers of Congress, and the Tenth Amendment made it clear that everything else was left up to the states or the people. Almost all of Washington's mischief would have been avoided had Congress stuck to its enumerated powers. Going back to that guidance would fix many of our problems. We can also be guided by the wisdom we've gained by watching government wreak havoc and conclude that less government is better.

These rules of thumb ought to guide our effort to put government in its place:

1. Government shouldn't do anything that individuals or the private sector can do.

2. If government involvement is needed, the involvement should be as local as possible.

Localize It

If you're an American, there's a good chance you have lived in more than one state. People move from state to state easily and often. But more likely, you've spent all your life as the resident of one country—even if you've traveled the world, you've probably only called the United States "home."

My point is that it's easier to go from one state to another than it is to move to another country. For geographic, logistical, economic, cultural, and linguistic reasons, switching your state of residence is far easier than switching your country of residence. This matters when it comes to public policy because the right to choose your government is a crucial part of being free.

Taxes, regulations, mandates, prohibitions, and government spending—all of which are compulsory for individuals—ought to occur on as local a level as possible. This allows more people to leave a given state if they're upset about the government's rules. Sure, you can leave the U.S. if you don't like ObamaCare's individual mandate, but that's very difficult for most people to do. Imagine trying to move your whole family to another country, find a job, and find a house, and rebuild your life.

If, however, you want to flee Mitt Romney's statewide individual insurance mandate or Massachusetts' high tax rates, New Hampshire is just a few miles away. Maybe it won't be painless, but it's much more reasonable. That's one reason to let state governments handle policy. This was part of the Founders' original plan. They created a federation of sovereign states united for the common defense and in a common economic market. They didn't intend that the United States be a nation in the same sense France was a nation.

One telling detail: before the Civil War, government documents used "United States" as a plural. "These United States are . . ." States weren't just administrative units of an all-powerful central government. They were sovereign governmental entities.

Federalism has many virtues. Most fundamentally, states that value different things can organize their governments around their particular values. We already see this in some issues. Maybe your state believes in a generous budget for public education, and your taxpayers don't mind footing the bill. Maybe your state believes in gay marriage. Maybe, like Utah, there's consensus for strict liquor laws. Or maybe the public opinion favors loose liquor laws.

It's easier for laws to match public opinion when the laws cover fewer people—even more so because it's easier for people to leave if they don't like the way things turn out. Of course, it's also easier for people to move into states where policies are more to their liking.

Another important concept: policy competition. Maybe your state has very lax building codes and safety regulations. If people feel too unsafe, they'll start leaving. Alternatively, maybe your state piles on the regulations, thus choking off business and fun. If you tax too much to expand welfare or universal health care, productive people will leave, and moochers will stay.

You sometimes hear the phrase "laboratory of democracy" used to describe these ideas. Different states can try different ideas, and we can watch which ones get the best results.

Competition can also be more local than at the state level. Take public education: why should towns send their money up to the state capital just to have it returned, with strings attached, for schooling? Why not let cities and towns fend for themselves wherever possible—not just in education, but also in road building, liquor laws, zoning, and more. It's easier to move from one town or city to another, allowing for even more experimentation.

Again, it boils down to this: if you have to have government do something, do it as locally as possible.

Start Abolishing Agencies and Departments

When it comes to rightsizing the federal government, let's start by abolishing unneeded and unconstitutional parts of the bureaucracy. We don't need fifteen cabinet departments. Most of these are unnecessary or redundant.

Consider the Department of Health and Human Services or the Department of Housing and Urban Development (HUD). How are health, human services, housing, or urban development the concern of the federal government? It's hard to think of matters more local, and there's no constitutional justification. Abolish both of these departments, and nearly every division within them.

The Department of Labor should also go, as should the Departments of Commerce and Transportation. The Education Department doesn't educate anyone. The U.S. Department of Agriculture doesn't grow anything. The Department of Energy was founded in 1977 to help promote energy independence. To the extent that any progress has been made toward this goal over the last thirty-six years, it has been entirely the result of recessionary decreases in overall energy consumption and (especially today) new oil and gas production that the department had nothing to do with in the first place. If any of these agencies do anything useful and appropriate for the federal level, fold them all into the Interior Department. Nine departments into one is a start. But we could consolidate further.

For instance, does the Department of Homeland Security (DHS) do anything that the Defense Department (DOD) or Justice Department (DOJ) (through the FBI) shouldn't be doing? We could abolish DHS, and roll its necessary and helpful functions into DOJ and DOD. The Department of Veterans Affairs could be a division within DOD, too.

This leaves an Interior Department (maybe), a Defense Department, a Justice Department, a Treasury Department, and a Department of State. We'll need to build a smaller table for the Cabinet room.

Many independent agencies exist outside Cabinet departments, such as the Export-Import Bank and the Environmental Protection Agency. Almost all of these can be axed, too.

The biggest reason to shrink the Cabinet and the other agencies is to get government out of where it doesn't belong. But you'll also save money by eliminating staff and redundancy. Fewer secretaries and fewer undersecretaries and deputy secretaries means fewer bureaucrats angling for ways to increase their power.

Washington Republicans talk about small cuts to government spending, and eliminating waste and redundancy. But we shouldn't shave off some small slice of domestic spending—we should leave only a small slice remaining.

Minding Our Own Business

The most unpopular part of the federal budget is foreign aid. Commentators like to respond by pointing out that foreign aid is only a tiny portion of the whole budget—$50 billion out of $3.8 trillion—or about 1.3 percent of the budget. But that still doesn't mean it's a good idea.

The Constitution empowers Congress to "provide for the general welfare of the United States," but not the general welfare of Bangladesh. There's no authority for foreign aid.

Personally, I'm all for foreign aid. There are starving people and sick people all over the world who don't have access to modern medicine and the bounty of the free world. I applaud everyone who gives his or her own money to worthy charities taking care of the world's downtrodden. But foreign aid ought to be voluntary, and done on the individual level. Here's the problem with U.S. foreign aid: it is governments giving money to governments. When individuals give foreign aid, it's people giving money to people.

When our government hands out foreign aid, the money comes from taxpayers, who were perfectly free to give their money to needy foreigners. The aid typically goes to foreign governments. Often, those foreign rulers use the money to enrich themselves and their friends. To make matters worse, foreign dictators often use this aid to strengthen their grip on power, thus hurting the very people the aid was intended to help. Under a system of private charity this would never happen. Congressman Ron Paul describes foreign aid this way: *It's poor people in rich countries (taxpayers) giving money to rich people in poor countries.* I couldn't agree more.

These days, the marginal U.S. foreign aid dollar is raised not through taxes, but through borrowing, leaving us in the perverse situation of borrowing from China to give to Ethiopia. And, as with much social welfare, foreign aid often undermines its own purposes and hurts the people it's supposed to help. Subsidizing despots doesn't help the people being starved by the despots.

Humanitarianism isn't the only reason for foreign aid. But if we're aiding countries in order to protect the United States—which is the argument for military aid to Taiwan or Israel, for instance—then we ought to be straightforward, and put the aid under our defense budget. Aid to Israel, of course, is a very sensitive issue with Jewish Americans. Being Jewish myself I understand why. But if we shrink government, American Jews will have a lot more money to donate to Israel on their own. Just because we feel an obligation to support Israel does not mean we have a right to force that obligation on the rest of the nation. Besides, we give far more aid to Israel's enemies than to Israel, so if we stopped all the aid, Israel and America would both be better off.

National Defense

The single most important function of the federal government is national defense. It's the main reason the federal government was created and it's the only reason it was given the power to levy direct taxes. That said, we currently spend too much money on the military, and cuts are long overdue. However, while the Defense Department is spending too much money, as a share of total federal spending, it's not spending enough.

For example, from 1792 to 1860, defense spending averaged 58.1 percent of total federal spending. Even after the rise of the welfare state, from 1945 to 2010 the average was 34.4 percent. I've excluded the periods that include the American Civil War and World War II. When John Kennedy was elected president in 1960, military spending was 50 percent of the federal budget. For fiscal 2012, defense spending represents just 19.5 percent of the budget. That is the lowest percentage ever. At a minimum we should increase that percentage back to its post–World War II average. However, since we also need to reduce military spending, we will have to reduce nonmilitary spending by an even greater percentage to achieve that goal.

Overreach

The United States has more than seven hundred military bases in 135 countries. More than two million men and women are currently active-duty soldiers, sailors, airmen, or marines, and many of them are deployed overseas. Even before 9/11, we had 250,000 U.S. troops deployed overseas— and this was during peacetime.

Most of these bases and these troop deployments do not advance

U.S. strategic interests. Think about our seventy thousand troops in Germany. How are we safer for having them there? If we brought them all home, how would the United States be endangered? Maybe we're there to help Germany or other European countries. In that case we should either leave their defense up to them, or send them a bill if they want us to stay.

While some bases are simply wastes of money, many bases around the world are trip wires for future wars. We put our troops in places with a history of violence, possibly provoking the locals and setting the stage for a full-fledged conflict. How would you feel if Iran was stationing troops in Canada? Or here? It's not hard for people to see us as colonial occupiers when our soldiers are patrolling their country.

The best example of this "trip wire" effect might be 9/11. President Bush liked to say al Qaeda attacked us because they hated our freedom. That might not be completely wrong, but it's definitely not a sufficient cause. Why didn't al Qaeda attack Switzerland? The Swiss are probably freer than we are. If al Qaeda hates freedom, they ought to be setting off bombs in Geneva and building cells in Gstaad.

One of Osama bin Laden's biggest gripes was that the U.S. had troops in Saudi Arabia, and that fact greatly aided his ability to recruit people to become suicidal mass murderers. It's no coincidence that fifteen of the nineteen hijackers were Saudis. I know how some people react when you point out the role of our foreign policy in inspiring the terrorist attacks. "How can you blame the United States for 9/11?" I know that's a powerful reaction, and rhetorically, it works wonders: Rudy Giuliani got a standing ovation during a 2008 Republican presidential debate for whacking Ron Paul in a similar way.

But explaining why a bad guy did a bad thing isn't defending the bad guy or the bad thing he did. Nor does it amount to blaming the victim or claiming that we got what was coming to us. I mention that deployments contributed to the anger behind 9/11 as a way of pointing out how much our deployments cost. Just because the terrorists hate something doesn't mean we should change our behavior, nor does it excuse theirs—but if our foreign policy makes terrorist attacks more likely, we need to ask what we're gaining from those policies.

Ron Paul does not blame America for the attacks—he blames the terrorists. His point is that we cannot ignore what motivated the terrorists to attack us, because doing so only increases the likelihood of it happening again.

I don't think we're safer because of our huge and dispersed deployments. The burden of proof is on anyone who says our soldiers in Germany, Japan, and Diego Garcia are protecting us from some threat. These troops are not preventing al Qaeda plots—the FBI is doing that, while our troops might be unwittingly inspiring the plots. And as far as the threat of some other nation attacking us—get serious. It's not likely.

The United States could kick the snot out of any foreign military that tried to mess with us. We would utterly annihilate an enemy who chose to attack us. We spend as much on our military—more than $700 billion a year—as the next twenty nations combined. U.S. military spending accounts for about 40 percent of all military spending on the planet. Think about it this way: We have eleven aircraft carriers in service. The rest of the world, combined, has ten—and most of those belong to peaceful allies like France, Brazil, Italy, the UK, and Spain. China doesn't have one, and neither does Iran.

If we focused our military on simply defending the United States, we would be a fortress.

I'm not saying we should totally withdraw and forget about the rest of the world. Spies and spy satellites are part of defense. But huge bases and deployments around the world don't make us safer.

Hyperinterventionism

Since the Cold War ended, the U.S. military has intervened in foreign countries constantly. Most notably, we have invaded or bombed Bosnia, Somalia, Kosovo, Iraq, Iraq again, Libya, and in late 2011, Obama even sent U.S. troops to Uganda.

These were not wars anyone started with us. While the second Iraq War was sold as a preemptive defensive strike, the rest of these U.S. invasions had no plausible connection to U.S. security. We typically invade countries not for hurting us or threatening us, but because their governments are bad governments.

I don't want to downplay the evils of Saddam Hussein, Slobodan Mi-
losevic, or Muammar Gaddafi, but the essence of our military policy is
that we will invade you and depose you if we object strongly enough to
the way you are running your country.

Think about the principle at play here, and imagine if the United
States weren't the dominant military in the world.

Europeans find the death penalty to be barbaric. In the United States
the government, between the state and federal level, executes hundreds of
criminals a year. What if France had a military that dwarfed ours, and
they gave us an ultimatum: stop executing your criminals, or we'll invade?
Does that seem morally justifiable?

Just fifty years ago, Jim Crow was widespread and racism was embodied in many state laws. What if the British had decided it had to use its
military to bring about regime change? We might laugh at these notions,
because we know that no country could push us around like that. But we
also don't believe that might makes right. So we need to reconsider this
practice of attacking any government that crosses our bounds of permis-
sible activity.

Sometimes military interventions are necessary, but our threshold
needs to be much higher than it is. For starters, presidents aren't allowed
to attack other countries on their own. They're legally permitted only to
defend the United States, unless they get a declaration of war from Congress. Do you know the last time Congress declared war? December
1941.

So, Korea, Vietnam, Grenada, Nicaragua, Iraq, Bosnia, Kosovo, Afghanistan, Iraq again, and Libya were all undeclared wars. Sometimes, as
in Afghanistan, Vietnam, and Iraq, Congress passed some vague "authorization" for war, but other times—as with Libya—the president acted illegally. The first threshold for a U.S. military intervention ought to be a
full-fledged congressional declaration of war.

And often—especially if it's outside of the Western Hemisphere—we
ought to get the rest of the world to agree. To ensure we're not simply
enforcing our will, we should get all the other major military powers on
board.

But these interventions into other regimes ought to be rare, and our
Defense Department ought to spend more time on defense, and much less
time on offense.

Military: Big Government Even a Republican Can Love

Republicans often fail to live up to their limited-government talk, but never are they as blatantly pro-government as on the question of the military. Somehow, a bloated military budget doesn't count as big government in their book.

The 2012 Republican presidential field was pretty embarrassing on this score. Tim Pawlenty, who was running as a fiscal conservative, said that he wouldn't shrink the military budget one penny. If he found waste, he would recycle the savings into new defense programs.

Mitt Romney said he would increase our military spending. Rick Perry's planned spending cuts would have left defense spending alone. The other candidates generally followed suit. Of course, Ron Paul was the candidate who made the most sense: "There's a difference between defense spending and military spending," he said.

Conservatives don't trust central planning and big-government solutions, but they trust the Pentagon to properly and efficiently dictate the shape of the world. Don't they see that the military operates under the same sort of limitations and prejudices as HUD or the Post Office?

I suspect the Cold War is the culprit. During the Cold War, elements of the Left were downright warm to the Soviet Union, while the Right was more hawkish. That disposition seems to have endured. Another cause: simple patriotism. Conservatives tend to be more jingoistic, and jingoism often manifests itself as hawkishness.

But a key driver of hawkishness in both parties is the military-industrial complex. Boeing, Lockheed Martin, General Dynamics, General Electric, Booz Allen Hamilton—all these industrial giants and Beltway Bandits profit from a large and growing military and homeland security apparatus. The congressmen, Pentagon officials, and congressional staffers who steer our military policy are the same people who later will be working for these companies. The result is an almost gravitational pull for a bigger military, which sets the stage for more militarism.

In addition, the military itself benefits from the largesse. Top brass live lavish lifestyles overseas and enjoy a level of prestige difficult to match in the private sector. Consequently, they go to great lengths to preserve their bases and maximize the number of troops under their command.

When you begin to consider the huge price tag of our militarism, you see another way in which it makes us less safe. Our Defense and Home-land Security budget in 2011 was $730 billion, or most of all discretionary spending. That's equal to 80 percent of all the money raised through indi-vidual income taxes.

So our militarism is inflating our spending, and thus increasing our debt. In other words, we're more in hock to China—probably the closest thing we have to a strategic threat in the world—because of our "defense." Even Hillary Clinton said so.

"It undermines our capacity to act in our own interest," she said of our debt. "It also sends a message of weakness internationally. It is very troubling to me that we are losing the ability not only to chart our own destiny, but to have the leverage that comes from having this enormously effective economic engine that has powered American values and interests over so many years."

Well said, Madame Secretary. Too bad you worked so hard to support the very policies that have helped create that threat.

Immigration Follies

If defense spending causes Republican inconsistency, immigration causes Republican idiocy. The issue screws up the party, because in primary con-tests, every Republican feels pressure to seem *tough* on immigration. That's how they show how much they love their country, even if *toughness* hurts the economy and fuels government growth.

Being "tough" on immigration means all sorts of things. It means ar-resting and deporting illegal immigrants. It means building a fence along the border. It means letting in fewer immigrants. Sometimes it even means cracking down on the use of foreign languages. These "tough" policies range from unrealistic to downright stupid. They're often rooted in racism, bad economics, or misplaced blame.

There are real problems in the realm of immigration: Our laws and our borders are porous; there's plenty of violence at the borders; some immi-grants, legal and illegal, are mooching off of welfare programs. We need to address these problems, but the "tough on immigration" approach rarely addresses them well.

To speak intelligently about immigration, you need to begin with the question *why are immigrants coming here, legally and illegally?* There are two main magnets drawing immigrants into the United States: economic opportunity and welfare.

When my grandparents came to United States, there were no food stamps, no Medicaid, no welfare. They came here because they thought there would be more opportunity and greater reward for their work.

But today, imagine if you are a poor person outside the United States. What do you see on the other side of the border? Free public education for your kids; free or subsidized health care; subsidized food; subsidized housing. I have no idea what portion of immigrants come here to work and what portion come here to mooch, but I do know the best way to keep the moochers out or get them to leave: turn off the magnets drawing them in.

We should end all these welfare programs. I don't want to end them just for immigrants, that would be difficult to pull off, and it misses half the point. We should end all these welfare programs because we can't afford them and they breed dependency, often hurting the people they're supposed to help. One benefit of ending them would be to reduce the number of freeloaders entering or staying in the country.

We'll still have immigrants, and that's good. People coming here will be coming here to work. Many of them will come from less free economies seeking greater reward for hard work. These are the people who will make us more prosperous.

Nobody's Taking Your Job

At this point, the average Republican politician starts fretting about "foreigners taking jobs from Americans." This is silly. First of all, you're not entitled to any job, so nobody is ever "taking your job." An employer always has the right to hire whomever he wants, and if the employer is smart that will be the person who will do the best job at the lowest price.

One anti-immigration argument is that immigrants drive down wages, and so keeping immigrants out of the country would lift wages. In some cases this is true, but not always. If you see an immigrant bussing a table at a restaurant for $8 an hour, you might think, "with tighter borders, a native-born U.S. citizen would be doing that same job for $10 an hour."

But that's not necessarily true. If restaurants' labor costs went up 25 percent, they might not be able to make a profit. If they then tried to raise their prices, they might not be able to attract customers. In other words, there are many jobs that simply wouldn't *exist* if cheap labor weren't available.

Think about lawn-mowing services. If these businesses couldn't hire cheap immigrant labor, they would have to raise their rates. At significantly higher raises, many homeowners would just mow their lawns themselves—or plant ivy.

So many things you can get today simply wouldn't be available with a smaller workforce. Other things would be more expensive. The profit the restaurateur makes wouldn't exist without immigrants. The guy who hires someone to mow his lawn today would be less productive without immigrants. That added productivity and the cost savings from the things we get cheaper thanks to immigrant labor—all that is added wealth, which is then invested, creating new jobs.

Then there is the example of illegal immigrants performing home child care. This happens all the time in border states like California, but the only time it seems to be discussed is when one parent runs for political office. Were it not for inexpensive illegal immigrant labor, many working parents might have to quit their jobs. That is because the higher cost of hiring legal help might offset the after-tax benefits of taking a job. So in this sense an illegal immigrant taking a job creates a higher-paying job for someone else.

In fact, there are many ways that the ability to hire illegal immigrants creates American jobs. If farmers had to pay higher wages to Americans to pick their crops, many would go out of business due to competition from less-expensive imported produce, as higher labor costs would price many domestic growers out of the market.

Paying low wages to immigrants to pick domestically grown fruit allows other higher-paying agricultural jobs to remain in America. Such jobs would be lost if we imported what Americans refuse to pick! Of course, if we get rid of the welfare state, Americans will no longer be able to choose to collect welfare or unemployment benefits rather than earn an honest living picking fruit.

Would some people lose out in the whole deal of letting in more immigrants? Sure. The guy who just wants to mow lawns and be paid for it handsomely, he loses. As for society, though, the more the merrier.

One particularly bad response to the fear of immigrants stealing our jobs is the proposal to punish all employers who hire illegal immigrants. So, on top of being tax collectors, attorneys, and spies, every boss now needs to be an immigration officer? The last thing we need to do is add to the government-imposed hiring penalty. Republicans should be for lowering the burdens government places on employers, not adding to them!

A final point on this question: blaming immigrants for unemployment is a distraction from the real drags on employment, which are regulations, taxes, and our messed-up monetary policy.

Solutions: Open Our Doors, Police Our Borders

Here's what we should do about immigration:

First, we should police our borders. Many of those troops we should bring home from Germany and Japan can be put on the border to keep out illegal entry. Second, we need to turn off the magnets of welfare and handouts. Then we should make it very easy for people to enter the country to live and work.

Here's another fix: amend the Constitution to end birthright citizenship. The Thirteenth Amendment was intended to ensure that freed slaves were citizens. But today it means that an illegal immigrant or a temporary visitor can get his child citizenship by giving birth on this side of the border. There's no good reason for this rule. If your parents aren't citizens when you're born, you should have to go through the citizenship process, too—which, of course, should be made more reasonable and efficient.

The result will be more legal immigrants and fewer illegals. This will give us more young people working, being productive, and creating wealth.

End the War on Drugs

I've left out the biggest magnet for illegal border crossing and the biggest cause of border crime: the drug war.

The problem is not drugs, but the war on drugs. Because drugs are illegal, criminals import them. Our efforts to keep out illegal drugs have just increased the profit margins of drug smugglers, pushing them toward more extreme and violent means. The costly drug war adds to our deficit and helps destroy inner cities, which hugely hurts our economy.

But simple border security considerations provide plenty of reasons to legalize drugs. Most of the effort that goes into getting around our border controls—digging tunnels, fighting border guards, establishing smuggling rings—involves the illegal drug trade. Also, were our border guards not so busy hunting drug smugglers, they would be able to focus more on controlling the flow of people in and out of the country.

The drug war has negative side effects throughout our culture. Conservatives are usually pretty good at seeing the unintended consequences of government policy, but when it comes to the fallout of drug prohibition, most conservatives are blind. *Drugs are bad, and so they should be illegal,* the argument goes. Conservatives don't believe that because *poverty is bad we need more welfare.* That is because unlike liberals, they see the unintended consequences of government antipoverty programs, which are that they create more poverty. But something about drugs instills conservatives with faith in government.

Sure, drugs are bad, but I think drug laws and their enforcement are worse. They turn the drug business into a criminal enterprise rife with violence. Look around a poor inner-city neighborhood, and see who has the cars, the women, the bling. Often it's the drug dealers. What sort of example does this set for urban youth?

It's unfortunate, but in our inner cities, the most entrepreneurial-minded individuals deal drugs. Wouldn't it be better if their talents were put to better use? And since dealing drugs is illegal, disputes are settled with violence rather then litigation (though sometimes I wonder which is worse). Think about it—if one drug dealer sells another some bad stuff, it's not like the buyer can sue the seller for breach of contract. All he can do is break his arm, or maybe cut it off with a chain saw. In fact, violence is a necessary part of the drug trade, as the fear of brutality is what keeps dealers "honest" with each other. It's not just the dealers themselves who are affected by the violence. Plenty of innocent bystanders get caught in the cross fire.

We know that prohibition increases criminality, because we saw it during alcohol prohibition. The Eighteenth Amendment was a boon to organized crime, which was fueled by profits from illegal liquor sales. There were an estimated 30,000 speakeasies in New York City during Prohibition. That exceeded the number of legal bars in the city before Prohibition. Making alcohol illegal actually increased its appeal. It was hipper to hang out at a speakeasy than a bar.

The real problem is that drug laws have turned a health problem into a crime problem. Our prisons are so overcrowded with drug offenders that oftentimes more violent criminals are let go to make room for them. Local police resources are overwhelmingly consumed fighting the drug war, leaving little left over for the crimes we fear most. In fact, it's estimated that drug addicts commit 90 percent of the robberies, as they need the money to pay the high cost of illegal drugs. The way I see it, if drugs were legal, they would be a lot less expensive, meaning addicts could support their habits without having to steal. I wouldn't be surprised to find out police forces themselves are rife with corruption, with many cops on the take. Corrupt police may actually protect the market share of the drug dealers who pay them from competitors that don't.

But if you still believe in the "war on drugs," let me ask you this: Do you really think we can win this war? Consider the place in the United States where drugs are most rampant—prison. The residents are locked up. They are regularly searched. Law enforcement is everywhere. Prison is less free than the most totalitarian countries in the world, yet drug use persists. How could our government possibly eradicate drugs in a free society if it cannot even do it in a prison?

Solution: Legalization

For starters, Congress should repeal all its drug prohibition laws. Drug regulation is a matter best left to the states.

On the state level, I would recommend leaving some drugs alone. Marijuana, for instance, is no more dangerous than alcohol and ought to be regulated. Getting high is probably less dangerous than getting drunk, so why should it be illegal? As it stands now, it's much easier to buy marijuana on a high school campus than alcohol. To buy alcohol, at least a kid has to convince a liquor store owner that his fake ID is legit. The storeowner also risks losing his license if he gets caught selling alcohol to underage customers.

On the other hand, the local high school drug dealer will sell to anyone with cash. And since the profits are so high, there are usually plenty of dealers. In fact, if an adult new to a neighborhood is looking to score some pot, all he needs to do is find the local high school. If we legalize marijuana, we take the profits away from the dealers; we can control its distribution much more effectively. Of course, kids will continue to smoke pot illegally, just as they drink alcohol illegally now, but the overall problem will be reduced.

States would probably want to prohibit minors from smoking pot and outlaw driving while high—similar to alcohol regulation. High schools could prohibit marijuana on campus. As a society, we could continue to frown on it and discourage people from smoking pot—or at least have a debate over it. Legalizing something isn't the same as encouraging its use.

Harder drugs are a more complicated answer. Heroin is far more destructive than alcohol or marijuana. But remember, much of heroin's danger results from its being completely illegal. People get killed buying and selling it because it's illegal. Heroin's dangerous to use in part because street dealers cut it with other substances.

So here's one idea to end to illegal heroin and cocaine trade: make them a prescription drug that any adult can get, but only in consultation with a doctor. Right now, you have drug pushers trying to get people hooked on heroin and cocaine. Under my idea, there would be no hard sell. A would-be drug user would have to go to a doctor for a prescription. The doctor would probably try to dissuade the customer from using drugs. If the customer insisted, the doctor would write the prescription, and the customer could get his heroin or cocaine at the pharmacy. At least this way the heroin would be pure, cutting down on other potential health problems that cost society even more money. And since the price would be lower, the addict could afford to support his addiction with income from a legitimate job instead of stealing. If drugs are legal, the problems fall mainly on those foolish enough to use them. By outlawing drugs, the problems fall on the innocent victims of drug-related crimes as well.

Before you freak out about scores of people opting to become heroin addicts, ask yourself how many people you know who are currently drug free, but who would start doing drugs if they were legal? Not many, I believe. Personally I have no desire to do heroin, and the fact that it's illegal doesn't even factor into my decision. Since I feel I'm a good parent, I'm sure my son will feel the same way. I have similar faith in my neighbors.

Of course, not everyone will exercise good judgment, but that is the price we pay for living in a free society. The benefits far outweigh the costs. In exchange for a few more users (possibly), we would be rid of most inner-city violence, border violence, and corruption in Latin America. Sounds like a good deal.

Prostitution

The drug war also provides an important lesson that carries over into other "social issues." Whenever government gets involved in telling people how to live their own lives—even if it's prohibiting unpopular activities like shooting heroin—constitutional limits on government power are eroded. This leads to the future growth of government. As government grows, liberty contracts. More government and less liberty always mean replacing the invisible hand with central planners. This makes everyone poorer.

So, if we want to restore a free market and revive our economy, we need to engage in a broad campaign to put government back into its place. A good place to start would be by ending our regulations of private citizens' lives.

Prostitution is like drugs in that it's a victimless crime, and our enforcement efforts hurt the economy and unnecessarily increase the size of government.

To the extent that there are victims and there is harm, prostitution *prohibition* is more to blame than prostitution itself. Of course, many women turn to prostitution to afford the high cost of illegal drugs. So by legalizing drugs we also reduce the number of prostitutes.

You always hear feminists talking about a "right to privacy," or how a "woman has a right to do with her own body as she pleases." In politics today, though, those phrases are just euphemisms for abortion. But abortion (which, we'll discuss more below) arguably involves an unwilling participant—the baby. Prostitution involves no unwilling participants (I'm not talking here about "human trafficking" or sex slavery).

As with drugs, much of the danger and harm surrounding prostitution stems not from the activity itself, but from its being illegal. In order to get any protection from abuse or being ripped off, prostitutes often need to work for pimps, who can be abusive and exploitive. Of course, prostitutes have limited legal recourse if their pimp is abusing them or ripping them off. As with drugs, much of the danger surrounding prostitution stems from its illegality. So one benefit of legalizing prostitution is that it puts the pimps out of business.

Selling or buying sex strikes most people as deeply wrong, but if you think it through, our laws are completely inconsistent on this score. Consider two hypotheticals:

First, imagine a man offers to pay a woman $100 to have sex with him. That would be illegal almost everywhere in the United States. But say he sets up a camera and films the act, posting the video on the Internet. Now it's not prostitution—it's pornography, which is legal to produce and distribute in the U.S. Does that distinction make sense? Similarly, if a john pays a prostitute to have sex with him they are both criminals and can go to jail. If a guy pays two people to have sex with each other and he films it, he's a producer, the participants are actors, and it's all legal.

Here's another, more common situation: what if there's a guy who simply wants to have sex. He's not looking for a wife, or even a girlfriend. He doesn't want company, or someone to talk to. He wants some sex, and he's willing to pay for it. What does he do today, if he's unwilling to break the law? He probably finds an attractive-enough girl, maybe one with low self-esteem, takes her out to dinner, tells her how interested he is in her, lies, implies he's interested in something more, and then tries to get her to bed. Then he never calls her again, leaving her with hurt feelings.

So, both the actual prostitutes and the unwitting prostitutes (the women who put out for a nice dinner and the false promise of a loving relationship) are exploited because prostitution is illegal. At least the actual prostitute knows exactly what she is getting herself into.

What about the situation of a kept woman? If a woman has sex with a man because he pays her rent, buys her a fancy car, jewelry, or a Louis Vuitton handbag, she is not breaking any laws. But if she accepts money instead, she is. Where is the consistency there? Oftentimes prostitutes get paid a lot less for doing the exact same thing some women do for far more valuable consideration.

The other victims of these laws are the sex slaves who are brought into the country by organized crime or other lowlifes, often on the promise of an honest job. That business would dry up were prostitution legal.

For some women, prostitution may be preferable to other ways of earning a living. Some might not do it full time, but occasionally to make ends meet or to afford an extravagant purchase. To deny her that opportunity is not fair. We might look down on her, but adults should be free to make their own decisions, even if we do not like what they decided. There are many reasons that a woman might choose to have sex that have nothing to do with true desire or love. A woman might have sex with a guy just to get back at his girlfriend. Should we outlaw revenge sex? If it's legal to have sex for revenge, it ought to be legal to have it for money.

What about a guy who just wants to have sex with a beautiful woman? If he looks like Brad Pitt, he can try his luck at a local bar. If he's rich enough, he'll have no problem finding a gold digger willing to accommodate his desire for a shot at a lavish lifestyle. If he's a rock star, he won't even have to look. However, if he is an average guy of modest means and below-average looks, what chance does he have of convincing a real hottie to go for a roll in the hay with him? Prostitution is likely his only shot. Why should society deny it to him, especially if there is a consenting adult willing to make his dream come true?

We ought to legalize prostitution. Sure, states should impose age limits—don't let underage girls do it. Under legalized prostitution, governments could prohibit public advertising and solicitation, in order to protect the sensibilities of those who would be offended, while allowing customers to find what they're looking for in the phone book or on the Internet.

Legal brothels could provide clean rooms, medical care for the prostitutes, and remove the need for women to walk the streets. Sell an iPhone app allowing a guy to find the nearest brothel, and get its ratings. Schoolteachers and public figures could still rail against prostitution and try to discourage everyone from participating. It would still be adultery for a guy to cheat on his wife with a prostitute. Legalizing prostitution isn't the same as endorsing prostitution, but it would make this business—which, after all, has been around longer than any other—much safer for everyone involved.

Gambling

Gambling is another victimless crime.

Currently, gambling is mostly handled on the state level, which is appropriate. But few states leave it alone. Think about the act of gambling: it involves somebody risking his own money, willingly, with another private party. Nobody is compelled to engage in gambling (unless you count taxpayers who were forced to invest in Solyndra and Chrysler).

The best way to think of gambling is as entertainment. Just as Michael Bloomberg might shell out $500 for a night of dinner and the opera, a man of different tastes might want to blow $100 drinking beer and playing blackjack—with the possible upside that he might leave with more than he came in with. Why should state governments prevent him from doing so?

I understand that for many people, gambling becomes an addiction. If someone is risking money he can't afford to lose, and is thus endangering his family, or threatening his ability to pay off his debts, then his gambling is a vice. But we need to remember that just because something is a vice, that doesn't mean government should prohibit it.

And state governments are among the last entities with moral authority on the matter of encouraging gambling among those who cannot afford it. What are lotteries but state-run gambling operations targeted at the poor?

A common joke about lotteries is that they are a tax on people who are bad at math. Take Powerball, the lottery operated by forty-two state governments plus D.C. and the U.S. Virgin Islands. The odds of winning the Powerball jackpot are 1 in 195 million. The average grand prize payout is $141 million, before taxes, which could cut the jackpot in half. That makes the expected value of a one-dollar ticket about forty cents. That's worse odds than any game you'll find in Las Vegas.

So, lotteries have worse odds than any casino, target the poor more than any casino, and are run by the same governments that outlaw or severely restrict gambling. In a free market, competitive pressures drive down the house's take. Because state lotteries are typically monopoly enterprises, there are no competitive pressures.

Right now we have states outlawing private gambling while running their own rigged games. I would do the opposite—legalize private gambling (prohibiting minors from gambling)—while ending all state-run lotteries.

Marriage and Babies

A properly limited government doesn't interfere with people's personal lives. To the degree government involvement is required, again, it should operate on as local a level as possible.

We've had a national debate over gay marriage for the past decade, with federal laws, court cases, and constitutional amendments all in the spotlight. But for the country's whole history, marriage has been a state matter, and it ought to stay that way.

These days, some gay marriage advocates are pushing to force all states to have gay marriage. Some opponents are pushing a constitutional amendment to make it illegal everywhere. Once again, federalism is the sensible solution.

If you're gay and you want to be married, move to a state where most people agree with you on this, where they've legalized gay marriage. If you think gay marriage is an abomination, and you don't want to raise your children or conduct your business in a place that forces you to recognize gay marriage, move to a state where marriage is strictly between a man and a woman.

The federal government shouldn't force states to recognize the marriage laws of other states; otherwise, that's the same as a federal law embracing gay marriage. The Constitution requires states to give "full faith and credit" to the "public acts" of other states. Congress could legislate that every state has to recognize any contract rights that went along with the marriage—inheritance, joint ownership of property, and so on—but that's different from acknowledging this union as a "marriage," legally equal to traditional marriage.

As far as the federal government is concerned, the prime effect of legal marriage involves the tax code: Can a couple file jointly? Can one person, upon death, pass on his wealth tax free to the other? In chapter 6, I prescribed the easiest way to deal with these questions: abolish the death tax and the income tax. Do that and gay marriage is really a moot issue.

Abortion is a more complicated issue, which you can't fully address without getting a bit philosophical. When does life begin? That's the crucial question, because even the most bare-bones government is responsible for protecting innocent lives. Is a fetus a person? What about an embryo? Is it manslaughter to kill a blastula?

I believe the most logical dividing line is viability. When could the baby have a decent chance of surviving outside the womb? I understand this line is moving, thanks to medical advances. A baby twenty-two weeks in gestation was born in 2007 and the doctors successfully kept her alive. Now she's a healthy schoolgirl.

After that baby left her mother's womb, the hospital could have let her die, but that would have been the moral equivalent of letting a car crash victim die when the hospital could have saved her. It makes no difference morally whether the mother wants the tiny baby or not, whether she spent forty weeks in the womb or only twenty-two.

So, once the baby has reached that point where it could survive, with medical assistance, outside the womb, that's a living baby. Yes, the little guy is depending on his mother for sustenance, but being dependent on others for your survival doesn't make you less than human. Would it be fine to stab someone to death because he's on a ventilator? Late-term abortion is analogous to that.

I would outlaw all third-trimester abortions, except to save the life of the mother. Of course, this is another state-level matter. Some states should be allowed to outlaw all abortions. Other states could have no restrictions. Others could impose parental-consent requirements for minors.

But moving abortion to the state level requires getting rid of *Roe v. Wade* (410 U.S. 113). When I ran for Senate, I described myself as pro-choice but anti-*Roe*. This confused the media, which isn't very good at nuance.

On the issue of federal funding of abortion the solution is simply: there should be none. Those who are morally opposed to abortion have every right to be outraged that their tax dollars are funding procedures they equate with murder. Regardless of your personal view on abortion, forcing those who oppose the procedure to pay for others to undergo it is wrong.

The Democratic Party holds it as a point of dogma that *Roe* is some glorious triumph in civil rights, but every honest legal scholar admits it was the height of judicial activism. Justices, clearly ideologically dedicated to protecting abortion, invented some constitutional "right of privacy" that included abortion at any point in pregnancy. Because this supposedly was a fundamental right, the court prohibited most state-level restrictions on abortion. Some of *Roe*'s abortion protections have been weakened, but the whole ruling needs to be scrapped, and the issue needs to be returned to the states.

One benefit of regulating marriage, prostitution, marijuana, and abortion at the state level is that they will then stop distracting us from addressing far more important issues on the federal level. In fact, conservative candidates who might otherwise win elections end up losing solely because of the Left's ability to scare voters that abortion will become illegal if the conservative wins. Images of back-alley abortions horrify voters, who end up voting for pro-choice candidates, even if they agree more with pro-life candidates on other issues. Plus the "end of legal abortions" scare is a big fund-raising gimmick for left-leaning candidates.

The irony is that conservative candidates lose elections on this issue, despite the fact that abortion will likely remain legal regardless of the outcome. When I ran for the Senate on the Republican Party primary, there were many Republican voters who said they could not support me because I was not pro-life enough, despite the fact that both of my major opponents were even less pro-life than I was. So they supported a fourth candidate who had no chance of winning, because he was 100 percent pro-life.

More Guns

The Second Amendment is the second for a reason. It's not the Eighth. It's not Twenty-Seventh. It's right up there, behind only one other entry in the Bill of Rights. The right to bear arms is almost as crucial to the preservation of a free republic as the freedom of speech, the freedom of the press, and the right to peaceably assemble.

The Second Amendment isn't about protecting hunters' rights. It's not even about self-defense primarily. It's about keeping the citizenry armed against tyranny. Read it: "A well regulated militia being necessary to the security of a free state, the right of the people to keep and bear arms shall not be infringed." You can't keep a government in check if the government thinks its citizens are defenseless. Today's government may be bad, and reasonably corrupt, but I doubt it represents the type of threat that would require armed rebellion. However, you never know what type of government might exist in the future, especially given the severity of the economic crisis that awaits us. One way to assure that such a tyrannical government never develops is to preserve a well-armed citizenry.

Practically, gun control makes us less safe. In a city where guns are illegal, muggers know their victims are defenseless. The worst recent mass shootings occurred in places where the shooters knew nobody would have guns: The Virginia Polytechnic Institute banned guns on campus, and so Seung-Hui Cho had ten minutes to go classroom to classroom killing students. In Norway, Anders Breivik went to an island and spent ninety minutes picking off sixty-nine people. The Columbine shooting happened in a high school, where guns are prohibited. In Newtown and throughout Connecticut, it is illegal for nearly anyone to carry guns on any elementary or secondary school campus, but that didn't stop the massacre at Sandy Hook Elementary.

Gun control primarily makes the law-abiding people less safe. After all, a guy carjacking your car isn't going to use a baseball bat to beat you into submission because carrying a gun is against the law. Law-abiding citizens obey gun control laws and criminals ignore them, just as they do other laws. The result: Criminals are armed and their potential victims are not. The biggest victims of gun control are probably women. Guns are the great equalizer. If a 200-pound man attacks a 110-pound woman, the woman doesn't stand a chance, unless she's armed.

You might be freaked out by the thought of a well-armed public, with people walking around armed everywhere. But think about this: 200 million cars are on the road in the United States. Any driver who wanted to kill a pedestrian or biker could do so with as much ease as a gun-toter could kill a bystander. We don't ban cars. We also don't ban big kitchen knives, but I could easily slit your throat if you were standing in front of me in the checkout line at Whole Foods.

Government can't eliminate weapons. It also can't eliminate deadly accidents, yet one favorite argument against gun control is the fact that a couple of hundred kids are accidentally killed each year by guns. But that's a fraction of the kids who drown or die in car crashes. Are we going to outlaw pools, beaches, and kids in cars, too? All of these statistics ignore the lives that are saved each year by guns. Many crimes are thwarted by gun owners and others never occur because guns act as a deterrent.

Agriculture

For thousands of years, farming was a viable occupation without government help. And farming has never been easier than it is today, thanks to advances in science and technology. So how is it that farming can no longer exist in a free market?

The history of U.S. agricultural subsidies is an inglorious one, and exemplifies how one government intervention creates problems that are subsequently used to justify further interventions until an entire industry has been reduced to abject government dependency and subsidy suckling. It began with the government encouraging overproduction to help the war effort during World War I. When the war ended, overextended farmers demanded relief, and it's pretty much snowballed from there.

The government's non-stop intrusion into agriculture has taken many forms over the last century—mass government purchases to manipulate prices, quotas, restrictions on farming, direct payments for farming (or for not farming), ethanol tariffs and mandates, and heavily subsidized crop insurance policies, which during the 2012 drought paid farmers twice as much as they would have actually earned had the drought not destroyed their crops, according to Iowa State agricultural economist Bruce Babcock.

The federal government has become so deeply immersed in agriculture that it seems impossible to extract. And although the argument for subsidy programs usually revolves around the bygone days of agrarian America, the programs chiefly benefit large modernized agribusinesses rather than family farmers.

Today, the federal government shells out as much as $30 billion each year in farm subsidies. Many of the programs (dairy and sugar policy, in particular) actually aim to keep prices artificially high, and these are the worst. They force taxpayers to make direct payments to farmers with one hand and then pay more for food (especially candy and milk) with the other. Taxpayers get dinged a third time because they're also paying for the federal food stamp program, which is required to help poor people pay the artificially high prices caused by these other government policies.

If the entire Department of Agriculture disappeared overnight, the whole nation would have more purchasing power and fewer people would need or receive government help.

Energy

Our energy follies create problems on foreign policy, debt, trade, and economic growth. Special interest politics and big government are to blame.

A rational energy policy would begin with freeing companies to drill for gas and oil and mine for coal. Right now, all sorts of federal laws and regulations leave fuel lying uselessly underground. According to the U.S. Geological Survey, the Arctic National Wildlife Refuge (ANWR) in Alaska contains an estimated 5.7 to 16 billion barrels of oil, yet federal regulations written to protect caribou prohibit drilling. In the eastern half of the United States waters in the Gulf of Mexico, federal law prohibits drilling. Off the Atlantic and Pacific coasts, drilling is severely restricted. The federal government owns so much land out West that it's sitting on an estimated 9 billion barrels of undiscovered oil.

Let's free this up for exploration. Of course, if a company causes a spill, it should be responsible for the damage. Right now, federal law limits the economic damages for which an offshore oil driller can be held responsible. Ironically, had we had fewer regulations, the British Petroleum (BP) oil spill in the Gulf of Mexico likely would never have happened.

Had there been fewer restrictions on shallow water drilling, BP probably would not have been drilling that deep in the first place, and had federal limits on liability not been in place, more caution would have been exercised. Of course, the political spin on the accident was that it proved that more regulation was needed. This is yet another example of government regulation that helped to create a problem being used to justify even more regulation to solve it. The real solution is to require the drillers who profit from the oil to bear 100 percent of the risk. But our regulations shouldn't keep these valuable resources off-limits.

Some reforms to our tax code would also help on energy. Right now, if a business makes a large capital investment—say a newspaper buys a printing press—the company doesn't get to deduct this expense from its profits. Instead the cost is slowly "depreciated," spreading the deduction over many years. Allowing businesses to immediately deduct capital investments would be particularly helpful for energy companies, which are very capital intensive.

Most important, we need to end all energy subsidies, for oil, gas, coal, solar, wind, geothermal, solar thermal, biomass, hydroelectric, nuclear, and whatever else you can name. Bureaucrats cannot possibly determine what sort of energy is most promising. The best judge of the most viable energy source is the distributed decision-making of a variety of investors all risking their own money.

Recent years have shown us what happens when politicians and bureaucrats pick energy winners and losers. Ethanol was the favorite fuel of environmentalists and farmers. Government pushed it on us like crazy. Today ethanol is widely derided for boosting food prices, causing environmental damage, and screwing up the tax code.

President Obama's first big energy subsidy was a taxpayer loan guarantee to solar company Solyndra. "It is here that companies like Solyndra are leading the way toward a brighter, more prosperous future," Obama said as he handed the subsidy to the politically connected solar company. Less than two years later, Solyndra went bankrupt.

Crashproof Yourself: Don't Go Chasing Subsidies

Yes, government has the ability to pick winners and losers, but government can't make a bad business into a fundamentally sound one. Serious investors don't bet on a company profiting for a few years, but on a company that's steadily growing. For this reason, avoid chasing subsidies with your investment dollars. In the middle of last decade, I saw plenty of people bet big on ethanol because both parties were subsidizing it, and even mandating it. Guess what? The subsidies caused a bubble and a rush on corn, which hurt the ethanol producers. Plenty of last decade's ethanol start-ups went bust, and now there's a congressional push to scrap ethanol subsidies. The government is clearly in bed with the banks. If you get in bed with the government you can guess what will happen to you. My advice is to avoid the sector completely. You also don't want your investments to depend on continued political favoritism. The long-term-care industry, for example, won a huge subsidy in ObamaCare: government-run (and thus subsidized) long-term-care insurance. But in late 2011, the Obama administration decided the program was too costly and just scrapped it by executive decision. If you live by the political winds, there is a good chance that you will die by them as well.

It's fairly simple: if a technology needs subsidies, it's a waste of money. If a technology is already profitable, it doesn't need subsidies. But energy subsidies don't just waste taxpayer money—they may also deter development of good new energy sources.

Government subsidies attract private capital. Who wouldn't loan money to someone sporting a government guarantee? This private capital would otherwise go somewhere else, to some company that seems like a good value proposition on its own merits. So subsidies actually slow down the development of new fuels and technologies because they push capital toward the politically favored instead of the economically promising.

The difference between private investors and bureaucrats allocating capital is that the former are guided by the profit motive. Since private investors put their own money at risk, they take precautions to limit losses. If an endeavor wastes resources, it is quickly abandoned. However, those that succeed in delivering value to consumers are expanded. Bureaucrats, however, have none of their own money on the line. They make decisions based on political considerations, even if taxpayer money is lost in the process.

The Environment

We need clean water. We need clean air. I love trees and birds and Siberian tigers as much as the next guy. But environmental policy has run off the rails.

The Environmental Protection Agency (EPA) is an unaccountable body that tramples on property rights and flouts the rule of law. Get a big rainfall? You'd better shoot any migratory birds before they land in your backyard, otherwise your land will be declared a protected wetland. See an endangered species anywhere near your land? You'd best "shoot, shovel, and shut up," as they say, or the EPA will come in and start saying what you can and cannot do with your land.

There are legitimate concerns about the environment, such as preventing pollution of our rivers and our air. But today's environmentalism is often just a front for socialistic tendencies. Politicians and leftists who want government to have more control over the economy and over our lives use the environment as the convenient excuse for seizing more power.

The mind-set behind modern American environmentalism is often simply an antihuman mind-set. Many of today's environmentalists see humans as "unnatural," and they subordinate human interests to the interests of other animals. They also espouse ideas that make little sense.

Consider the Endangered Species Act. There's some sense here: we should make sure we don't wipe out species if we can avoid it. Many species are crucial because we eat them—or we eat the things that eat them. Many species are important to us, because we simply enjoy the fact that they are around, such as tigers and gorillas. If a species is important to us, there will be people or groups with economic incentive to protect them. The law should allow these people to pay to protect these species.

But the notion that we should sacrifice our happiness, health, and wealth for other species is one that makes no sense. If we need to hurt some bird species with DDT in order to clear out the mosquitoes that spread malaria, then so be it. If building housing necessarily hurts the snail darter, then too bad for the snail darter.

The confusion at the heart of twenty-first-century environmentalism is this: we need to protect nature in order to maintain our standard of living; environmentalists sometimes think we need to sacrifice our standard of living in order to protect nature.

More species are extinct than still exist. In fact, scientists estimate that 99.9 percent of all the species that have ever existed are already extinct. Extinction is a natural part of evolution. The world is in a constant state of flux. Those species that cannot adapt die out, making room for those that can. In some cases extinction is a good thing. I'm sure all of us are glad that dinosaurs are extinct. *Jurassic Park* was an entertaining movie, but would you really want to experience being chased (or eaten) by a T-Rex in real life?

There are currently over 1.7 million species of plants and animals. Each species also contains many subspecies. For example, there are 141 subspecies of owls. I like owls. As far as birds of prey go I think they're really cute. But I also think 140 subspecies (or fewer for that matter) would be more than enough. Remember all the controversy over the spotted owl. In February 2008, a federal judge reinforced a U.S. Fish and Wildlife Service decision to designate 8,600,000 acres in Arizona, Utah, Colorado, and New Mexico as critical habitat for the spotted owl, making the area off limits to the logging industry. We cannot afford to place the mere existence of every single subspecies above the well-being of mankind.

Some environmental policy—like preventing air pollution or river pollution—may need to be done on the federal level. Most of it should be done on the state level. Much of it can be left to the markets.

But the antimarket, pro-government environmentalists need to be ignored. Their real agenda is to destroy private property rights, but they realize that most Americans will not buy into that kind of overt socialism. So they wrap their socialist agenda in an environmental package, making it much easier to sell to the public.

Housing

Because it was a major determinant of our recent financial maladies, I have to address housing.

Liberals blame the housing bubble and burst on greedy banks, but as discussed earlier in this book, the blame rests on tax policy, Fannie Mae, the Federal Reserve, and other government policies aimed at "promoting home ownership" and subsidizing banks.

Having figured out how we got here, we should figure out what to do next. Liberal politicians and journalists have chastised Obama for not "doing more about foreclosures" or trying harder to "keep people in their homes." Obama, in fact, has rolled out a handful of programs aimed at keeping people in their homes—pushing banks to write down principal or refinance underwater homeowners. Always pitched as pro-homeowner, these policies are basically bank subsidies.

The banks benefit from these measures aimed at preventing foreclosures, while everyone else—current homeowners and would-be homeowners—suffers.

If you are in a $200,000 home on which you owe $300,000, are you really helped by government efforts to prevent default and inflate your home value? Often, these programs keep you making monthly payments for a few more months (together with late fees) until you eventually default anyway. Former Treasury Secretary Timothy Geithner tactlessly but accurately referred to this policy as "foaming the runway" for the banking industry's crash landing. Sure, government can slow the collapse of housing prices by delaying and preventing foreclosures, but does that help anyone?

Many people deep underwater who are struggling to make payments would be better off defaulting. Walking away from your underwater house and taking a ding on your credit score is often financially more beneficial than scraping away to make payments on a house that's not really an asset at all, but a liability.

In fact, if you're already deep underwater, letting your home's value collapse might be the best thing the government can do for you. If you owe $300,000 on a home valued at $100,000, what does the bank want to do? Would they really want to take over your house? All they can do is sell it for $100,000, minus the legal and brokerage costs of doing so. In reality, the less your house is worth, the more leverage you have with your lender. Once you're underwater, the deeper the water, the better. It's obvious that low home prices benefit buyers. Less obvious is the fact that they also benefit underwater homeowners, who are effectively buyers when renegotiating a mortgage.

The best option for the bank might be to tear up your existing $300,000 mortgage and offer you a new one for $80,000, provided that you come up with a new $20,000 down payment. After all, that's the best the bank could do in foreclosure, but with a lot less hassle. This type of modification would happen on its own with no government action required.

Some mortgages are known as "recourse loans," which means the bank can seize your other assets (like your savings account or your engagement ring) if you walk away from an upside-down house. If your mortgage is recourse, and you have other assets for the banks to go after, they have little incentive to agree to such a deal. However, if it's non-recourse—meaning the only thing the bank could get is your house—what other choice does the bank really have?

If you do not even have the $20,000 to put down, maybe it's better for the bank to foreclose and sell the house to an investor who has the money.

In fact, with you as a tenant, the property is a much better investment, and as such, easier for the bank to market. Being a homeowner requires the resources necessary to maintain the property. If you do not have them yourself, better to rent a house from someone who does.

If, on the other hand, government efforts are successful in temporarily boosting real estate prices by 25 percent, what good does that increase do for the homeowner upside down by 50 percent? If a property's value rises back to $250,000, how is the guy who owes $300,000 any better off? From a net worth perspective, being negative $50,000 is the same as being negative $100,000.

In any event, if the bank doesn't want to play ball, the homeowner shouldn't be afraid to walk away, and the government shouldn't consider it a crime if they have to move. But the weaker the real estate market, the more likely the bank is to work out a deal. Even if you turn the deal down and walk away, you can always buy any one of a number of cheap houses. Your credit might have a ding from a foreclosure, but in a really depressed market, if you can come up with a good enough down payment, you still might find a cooperative seller. Perhaps he will carry back a second mortgage, sweetening the pot for a lender worried about a previous foreclosure. However, with so many people walking away from mortgages, I doubt one foreclosure will carry anywhere near the significance with lenders that it used to.

The bottom line is that real estate prices are going to come down. For some people, that's bad news. For many people—current homeowners underwater on their mortgages and all prospective homebuyers—that's good. Do we panic to make sure gasoline prices or beer prices don't fall? Falling home prices isn't a societal calamity.

The very idea that government has to keep current homeowners in their homes is absurd. What if someone bought a house he really couldn't afford? What right does such an individual have to live in a home he never should have bought in the first place? He may have lived there for a few years, but now it's time to move. People move all the time; it's not so terrible.

More than one-third of Americans are renters. I was a renter for most of my life; it didn't seem to hurt me. In fact, there are plenty of renters who sat out the real estate bubble, as they did not want to commit to mortgages they could not afford. Instead, they have been saving their money, patiently waiting for lower prices. If prices were allowed to fall, those renters would be able to buy. Why should a renter waiting to buy be taxed to keep a homeowner in an overpriced house he cannot afford? By trying to keep irresponsible owners in their homes, policy makers are keeping more responsible buyers out.

But that's the way our economic policies work: government intervenes to benefit special interests and tap into popular fears—all to the detriment of society's wealth.

Former Federal Reserve chairman Alan Greenspan has actually argued that the federal government should buy and destroy surplus houses as a solution to the housing crisis. According to Greenspan, the problem is that prices are too low. If we reduced the supply of houses, prices would rise. While Greenspan is correct, the destruction of our housing stock so that the remaining homes will be more valuable is the ultimate in economic folly.

The one benefit that we received from the housing bubble is more houses. These houses are assets. Sure we should have used our resources for other purposes, and would have without Alan Greenspan's irresponsible monetary policy, but since the houses are here, we might as well enjoy them. Since we no longer have to build houses, we can now use our resources to produce other things.

However, if we followed Greenspan's advice and destroyed them, all of the money spent building them would have been a complete waste. I guess instead of building houses, Greenspan would prefer that we had spent all of his cheap money washing the rocks on the moon. Then we would have absolutely nothing at all to show for all our efforts.

Of course, because interest rates remain artificially low and the government continues to subsidize housing, the homebuilding industry continues building them. Now that makes no sense at all. If we have so many houses that some economists thing we should destroy those that already exist, why should we waste scarce resources building more? After all, we are only adding to supply in a saturated market.

Greenspan makes the foolish Keynesian mistake of valuing work as an end rather than a means. Society advances based on its ability to turn scarce resources into consumer goods. Existing houses are wealth. They provide shelter. Scarce resources were required to create them. The greater the supply of house the lower their price. Low prices are a good thing, as they mean more people can afford to buy homes. Lower home prices mean consumers will have more money left over to buy other things.

Reducing the supply of houses to increase home prices just makes us poorer. Ironically once those houses are destroyed, the homebuilding industry would then devote scare resources to rebuild them—resources that otherwise would have been available to satisfy some other human desire.

Greenspan's plan is similar to what Roosevelt did during the Great Depression with agriculture. According to Roosevelt, food prices were too low, so he destroyed crops and livestock in an effort to increase prices. His plan worked, and as a result food was much more expensive than it otherwise would have been. Obviously, during tough economic times, lower food costs would have been one of the few benefits easing the burden of the unemployed. However, Roosevelt extinguished that light. The fact that houses are now less expensive for those who want to buy them is one the bright spots in an otherwise gloomy economy. Fortunately, Greenspan's plan has yet to see the light of day. The irony here is that not only is Alan Greenspan the principal architect of the housing bubble, but his plan to clean up his mess would rob society of the lone benefit of this incompetence—the houses themselves.

Reforming Politics

This book has laid out deep problems in our monetary policy, bank regulations, spending, taxes, energy policy, foreign policy, social policy, housing policy, and much more. These problems all reflect a broken political system.

In viewing our system as broken, I agree with most of the media. But their solutions are almost always bad. Journalists and many politicians are always pushing for "campaign finance reform," which typically amounts to free-speech restrictions, incumbent protection measures, and laws that privilege media corporations as the only businesses allowed to comment on politics.

I'm even skeptical when politicians bring up reforms I agree with. I would love a balanced budget amendment to the Constitution, but I know that politicians bring it up as a way to avoid having to balance the budget. Politicians know the public thinks government should spend no more than it taxes, but they also don't want to vote to cut any specific programs. So, they campaign in favor of a balanced budget amendment, knowing it will never get a supermajority in both chambers of Congress.

My favorite reform would be term limits for Congress. We should have a citizen legislature, not a Congress filled with people making a career out of politics. America shouldn't have *any* career politicians. Our representatives ought to sit a few years—out of a sense of public service, like volunteering at the local library—and then go back to their real jobs. Citizen-legislators wouldn't hang onto their jobs with all their might.

That would give us a legislature of people more likely to know how the real economy works. We do not want our legislators to simply pass rules and regulations, but to abide by them as well. In fact, knowing that they might have to do so would be a powerful incentive to vote against such regulations. If they had to spend more time in the real economy, not only would they understand it better, but they would also appreciate how much government screws it up.

The real reform of our government will come only when politicians are forced to change. Right now, there's no accountability for bad governance because we just keep borrowing, inflating, and consuming. That's going to change some day, and the sooner it does, the better.

Putting Government in Its Place 2.0: Sequestration

In Europe, they were going through "austerity." That might sound like it consists mostly or entirely of spending cuts—and some pundits, such as Paul Krugman, have suggested that this is the case. But it isn't. In fact, in many European countries, most of it has come in the form of tax increases.

But on this side of the pond, as New Year's Day approached after President Obama's re-election, America was facing its own "austerity" crisis. It was a joke compared to the reality faced by Greece and other European nations, but that didn't stop Fed chairman Bernanke from calling it "the fiscal cliff." This cliff was actually a combination of tax increases (the expiration of the Bush-era tax rates, the ending of a two-point payroll tax holiday) and tiny spending cuts known as sequestration.

Congress resolved the tax issue quickly by allowing income tax rates to increase only on small businesses and high wage-earners. Sequestration was put off until March 2013.

In reality, the "fiscal cliff" was never a very big deal. The real problem was and still is the mountain of debt that made such a standoff necessary. The spending cuts of sequestration were a sideshow that had little to do with this. Neither the high-income tax increase nor the spending cuts, would do anything near to the damage that our $17 trillion debt threatens to do. The biggest problem with the sequester cuts is that they were much too small.

Still, there's a lesson to be learned from sequestration. Even though it didn't involve real spending cuts—in fact, it was a cut of less than 3 percent to *projected* spending—it's the closest thing to a real cut we've seen in ages. And as it approached, we got a good look at all of the empty scare tactics that opponents of fiscal restraint will employ whenever a real opportunity to cut spending arises.

Sequestration had its origins in the debt ceiling deal of 2011. Congress kicked the can down the road by allowing the U.S. Treasury to borrow more money and accumulate a total debt of up to $16.7 trillion. But in exchange, House Republicans demanded some modest spending cuts. These were to be determined by a "supercommittee" whose nominal purpose was to agree on $1.5 trillion in bipartisan spending reductions over the next ten years.

Sequestration was merely the penalty in case the supercommittee failed—an across-the-board cut set to hit both the Republicans' sacred cows (military spending) and the Democrats' (domestic discretionary spending).

Needless to say, this convoluted arrangement failed. If the federal government's massive, economy-threatening debt was not enough to produce agreement on even such a tiny spending cut, then there's no reason to think that a gimmick like sequestration would do it. In fact, the chief effect of the supercommittee's creation was to allow members to hold fundraisers and thus take advantage of their life-or-death power over key parts of the budget.

Then Republicans made a strategic decision in early 2013 to bite the bullet and let sequestration happen, military contractors be damned. The results were both illustrative and entertaining.

As the tiny cuts of sequestration loomed, President Obama and his cabinet members began to predict a catastrophic disruption of Americans' daily lives. If the federal budget was a mere $3.5 trillion this year, as opposed to $3.6 trillion, then 40,000 teachers would lose their jobs. Crucial flood-prevention measures would lose funding. Wait times in airport security lines would increase to at least one hour. Waits at the border would increase to four hours.

In their last minute preparations for sequestration, federal agencies scrambled to protect their budgets by employing what's known as the "Washington Monument Strategy." The idea is that when there are modest spending cuts, you apply them in whatever way will maximize the pain for the general public. By inconveniencing the unwashed masses as much as possible, you force them to the conclusion that not one hair on the federal government's head may be touched without grave consequences to their lives.

This was about much more than the difference between spending $47.2 trillion over the next ten years versus $48.3 trillion. This was about the principle of whether spending should ever be cut by even the smallest amount.

Put yourself in the shoes of a senior bureaucrat who is told he must cut out a few billion dollars for the year. Instead of cancelling unnecessary conferences for government workers or furloughing the janitors over Christmas, you start releasing prisoners, furloughing air traffic controllers, and shutting down famous monuments to tourists visiting Washington—whichever is within your agency's power. Various agencies did all three of those things to prove their own importance to the public.

The Federal Aviation Administration did in fact indiscriminately furlough air traffic controllers at the busiest airports, despite the fact that it got a budget increase even after sequestration. The Department of Homeland Security released detainees who were awaiting deportation, some of whom had criminal records. Agriculture Secretary Tom Vilsack warned that he would have to shut down U.S. meat production for eleven days and furlough 6,000 food safety inspectors.

They couldn't shut down the Washington Monument itself (it was already closed due to earthquake damage), but President Obama made a point of shutting down White House tours, even though the move saved the government almost nothing. Had the president really wanted to cut trivial White House expenses, he could have at least fired the official White House dog handler, who is paid $102,000 per year. The president has two daughters—I'm sure between them they can handle walking and feeding one dog.

Congress asked all the agencies affected to help them reprogram money so that they would have the needed flexibility to make the cuts in the least disruptive way possible, but nearly all of them refused. That would have defeated the purpose. With any luck, the bureaucrats would cause an airline accident, a released prisoner would commit a violent crime, or someone would get mad cow disease from a bad steak. That would mean everybody gets a bigger agency budget next year.

For all of this nefarious behavior by bureaucrats, sequestration proved to be a dud. The public barely noticed after it began in March 2013. For all the bureaucrats' efforts to cause substantial pain, they could not do so. Why? Because America doesn't need them to thrive and prosper. In most cases, it's far better off without them.

That's the first and most important lesson of sequestration. The second lesson comes from those areas where the public did notice the pain and inconvenience—for example, through the unnecessary flight delays deliberately caused by the FAA for a couple of days through strategic furloughs of its most essential workers. The lesson here is that a large government cannot be trusted to look out for the public welfare.

Sequestration highlighted the fact that government is society's worst institution for allocating resources within the economy. Many of its functions could be replaced by institutions anchored to the reality of the free market, which operate from a rational profit motive that can't afford to brook so much bureaucratic nonsense. If we had private air traffic controllers—as they do in Canada—we wouldn't be at the mercy of people who behave so irrationally.

Airlines make money by moving people efficiently from one place to another. Government, on the other hand, "makes" more money when it acts as an obstacle to efficient transportation. Sequestration proved that government is not only incapable of distinguishing important functions from unimportant ones, but also that it is unwilling to do so because it operates based on an incentive structure that is counterproductive to fulfilling citizens' needs. And we saw the same effect in late 2013 during the government shutdown.

Perhaps, someday, a future generation of libertarian professors will teach students about the dire predictions that led up to sequestration, and hold it up as an inglorious example of how smoke, mirrors, and scare tactics preserved the Leviathan for so long.

12

America Is Bankrupt:
Time to Admit It

EVERYONE KNOWS OUR NATIONAL DEBT is huge. It's so large that it's hard to comprehend the size.

Both parties say they want to reduce the debt, but neither party means it. When Democrats talk about deficit reduction, they mean that they want to increase taxes. When Republicans talk about deficit reduction, they mean they want to attack Democratic spending. But realistically, neither party, in its current form, is capable of addressing the national debt, because the problem is so huge and the steps needed to address it are so extreme.

Next year, we'll pay about $450 billion in interest. We'll make these payments by borrowing the money. But in the not-so-distant future, interest rates will rise, making our debt service even more crippling. Given our current national debt, and where it's headed, if interest rates go where I think they'll go, we are going to have a situation where debt service is equal to our current tax revenue.

In brief: we're going broke. We can't afford our debts. America is bankrupt. It's time to admit it.

Massive Debt

The national debt is $15 trillion. Let me try to put that into perspective.

All federal tax revenue in 2011 was $2.2 trillion—less than one sixth of the total national debt. The $17 trillion gross debt amounts to $148,000 per taxpayer.*

The richest person in America, Bill Gates, has a total net worth of $59 billion. If he donated every dime to the U.S. Treasury in order to pay down the national debt, he couldn't even retire one half of 1 percent of it. Put another way, he could pay two months' worth of interest. If Obama confiscated all the wealth—not income, but *wealth*—of the fifty wealthiest people in America, he could use that $700 billion to pay down about 5 percent of the national debt.

In fiscal year 2011, taxpayers paid $454 billion in interest. That's 20 percent of all federal receipts. It's more than twice as much as Washington collected through the corporate income tax.

But even these numbers on the national debt understate Uncle Sam's obligations. The $17 trillion actually represents the tip of a very large iceberg. When off-budget and contingent liabilities are factored in, total federal liabilities exceed $100 trillion. Nobody knows the future obligations of our entitlement programs. Medicare budget projections regularly come in extremely low. Medicare costs rise as health-care costs rise, and that's not something we can predict. Plus, ObamaCare created new federal health-care obligations that will only accelerate the rate of increase.

What about all those student loans, with total guaranteed obligations now exceeding one trillion? Thanks to Obama's new limits on repayment obligations, a significant percentage of this total will now fall on taxpayers. And since the program itself makes it even easier for colleges to increase tuitions, the size of this obligation will now grow faster as well.

It is also clear that more financial bailouts are coming. Fannie Mae asks for a new multibillion-dollar bailout every few months. The FHA has also climbed board the bailout bandwagon. Some big banks are liable to fail as well. Since the FDIC will lack the resources to cover insured deposits, that's yet another bailout waiting in the wings. The FDIC is not the only federally backed agency that will need a bailout. The Securities Investor Protection Corporation (SIPC) insures individual brokerage accounts of up to $500,000 in value. The Pension Benefit Guarantee Program

---

* When the first edition of *The Real Crash* went to press, the debt was $15 trillion and $133,000 per taxpayer.

(PBGP) puts federal guarantees behind billions of dollars of defined benefit pension programs. In a downturn as severe as the one I see coming, both these agencies will require bailouts as well. And who knows what the next Detroit-type bailout will be, or Katrina-level national disaster?

What about the U.S. Post Office? Its ability to raise stamp prices is limited to official inflation figures. However, those figures do not even come close to tracking increases in postal costs. As a result, the Post Office is proposing shutting down branches and ending Saturday mail delivery. Higher prices and reduced services are a postal tradition. (Remember when there were two deliveries per day, morning and afternoon mail?)

In the meantime, the Post Office is trying to make ends meet by selling "Forever Stamps." These stamps sell for the same price as regular stamps, but can be used to mail letters even when future stamp prices rise. The problem is that the revenue generated from those sales is spent to cover the cost of current deliveries. When postage rates finally jump, rather than buying higher-priced stamps, customers will simply use the Forever Stamps they have already purchased. The Post Office will then have to deliver mail but will collect no new money for doing so. A taxpayer bailout is all but assured.

Amtrak probably has another bailout coming as well, along with state governments, including their public pensions.

Obama has proposed a federal infrastructure bank. His allies have also called for a "Green Bank." These are ideas that would expand federal exposure to private debt in risky markets. Obama also has ramped up the existing government credit agencies like the Export-Import Bank.

The problem is that the U.S. government stands behind so many contingent liabilities waiting to explode that there is no way to tell which one will blow up next. Systemic shock could trigger multiple contingent liabilities simultaneously. In fact, in such a crisis they are likely to fall like dominos.

The bottom line is that our national debt substantially understates true federal liabilities. If the U.S. government were a private company being audited by standard practices, it would be considered much further in the red than official national debt figures show. In fact, it would be shut down and its key executive prosecuted for fraud.

But still, Uncle Sam is able to borrow at near-zero interest rates. This makes it nearly affordable for us to pay what we owe. The disturbing news is that interest rates will rise. When we have a national debt seven times our annual tax receipts and interest rates start doubling and tripling, things will get ugly. At some point, the charade will be up, and we'll have to admit that we're broke.

Pensions

We've covered most of the debt traps, like Social Security, Medicare, and overspending in previous chapters. Let me just make a quick note here about another ticking time bomb: public employee pensions.

State and local governments will come up about $2.5 trillion short of the pension obligations to their government employees, according to a 2011 assessment by New Jersey's former pension boss.[1] Thanks to an incestuous relationship between public employee unions and the politicians they help elect, generous pension benefits have been promised to government employees. However, to avoid the wrath of private sector voters, such benefits have not been properly funded. The liabilities have merely been put on the backs of future taxpayers. Well, the future is here and the taxpayers cannot afford to pay the bills.

A 2010 study by the Pew Center on the states found that only ten states had their pensions funded at 91.6 percent or more. Only three states were fully funded. Illinois has no way to pay for 46 percent of its $119 billion public-employee pension obligations. California's shortfall is $59.5 billion according to the Pew Center. New Jersey's shortfall is $34.4 billion.

These numbers reflect a snapshot taken in 2009, but things are deteriorating rapidly. In the State Employees' Retirement System of Michigan, for instance, unfunded pension liabilities jumped from $3.1 billion in 2009 to $4.0 billion in 2010.[2]

States are already bailing out local pension plans. Pittsburgh officially asked Pennsylvania to bail out its pension plan. The next question is whether the federal government will bail out state pension plans. Obama's 2009 stimulus bill dedicated huge sums to fill local and state deficits. In 2010, Congress passed a special bailout just for state and local employees.

So, will Washington run to the rescue of failed state-employee pension plans? Republicans in both chambers have introduced bills to prohibit bailouts of state pension plans. But of all things where you might be tempted to trust Republicans, blocking bailouts should be one of the last.

I wouldn't be surprised to see a Republican president push a federal bailout of state and local pension plans, calling on conservative-sounding rhetoric about states' rights and local control—and under pressure from investment firms that depend on state pension funds for business.

In any event, public pensions are another reason our actual debt—measured by unfunded obligations—is much bigger than anyone admits.

Running out of Capital

Here's the detail that nobody wants to admit, because admitting it will knock down our house of cards: There is no solution to our current economic problem that doesn't involve much higher interest rates. The biggest problem underlying the U.S. economy is artificially low interest rates. They are the root cause of the macroeconomic imbalances that are crippling us. Until rates are allowed to rise to reflect a true market price, a real economic recovery cannot take place.

Americans aren't saving. In September 2011, the government reported that Americans had saved 3.6 percent of their income, the lowest savings rate since 2007.[3] But that rate has been low and generally falling for decades. In the early 1980s, personal savings rates were above 11 percent. During the Greenspan dot-com bubble, they were down below 4 percent. At the height of the housing market, the rates got down below 1 percent. After a slight rebound after the credit panic of late 2008, people in 2011 once again gave up on saving.[4]

This aversion to saving isn't just some bizarre self-destructive trait of Americans. It is a semi-rational response to market conditions—market conditions that have been rigged by the Federal Reserve.

Low interest rates discourage people from saving. When I first wrote this chapter, I was having a very hard time finding a bank that would pay me even one percent for savings deposits. Meanwhile year-over-year inflation had been 3.86 percent—and that's measured by the CPI, which grossly underestimates the true inflation rate. If I had put my money in a savings account, it would have bled more than 2.5 percent of its value each year. So it's no mystery why many people forgo saving.

Of course, in an economy where the market sets interest rates, such low interest rates would occur only if there was a huge glut of savings relative to demand for borrowing. Think about it—interest rates are the price that lenders charge to loan out their savings. Low prices in anything signify a high supply relative to demand. But we don't have a high supply of savings to loan out, so how do we get low interest rates?

The answer is Fed manipulation.

The Federal Reserve sets interest rates by setting the discount rate (at which banks borrow from the Fed), and by targeting the federal-funds rate (at which banks borrow from one another). The Fed works toward its target fed-funds rate by buying or selling U.S. Treasuries and other securities. By buying up securities, the Fed injects more cash into the banking system.

Greenspan and Bernanke have kept the fed-funds rates below 4 percent for most of the past twenty years. Since the credit crisis, rates have been down around zero. So the Fed has successfully injected more reserves into the banking system and thus lowered interest rates. Most mainstream economists—and certainly Ben Bernanke—seem to think this is the path to recovery. But it's not. Artificially low interest rates are one of the biggest obstacles to recovery.

What do I mean by "artificially low"? I mean we have extra money showing up without anyone saving.

Absent Fed manipulation, big cash stockpiles represent savings, and thus the potential for future consumption. But when those cash stockpiles come in the form of Fed injections, rather than individual savings, they don't represent deferred consumption. They just represent a diluted dollar. This money won't really be invested in the economy. Banks are likely to use this free money from the Fed to buy U.S. Treasuries (that is, finance the national debt), and get a couple of cents' interest. It's free money with low or no risk, but it also provides zero economic value to the country.

Interest Rates Will Rise

So these artificially low rates don't finance anything useful, and they actually crowd out real savings, thus preventing Americans from ever getting to the point where they can afford to spend.

At low interest rates, banks don't see an incentive to lend to small and medium-sized businesses. Instead, credit is directed toward Wall Street, where it finances nonproductive speculation, or toward homebuyers or students sporting government guarantees. Major corporations with access to the bond market can refinance at lower rates, using the savings to buy back stock. However, stock buybacks do not grow the economy. In the meantime, small and medium-sized businesses that cannot sell bonds and have no government guarantees get shut out of the credit market. What good do these low rates do business if they can't get a loan?

Banks have no real funds to loan out, because anyone wishing to get a decent return on his money feels drawn toward the stock market, hoping to get on the upside of one of its wild swings. So Fed rate manipulation encourages speculation over investing or savings. With inflation exceeding interest rates, there's little reason not to just spend away—because it's hard to make your money grow.

More money in the economy makes the dollar less valuable. This means Americans are losing purchasing power. In other words, the Fed's activities make people poorer.

Poorer people dedicating more of their money to consumption, combined with less saving, less investment, and more speculation—does that sound like the foundation for a recovery to you? To me, it sounds like the same thing that got us into trouble.

When government fools with prices, it causes wealth to be misallocated. It's no different with interest rates, which are the price of borrowing. The definition of a healthy economy is when resources flow to wherever they do the most good. The only way to recover is to stop the misallocation of wealth that the Fed has been causing for twenty years.

That will require interest rates to rise.

If the Fed stopped playing with rates and the money supply, that's exactly what would happen. If banks weren't getting free money from the Fed, they would need to turn to depositors for money. This demand for deposits would drive up the interest paid on savings. With higher rates, more people would save, and lending capital would go up. At higher interest rates, it would now be worthwhile for banks to invest in growing small businesses. This would spur job creation. Higher rates would also raise the bar on speculative activity, tilting the playing field back in the direction of legitimate business investment. Credit formerly used to finance mere speculation will be freed up to finance legitimate capital investment instead. While the former enriches some at the expense of others, the latter benefits everyone by increasing production, creating jobs, lowering prices, and raising living standards.

Even if you don't agree with me that we need higher rates to stop mal-investment, you should understand that higher rates are coming anyway. If we keep spending and keep borrowing, and if we pay off that debt by borrowing some more, sooner or later, lenders will start to worry more about whether we can pay them back. They'll start charging us higher interest to compensate for the risk.

So if higher interest rates are the road to recovery for Americans, why is the Fed blocking the way? Because what is good for the long-term health of the U.S. economy is devastating for the phony economy the Fed is trying to preserve, and absolutely terrifying for Uncle Sam. Do the math. In fiscal 2011, interest payments amounted to about 3 percent of the national debt. A fair guess would put the debt in 2020 at about $24 trillion. If interest rates were 7 percent (which might be low), payments on the national debt would equal $1.68 trillion per year, which is more than all appropriations that year, according to the FY 2011 budget. It exceeds all Social Security outlays plus all Medicaid outlays.[5]

In this scenario, to simply keep the debt from increasing in 2020, we would need to eliminate all discretionary spending and cut entitlements by 15 percent. Imagine that: the whole purpose of our federal government would be to tax people and then make payments to seniors and to creditors, the majority being foreign. Alternatively, we could increase taxes—on everyone, not just rich people—by nearly 50 percent.

We're not likely to do any of these things or any sufficient combination of them, and so the national debt will keep rising, digging us into a deeper hole. Politicians all talk about shrinking the national debt, but there's no reason to believe anyone can actually shrink it—or even slow its growth. In short, we've got debts we can't pay.

Bankrupt

America simply cannot pay its bills much longer. Our government has promised too many people too many things. Most of our budget these days is dedicated to "entitlements," which politicians tell people are their

due. You get your Social Security statements, asserting you will get a certain amount of money when you turn sixty-five. Anytime someone suggests reforming Medicare, demagogues accuse the reformer of taking
away "your Medicare."

Our highway "trust funds" and federal pension payments are other
long-standing obligations. Government has also bred dependency in all
corners of the country, from the poor relying on federal social programs
to corporations relying on their handouts.

On top of all of this is our national debt—money the Treasury has
borrowed with the promise to repay.

We can try to skim "wasteful spending," and hike taxes on the rich
all we like, but soon, we'll have to admit that something's got to give. We
simply cannot meet our obligations. Somebody is going to get shortchanged.

Here's my question: Why should we honor our Chinese creditors over
our own seniors? I wouldn't have borrowed the money from the Chinese
or created Social Security, but now that we're in a jam, I'm not convinced
that American seniors who have been paying taxes their whole life should
bear the consequences of Washington's fiscal incontinence, while Chinese
bondholders are made whole.

Recently, the youth rioted in Greece over "austerity" plans of tax hikes
and benefit cuts. Are they spoiled, entitled kids? Sure. But they also have a
point. They know that they are taking the hit so that Greece's creditors—
largely German and Swiss banks—don't suffer too much.

America will be in a similar position soon, and I do not expect Americans to take austerity measures (designed to benefit the Chinese) any better than the Greeks did.

When a person has debts he cannot repay, he declares bankruptcy. He
then formulates a plan for repaying his creditors to the greatest extent
possible, but all of them take a haircut.

It's time for the United States of America to declare bankruptcy.

Perception Versus Reality

Numbers don't lie—and the numbers show that we are already bankrupt.
But for now the perception of solvency remains. The problem is that this

perception will soon change. For a while, people perceived subprime borrowers with teaser rates to be creditworthy. For a while the same perception existed for the Greek government.

Perceptions can change quickly, and they often do. Remember America's solvency is built on the shaky foundation of low short-term interest rates. The only way we can pretend to pay our bills is by borrowing the money required to do so at near-zero percent interest rates. I say pretend, because if you have to borrow money to repay your debts, you aren't repaying anything. However, the pretense can only be maintained so long as rates remain low and our creditors cooperative.

As previously discussed, I believe that the U.S. Treasury is running a giant Ponzi scheme. The national debt always goes up. Even during the Clinton years when the budget was supposed to be in surplus the national debt rose every year. When a Treasury Bond matures, the government sells another one to pay it off. When an interest payment comes due the government borrows the money required to pay it. This is precisely the same way that Bernie Madoff ran his investment business. It "worked" great for a while, until too many people wanted their money back.

What happens when America's creditors want their money back? For now the U.S. is able to finance its deficits largely by selling T-bills. It does this because T-bill rates are much lower than T-bond rates. This helps make our current deficits smaller. The risk is that when rates eventually rise, future deficits are much larger. Politicians, however, are doing what is politically expedient rather than what is financially sound. This is the same mistake homeowners made with adjustable rate mortgages. They traded lower initial payments for higher future payments. The problem was that once those higher payments kicked in, many borrowers could not afford to make them. The predictable result was default.

As the dollar falls, eventually even the CPI-measured inflation rate will rise to unacceptable levels. Then our creditors will no longer be willing to lend us money at such low rates. When that happens, it's not just interest payments that will be due, but principal payments as well.

For example, given the short maturity of our debt, it's very possible that in any given year, over $5 trillion in debts will mature. Since that is more than twice annual tax receipts, where will the money come from to pay it? The answer generally given is that we will not have to pay it, as we will simply borrow the money. But what if we can't? What if our creditors

do not want to roll over low-yielding debt in a high inflationary environment? This book is called *The Real Crash* for a reason. This is the reason.

The idea that America can borrow forever, without ever having to pay
any of the money back, is absurd. Inherent in that assumption is that the
rest of the world is willing to lend without ever getting its money back.
This overlooks the most important aspect of the lending process, the part
where you get your money back. Anyone can make a loan. The key to the
transaction is making sure the borrower actually pays you back. If you do
not get paid back, it's not a loan; it's a gift. When our lenders discover
they are really benefactors, the gifts will stop coming.

At some point the Fed is going to be confronted with the reality it has
worked so hard to postpone facing. The Fed's ability to keep rates low is
predicated on its commitment to containing inflation. Since its commitment is no more than a smoke screen, its credibility is based on a lie. However, most people do not realize it is a lie. That is what is going to change.
The Fed can keep rates low only as long as our creditors remain confident
in its commitment and ability to contain inflation. But despite its loud
inflation-fighting bark, the Fed has no bite. In fact, the main reason the
Fed pretends there is no inflation is that it knows it is not prepared to fight
it. It pretends inflation does not exist, so it doesn't have to deal with it. But
it must maintain the illusion that it will, so it lies and hopes for the best.

At some point, trailing CPI will be so high that the Fed will be forced
either to raise rates sharply or lose all remaining credibility on containing
inflation. If trailing CPI is 5 percent, and the Fed is forced to raise rates to
contain it, moving rates from 0 to 25 basis points will not cut it. The Fed
will have to be much more aggressive. Even moving rates to 3 percent would
not suffice, as rates would still be negative. Negative rates will only fuel
even more inflation, not fight it. Getting ahead of the inflation curve might
require a 7 percent fed-funds rate. However, at 7 percent we can no more
afford to pay the interest on our debt than Greece could afford to pay the
interest on its debt.

If you recall, for years before the Greek debt crisis erupted, the Greeks
enjoyed record low-interest rates. As such, they were able to feign solvency
just as America does now. Servicing the debt was no problem as long as
rates remained rock bottom. But rock bottom rates rested on the false
premise that the Greeks were actually good for the money. Low rates in
America rest on the same false paradigm. Once this premise was chal-

lenged, the Greek house of cards collapsed. Greece could not roll over maturing debt at the same low rates, and it lacked the revenue to pay higher rates. As this became apparent the process fed on itself, and a crisis quickly emerged.

The main difference between Greece and America is that Greece cannot print euros. However, the fact that the Fed can print dollars will be of little consolation to our creditors. It may provide a certain degree of comfort now, but that will change once the pain of dollar depreciation sets in.

When America's creditors finally say *no mas*, the game, as they say, will be over. The music will stop and the piper will look to be paid. When I raise the obvious point to my fellow financial pundits, it's generally dismissed on the theory that it will never happen, as the Fed will keep rates low indefinitely. Rates can no more stay low forever than real estate prices could have risen forever. It is also interesting that the same folks who believed the latter are now arguing the former.

Unfortunately, the only way the Fed can keep rates artificially low as inflation rises is to create even more inflation. Our creditors are only willing to lend us money at low rates because they believe inflation is not a problem, and that were it to become one, the Fed would quickly extinguish it. Once they discover otherwise, our creditors will refuse to lend.

So to keep rates down, the Fed will have to buy any bonds our creditors refuse to roll over. The problem is that the more money the Fed prints to pay off maturing bonds, the more inflation it must create to buy them. This process feeds on itself. Soon it's not just Treasuries the Fed has to buy, but all dollar-denominated debt. No private buyers will purchase corporate or municipal bonds at rates far below the official inflation rate. That is when its balance sheet really explodes. Soon the inflationary fire threatens to burn the dollar and our entire economy to a cinder. At that point the only choice is between hyperinflation and default. This is the rock and the hard place the Fed will eventually be between.

Whatever it decides to do will set the real crash into motion. If the Fed does the right thing and raises rates aggressively, it will prick our bubble economy. The banks that were bailed out with TARP will fail again, but this time none of them will get bailed out. The Fed cannot ease and tighten simultaneously. If it's raising rates and contracting money supply, there is no money to finance another round of bailouts. Under this scenario, real estate prices will have another big lag down, unemployment will spike up, and the federal and many state governments will be rendered insolvent. The ensuing economic contraction will be much sharper than the one experienced in 2008. The bad news is this is actually the rosy scenario. The far bleaker outcome results from the Fed's refusal to allow this scenario to play out. If the Fed continues to inflate to delay the process, the result will be hyperinflation and the complete collapse of our economy and way of life.

Restructuring the National Debt

So we need to admit the obvious. There is simply no way American taxpayers can repay the money the federal government has borrowed. That means our creditors are going to take huge losses. There are really only two questions left unanswered.

The first is what form those losses will take. Either our creditors will not get all of their money back, or the money they get back will buy much less than they expect. So either we default or we inflate, but honest repayment isn't even an option. Given a choice between the two, default is by far the better choice, even for our creditors. The second question is one of timing. Will we default to avoid a crisis or in reaction to one? Will we default on our own terms or on those imposed upon us by our creditors? I would argue that the sooner we default the better, and that the terms will be more favorable when we are the ones proposing them.

Now by "default," I'm not talking about walking away from all our obligations entirely. But I am talking about a restructuring where creditors are paid less than they are owed.

If our government owes you money, you're not going to get 100 cents on the dollar. You might get thirty cents on the dollar. Depending on who you are and the nature of the U.S. obligation to you, you might get more or less.

There's a good debate to have on how we should decide whom to pay and how much. Usually a bankruptcy judge handles this sort of thing, but since we are the United States of America, no judge is going to preside over us. As a result, we get to decide for ourselves what's most fair.

If we're going to means-test Social Security benefits, which we should, maybe we ought to means-test other obligations? Huge, profitable banks could get less than old ladies holding on to savings bonds. That might be fairest. Or maybe we give preference to Americans over foreigners.

Probably, we should treat everyone as equally as possible, but things get more complicated when we acknowledge that T-Bills and Treasury Bonds aren't the only obligations we have, but that some of our spending is also a sort of obligation, too.

None of these are easy questions. But we can't start having an intelligent conversation as long as we keep pretending that we can meet our obligations. That's why we need to begin by declaring bankruptcy.

Default's Bad, but There's No Alternative

I know exactly how the economic pundits will react when they hear my recommendation.

Peter Schiff is saying we should default! This is the height of irresponsibility! How dare he even utter such words!

We saw similar hysterics around the 2011 debt-ceiling debate. The one thing on which all leaders in both parties agreed was that default was not acceptable. Both sides, in fact, attacked the other by saying the other guy was "willing to default rather than cut spending," or "willing to default rather than let tax cuts expire for the rich."

Default was the only taboo. But what do we do when our taboo is inevitable? In fact, by putting the default option on the table in the first place, we let our creditors know just how low they actually sit on the repayment totem pole. From their perspective, this should have been an official admission that we were running the world's biggest Ponzi scheme. We put our creditors on notice that default was inevitable. Our leaders could have taken default off the table by stating that we would prioritize payments on our debt over all other government expenditures. They did not do that. Remember, the debt ceiling is self-imposed. Failing to raise it merely amounts to our own refusal to borrow. However, what happens when we hit the "lending ceiling"? That is a ceiling we cannot breach, as we lack the ability to lift it. Our creditors already know the answer because we told them. If they refuse to lend us more money, we will refuse to pay them back the money we have already borrowed!

Again, if we tried to pay off our debts we would basically have to scrap everything the government does, but keep taxes high. The only functions of government would be to collect taxes and then cut checks to our creditors. We would be a colony of China and Wall Street. How long do you think that would last?

And hiking taxes 50 percent just to keep the debt at its current level? That's not going to work either. You'd get *Atlas Shrugged* at that point, with all wealth creators fleeing the country or diving into the black market.

The only feasible way to keep making our payments is through massive inflation. But massive inflation is effectively defaulting. Sure, we'll pay off your bond, but with dollars that are worth half as much, or less. Sure, you get your Social Security benefit, but we'll make sure the cost-of-living adjustments don't really match the cost-of-living increase we've caused with our printing press.

It's not even in the realm of possibility that we can pay off this debt. The sooner we admit it the better. If we declared bankruptcy today, while our outstanding debt is "only" $15 trillion or $16 trillion, our creditors and we would be better off than if we waited until the debt hit $20 or $25 trillion. It's not about whether default is good or bad. It's about whether default is better than the alternative. The truth is that inflation is worse than restructuring. The collateral damage to our economy, and real losses to our creditors, will be far greater if we inflate. Right now, we're not trying to right the ship. Every year, we expand the deficit and accelerate the growth rate of the debt. Not only are we not shrinking the debt, we're not even slowing down its growth.

Bipartisan crowing about deficit control always ends up in some embarrassing farce, like a commission, a super-committee, or some agreement to shrink the planned increases in discretionary spending. However, any recommendations to cut are routinely dismissed, and the hard choices are postponed yet again.

Even if we do get some kind of agreement, the numbers are too trivial to matter. Politicians try to make the number sound large by proposing cuts over ten-year time horizons, as was the case with the $1.2 trillion in automatic cuts agreed to in 2011 as part of the deal to raise the debt ceiling. Over two hundred billion of the so-called "cuts" merely represented reduced interest payments on smaller deficits, with the remaining trillion spread over ten years. None of the "cuts" represented actual reductions in government spending, but mere reductions in the rate of increase in that spending. The only "cuts" that count are those made in the first year. However, nothing whatsoever was cut in 2012. So Congress was able to claim credit for cutting spending without ever cutting anything. It's easy to vote for spending cuts that take place years in the future knowing they are unlikely ever to be enacted. One Congress cannot bind a future Congress to honor its budget proposals, so all they really amount to are suggestions. There will always be some excuse to postpone the cuts.

So everybody is just pretending they can fix our debt problem. Republicans talk about a balanced budget amendment. But they know this is a harmless way to win points. It takes sixty-seven votes in the Senate and 290 votes in the House in order to *propose* a constitutional amendment. After that, thirty-eight states would need to ratify the amendment.

With that high a threshold, Republican lawmakers are free to posture and rail as much as they like without a serious threat of ever being bound to a balanced budget.

The Democrats' game of pretend focuses on taxing the rich. They talk as if our debt would go away if only we let the Bush tax cuts expire, sending the top rates up a few percentage points. But if you wanted to balance our budget by squeezing the rich, you would need to tax almost all of their income, at which point you would see their taxable incomes shrinking. If you hiked everyone's taxes significantly, you could balance the budget, but you'd have to increase everyone's taxes a lot.

These debates—GOP calls for a balanced budget amendment, and Democratic class warfare tax hikes—are how politicians pretend that our debt is manageable. Everyone wants to pretend that we can actually repay our debts. We can't.

From a moral perspective, we shouldn't worry, either. The immoral thing was making the promises Congress has made—saddling future generations with debt for unsustainable programs. And I don't feel too bad for our largest foreign creditors taking a haircut. They had access to our budgets. They could read my books. They knew they were lending to a fiscally crippled nation.

And what about our credit rating and our ability to borrow again in the future? Sure, a default would make it harder for us to borrow cheaply. Like the guy who strategically walks away from his mortgage, we would default knowing that our future borrowing costs will go up, but calculating that it's still the smarter move. Anything that prevents the U.S. government from borrowing money is a good thing. First, the money borrowed is used to grow the government at the expense of the economy. Second, the money has to be repaid with interest. I do not want the U.S. government obligating me to repay loans to finance government expenditure I would prefer not to have been made in the first place. If our government were run properly, we wouldn't be constantly borrowing. Uncle Sam would borrow for the short term to cover emergencies. And after we had rebuilt a government limited in its scope and disciplined in its spending, lenders would see us as a safer bet than we are now.

Liquidation

Now imagine a bankrupt United States of America. Instead of playing pretend and tweaking our current system of government and finance, we could rebuild from scratch.

To pay what we could to those whom we owe, the U.S. government would have to sell off assets and shut down entire agencies and departments. The agenda I discussed in chapter 10 would be not only feasible in case of bankruptcy, but imperative.

All nonessential expenses would be ended, having been handed to the states and the private sector. Federal lands and federal buildings would be auctioned off. Federal subsidy programs would be wound down. In a quick but orderly fashion the government would liquidate everything it could.

After we've sold what we could and repaid what we could, we'd cancel our debts. The slate would be wiped clean. Like a business cleared of its malinvestments, the U.S. government would be liberated from Washington's last century of lousy decision-making. This would be the opportunity to set the ship straight.

Programs like Social Security and farm subsidies survive today not because people think they're a great idea, but because there are vested interests defending them, and reformers are dismissed as radical. If bankruptcy drove us to slash these programs, do you really think we would create them again later on, especially knowing what we know now?

As the U.S. government spent a few years in bankruptcy, local governments would step up and provide the important services Washington has been providing. Nonprofits and church groups would spring to fill the voids left when programs like Medicaid must be shelved. And businesses and families that have grown dependent on government would become more self-sufficient.

Those industries that have been propped up by government, like renewable energy and even much of the financial sector, would shrink, rearrange themselves, or even disappear. Wealth would steadily start allocating itself according to economic value, rather than political favor.

We wouldn't find ourselves in the midst of *Mad Max* or some other postapocalyptic world. There would be no cannibalism, and our buildings would not begin crumbling. There would be some "austerity" in this period, but that would be the fever ridding the economy of its toxins.

Let me ask you: What is the alternative? Pretending and pretending that we can repay our debts until one day, bam, like Greece, our creditors make a run on the bank? Or do we try to inflate our way out of the debt, risking hyperinflation and complete collapse?

Our economy and our government are in a car that is out of control, accelerating down an icy hill. I'm saying we need to steer it into the ditch before things get even worse. We're not going to avoid this crash. The best we can do is try to control it ourselves and brace for the impact.

America is Bankrupt 2.0: We Are All Detroit Now

Detroit was once a great city. It was the place where Americans' cars were built. In the 1960s, its citizens enjoyed the highest per capita income of any major city in America. Detroit is now a depressing ruin and a grim milestone along America's path of self-destruction.

When we talk about America staring down the next big bubble—the "government bubble"—Detroit provides an example in miniature. Like many municipalities, it has been struggling through the late stages of too-big government. Like others, it reached a point at which it owed so much to its retirees that it could no longer provide basic services to its citizens, not even by imposing draconian tax rates on people who literally lack the money to pay.

In perhaps one of the greatest spin campaigns ever, these reductions in government services have resulted in the Left proclaiming Detroit to be the most libertarian city in America—the lesson being that libertarianism is dangerous. Of course Detroit, with one of the highest tax and regulatory burdens of any city in the nation, is hardly a libertarian paradise.

Detroit does not lack government services because its government is too small. It's because the government grew so large that it destroyed the tax base necessary to sustain itself. Like a parasite that has killed its host, Detroit can no longer survive. Detroit calls into question the Left's mode of governance, and liberals have responded by covering their eyes and deliberately drawing the wrong lesson from the crisis.

Had Detroit truly been a libertarian city all along, the tax base would still be healthy, and the government would have plenty of resources to provide the necessary (and limited) public services that even libertarians support. But because it is one of the most socialist cities in America, it is now broke and lacks the resources to even operate the streetlights.

Meredith Whitney, in her book *The Fate of the States*, writes that "inside of just one decade, government pension funds" at the state and local level "went from being fully funded to being underfunded by nearly $1 trillion." This is manifesting itself all over America in different ways. She notes that in the 2013 forest fire season, California's Contra Costa County could only afford 261 firefighters—most of its money is tied up in paying six-figure annual pensions to 665 retired firefighters.

And municipalities that can't cut services any further are declaring bankruptcy—beginning with Vallejo and Stockton, also both in California.

But Detroit's bankruptcy of July 2013 was the biggest ever of its kind. It was the predictable result of a city that had cannibalized itself—that had gorged itself for so long on its citizens' money, prompting them to run for the city limits and exacerbating the problem still further with each departure.

When Detroit lost its main industry—the automakers—its economy began to decline. By the time it declared Chapter Nine bankruptcy on July 18, 2013, its population was less than 700,000—a bit more than one-third of what it had been at its peak in 1950. It had an astounding 78,000 vacant buildings, 38,000 of which were deemed unsafe, and 66,000 vacant and blighted lots.

According to a *Detroit News* report in October 2012, 40 percent of the city's remaining residents were planning to leave within the next five years.

In a great example of truth being stranger than fiction, Detroit has literally "gone to the dogs," as packs of stray pit bulls and other canines roam the streets, making the city look like a studio back lot for the production of some kind of postapocalyptic sci-fi horror film.

The city didn't just lack money, industry, and jobs—it also lacked hope. Howard Dean, the former Vermont governor and presidential candidate, told an MSNBC panel that the city could be saved because housing prices there have hit rock bottom. What he was forgetting is that there's a reason those houses are so cheap—no sane person would move there if given a choice to live anywhere else.

The loss of industry was hard on Detroit, but things never had to get this bad. And if you look at Detroit's neighboring counties—Oakland and Macomb—things aren't so bad there, even though they lost thousands of jobs in the exact same industry. Detroit ended up where it is now because its city government worked so hard to hasten the demise at every step along the way.

The city payrolls stayed fat for far too long, even as the city's population vanished. In order to remain grossly overstaffed and to pay for the excessive pension promises to retirees, Detroit's central planners imposed ever-higher taxes on an ever-shrinking and ever-poorer population. They sought to squeeze blood out of the stone, raising nearly every tax they could to the maximum statutory rate allowed by Michigan law.

By 2013, Detroit's per capita tax burden was twice as high as Livonia, one of its nearby suburbs, even though Detroit residents by then had only half Livonia's per-capita income. In fact, Detroit owes over 100,000 creditors $18 billion dollars. That amounts to a total per capita debt of $26,000—every man, woman, and child in the city, not even including their share of state and federal debt. But when you consider that 47 percent of Detroit's population is functionally illiterate, and less than half of the adult population is employed, even the expression of not being able to get "blood from a turnip" seems inadequate.

Detroiters, rich (what few remained) and poor, were being soaked to pay for more than forty overstaffed and inefficient city government agencies that provided them with sub-par or nonexistent services. Hundreds of millions were wasted revitalizing the downtown area of a city whose residential areas were emptying out. Detroit built a stadium and casinos and developed corporate welfare packages to lure in the headquarters of big businesses.

Meanwhile, even the simplest government tasks were performed with a maximum amount of waste. Detroit had 151 employees working to print the checks for its own staff. Each paycheck cost $62 in administrative costs—four times as expensive as the average employer and 3.5 times as expensive as the average city.

But that's not all. The long-suffering residents of that city were also being overtaxed to pay for overgenerous retirement packages that had been promised when times were better and when Detroit's city government was even more overstaffed than it is today. By the time it went bankrupt, Detroit had made drastic personnel cuts through attrition and negotiated early retirements, reducing its payroll by 38 percent between 2000 and 2011. Yet even after those reductions, Detroit was still one of America's most overstaffed cities. By 2011, there was still one city employee in Detroit for every fifty-five residents—the second worst ratio (after wealthy San Francisco) for any city its size. And Detroiters weren't just paying that reduced workforce—they were also still paying pensions and health care for the workers who had been there in 2000, when there was one city employee for every thirty-five residents.

To keep making payroll and pension payments, the city did what many cities and states have done—it stopped contributing to its pension funds for current employees. Then it began skimping on city services. Violent crime soared, with police response times of nearly an hour for 911 calls in early 2013. The city began turning off and choosing not to fix thousands of streetlights to save money.

Detroit shut down two-thirds of its parks in 2009, and by 2013 was planning to shut down or limit access to nearly all of those remaining. Half of the city's residents stopped paying their ridiculously high property taxes. As one resident told the *Detroit News*: "Why should I send them taxes when they aren't supplying services? It is sickening. . . . Every time I see the tax bill come, I think about the times we called and nobody came."

As Michigan governor Rick Snyder noted in his letter authorizing the city's emergency manager to file for bankruptcy, Detroit could meet neither its obligations to citizens nor to creditors. Moreover, there was no tax increase high enough, and no spending cut deep enough, nor any combination of the two, that could possibly be large enough to save Detroit from its $18 billion in accumulated obligations.

Obama's former auto bailout czar, Steve Rattner, even suggested in *The New York Times* that Detroit be given disaster aid, as if it had just been hit by a hurricane. However, there is nothing natural about this disaster. It is entirely man-made. As neither this sort of creative bailout nor any other seemed forthcoming, bankruptcy was the only choice.

Besides, if the federal government gives in to political pressure and bails out Detroit, the problems for the city and the nation will only get worse. Incompetent and corrupt city officials will remain in power, and municipal labor unions will retain their vise-grip on taxpayers. On a broader level, the inherent moral hazard will only encourage more cities to overpromise and over-borrow, confident that the Federal government will bail them out too. It's the same problem that Europe has with Greece, only we have a lot more cities like Detroit than Europe has nations like Greece.

The bankruptcy also has broader implications for the municipal bond markets. A court challenge sought to place pensioners ahead of bondholders. Politically this is a popular position for politicians to take. But if they succeed, municipal bond yields will rise across the nation as creditors of other troubled municipalities (including really big ones like Chicago) receive a massive wake-up call. A bailout might mitigate the damage for muni bonds, but an effective, implied federal government guarantee on muni bonds would send treasury yields rising, lifting the entire yield spectrum with it.

Regardless of how the politics play out, Detroit's bankruptcy provides more evidence of the risks inherent in the muni-bond market—and it validates my general advice to avoid the sector entirely. Either by default or inflation, muni-bond buyers will suffer significant losses.

It's easy to laugh at Detroit—a poorly run city by all accounts. You can make fun of the liberals who ran it, or (if you're especially cruel) even the residents who had the misfortune of living there. But you shouldn't.

It's a little harder to learn the lessons of Detroit. It hurts a bit to admit the reality. Because this isn't just about Detroit—this is you, America.

Detroit's situation, with a massive, unpayable debt of five to six times its annual operating budget, loosely mirrors the federal government's situation. Just multiply all of the dollar amounts by a thousand, and you're in the ballpark.

There are a few important differences, of course. Unlike Detroit, which only has to pay for its own employees' retirement and health care, the feds are on the hook for *everyone's* retirement and health care through Social Security and Medicare.

And then there are a lot of similarities. Like Detroit with its pensions, the feds aren't contributing a dime to the trust funds that supposedly undergird its much, much larger retirement programs. For decades, they have been spending all the money dedicated to those programs, and they'll have to borrow every dime of it back—adding to our $17 trillion debt—if they're going to honor those programs' promises.

Like Detroit, the federal government is spending so much money on frivolities—government employee conferences, foreign wars with questionable value to America's interests—that it can't even spare money for services the federal government is nominally justified in providing. It can arm rebels in a protracted Syrian civil war, drop bombs on Libya, and rebuild Afghanistan, but it can't police our southern border against drug and human smugglers. Despite the robust role government has taken in regulating the financial industry, it can't catch obvious billion-dollar frauds like Bernie Madoff. And as Warren Buffett has famously noted, the federal government wasn't even able to police the government-sponsored Fannie Mae and Freddie Mac businesses, even though an entire regulatory agency exists for that sole purpose.

For now, the federal government is safe. It isn't like Detroit in that, at least as long as Europe remains a wreck, it can continue borrowing money from abroad. And importantly, the federal government controls its own currency. It can print more money, devalue its citizens' wealth, and prevent reality from crashing down for even longer than the decades Detroit had before its fall.

But this can only go on for so long. And by the time it's done, we will be lucky indeed if Uncle Sam is wise enough to learn from Detroit. When the day of reckoning comes and interest rates rise, America needs to follow Detroit into bankruptcy.

If America is not as smart as Detroit was, then things are going to be much, much worse. Get ready for the Real Crash.

13

Investing for the Crash

IF YOU ARE PAYING ATTENTION TODAY, YOU KNOW that the U.S. economy and the world economy are in incredible flux. You're worried about your home. You're worried about your job. You're downright terrified about your investment portfolio and your retirement account. People are asking how to protect themselves from the turmoil, and maybe even profit from the dramatic changes and pervading uncertainty.

The central problem is this: what was previously safe may no longer be safe. Safety used to be defined by the dollar and U.S. Treasuries. As I laid out in the previous eleven chapters, the dollar is not safe, and the U.S. Treasury market is the next bubble waiting to burst. In short, nothing is safe.

Amid the flux, there's some consistency. The trends and the dynamics shaping the economy today are the same ones that have prevailed for over a decade. When it comes to how to invest for the long term, I've been giving my clients the same advice for ten years. What I predicted a decade ago regarding the future of the United States and the global economy has been playing out before our eyes. Some of it has happened more quickly than I expected. Some of it is happening more slowly.

Not all of the advice I gave in the first edition of *The Real Crash* has made you money in the year and a half since its publication. In fact, if you bought it the day it was published, you're probably behind at this point. There are reasons for that, which I'll get into shortly.

But first of all, let's put this into perspective: The recommendations I offered were never intended for a period as short as just a year and a half.

And many of them now represent even better investments than when this book was first published. There are more favorable valuations now—so you can get in closer to the bottom.

But I believe strongly that these are solid investments. I'll explain in this chapter why that's true even if I'm wrong about the severity of the coming crash. I'm not recommending an all-or-nothing bet on an economic apocalypse that will leave you in pain if a miracle occurs and the economy is saved. But when the real crash does happen—and I do think it will—I believe the advice I'm giving you is the best way to protect your wealth and leave you ahead of the game.

Thinking Long Term

Investing isn't gambling. But in at least one respect it is a bit like playing poker. What matters is not the number of hands you win or how big your stack of chips grows while you're still sitting at the table. What matters is how big the stack is when you cash out. If you've played poker, you know that playing a sound strategy might mean that you lose a few hands. Playing dumb might win you some hands. But over the course of the night, it's the player who best understands the game who goes home a winner.

Now, if you crafted the perfect Peter Schiff portfolio for yourself in 2012, you've had a few major factors working against you. We have since had a big run in the U.S. stock market. It has hit new highs and outperformed (in real terms) all of its world peers. I recommended foreign stocks, which I believe will, in the long run, outperform the U.S. market. (I did warn that if you're in American investments you should pick U.S. stocks over bonds, and in that I was right.) I also recommended gold as part of your portfolio, and gold has not performed well during this short period.

So I was in some ways wrong as far as the last year and a half goes—but in the long run, I'm still confident that I will be proven right. In fact, the advice I offered then is even more appropriate as this second edition goes to print. Gold is cheaper, so what better time to add it to your portfolio? And foreign stocks are now trading at cheaper valuations relative to U.S. stocks.

The deception behind the current U.S. economic expansion must be understood, because it's a temporary speed bump for your portfolio. All year, right up until September 2013, the idea that the economy was really coming back pervaded the market.

But you know who didn't believe that? Fed Chairman Ben Bernanke. He proved it in September 2013, when the Fed announced that there would be no tapering off of Fed monthly asset purchases. He argued that he couldn't do it because of signs of weakness in the economy. But that renewed weakness—and he specifically referenced rising interest rates—was the result of his own posturing and the threat of tapering that he had made earlier. In fact, by citing rising interest rates as a reason not to taper, Bernanke revealed the conundrum the Fed faces. Interest rates rose because he threatened to taper. Because rates rose, he could not carry out his threat. The Fed cannot taper without causing rates to rise, and the Fed knows that rising rates will derail the recovery.

This is why I believe the Fed will likely reverse course on tapering, especially given its renewed commitment to keep interest rates near zero.

Some experts have likened the stimulus of quantitative easing to training wheels on a bike. What they fail to understand is that the stimulus is the only wheels the bike has.

The larger problem, however, is that the bike is cycling toward a cliff, so the wheels must be removed to avoid going over the edge. It will cause a painful fall for the rider, but not nearly as painful as going over that cliff. (For a good idea of the near unanimity of "expert" opinion as to the certainty of a September taper, go to YouTube and check out "Peter Schiff Was Right, Taper Edition.")

As we noted in an earlier chapter, the result of the Fed's pump-priming has been a mere reflation of well-known asset bubbles—especially U.S. stocks and real estate. Conservative investments return almost nothing, forcing investors to behave more aggressively, in stocks or speculative real estate. Mortgage rates continue to be historically low, so speculators are stoking the housing market. As a result of low interest rates, U.S. companies are also borrowing money, hand over fist, to buy back their own stock. All of these things are raising asset prices without creating real value or contributing to genuine economic growth.

The result is that there is no economic recovery underway. In reality, we're just drifting, and even worse, sinking from the weight of government debt. The few bullish signs in the economy—namely, the rise in the stock and real estate markets—are actually the result of expansionary monetary policy, not a sign that it's finally time to cut it off. This is the open secret that we are likely to discover soon.

The action in the currency markets is consistent with this theory. In 2013, as currency traders started to factor in the tapering, they went back into the dollar, which they expected to strengthen relative to other currencies. This undermined investment in many emerging-market countries that had been printing money in an effort to keep their currencies from rising too much against the dollar so as to keep exports to the U.S. strong. But with Bernanke's surprise announcement in September, the dollar tanked. And over time, as the market figures out that the Fed has no exit strategy for unloading the debts it has purchased—now or ever—the dollar will weaken still more. I believe that central bankers in emerging markets will feel once-bitten, twice shy. They will choose not to compete in the race to the bottom against our currency. They won't be printing money and buying nearly as many dollars as they did last time around. This will cause the dollar to fall still further, possibly leading to a rout as everyone flees investments with dollar-denominated returns.

The bond market also shows obvious signs of dependency on continued quantitative easing. Beginning in Spring 2013, when the Fed started talking about tapering its purchases of government debt, the yield on the 10-year Treasury nearly doubled from 1.6 percent to 3 percent by September 2013. Once the word came down that there would be no tapering, yields headed back down to 2.5 percent. When a taper was announced in December, they'd hit 3 percent again. But the Fed is dangerously close to losing control of long-term interest rates, if it has not done so already. Once the markets figure out that quantitative easing is actually bearish and not bullish for bonds, because it means more inflation and a weaker dollar, the party will be over.

As I've noted earlier, the Fed is walking a fine line here. It's trying to keep interest rates down while maintaining the pretense of an exit strategy from all the debt it has purchased. If people start to perceive that it's actually monetizing the debt, the consequences will be grave. The value of the dollar will fall further, requiring even more energetic intervention in order to avoid losing control of interest rates. Yet at the same time, a failure to tighten and raise interest rates will lead to rampant inflation.

Gold has not been performed well since peaking near $1,900 an ounce in

August 2011, but here too we see the Fed's fingerprints. After that summer spike, gold mainly traded in a $200 range between $1,500 and $1,700 until April 2013, when Goldman Sachs issued its sell recommendation and the Fed started talking about tapering. This sent gold plunging by over $200 per ounce in less than two weeks, and marked the beginning of a four-month decline that ended with gold approaching $1,200 in early July.

But the sell off in gold was based on the false narrative that the U.S. economic recovery was gaining momentum and that the Fed was preparing to end QE and raise interest rates. None of these assumptions were correct. However, it resulted in panic-selling and an incredible buying opportunity. My take is that speculators, who watched from the sidelines for over ten years as gold rose from below $300 per ounce in 2001 to over $1,500 in 2011, only to pile into the market though exchange traded funds, such as GLD, panicked. The Goldman sell and the Fed taper talk pushed gold though key technical support levels, triggering a wave of selling.

However, while the speculators were bailing out, real investors were taking advantage of the sale. Physical gold was disappearing from the market, and premiums on bullion coins rose sharply. The physical market was so tight that some coins were unavailable and delivery times that used to take less than a week required six weeks or more.

The speculators never really understood the gold trade. If they had, they would have begun buying ten years earlier like I did. They only jumped on the train because in early 2011, it was the only trade that was working. At that time, gold trading at $1,500 was 50 percent above its 2008 high, while the Dow Jones was still about 10 percent below its 2007 peak. Plus, since some high-profile hedge funds that made billions shorting subprime were big buyers of gold, it seemed like the smart thing to do. However, as these new fair-weather gold friends had no real conviction, they bailed at the first sign of trouble. As a result, gold has moved from weak hands to strong ones.

Once gold speculators discover that their premise is false, it will be expensive for them to reestablish their positions. The gold they sold on the way down is unlikely to be for sale on the way up. This will be particularly problematic for shorts looking to cover their positions. The investors who purchased, including central banks, likely have no intention of selling. In addition, gold mining companies have shut down higher-cost mines, and pared back their capital spending and exploration budget. As a result future supply will be insufficient to meet future demand. As speculators return to a supply-constrained market, I expect prices to surge. It could be the mother of all short-covering rallies.

So all of the themes I stressed in the first edition, which I lay out in greater detail below, still apply. You should invest in commodities, emerging markets, and developed foreign stock markets—especially in the foreign stocks of companies that pay dividends and do not rely on the U.S. consumer, whose purchasing power could soon take a sharp dive.

As far as temporary losses are concerned, look to the head fake of the 2008 crisis, when investors relied on the reputation of the United States and became even more scared about foreign investments than domestic ones. For a brief moment, gold and foreign stocks took a serious beating. At that time, I was pounding the table for investors to buy gold and foreign stocks. In hindsight, we now know what a good call that was.

Before going into this investment advice, I'd just like to add one more note. Some people have complained about the first edition of this book that there wasn't enough specific information on what to do. It's actually pretty simple to tell you what to do with your money, but I don't know your personal situation. And I can't get too specific (recommending individual stocks, for example) for regulatory reasons. Also, as I write this, I don't know exactly when you'll be reading the book. Even if the exact timing doesn't change the broader strategy, the specifics (for example, what Australian companies and what gold mining stocks should you own) could change dramatically.

So I aim here to lay out a broad strategy. If you want more specific advice, you'll need an advisor. It doesn't have to be me, but I have developed specific investment products tailored to what I believe will happen, as outlined in this book. If you like to handle your own investing, you don't even need to hire me to benefit from these—we have launched mutual funds for this specific purpose, which you can buy without even having an account at Euro Pacific Capital.

But either way, this isn't a place where I can offer specific investment advice for your situation—only broad guidelines from which you can learn.

What Is Investing?

Politicians are skilled at mangling the meanings of words. Two of the most frequently distorted words in recent years are "investment" and "speculation." Politicians know that investment carries a positive connotation, and speculation a negative one. So President Obama uses the word "investment" to refer to any government spending, while congressmen use the word "speculation" to describe any financial activity they want to attack.

But these terms have real meaning, and we need to set them straight.

When considering a more meaningful and traditional understanding of the word *investing,* I recall a story my father once told me. When he got into the investment business, the first question clients would ask when considering an investment was "What does it pay?" That's the idea of investing: you buy something, and get paid for owning it.

If you buy an apartment as an investment, you're collecting rent. If you buy a bond, you collect interest. Some stocks pay dividends, too. This is what my father's clients were asking with the question, "What does it pay?"

Speculating is something different—and it is commonly mislabeled as *investing.* Just like politicians, your stockbroker also realizes that speculation has a negative ring to it. So the best way for him to get you to speculate is by convincing you that you're investing. But if you buy an asset simply because you hope that you will be able to sell it for more at some later date, you're speculating. For many people today, this is the definition of investing: buy low, sell high. But it's more properly called *speculating,* because it is based not on some underlying value in the asset, but on the hope that somebody else will pay more for it than you did. Stock and real estate bubbles of recent years were rife with speculation disguised as investment.

In contrast to my father's experience, when modern stockbrokers bring stock ideas to their clients, the first question the client typically asks is "What is the price?" The idea is that a low price somehow indicates more upside potential than a high one. In truth, a stock price on its own reveals nothing about the underlying value of the shares. A company with a share price of $100 may be very cheap, while another with a share price of only $5 may be prohibitively expensive. A share price only conveys meaning when expressed relative to another variable, such as earnings, book value, or sales. You also need to know the total number of shares outstanding to figure out the market value of the company.

The rise of speculation over investing has changed the shape of the market. Consider AT&T stock and AT&T bonds. It used to be that when you bought a stock, the company would pay you a decent dividend in order to make up for two downsides relative to a bond: you were bearing the risk (you might not get your money back), and you weren't getting interest payments.

Today, it's backward. Investors see the stockholder as the privileged one, because he gets a share of the company's growth. In that light, he doesn't need to be compensated. Bondholders are considered the chumps: lending the company money, but not getting a cut when the company grows. You can sense the underlying fallacy here: the belief that stocks always go up.

Of course, many stocks are down today compared to the year 2000, but very few of the companies behind them went bankrupt. That means shareholders have often lost value, but very few bondholders were left in the lurch. Meanwhile, shareholders often haven't been getting paid. Dividends were discarded as old-fashioned during the dot-com boom. Dividends are slowly creeping back into vogue among U.S. companies. One reason I advise clients to buy foreign stocks is that they are more likely to pay dividends, and higher dividends as well. (There are plenty of other reasons, but I'll get to those later.)

How to Think About Investing

You need to have a long-term time horizon in order to invest well. If your time window is just a couple of years, you can't really do any investing. Sure, for a couple of years you could speculate (betting a stock will go up). But there is also a good chance that stock prices will fall instead. With a short time horizon, you may not own your shares when the market eventually recovers. In reality, under these circumstances, it's just better to save.

The reason: in the short term, there's too much "noise." A good investment strategy could, at any given point, be a money loser. Only over the long run will the strength of your strategy really pay off. As an analogy: the best shooter in basketball could have an awful game. Over the course of the season, though, he'll have the best shooting percentage.

So, if we're looking over the long term, here's the question you need to ask: how will the world be different in ten or twenty years than it is today? Geopolitically, here's what I believe.

Right now, the United States is the center of the economic world. We are perceived to be the richest country, and the dollar is the reserve currency. We don't have to make anything but can still buy everything. Our interest rates are low, and so we can borrow like crazy.

But America's position in the world is going to change. We're living beyond our means, which is something one cannot do forever. Either gradually or abruptly, our ability to consume without producing will come to an end.

Americans can only live beyond their means because much of the rest of the world is willing to save up for now and live beneath its means. Elsewhere in the world, there are more creditors than debtors, and there is pent-up demand and excess production. In the future, these economies will see a surge in demand, while ours will see demand fall.

As this second edition goes to press, there are signs already that China is reaching this threshold. In mid-November of 2013 all 376 members of the "communist" party's central committee concluded a key four-day economic policy meeting know as the "Third Plenum" by pledging to allow market forces to pay a great role in the economy.

The irony, of course, is that as the Chinese Communists have agreed to allow market forces to play "a decisive role in allocating resources," American "capitalists" are taking the opposite approach, with ObamaCare being the latest example of the state taking a greater role in the allocation of heath care and the pricing of insurance.

The significance of this meeting cannot be underestimated. The 1978 Plenum, two years after the death of Mao Tse Tung, was where Deng Xiaoping began the historic transformation of China's economy. The 1993 Plenum led to China's entry into the World Trade Organization.

A week following the conclusion of this recent Plenum, in a guidebook released explaining the reforms, Zhou Xiaochuan, governor of The People's Bank of China (PBOC) wrote:

"We will increase the role of market exchange rates, and the central bank will basically exit from normal foreign-exchange market intervention. . . . The central bank will "establish a managed floating exchange-rate system based upon market supply and demand."

And in a shocking admission, almost unnoticed in the American press, Yi Gang, a deputy governor at the bank said, "It's no longer in China's favor to accumulate foreign-exchange reserves."

In truth, it has not been in China's favor to accumulate foreign-exchange reserves for a long time. Personally I think the BPOC has known this for a while, but if they are admitting it publicly, it must mean they are getting ready to exit the dollar-buying business. Of course if they are no longer buying dollars, that means they will no longer be buying Treasuries or U.S. mortgage-backed securities either. While Fed officials were talking about tapering, China was actually getting ready to do it.

And this would be the mother of all tapers—unlike the Fed, China is talking about going cold turkey! If it's "no longer in China's favor to accumulate foreign reserves" then they can no longer act as America's banker as the only way they can lend us more money is to keep increasing their reserves. In fact, if they are going to let market forces determine exchange rates, then China no longer has to buy dollars. The sole reason behind dollar purchases was to prevent market forces from increasing the value of their currency.

At the time of this announcement in November 2013, China's foreign exchange reserves stood at $3.66 trillion (almost as large as the Fed's balance sheet at that time). During the third quarter of 2013 those reserves grew by $163.3 billion. That means that while the Fed was buying $85 billion per month with its official QE program, China's unofficial QE program amounted to more than $54 billion per month! Since China does not publish the details of those purchases, we do not know for sure what percentage are U.S. dollars. But I'm sure it is substantial—perhaps 50 percent if not considerably more.

Also, since the PBOC has correctly concluded that expanding their balance sheet is not in China's interest, perhaps they have also correctly concluded that shrinking its balance sheet is. If my guess is correct, while the Fed was bluffing an exit strategy, China was actually preparing for one.

During Operation Twist, as the Fed was swapping short for long-term Treasuries, China was likely taking the other side of those trades. As a result, China no longer needs to sell Treasuries to unwind its balance sheet. All it needs to do is let them mature.

So if China tapers its purchases of U.S. Treasuries by about $30 billion per month, and potentially demands repayment of hundreds of billions more that mature, how is the Fed supposed to taper its bond-buying program? The answer is, it can't. That is why I predict that a Yellen-led Fed will have to reverse course on its December announcement.

On a separate but important note, the Third Plenum also resulted in a relaxation of China's controversial "one-child policy." Under the relaxed policy, couples where at least one parent is an only child will be allowed to have two children. This will result in millions of additional births. With more of their own to take care of, China will have even more reasons to stop supporting Americans.

All of this, of course, is good news for the Chinese and bad news for Americans who depend on China's largesse. For China, a stronger yuan means lower consumer prices, more domestic capital investment, a more efficient allocation of resources, and a higher standard of living. For America, it means a weaker dollar, higher consumer prices, higher interest rates, and a lower standard of living.

You want to be invested in businesses whose customers will be richer in the future. That is, you want to be investing today where people are saving and producing, so that tomorrow, when they're ready to spend, you're getting some of that money. So there's your first hint.

The typical American is drowning in debt. The typical Asian is floating on a sea of savings. Here's one representative detail: 90 percent of cars in China are purchased with all cash. Eighty-five percent of cars in the United States are bought with auto loans. Think about what this means for future consumers in both countries. Not only can today's Chinese car buyers actually afford their cars, but tomorrow's will be able to trade up for newer ones without owing anything.

Disposable income will be even higher in countries when they stop sending all their money to the U.S. Treasury. This money will go toward consumption, or investment that is more likely to be at home.

Bottom line: purchasing power is shifting. You should try to invest in companies that will benefit from this shift. These will primarily be foreign companies. Of course, many foreign companies sell to the United States. These aren't the businesses I'm talking about. Also, some U.S. companies might be wise investments if they sell mostly to the economies where demand will skyrocket. However, my fear here is that as the U.S. economy comes under more pressure, politicians will scapegoat those corporations that manage to profit while "the rest of us" suffer. This could provide political cover for a "windfall profits" tax that could undermine the earnings of U.S exporters.

If my theory about purchasing power shifting to developing nations is correct, then raw materials should be a major beneficiary. If China and India start spending more money, the demand for raw materials will go way up. People who have never owned cars before, or a dishwasher or washing machine, will start buying them. The materials to make this equipment, and the fuels to power them, will become scarcer. Yes, they are spending a lot of that money making stuff for Americans, but the stuff they make for themselves will be far more resource-intensive.

Also, as people get richer, they eat more, and they eat more complicated food. For example, wealthier societies generally consume more meat. Raising a cow or a pig requires plenty of grain. You consume more corn when you eat a steak than when you eat the corn directly. So we should invest in agriculture.

A Few Good Countries

I don't settle lightly on which countries and currencies I'm willing to invest in. I study their monetary policy, their regulation, their taxes, their political stability, their natural resources, and more.

The countries that I am most optimistic about in 2013 are the same ones I favored in 2008. Some are weaker or stronger than they were six years ago, depending on how their governments and economies reacted to the 2008–2009 recession. Also, with the U.S. closer to the Real Crash, I put more importance today on the country's dependence on U.S. purchasing power.

Here are some of the countries I like, and a few reasons why I like them:

Australia

Australia is a little bit like what we wish the United States was. It's a large, English-speaking country with robust finance and plenty of natural resources. But Australia has some strengths we lack.

The Aussies didn't have a recession in 2008–2009. Their strong banking system was one reason, but most important was their export market: most of their exports go to Asia. So while Americans were panicking and scrimping, and losing houses, the Chinese were buying—and so Australia was selling.

Australia's huge supply of natural gas is another key. The country isn't as sensitive to oil price shocks or disruptions in fuel shipments. The government has forced its agencies to trim 1.25 percent to 1.5 percent of their operations costs—which is not a huge amount, but most countries are moving in the opposite directions.

The Australian dollar gained 60 percent on the U.S. dollar from its late 2008 lows to its late 2011 lows, and although it pulled back in 2013 when Fed tapering was in the cards, it has held most of these gains for the long term. Moreover, as this book was going to press, Australians elected a government that will scrap Australia's carbon tax and help it remain a powerful force in manufacturing.

Singapore

Singapore arguably has the freest economy in the world, which is one reason Singaporeans are getting richer. Since 2000, Singapore's GDP has more than doubled, and it hasn't shown signs of slowing. The country is at full employment and the Singaporean people have high personal savings rates.

These people will pick up a tiny bit of slack in consumer demand when U.S. demand drops off. But Singapore is most promising not because of the wealth of its people, but because, like Australia, it is selling to a booming region of the world.

Singapore has a huge trade surplus (on a per-capita basis). While much of that is due to exports to the U.S., the growth in the rest of Asia is a huge factor, too. These guys are manufacturing for sale to China, Australia, and India.

Hong Kong

A model of capitalism, Hong Kong has low taxes and low regulation, making it the corporate Mecca of Asia. The Hong Kong Stock Exchange is the fifth largest in the world, with a total market capitalization of $2.7 trillion as of late 2011.

This little tip of land in China is politically an odd creature. It is under Chinese rule, but its constitution dictates that Hong Kong will have a capitalist economy. This helps explain the booming wealth there as well as corporations' eagerness to set up headquarters.

Unsurprisingly, half of Hong Kong's exports (if you can call them that) go to China. The United States and Japan are its other big export markets, but as manufacturing moves to Mainland China, Hong Kong is becoming more service oriented.

New Zealand

Another small Pacific nation with huge upside potential, New Zealand has seen its GDP more than double since 2000. Since a downturn in 2009, economic growth has been flat, but it could rebound.

Steadily shifting from agriculture to manufacturing, New Zealand is pursuing free-trade agreements around the globe. In 2008, the New Zealand–China Free Trade Agreement became China's first free-trade agreement with a developed nation.

If New Zealand becomes a major exporter to China and Australia, it is poised to boom.

Switzerland

If the United States is the Prodigal Son, Switzerland is the brother who stayed true to his roots. The Swiss still adhere to many of the principles on which both Switzerland and the United States were founded, including federalism and staying out of entangling alliances.

Switzerland has never joined the European Union (EU), much less adopted the euro. It has long been home to some of the most successful banks and insurers, but drug and chemical companies are also thriving there.

Sitting smack in the middle of Europe, it is subject to some of the continent's turmoil, but the country's fierce independence makes it something of an oasis. It is far easier to do business in Switzerland than in the EU.

Norway

I call Norway my European secret. Like Switzerland, Norway held on to its currency, the krone. The country is also a leading oil exporter, and is flush with fish, forests, and minerals.

Again, being in Europe and relying on Europe for exports is a handicap. But when you're selling fuel and other natural resources, the relevant market is global, so Norway should be able to make adjustments if Europe falls into a deep funk.

Also, having learned firsthand the problems of the social welfare state, the nation has sent its political pendulum swinging in the other direction, as its September 2013 election demonstrated.

The Netherlands

You may know that the United States is the world's leading agricultural exporter, and that France is number two. You probably didn't know that the Netherlands is in third place. Also surprising: Netherlands' Groningen natural gas field is Europe's largest.

The Netherlands has a stable economy and is an active trading partner, boasting a trade surplus. Yes, they scrapped the gilder for the euro, but for those looking for some euro exposure, the Netherlands is a good place to get it.

Canada

Manufacturing, mining, drilling, extraction, and logging—Canada does all the things the United States seems to be moving away from.

Look at Canada's economic growth figures and you would think it was some developing country, having doubled its GDP between 2002 and 2010. The country's banking system is also on far firmer footing than is the U.S. system. In per-capita GDP, Canada could catch up with the United States in purchasing-power terms any day now—in nominal terms, it already has.

Canada's weakness is that it depends so much on its big brother to the south (us). However, as trade with the U.S. slows, trade with other developing economies will rise to fill the void.

China

This whole book has been about the harm that the U.S. government does to our economy. So how can I advise you to invest in a communist country like China?

First, you need to understand that no country is perfectly free, nor will there be a perfectly free market until Schiffistan is created. If you're looking for a place where wealth can be created and expanded, look to the freest economy.

When judging countries on this basis, remember there's a difference between political freedom and economic freedom. That is, capitalism and democracy are not the same thing. Think about the United States in the nineteenth century. We were far less democratic. Women couldn't vote. Men couldn't vote until they were twenty-one, which meant they had probably been in the workforce for at least five years. Literacy tests, poll taxes, and property requirements denied many people the vote. Senators were chosen by state legislators rather than by popular election. The Electoral College was actually a group of elites gathering to choose the president.

While we were much less democratic, the economy was a lot freer. We were less regulated, less subsidized, and less bailed out. Taxes were a tiny fraction of what they are today.

Similarly, China is not a free country politically. Dissidents are jailed and the Internet is censored. But China is no longer a command economy controlled by the state or the Communist Party. In many ways, their economy is freer than ours. Resort mogul Steve Wynn has moved much of his business to China in part because, as he puts it, "The governmental policies in the United States of America are a damper, a wet blanket. . . . They retard investment; they retard job formation." Reiterating that sentiment, Coca-Cola CEO Muhtar Kent told the *Financial Times* in September 2011 that in many respects it's easier to do business in China than in the United States.

No, I'm not saying China is the land of the free. I'm saying many countries, including China, are more fertile ground for economic growth.

The Three-Legged Stool

Any investment portfolio needs to be balanced. I like the standard image of a stool, with three legs. If one is missing, the whole thing is unstable. Many advisors and brokers know that balance is needed, but anyone today relying on conventional wisdom is building the stool with rickety legs.

My strategy is a stool with three solid legs: (1) quality dividend-paying foreign stocks in the right sectors; (2) liquidity, and less volatile investments, such as cash and foreign bonds; and (3) gold and gold mining stocks.

I recommended this strategy in both versions of *Crash Proof* and in *The Little Book of Bull Moves and Bear Markets.* Because the real crash that I have been helping people prepare for has yet to occur, I see no reason to change course now. In fact, the parts of my forecast that have already come true merely strengthen my resolve as to the appropriateness of my approach. In any event, since I have already done a pretty good job of building a case for this strategy in my prior books, I will here merely outline that strategy. Again, I wish I could personally look at your situation and tell you exactly what to do, but both government regulation and practical considerations won't allow that. You can call one of my investment companies if you want more specific help (the phone numbers appear at the end of this chapter). What follows are general guidelines. And for a more complete explanation, I would encourage you to read my earlier books, *Crash Proof 2.0* and *The Little Book of Bull Moves and Bear Markets.*

Dividend-paying stocks in business whose customers are getting richer

Remember, the best reason to buy stocks is not simply because you think they'll go up—that's speculation—but because they pay dividends. So find those companies and industries whose customer bases are becoming richer and are building up cash: the ones selling cars to the Chinese, or air conditioners to the Indians. You don't know how soon these stocks will climb in value—it might be three years from now, or it could be ten years from now. But if you're in it for the long term, the dividends make it worth the wait.

I reject the stock strategy most professionals advise. They say, hey, you're young, make risky investments in stocks, and sell them later on when they're priced higher. If there are no dividends, even in the future, this looks a lot like a Ponzi scheme. Nobody's buying these stocks in the expectation of getting paid—they're buying these stocks in the expectation that someone will be willing to pay a higher price later on. It's called the Greater Fool theory.

Think about investors who bought into this Wall Street myth in 2000. They piled into non-dividend-paying stocks, hoping to cash out big gains in 2012, then roll their windfalls into bonds and certificates of deposit (CDs) living off 7 percent interest rates. Not only did the gains never materialize, but interest rates on CDs these days are practically zero. The only way to even get a 3 percent return on bonds is to assume a lot of interest-rate risk. These individuals are now stuck. There are no greater fools offering higher prices for their shares, and even if they could find a few, there are no conservative ways to generate income from the proceeds. Their only choice now is to postpone retirement, perhaps indefinitely, and hope for a miracle—not exactly what they thought they were signing up for.

Dividend-paying stocks, on the other hand, are real investments because they pay you to own them. Even if you don't need the income now, the dividends are great, because you can reinvest them. This makes your portfolio grow even if the share price stays flat. Then once you retire, you start living off the dividends, perhaps without ever having even to draw on the principal.

Liquidity and stable investments

Most people don't see bonds as investments, because they confuse speculation with investing. However, bonds can play a valuable role in an investment portfolio. Then again, just because some gentlemen might prefer
bonds, you shouldn't fool yourself into considering them safe.

In a normal economy, Treasury bonds or blue-chip corporate bonds
are a standard safe play: you collect a little bit of interest, and bear almost
no risk. But over the next twenty years, the biggest threats to your wealth
could be runaway inflation and skyrocketing interest rates. So a long-term
bond at today's super-low interest rates could end up losing you a bundle
in real terms.

First, as yields rise, bond prices fall. The longer the maturity, the
sharper the fall. Sure, if you hold a bond to maturity you will eventually
get your money back (assuming no default), but thirty years is a long time
to wait if you're collecting a submarket rate of interest while inflation eats
away your purchasing power. And if you need to sell before maturity, you
could take a real bath even in nominal terms.

Of course, the greater risk in bonds is the value of the currency in which
they are denominated. As this book has repeatedly asserted, the dollar is
risky. And as this edition goes to press, and people start to see that the Fed
has no exit strategy, currencies in emerging markets will begin to recover.
Where they had once counteracted the dollar's weakness by printing more
money and buying U.S. Treasuries, they may not do that again. The money
won't be recycled into the U.S. Treasury market. That will cause the dollar
to fall still further, and scare everyone about dollar-denominated investments.

If you dislike the dollar, you really have to dislike dollar-denominated
bonds. Such bonds merely represent future receipts of dollars. The only
thing worse than being paid a dollar today is being paid a dollar in the
future. Therefore, when it comes to bonds, I prefer short maturities, and
non-dollar denominations. As interest rates rise and short-term bonds
mature, we can roll over our principal into higher yielding paper. If rates
rise high enough, we can lock them in by lengthening the maturities of the
replacement bonds.

An added benefit of short-term bonds is that they have lower volatility and lots of liquidity. In fact, in many cases you do not even have to sell them, as you can simply let them mature at no cost. This gives you some dry powder if you get a big sell-off in stocks or precious metals—it puts you in a position to take advantage of the bargains.

Buying foreign bonds is a bit harder than just buying U.S. bonds, so you need a broker who can execute these trades. Generally, to buy them directly you need a lot of money, especially if you want to diversify. For some people, mutual funds are the way to go. If you buy one, make sure it does not hedge to the U.S. dollar, that it owns the right currencies, and that its portfolio has a short duration. It just so happens that I manage a mutual fund of my own that covers all of those bases for you. You can get more information at www.europacificfunds.com. Read the prospectus carefully and consider the risks before investing.

Another type of bond that provides better inflation protection is a convertible bond. Such bonds allow the holder to convert to common equity at a specified conversion price. For this added upside, there is generally a trade-off in the form of reduced interest payments, but if you buy the right stocks, the potential future benefits outweigh the current costs. If there is a lot of inflation, you convert your bonds to stock, and replace your low fixed coupon with a higher dividend. That is because inflation will allow a company to raise its prices, and pass on those higher prices to its shareholders in the form of higher dividends. Bond interest payments, however, are fixed, as is their principal at maturity, and both are eroded by inflation. In that way, inflation transfers wealth from bondholders to equity holders. The convertible feature allows bondholders to join the winning team even after it's clear which team won.

I believe that Treasury Inflation-Protected Securities, known as TIPS, should be avoided. These are bonds issued by the U.S. Treasury where coupon and principal payments are adjusted upward based on the Consumer Price Index. As previously discussed, this government-calculated index grossly understates the true rate of inflation, making TIPS a sucker's bet. It's akin to hiring the proverbial fox to guard your henhouse. Also, there are adverse tax effects that only compound this problem.

Of course, the most obvious way to stay liquid is to hold cash. But the argument not to denominate bonds in dollars can also be applied to cash. Sit on an account of dollars, and it will retain its nominal value, but you'll be losing purchasing power. You'll be getting poorer. As far as I'm concerned, betting on the dollar going down now is easier than betting against housing in 2006.

So, I hold foreign currencies. The Swiss franc has been one of my favorites. So has the Australian dollar. Politics shake things up, so you have to stay on your toes, but I'm always looking for foreign currencies to hold—not for the sake of currency speculation, but for a relatively safe, liquid store of wealth.

The main reason for holding cash is to be able to spend right away. First, you may have an emergency: you may lose your job or crash your car. But from an investing point of view, you want cash so that you can pounce on opportunities when they arise.

People are often forced to sell assets, like houses, stocks, or bonds. Maybe they're heavily leveraged, and their debt is due. Maybe they experience a shock. We saw plenty of this during the credit crunch and the spectacular housing collapse of late 2008 and early 2009. You get good deals from distressed sellers not only because they have to sell, but because other would-be buyers are often scared away by collapsing prices. As Warren Buffett says, be greedy when others are scared. Of course, if you are all-in with no cash on the sidelines, you may be among those who are forced to sell at an inopportune time, with someone else taking advantage of your misfortune. Having liquidity helps you avoid getting into this predicament.

Gold

If you bought gold in the beginning of 2000, your investment had grown more than 550 percent by the time the first edition of this book was published. As the second edition goes to print, gold has pulled back from the days when inexperienced gold speculators really were running to gold out of fear. So at this point, you would have only gained about 300 percent. But if you bought a Standards & Poor's (S&P) index fund in 2000, your investment was up less than 20 percent as of the moment stocks reached their all-time high in September 2013. Put another way, the gold investment was far better. Over the past decade, gold has outperformed any stock market.

I'd add that with gold, it's important to understand that ups and downs are a fact of life. When my earlier book, *Crash Proof*, was first published, the NYSE Gold Bugs Index of mining stocks (HUI) was trading around 350. It hit a high of near 520 in 2008, then plunged 71 percent when the crisis hit—worse than the 57 percent decline in the S&P 500. But by September 2011 the HUI had hit 638, 23 percent above its 2008 peak, even as the S&P 500 was still 13 percent below its 2008 high. Gold and gold stocks were the wrong assets to own going into the crash; they were the best assets to own coming out of it. If you bought gold at its 2008 peak price of $1,000 (it fell to $700 later that year) you are still ahead now. Of course, you did even better if you bought gold at $650 per ounce when *Crash Proof* was first published.

Comparisons between gold and stocks are just for purposes of illustration. I don't really think of gold as an alternative to stocks. I compare it to dollars, euros, and yen. In other words, I compare real money (gold) to fiat money (currencies).

Remember our discussion of money from chapter 5. Money is a store of value. You should think of gold as a store of value. Which preserves its value better, paper currency or gold? The data makes that clear—an ounce of gold gets you four times as many dollars today as it did thirteen years ago.

It's no wonder. Which would you expect to hold its value more: something that can be printed at near-zero cost, or created out of thin air with some computer keystrokes at the Federal Reserve, or a rare element that must be mined at substantial cost?

Most investment professionals will try to convince you that holding gold is a bad deal by pointing to its value in 1980. They will tell you that if you paid $800 for gold in 1980, adjusted for inflation you're still down. In fact, every time gold makes a new high, the media always qualifies the record by calling it a new "nominal high." But those same reporters never qualify the Dow's new highs, even though that index had to climb as high as 15,000 in 2013 to take out its inflation-adjusted 2000 high of 11,772.98.

By selecting 1980 as a benchmark, gold critics are picking a price at the very top of a ten-year bull market that saw gold prices soar from $35 per ounce to over $800. If they started their reference period in 1970, the results would be very different. Arguing that gold is a bad investment based on its relationship to its 1980 spike high is like arguing that stocks are bad investments today because the NASDAQ was at 5,000 in 2000. Sure, if someone was dumb enough to buy all their gold in 1980 and then hold it through a twenty-year bear market as the Dow Jones rose from 700 to 11,000, they deserve to lose money. But it's not fair to blame their losses on gold.

The key to gold is knowing when to hold it and when to use it to purchase stocks or other assets. To do that, you need to understand where you are in the cycle and how future fundamentals might alter it. As far as I'm concerned we are much closer to 1970 than 1980. I think the fundamentals for the U.S. economy are much worse and the fundamentals for gold much better now than they were then.

It is also interesting that all these so-called experts who missed both the stock market and real estate bubbles are convinced they see a bubble in gold. In fact, this gold-bubble talk has been around since gold hit $500 per ounce. With gold trading at $625 per ounce on April 26, 2006, I wrote a David Letterman–style article titled "The Top Ten Signs of a Precious Metals Bubble" to poke fun at those convinced gold was a bubble about to pop. (If you want a good laugh just Google the title.)

One of the main flaws in the gold-bubble hypothesis is that while a lot of people are talking about gold, few are actually buying any. Bubbles are built on actions, not words. For gold to be in a bubble, many of the people talking about gold are actually going to have to buy some. In fact, given the magnitude of the ten-year bull market, it's amazing just how few investors, retail or institutional, own gold. The low P/Es (price-to-earnings ratio) of the major gold stocks and the lack of interest in the more speculative names prove that there is far more fear than greed in the gold market—hardly the attitude one would expect in a bubble. The fact of the matter is that gold's rise merely reflects the loss of value of fiat currencies, and the reasonable expectation of even greater losses in the future.

I also find it very funny when all the experts who haven't bought a single ounce of gold try to explain why others are doing so. You would think they might ask one of us instead. Since they contend there is no inflation, they assume investors must be buying for some other reason. Their explanation usually boils down to uncertainty. The theory is that since investors are worried about the economy, political unrest, and the stock market, they buy gold to guard against those uncertainties. As someone who has been buying and advising others to do likewise for ten years, uncertainty has nothing to do with it. In fact, it is the things that I am certain about that cause me to buy gold. I'm certain central banks will continue to debase their currencies. So the real reason investors are buying gold is that they correctly perceive the inflation threat being missed by those who aren't buying gold.

In addition to owning physical gold, your gold holdings should include gold mining stocks. Because of the skepticism with which most investors view the gold rally, few have been willing to assign high P/Es to gold-mining stocks. This is because investors believe higher gold prices are un-sustainable. The expectation is for gold prices and therefore earnings to drop below where they are in late 2013. This irrational fear has created a great buying opportunity. In fact, the underperformance of gold stocks versus the metal has been historic, creating a rare opportunity for those who have missed much of the gold rally to catch up.

Today, these stocks don't generally pay high dividends, so there's an element of speculation going on, but I expect they will be well positioned to raise their dividends as gold prices rise. Knowing which gold stocks offer the best potential is more complicated. Some carry far more risk than others. Many, called exploration stocks, may not even own any gold, just the prospect of finding some. Therefore investors need to be careful.

As gold plunged in the spring and summer of 2013, gold stocks fared even worse, with the HUI dropping 40 percent in four months. As gold prices fell, forecasts for even greater future declines caused investors to question the very viability of many miners. After all, mining costs had risen so much over the years that most mines cannot sustain profitability if sub-$1,200 gold price forecasts came true. Lost in these forecasts was the fact that the prospect of widespread bankruptcy in the gold mining sector would portend a collapse in the supply of gold and therefor a sig-nificant rise in its price. It's also ironic that gold miners have been the victims rather than the beneficiaries of rising inflation. That is because while inflation has resulted in a significant increase in the cost of mining, the fact that so many investors still believe that inflation does not exist, gold demand remains low, and the prices the miners receive for their gold do not reflect inflation nearly as well as their input cost to mine it. How-ever, when investors see though the government's inflation con, ignore of-ficial measures such as CPI, and open their eyes to reality, the price of gold has a lot of catching up to do. That is when the miners really start to make money, as the price of gold should rise much faster than the cost of min-ing it. That is when gold mines will finally live up to the expression and become "gold mines."

If you think of building a gold mining portfolio as building a pyramid, senior producers, those with plenty of proven resources, would form its base. Then you would add additional exposure with mid-tier and junior producers. The very top of the pyramid would consist of exploration companies. If one hits it big, it's a home run. Of course, if you strike out you can still win the game with plenty of base hits from the more reliable batters in your portfolio. You can also diversify your exposure to the exploration sector so that not all of your money is riding on the same stock.

If you do not want to do the research necessary to create your own mining portfolio, there are plenty of diversified mutual funds that will do it for you. My company actually launched a gold mutual fund (EPGFX) after the publication of the first edition of this book. Read the prospectus and consider the risks before investing. You still need to research all such funds, but this involves considerably less work, and far less monitoring once you find a manager you can trust. The key is to understand the risks, and to adopt a strategy that bests suits your goals.

In addition, my firm offers physical gold though the Perth Mint Certificate Program. Through that program, our clients can have their precious metal stored in the Perth Mint in Australia, often free of storage charges. The deposits are guaranteed by the Government of Western Australia and reinsured through Lloyd's of London. I think it's a very secure way to store bullion overseas. My personal feeling is that it makes sense not to keep all your gold in the same place, and it's particularly important to have some stored out of the country. It's always possible that things could get so bad here that you might need to flee. If things really do get that bad, there is a good chance it might be very difficult, or even illegal, to take your gold with you. Therefore it's a good idea to have some waiting for you on the other side of the border.

Some of you may want to have some physical bullion in your possession, and this can be safely obtained though Euro Pacific Precious Metals, which sells bullion for physical delivery to your doorstep.

I set this company up as a result of the many horror stories I had been told by investors who had followed my advice to buy physical precious metals, but were sold overpriced numismatics instead. The problem is that the firms that advertise so heavily are the very firms that use high-pressure sales tactics to push investors into high markup "collector" coins of dubious investment value. They do this because the sales commissions on legitimate bullion coins and bars are much smaller, and insufficient to cover their big advertising budgets.

As a result, these are often the same dealers recommended by some of the most trusted conservative talk radio hosts. It's a very cozy relationship, where dealers exchange advertising dollars for endorsements. However, it's the host's audience that gets stuck with the bill when they overpay for their coins.

The problem is that listeners trust the hosts, who they assume are making recommendations with their audience's interest at heart. This marketing strategy works even better given that the hosts often warn about the problems in the U.S. economy and advise owning gold as a safe haven. This advice is sound; it's the execution that is not.

Buying gold as an inflation hedge is a good idea, but paying a 70 percent markup to buy a "rare" coin instead is a terrible idea. For a more detailed analysis of the pitfalls of the precious metals market, I have written a special report that can be downloaded free online at www.goldscams.com.

Building Your Stock Portfolio

The key to building a diversified stock portfolio centers around four components: countries, currencies, sectors, and individual stocks (in that order). This is what the investment community would refer to as a "top-down" approach. First, decide which countries you feel are the most stable, and have a combination of monetary and fiscal policy conducive to maximize economic growth. Then decide which currencies offer the best prospects of preserving their value.

Often the best countries will also have the best currencies, but you have to remember that although a company is located in a country you like, it still might derive most of its income in a currency you don't. For example, you may like Australia, but what if the Australian company you buy derives most of its income in the UK, and you do not like the pound? Alternatively, you may not like the euro and might be inclined to avoid Germany for that reason. However, in so doing you might miss an excellent German company selling into the Chinese market and earning its revenue in RMB (renminbi).

Once you have figured out the countries and currencies you like, you can narrow down your investment universe by eliminating those sectors you think are poorly positioned given the macroeconomic fundamentals at play. Once you have established the sectors you most want exposure to, you're ready to select your stocks. Of course, stock selection is the hard part. The rest is easy if you understand the big picture.

An easy way to skip the hard part is to buy exchange-traded funds or mutual funds that focus on the countries, currencies, and sectors you have determined offer the best potential. However, this often involves more research than you might think, as funds may have portfolios that do not necessarily reflect their names. Also, fund managers often care more about short-term rather than absolute performance, and as such tend to chase fads and ignore value. But for an investor, it's absolute long-term returns that count. It does you no good if you get a big short-term rally in stocks that ultimately crash and burn while they are still in your portfolio. However, it does a lot of good for your fund manager, who gets paid on relative rather than absolute performance.

Crashproof Yourself: Hold Some Dollars

There is one caveat when it comes to cash. If you live in America and have expenses in dollars, it makes sense to keep some dollars lying around. Remember, this leg of the stool is partly about liquidity. You should have some dollars because you never know when you'll need money, and regardless of long-term trends, you can never guess where a currency will be at any given moment in time. If you need money at a time when the dollar happens to be high, you want to have dollars to spend. In general, a diversified basket of currencies held for the long term allows you to spend the most valuable currency at any given moment. In addition, many of your own expenses—mortgage payments, monthly tuition bills, or car insurance—are likely fixed in dollar terms, at least for the short run. Having a set amount of dollars to cover such expenditures for at least six to twelve months is a good idea and provides some peace of mind.

Again, I have provided more detailed information on the portfolio-building process in my earlier books. Earlier in this chapter, I listed some of my favorite countries, so those nations and their respective currencies are a good place to start. The next step is picking the sectors. Of course, I have no idea when a particular investor will be reading this book, so the best sectors may change based on changing circumstances and valuations.

At the moment I prefer raw materials, energy, manufacturing, chemicals, agriculture, infrastructure, utilities, and technology. I would avoid banking and finance, Internet, residential property, or any fad-type sectors where stocks trade at high multiples with no yield. When it comes to individual stocks, here again circumstances may change based on when this book is read. Besides, securities regulations prevent me from including any specific stock recommendations in this book, because I cannot determine suitability without first knowing the investor. My stock recommendations and strategic advice on building a stock portfolio are available through my brokerage company, Euro Pacific Capital, after suitability has been determined. Read the prospectus carefully before deciding if these funds are suitable for you.

What If I'm Wrong?

So what if the United States doesn't go bankrupt? What if the dollar doesn't collapse? What if our economy remains stable? What if the Dow Jones resumes its climb?

My investment strategy still works in that case. It's not as if foreign stocks will fall because U.S. stocks are strong. Foreign stocks tend to go up when the Dow goes up. The only time they would diverge is if China and the rest of the world deliberately decoupled from the U.S. economy. In that case, the divergence is likely to work in your favor as foreign stocks rise and domestic stocks fall.

So, even if U.S. stocks climb over the next decade or two, you won't necessarily be losing money if you're mostly in foreign securities. And if the recent trend of rising U.S. and global stock prices continues, the dollar will fall. Therefore, those who invest in foreign stocks will have the currency winds at their backs.

Even if the U.S. economy does well, do you really think it will do better than Asia? First, consider the baselines. The U.S. starts off so much bigger, it's harder to get any decent percentage of growth. Second, consider the debt and savings differences.

I'm perfectly willing to admit, as I noted above, that over some short-term time window, my strategy can lose money. But you can't do serious investing unless you're willing to ride out unpredictable short-term ups and downs. You shouldn't check your stocks every day or get emotional about the fluctuations.

Checking your stock price doesn't tell you as much as you think. The price of a stock doesn't tell you the value of the company. It tells you what you could get if you sold your shares at a particular instant in time. A drop in price could simply reflect that someone had to sell today—maybe to meet a margin call. A rise in price might be the result of someone who just came into a bunch of cash and was looking for securities to buy up. Maybe a big mutual fund just picked up or just dropped a stock—that could move the price without reflecting anything about the stock's actual value.

I have confidence that my approach is the best approach toward long-term investing. I'm even more confident, though, that you'll do okay with my approach even if I'm wrong about my dire outlook for the U.S. economy. A portfolio of foreign stocks and bonds does not need the U.S. economy to fail for it to succeed. However, if I am correct, and the U.S. economy does fail along the lines I have predicted, that is when my investment strategy would be most effective.

The Rules Have Changed

If I can impress one notion on you in this chapter it's this: what used to be safe investing isn't safe anymore.

Even something as basic as "saving" doesn't mean what it used to mean. The standard way to save is to put your money in a savings account, which today also means earning near-zero interest. But this is really a bet on the dollar retaining its value. That's not a good long-term bet to make, but under conventional wisdom it is considered the safest thing to do with your money.

Remember those SEC and FINRA rules I wrote about in chapter 5?

They fail to address the rule of the value of the dollar itself. They are grounded in the soundness of the dollar and the supremacy of the U.S. economy over other economies. What the conventional wisdom regards as safe, I regard as risky. What the conventional wisdom regards as risky, I regard as relatively safe. The bottom line is that, thanks to our reckless Fed and our profligate government, no investment can truly be considered safe.

Sadly, as previously discussed in chapter 5, U.S. regulations don't allow me to do everything I would like to do for my clients—"consumer protection" regulations often protect consumers from making money.

Recall my experience with the hedge fund we helped set up in 2006 to bet against subprime mortgages. While several Euro Pacific Capital clients cleaned up, far more clients missed out on the opportunity as a result of all the regulations that limited our ability to market the product. In addition, securities regulations passed pursuant to the anti–money laundering provisions of the Patriot Act have made it very expensive for me to service foreign accounts from the United States.

In response, I've set up another business, called Euro Pacific Bank, Ltd. This offshore bank operates out of the eastern Caribbean nation of St. Vincent and the Grenadines, and offers an array of banking and investment services and products far more robust than what is available to my U.S. clients. In addition, strict bank secrecy laws protect customer privacy.

Unfortunately, the same U.S. regulations that forced me to move this portion of my business offshore also prevent me from offering any of these enhanced services to Americans. Euro Pacific Bank cannot accept accounts from American citizens nor from foreign citizens residing in the United States. However, foreign citizens who have joint U.S. citizenship may open accounts, provided they are living abroad.

One unique feature of my offshore bank is that clients can choose to hold their deposits in gold that can be accessed using a debit card linked directly to their accounts. Since our card is accepted at over 30 million retail locations and 1.4 million ATM machines worldwide, this makes spending your gold as easy as swiping your debit card. Ironically, when I wrote *Crash Proof,* I predicted that eventually banks would offer this type of service. Little did I know that I would be the one to blaze the trail.

Decoupling

Consider the image of a train. The U.S. economy is coupled with other economies. The U.S. is not the engine; Asia might be. We might actually be the caboose. But the point is, the rest of the world still chooses to be coupled to us. China still pegs its currency to the dollar. It still buys up U.S. Treasuries. Foreign manufacturers still sell to Americans on credit.

What would you do if you were Asia? Pretty soon, it seems to me, you would decouple from the U.S., and pull away.

Many feel that the events of 2008 prove my "decoupling theory" wrong. I disagree. I think those events prove just how important it is for the rest of the world to decouple. If I am correct about my train analogy, the American caboose is slowing the global train down.

Given that Asian nations are bearing the lion's share of the load, it's a pretty good bet that they will choose to decouple first. They could stop buying our debt and propping up our currency. They could start making things for themselves or other non-U.S. consumers.

When this happens we won't have much say, and will merely watch from a distance as the global train pulls away without us. Then the dollar will no longer be the reserve currency, and our house of cards economy will come crumbling down.

I said this at the beginning of the book, and I'll say it again now: the real crash I'm preparing for hasn't come yet. *Crash Proof* wasn't subtitled "how to profit from the stock market crash," or "how to profit from the housing bubble bursting." The subtitle was "How to Profit From the Economic Collapse." That collapse has barely begun.

My investment strategy has been about how to profit from the crash of the U.S. economy. Before that collapse is complete, U.S. bonds and the dollar will crash. That is the opposite of what happened in 2008. The fact that this hasn't happened yet—that the dollar hasn't been wiped out and that the U.S. government can still borrow cheaply—doesn't make me wrong. Look how long real estate prices rose while I was warning about the bubble.

For the U.S. economy, things won't be pretty when this bubble finally bursts. How will you prepare? The bottom line is to remember that when the dust settles, Americans are going to be a lot poorer. There will be a major realignment in global living standards. The instrument that will realign them is exchange rates. The dollar will fall as other currencies rise. The rest of the world will enjoy purchasing power once enjoyed by Americans. The key is to figure out which currencies will gain the most from the dollar's demise, and which nation's living standards will rise the most as America's falls; then align your investments to be on the receiving end of this historic wealth transfer.

The Poor Man's Investment Strategy for the Real Crash

For those of you who have no money to invest, the bright side is that you also have no investments to lose. That does not mean that there is nothing you can do to prepare for hard times. My guess is consumer prices will surge, and if the government responds with price controls, there may be shortages as well. Therefore, buying in bulk now and stocking up makes a lot of sense. Not only do you save money on volume, but you lock in prices before they rise.

Think of it as a poor-man's investment strategy, with the added twist being that any returns are tax free. For example, if you buy a box of cornflakes today and eat it two years from now when the price of a new box is 40 percent higher, that's a 40 percent tax-free return. It's tax free because eating an appreciated box of cornflakes is not a taxable event. If we end up with price controls, it's not just money you save, but the time you might otherwise spend waiting in line to buy your box. Because taxes could be much higher in the future, your tax savings are magnified.

There are many other items you can stock up on other than nonperishable foods. Batteries and toiletries come to mind. Some things like wine actually improve with age. You can even store things you do not use yourself, such as cigarettes, as you could use them to barter for those items you do use.

It's also a good idea to be armed, and to have an ample supply of ammunition. Even if you never use them, bullets will likely turn out to be a good investment. In fact, I first recommended stocking up on bullets in the original version of the *Little Book of Bull Moves in Bear Markets* and ammunition prices skyrocketed soon after it was published—not because of the economic crisis I had forecast, but because President

Obama's election caused gun owners fearful of stricter controls to stock up on ammunition.

America's Future

The 1950s gave rise to the expression Ugly American. The term was originally coined because of the seemingly arrogant behavior of American tourists traveling abroad. At that time Americans enjoyed a living standard unmatched anywhere else in the world. Limited government maximized freedom and economic growth. As a result, our industrial might lifted the purchasing power of the dollar relative to foreign currencies, allowing middle class Americans to feel like tycoons when traveling abroad. Even college kids spent their summers backpacking around Europe for a mere five dollars a day. This gave Americans a feeling of superiority that often produced resentment.

My main point in bringing this up is not merely to lament a bygone era, but to show that the same thing is about to happen again, only in reverse. A collapsing dollar is about to turn the United States into the world's largest bargain basement.

However, it's not just foreign tourists who will be able to go on shopping sprees, but those Americans who have the foresight to get out of U.S. dollars before the collapse. You do not have to be a tourist to enjoy the bargains, just be in possession of their currencies or precious metals to pay for your purchases.

One last thing to consider when it comes to your investments—make sure to warn your family and friends. If you arrange your investments in a manner that allows you to prosper while most other Americans go broke, many of those closest to you will likely share their fate. Unless you want lots of people borrowing from you, are willing to pick up every dinner check, or go on vacations without your friends, you had better make sure that your inner circle is similarly prepared. That means helping to educate them to understand the nature of the problems, and more important, how they can protect themselves financially. In the end, of course, you can lead a horse to water, but you cannot make it drink. However, at least your family and friends can't blame you for keeping your insights to yourself.

The bottom line is that a major economic event looms on the horizon. Knowing about it is one thing—being prepared is another.

For those interested in implementing any of my investment strategies, you don't have to do it through me or any of my companies. But if you do come to us, you can count on the fact that we won't look at you like you have three heads, the way many brokers will if you tell them you're worried about the real crash hitting.

I believe strongly in the predictions I've made in this book, and I've backed it up by developing multiple investment tools designed to weather what's coming. And if you like to do things yourself, we have launched mutual funds that you can invest in without having an account with me.

If you do want to invest through my companies, here is the contact information for them, along with brief descriptions.

Euro Pacific Capital, Inc.
www.europac.net
1 (800) 727-7922
A full-service brokerage firm offering U.S. investors brokerage and managed accounts, mutual funds, research, and private placements. Minimum account size is $25,000. Member SIPC.

Euro Pacific Asset Management, Ltd.
www.europacificfunds.com
1 (888) 558-5851
An Asset Management company offering U.S. investors direct access to my proprietary mutual funds without having to open a separate brokerage account. The minimum account size is $2,500.

Euro Pacific Precious Metals
www.europacmetals.com
1 (888) 465-3160
A precious metals dealer offering physical delivery of bullion coins and bars at competitive prices.

Euro Pacific Bank, LLC
www.europacbank.com
1 (784) 453-2086
   A full-service offshore bank offering non-U.S. clients brokerage
and managed accounts, mutual funds, bank accounts, precious metals, trusts services, and gold-backed debit cards.

Euro Pacific Canada, Inc.
www.europac.ca
1 (888) 216-9779
   A full-service brokerage firm offering Canadian investors brokerage and managed accounts, mutual funds, research, and private
placements.

Epilogue

WHEN A DISEASE HITS A healthy body, the body responds with antibodies tailor-made to kill the specific malady. So it often is with the body politic.

I'm not talking about the political class. Our politicians and pundits have reacted to the financial crisis and economic downturn by blaming "greedy bankers," and scapegoating the Chinese.

It's the grassroots that have responded to our economic misadventures in a way that could help solve things. Economic anxiety has helped energize Americans in ways that we haven't seen for decades. The crisis, as former White House chief of staff Rahm Emanuel likes to say, presents an opportunity for the severe changes we need if our economy is ever to be healthy—the changes I've proposed in this book.

On one side of the political spectrum, we have the emergence of the Tea Party, which began as a libertarian reaction to the massive financial bailouts engineered by the Bush and Obama administrations. Gradually, the Tea Party evolved beyond its fiscal roots to include a broader swath of conservatives who had become disenchanted with the policies of the mainstream Republican party under George Bush, and who then became infuriated at the increasing governmental activism under Obama (in particular his encroachment into health care). Although the Tea Party ideas have successfully moved into the mainstream, its adherents maintain a commitment to outside-the-box political engagement and an urgency that is not visible among rank-and-file Republicans.

As the Tea Party movement began picking up more and more social conservatives and foreign policy hawks, the growing numbers of libertarians have begun forming their own political bloc, who are increasingly making common cause with liberals opposed to U.S. adventurism overseas. The election of Rand Paul to the U.S. Senate in Kentucky marks one step in this process of making converts to the libertarian cause, and he brought it much publicity with his winter 2013 filibuster in which he called for limits on the Obama administration's policy of targeted assassinations. Congressman Ron Paul made converts as well with his 2012 repeat run for the presidency. Judge Andrew Napolitano, a dyed-in-the-wool libertarian, has an extremely popular daily program on a national news network (Fox Business), a reality that would have seemed like fantasy a few years ago.

On the other hand, late 2011 saw left-leaning young people surge into the streets to engage in wide-scale protests against what they believe to be economic injustice. The narrative that dominates their thinking holds that our government is controlled by the ultra-wealthy who have gotten richer by avoiding taxes, exploiting workers, shifting U.S. jobs overseas, and receiving bailouts from Washington. Although the "Occupy Wall Street" protesters come in all shapes and sizes, there is a poster child stereotype: a recent college graduate with nearly six figures of student loan debt and no serious job prospects. This person feels that they have been robbed of their birthright in exchange for a crushing debt burden. Though their outrage is generally directed at capitalism, it's the *absence* of capitalism that has produced the conditions they now protest. By preaching capitalism, but practicing something else, our leaders on the Right have tarnished the reputation of free markets.

As the economy continues to stagnate, as I'm sure it will, the broad electoral center will also become eager for radical change. It is safe to assume that these contrasting ideologies will compete for the affections of those increasing numbers of rank-and-file Americans who are willing to consider fundamental change.

The stage is set for a revolution in America.

Jefferson or Lenin?

The question is, which revolutionary year will be our template, 1776 or 1917? In other words, do we follow the principles established by our

founders, who two hundred and thirty years ago conceived a bold experiment in capitalism and personal liberty, or do we man the barricades with
the Bolsheviks, who tried to throw off centuries of aristocratic oppression
with a classless society and a dictatorship of the proletariat? For this decision, I can only hope we let history be our clear guide.

In the one hundred and seventy-five years or so that followed the establishment of the United States, our country experienced nearly unending
growth in prosperity. The road was far from smooth and the arrows did
not always point up. We were periodically beset by horrific panics, recessions and depressions, not to mention civil wars, external wars, and wars
of continental conquest that don't look particularly good on the national
highlight reel. But the upward economic tide was unmistakable.

By the turn of the twentieth century, the United States had developed
the greatest industrial economy the world had ever seen. In just a few generations capitalism and free markets had created a genuine middle class
that enjoyed amenities never before dreamed of by prior generations. In the
process we created entire industries and flooded the world with low-cost,
high-quality merchandise. America was largely responsible for all the great
advances that revolutionized lifestyles in the modern world: electrification,
the telephone, the lightbulb, radio, refrigeration, air-conditioning, automobiles, airplanes, and more. And we did this by offering the highest wages
in the world (without any government mandates to do so). Immigrants
couldn't get here fast enough.

A bit of revisionist history has arisen regarding the development of
America's economic success. According to many left-wing theorists, the
benefits of capitalism never extended to the middle and lower classes until
the government and organized labor forced redistribution of the wealth
that the rich had previously extracted from the poor through exploitation.
According to this line of reasoning, most Americans got progressively
poorer and working conditions steadily declined until sometime after the
1920s or 1930s, when the highly progressive taxes and more generous welfare state policies of FDR's New Deal combined with the increased power
of organized labor to claw prosperity from the miserly hands of the rob-
ber barons. But that's not what happened.

Prior to any government or union involvement, the workers at Ford
Motor Company made twice as much on an inflation-adjusted-after-tax
basis in 1915 as their union successors did in 2010. Wages rose and prices

fell because of gains in productivity, not because some bureaucrat or union official mandated it. And while it's true that the height of middle-class prosperity may not have peaked until the 1950s or 1960s, this was not because government redistribution policies made it so, but because those policies had yet to inflict most of their damage.

On the other hand, the Russian Revolution, despite its lofty goals and stirring rhetoric of justice and equality, had a somewhat spottier record of achievement. The concentrated focus of the best minds in academia, countless five-year industrial plans, massive purges of anyone who harbored views different from the Party, the reorganization of society to promote production and efficiency, and wholesale dislocations of ethnic groups and entrenched power centers were utterly incapable of raising living standards of a population that had previously been stuck in the Dark Ages.

After just seventy years of misery, failure, and oppression the Soviet Union collapsed. It is no accident that its single most important contribution to industrial production came in 1947 when Mikhail Kalashnikov designed the AK-47, the world's most durable assault rifle. (Governments may not be competent at much, but they have always been good in figuring out how to kill people.)

Squandering Our Riches

After World War II, America benefited from a unique position. We were the only industrial power that survived the catastrophe unscathed. This advantage allowed U.S. manufacturers to enjoy unchallenged global market dominance for a generation or more. We were also in possession of the world's reserve currency, which gave our government a considerable degree of fiscal latitude in running up deficits and charging our debts to others. Unfortunately, in the ensuing sixty-plus years, these advantages have been squandered.

While it is true that free market capitalism lifted all boats, it was apparent that some boats were lifted higher than others. Those that contributed the most gained the most. But natural envy, plus the very bad ideas of a few unfortunately influential academics and demagogues set the stage for more redistributionist policies. All sorts of benefits were promised, the cost of which would be paid for by taxing the rich.

By 1944, the top marginal income tax rate peaked at 94 percent, then fluctuated between 82 percent and 91 percent between 1946 and 1963, before falling to 70 percent, where it generally remained until 1980. The fact that the current top federal rate is now "only" 39.6 percent (actually 42.5 percent when both portions of the Medicare tax are factored in, and still more when state income taxes that did not exist back then are factored in) has led the Occupy Wall Street crowd to argue that our current problems result from this differential.* They argue that the reason the economy was better in the 1950s and that the gap between rich and poor was smaller is that taxes on the rich were much higher.

Among the many flaws in this redistributionist argument is that it ignores a huge chunk of history: that part before 1913, when the rich paid no income taxes at all. Living standards of the poor and middle class rose much faster during the nineteenth than the twentieth century. The main differences were taxes, redistribution, and the Federal Reserve.

It also ignores the fact that while marginal rates were higher in the past, a more liberal tax code made it much easier to reduce taxable income. So despite higher marginal rates, for most high-income taxpayers, the effective tax rates of the past were actually quite a bit lower than they are today.

Another popular left-wing narrative is that the rich succeed as a result of government services paid for by lower and middle-income workers. The argument, popularized by Harvard law professor Elizabeth Warren during her 2012 U.S. Senate campaign, is that without roads, schools, infrastructure, police, social safety nets—all of which are paid for by taxpayers—the rich would be unable to amass their wealth. As a result, they owe a debt to society that must be repaid in the form of higher taxes.

Despite the fact that in earning their wealth rich people already benefit society by providing it with goods, services, and jobs, the claim that government programs are responsible for their success is false. Sure, by preserving the rule of law, enforcing contracts, and protecting private property, government creates an environment in which capitalism can flourish, but this has been true in America since the birth of the Republic, and government provides these services at very low cost. But aside from

---

* The first edition of *The Real Crash* went to press before these rates were raised by 4.6 percent in the January 2013 tax deal.

that, most wealthy Americans amass their fortunes *despite* the expanded role of government, not *because* of it.

History proves that it was easier to become rich in America before the New Deal and Great Society programs were enacted than after. Of the thirty richest Americans in history (figured in real dollars) only three were born in the twentieth century: Sam Walton, Warren Buffett, and Bill Gates. Of those three, only Bill Gates was born after World War II. None of the remaining twenty-seven on the list was born after the Civil War. The greatest American fortunes were amassed during the nineteenth century when the U.S. government was its smallest. These men earned their fortunes not by extracting wealth from society, but by improving the lives of their fellow Americans—giving them oil, railroads, and steel—at a faster rate than anyone's living standards have ever been improved before or since.

In the twentieth century, we replaced the free-enterprise ideas of Adam Smith and Thomas Jefferson with the notions of Karl Marx and John Maynard Keynes. Given that we still retain a good deal of our entrepreneurial spirit and at least some of the benefits of true capitalism, these ideas have not been nearly as destructive here as they were in Russia. But their effects have been steadily growing.

The New Deal, The Fair Deal, The New Frontier, and The Great Society all placed government successively closer and closer to the center of the economic equation. As a result, government debt and spending took ever-greater bites out of the economy. We have now reached a point where current levels of debt are completely unsustainable. Although we are bigger and more economically integrated than Greece, our disease is identical. We have been given a warning about our potential future. I can only hope we are smart enough to see it.

At present we have come to a fork in the road. Neither path is particularly inviting. Both involve rough terrain and bumpy, uncomfortable rides. The left fork is a one-way road to economic disaster. The other leads, eventually, to a much better place. Our choice. I wrote this book to lay out all the compelling arguments for taking the right one.

Addendum

The past four years since the publication of the first edition of this book, and especially the last two since the publication of the second, have been extremely frustrating for investors who have structured their portfolios around the belief that the current experiments in central bank stimulus, the anti-business drift in Washington, America's mediocre economy, and unresolved debt issues would push down the value of the dollar, push up commodity prices, and favor assets in economies with relatively low debt levels, smaller governments, and higher real growth. That's because between the beginning of 2011 and the end of 2015, the Dow Jones Industrial Average rallied 70.82 percent while investment returns in the rest of the world have been largely stuck in the mud. This dominance is reminiscent of the five years from the beginning of 1996 to the end of 2000, when the Dow rallied 130.60 percent while overseas markets languished. Although past performance is no guarantee of future results, a casual look back at how the U.S. out-performance trend played out the last time it had occurred should give investors much to think about.

The second half of the 1990s was the original "Goldilocks" era of U.S. economic history, one in which all the inputs seemed to offer investors the best of all possible worlds. The Clinton administration and the first Republican-controlled Congress in a generation had implemented policies that lowered taxes, eased business conditions, and encouraged business investment. But, more importantly, the Federal Reserve was led by Alan Greenspan, whose efforts to orchestrate smooth sailing on Wall Street led many to dub Mr. Greenspan "The Maestro."

Toward the end of the 1990s, Greenspan worked hard to insulate the markets from some of the more negative developments in global finance. These included the Asian Debt Crisis of 1997 and the Russian debt default of 1998. But the most telling policy move of the Greenspan Fed in the late 1990s was its response to the rapid demise of hedge fund Long-Term Capital Management (LTCM), whose strategy of heavily leveraged arbitrage backfired spectacularly in 1998. Greenspan engineered a $3.6 billion bailout and forced sale of LTCM to a consortium of Wall Street firms. The intervention was an enormous relief to LTCM shareholders but, more importantly, it provided a precedent that the Fed had Wall Street's back.

Not surprisingly, the 1990s became one of the longest sustained bull markets on record. But in the latter part of the decade the markets really started to climb in an unprecedented trajectory. As the bubble began inflating in earnest Greenspan was reluctant to follow the dictum that the Fed's job was to remove the punch bowl before the party got out of hand. Instead he argued that the Fed shouldn't prevent bubbles from forming, but simply clean up the mess after they burst.

But while U.S. markets were taking off, the rest of the world was languishing, or worse:

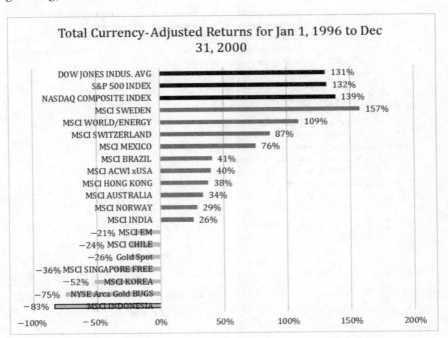

Total Currency-Adjusted Returns for Jan 1, 1996 to Dec 31, 2000

But then a very funny thing happened. In March 2000, the music stopped and the dot-com bubble finally burst, sending the NASDAQ down nearly 50 percent by the end of the year, and a staggering 70 percent by September 2001. When investors got back into the market their values had changed. They now favored low valuations, real revenue growth, understandable business models, high dividends, and low debt. They came to find those features in the non-dollar investments that they had previously avoided.

Over the seven years that began at the end of 2000 and lasted until the end of 2007, the S&P 500 inched upward by just 26.41 percent, for an average annual return of only 3.4 percent. But over that time frame the world index (which includes everything except the U.S.) was up 109.2 percent. The emerging markets, which had suffered the most during the five prior years, were up a staggering 348.9 percent. See table below:

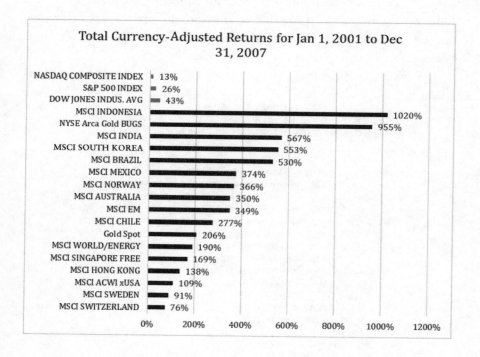

Not surprisingly, the markets and asset classes that had been decimated by the Asian debt and currency crises, delivered stunning results. South Korea, which had fallen 52 percent in the five years prior, was up 553 percent from 2001–2007. Brazil, which had risen 41 percent, notched a

530 percent return, and Indonesia, which had fallen by 83 percent, sky-rocketed by 1,020 percent.

The period was also a great time for gold and gold stocks. The earlier five years had offered nothing but misery for investors like me who had been convinced that the Greenspan policies would undermine the dollar, shake confidence in fiat currency, and drive investors into gold. Instead, gold fell 26 percent (to a twenty-year low), and shares of gold-mining companies fell a stunning 75 percent.

But when the gold market turned in 2001, it turned hard. From 2001–2007, the dollar retreated by nearly 18 percent (FRED, FRB St. Louis), while gold shot up by 206 percent, and shares of gold miners surged 955 percent. As it turned out, we weren't wrong about the impact of the Fed's easy money, just early.

2010–2015

In recent years, investors who have looked to avoid the dollar and the high-debt developed economies have encountered many of the same frustrations

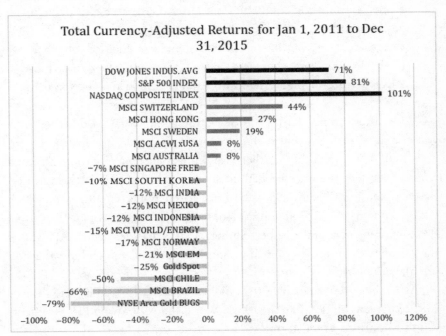

Total Currency-Adjusted Returns for Jan 1, 2011 to Dec 31, 2015

that they encountered in the late 1990s. Foreign markets, energy, commodities, and gold have either gone nowhere, fallen a little, or gotten completely crushed, while the dollar and U.S. markets have surged as they did in 1996–2000.

It is said history may not repeat, but it often rhymes. If so, there may be a financial sonnet brewing. There are reasons to believe that relative returns globally will soon turn around much as they did back in 2000, perhaps even more decisively this time than last.

Just as they had back in the late 1990s, investors appear to be ignoring flashing red flags. In its Business and Finance Outlook 2015, the Organization for Economic Cooperation and Development (OECD), a body that could not be characterized as a harbinger of doom, highlighted some of the issues that should be concerning the markets. Reuters provides this summary of the report's conclusions:

- Encouraged by years of central bank easing, investors are plowing too much cash into unproductive and increasingly speculative investments while shunning businesses building economic growth.
- There is a growing divergence between investors rushing into ever-riskier assets while companies remain too risk-averse to make investments.
- Investors are rewarding corporate managers focused on share-buybacks, dividends, mergers and acquisitions rather than those CEOs betting on long-term investment in research and development.

While these trends have been occurring around the world, they have become most pronounced in the U.S., making valuations disproportionately high relative to other markets. Looking at current valuations through a long-term lens provides needed perspective. One of the best ways to do that is with the Cyclically-Adjusted-Price-to-Earnings (CAPE) ratio, which is also known as the Shiller Ratio (named after its developer, the Nobel Prize–winning economist Robert Shiller). Using 2015 year-end CAPE ratios that average earnings over a trailing ten-year period, the global valuation imbalances become evident:

As of the end of October 2015, the S&P 500 had a CAPE ratio of over 25x, 26 percent higher than the MSCI World Index of around 19.9 percent. (High valuations are also on evidence in Japan, where similar monetary

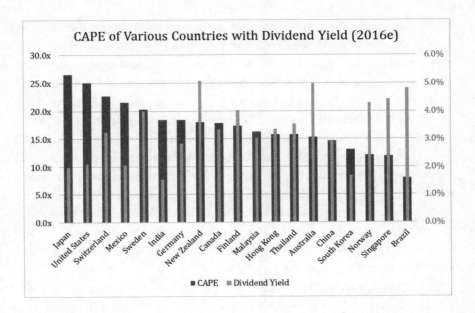

CAPE of Various Countries with Dividend Yield (2016e)

■ CAPE ▪ Dividend Yield

stimulus programs are underway). On a country-by-country basis, the U.S. has a CAPE that is at least 40 percent higher than Canada, 64 percent higher than Australia, 39 percent higher than New Zealand and Finland, and over 70 percent higher than South Korea, Norway, and Singapore. Yet these markets, despite the strong domestic economic fundamentals that we feel exist, are rarely mentioned as priority investment targets by the mainstream asset management firms.

In addition, at the end of 2015 U.S. stocks offered some of the lowest dividend yields to compensate investors for the higher valuations (see chart above). At the time the 2016 estimated 2.1 percent annual dividend yield for the S&P 500 was far below annual dividend yields of Australia, New Zealand, Finland, and Norway.

If a dramatic shock occurs as it did in 2000, will investors again turn away from high leverage and high valuations to seek more modestly valued investments? Then, as now, we believe those types of assets can more readily be found in non-dollar markets.

Another similarity between then and now is the propensity to confuse an asset bubble for genuine economic growth. The dot-com craze of the 1990s painted a false picture of prosperity that was doomed to end badly once market forces corrected for the mal-investments. When that did occur, and stock prices fell sharply, the Fed responded by blowing up an even bigger bubble in real estate. When that larger bubble burst in 2008, the result was not just recession, but the largest financial crisis since the Great Depression.

But once again investors have mistaken a bubble for a recovery, only this time the bubble is much larger and the "recovery" much smaller. The approximate 2 percent annual GDP growth experienced during the most recent "recovery" is approximately half of what we saw in the late 1990s. In reality, the Fed prevented market forces from solving acute structural problems while producing the mother of all bubbles in stocks, bonds, and real estate. As a result a return to monetary normalcy is now impossible without pricking those bubbles. Soon the markets will be faced with the unpleasant reality that the U.S. economy may now be so addicted to monetary heroin that another round of quantitative easing will be required to keep the bubble from deflating.

At the time I write this in January 2016, the current bull market in U.S. stocks has gone on for nearly seven years. Given that high asset prices are one of the pillars of support the Fed has erected to prop up our weak economy, it is likely that the Fed will unleash another round of quantitative easing as soon as that support gives way. The realization that the markets gains have been solely dependent on the Fed's support should seal the dollar's fate. Perhaps a glimpse of what lies ahead occurred on the very first trading day of 2016, when the S&P dropped by 1.5 percent, notching the worst opening day since 2001 when it dropped by 2.8 percent. In fact, as the days and weeks progressed, Wall Street rang in the worst start to a new year in the history of the stock market. Life on Wall Street without the artificial sunshine of easing monetary policy can be a bleak prospect.

But bigger than the reversal in stock market gains will be a change in direction in currency valuations. Once the dollar rally runs out of steam, a process that may have already begun, so, too, should the fortunes of U.S. markets relative to foreign markets. If I am right, we may be about to embark on what could become the single most substantial period of outperformance of foreign verses domestic markets.

While the party in the 1990s ended badly, the festivities currently underway may end in outright disaster. The partygoers may not just awaken with hangovers, but with missing teeth, no memories, and Mike Tyson's tiger in their hotel room.

When the Fed finally did get around to raising interest rates on December 17, 2015, a liftoff that I likened to the launch of a hover board rather than a rocket ship, most stock market investors were reassured by the historical tendency of bull markets to continue climbing during the early years of a tightening cycle. However such complacency is hardly warranted when one considers the stark differences between this potential tightening cycle and all others that have preceded it.

Not only did the Fed keep rates much lower for much longer than in any prior easing, but the first tightening did not begin in December with the first official rate hike, but over a year earlier, and the market and the economy have already shown an inability to handle it.

Zero percent interest rates were not the only means by which the Fed provided stimulus. We also have to account for the effects of QE and forward guidance of the Fed. Changes in those inputs over the past year have already created conditions of monetary tightening.

QE has been the process by which the central bank expands its balance sheet (otherwise known as printing money) to buy government and asset-backed bonds on the longer end of the duration spectrum. In so doing, it is able to help hold down long-term interest rates, a result that would be difficult to achieve by changes in the federal funds rate. Zero percent interest rates represent a loose monetary policy, but once at the zero lower bound, QE is the way the bank eases even further. Another way is with negative interest rates, a disasters trail currently being blazed by the Japanese and various European central banks, and one that Janet Yellen recently admitted the Fed is actually considering following.

Another big input is the Fed's "forward guidance." This comes in the form of official and unofficial pronouncements from top Fed policy makers as to the possible trajectory of interest rates in the future. If the Fed communicates that rates will stay low, or QE will remain in place, for some time, then policy becomes looser still. Such assurances effectively remove near term interest rate risk, which is supposed to stimulate financial activity. Ever since the financial crisis of 2008, the Fed has engaged in unprecedented forward guidance, without which monetary conditions could have been expected to be tighter.

To account for these important factors, University of Chicago professors Cynthia Wu and Fan Dora Xia, constructed a model for the "Shadow Rate." While the Fed funds rate has remained between 0.0 percent and 0.25 percent ever since November of 2008 (Federal Reserve Board), the

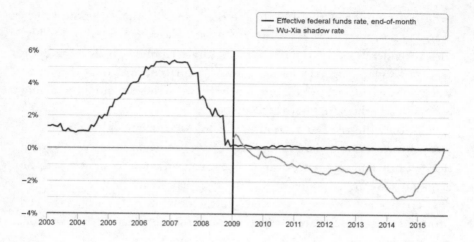

Shadow Rate moved much lower, factoring in the effects of QE and forward
guidance. That rate got as low as −2.99 percent in May of 2014. (Federal
Reserve Bank of Atlanta, CQER, Shadow Rate)

But the Fed's QE tapering campaign, which gradually reduced the
amount of securities purchased monthly by the Fed, effectively began a
campaign of monetary tightening that helped push the Shadow Rate
sharply higher even as the Fed funds rate itself did not budge. After QE
was officially wound down in October 2014, the Fed began to change its
forward guidance to actively suggest that a long-term campaign to lift interest rates would begin in 2015. This also worked to help tighten monetary conditions. As a result, the Shadow Rate moved up from −2.99 percent
in May of 2014 to just −.74 percent in September of 2015, (FRB Atlanta,
CQER, Shadow Rate) an increase of 225 basis points in just over a year.

This is a fairly robust tightening trajectory that can be said to have clearly
taken a toll. In 2015, the major market index, the S&P 500, has essentially
been flat. While in contrast, it had been up by double digits in five of the last
six calendar years. Similarly, GDP growth has slowed considerably since the
QE program was finally tapered down to zero in October of 2014.

Yet U.S. stock market investor's continue taking comfort in the fact
that historically markets have not peaked until 12 to 24 months after the
Fed begins to tighten. But their compliancy assumes the tightening cycle
started with the first official rate hike. But if it really began with the increase in the Shadow Rate, then the December 2015 rate hike actually oc-

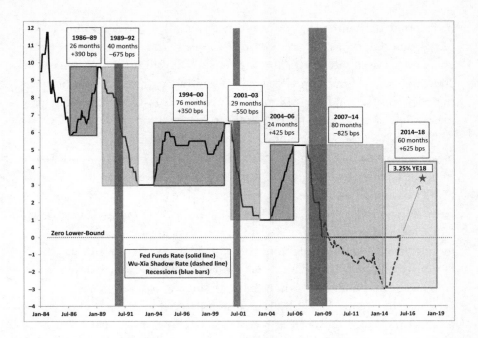

curred 19 months into the tightening cycle! Plus, given how overvalued stocks were at that time, and the amount of corporate debt accumulated to finance share buybacks, the current bull market may be far more vulnerable than most prior bulls to higher interest rates.

The last three times that the Fed had conducted a rate tightening cycle (1986–1989, 1994–2000, and 2004–2006), the increases in rates averaged 388 basis points. But those moves upward occurred when QE did not exist and when forward guidance was hardly a factor (the Fed only started doing press conferences in the last few years). So the tightening that has occurred to the Shadow Rate in the last year is already 58 percent of the size of the average of the last three tightening cycles.

If the Fed does as it has suggested it will, and takes fed funds up to 2.6 percent by the end of 2017 (which is the Fed's own median forecast), then the total effective move (that includes the tightening of the Shadow Rate) would be a tightening of 559 basis points, well larger than the average of the last three tightening cycles. Does anyone really believe that our fragile and slowing economy can deal with that kind of headwind?

Generally, the Fed tends to wait until the economy is on solid footing before tightening. For instance, in the twelve months prior to the 390 basis point tightening that occurred between 1986–1989, real GDP was 3.2 percent. GDP was 2.65 percent in 1993, the year before a six-year tightening cycle raised rates by 350 basis points. GDP was a solid 4.3 percent in 2003, the year before Alan Greenspan began raising rates in 2004, a move that took up fed funds by 425 basis points. But 2015 GDP, that grew by a mere 1.8 percent, was not nearly as robust.

But what's more concerning is the magnitude of the easing cycle that has gotten us to this point. It began in 2007, lasted a full 80 months, and took the effective fed funds rate (accounting for the Shadow Rate) down by 825 basis points. In contrast, the prior two easing cycles averaged 612 basis points and 34.5 months. This huge dose of stimulus is certain to have caused distortions in the economy that won't be seen until we get more normalized levels of monetary policy. As Warren Buffet has most famously quipped, "We have to wait till the tide goes out before we see who has been swimming without bathing suits."

Since the Second World War, recessions have begun, on average, every seven years. Since the current recovery is already seven years old, how much longer should we expect this historically anemic recovery to last? If the slowdown occurs in 2016, can we really expect the Fed to remain on the sidelines and risk the possibility that the economy goes into a recession during a presidential election year? Both the chairperson and vice chairman of the Fed are solidly associated with the left side of the political spectrum. Should we expect that they would be hesitant to support the markets and the economy and thereby create conditions that might help Republicans take the White House?

Nevertheless, most people assume that rates are on the way up to 2 percent or more. But from my perspective it's much more likely that the rates never get close to that level. I would argue that any positive rate of interest would be enough to stop this economy cold. Years of negative rates have so corrupted our economy that I believe it is now fully addicted and cannot survive under any other condition.

Since this historically weak recovery is already decelerating, one might expect the removal of stimulus could cause the next recession to start quicker and be far deeper than any experienced in the past. Since the Fed may recognize this, the next easing cycle could likely start much sooner, and the accompanying monetary stimulus be much larger than just about anyone believes.

Each of the last three easing cycles took rates lower than where they were at the end of the prior easing cycle. Given that the fed funds rate went to zero (and the Shadow Rate got to as low as −2.99 percent), one shudders to think how low the Fed is prepared to go the next time around. That is precisely why savvy investors need to prepare themselves now for an outcome few others actually expect. As was the case with the subprime short, the biggest profits come from correctly anticipating unexpected outcomes.

Appendix I: Letters to Investors

TO: Euro Pacific Capital client

FROM: Peter Schiff/Euro Pacific Capital

RE: Profit from the Coming Real Estate Collapse

[This is a somewhat complicated e-mail, so please be patient reading this. I believe there may be a once-in-a-lifetime opportunity in the real estate market. Real estate is way overpriced, and may be due for a huge decline in prices. If you agree with me, and would like to find ways to profit from the coming drop in prices, read on.]

August 22, 2006
Dear Client,

For the last several years I have watched in amazement as speculators helped inflate the biggest real estate bubble in memory. However, recent evidence suggests that the bubble has finally reached the limits of its expansion, and is on the verge of bursting. When it does, the losses will be enormous, both for those who bet on it, by buying real estate, and those who financed it, by granting mortgages. It is from the latter group, the financing sector, where I believe the greatest profit opportunities are likely to develop in the real estate debacle about to unfold.

Most people looking to profit from a decline in housing are looking for ways to short houses themselves (if this were possible). Another idea is to short those publicly traded companies that build and sell them. Often overlooked, however, are the incredible opportunities involved in the mortgage market, especially mortgage paper that has financed real estate transactions, particularly in the risky, subprime market.

I believe there is a brief window of opportunity to profit from potential difficulties in this shaky market, as the decline in real estate prices starts to pick up steam. Surprisingly, these mortgages still command investment grade ratings; in reality, they should be trading as junk. Further price declines in the housing market, coupled with increasing interest rates, will see a dramatic increase in defaults, especially as all those "no money down, interest only ARMs" begin to reset at much higher interest rates.

If I am right, the value of these mortgages will soon plunge.

In the coming weeks and months, we will actively be looking for the best ways for investors to profit from falling real estate prices, rising interest rates, and the wave of forecloses likely to follow.

If you wish to learn more about any opportunities we might develop, it is essential that you answer the question below and return to me by e-mail. Only if you have done so in advance, will I be allowed to share with you any opportunities that we develop. These opportunities are likely to be in special limited partnerships, or private placements. According to SEC and NASDAQ rules, I can only offer information regarding private placement opportunities to those investors with whom we have a preexisting relationship, and who we know to be both an "accredited investor" and "suitable" for any proposed investment.

As you are already in our proprietary database, the preexisting relationship criterion is already satisfied. However, if you are not a current client of Euro Pacific, I do not know if you are accredited, or what type of investments might be suitable for you. It is important that you inform us now, if you think you might have any interest in such a product in the future. Once we actually have an investment product available for investors, we can only offer it to those investors who are on record with us as being "accredited." We must have your status "in advance" before we can legally offer any such product.

If you would like to personally discuss some of my ideas about real estate, or have any questions about "accredited investor" status, call me directly at 1-800-727-7922.

In order to be an "accredited investor," one of the following two criteria must apply:

1. Net Worth, excluding your primary residence, of one million dollars.
2. Annual income of over $200,000 for each of the last 2 years.

If either applies, you are an "accredited investor." Please check below which applies.

[ ] Yes, I am an "accredited investor," as defined. I am not an existing Euro Pacific client. I would like to be informed about any future private offerings you might have.

[ ] Yes, I am an "accredited investor," as defined. I am a Euro Pacific client. Please send me information about future private opportunities as they become available.

[ ] No, I am not accredited, but would like to know about opportunities that are not solely restricted to accredited investors.

Very Important: All of the information that you provide us with will be held in the strictest confidence and will not be shared with any other companies. Also, answering the question above does not obligate you in the slightest way to participate in any private deals we might develop. It simply allows us to share details of those offerings with you, and gives you the opportunity to participate if you so choose.

I believe the current situation is a rare opportunity to profit from a real estate market that is grossly out of balance. I have been waiting a long time to try to develop a strategy to capitalize on the bursting of the real estate bubble, but the timing had to be just right. I believe the time is now! My team and I at Euro Pacific will be working overtime to try to identify and develop an investment vehicle to capture the potential profits resulting from the declining real estate market.

I urge you to answer the question above, and return to me. If you think the real estate market is in trouble, and would like to consider ways to profit from it, just return this e-mail to me. If you do not return this e-mail, and are not a current Euro Pacific brokerage client, we will not be allowed to show you any of these offerings.

Sincerely,

Euro Pacific Capital

October 13, 2006
Dear Client,

At last I have found an investment that I believe will make money if the real estate market declines. In fact, we believe the decline has already started, and we need to act fast.

The investment is a private placement, limited partnership limited to 99 "accredited" and "suitable investors." The normal minimum is $1,000,000. However, we have made special arrangements with the general partner to accept as little as $100,000 for clients of Euro Pacific Capital.

The deal is a little complicated, so bear with me. PLEASE CALL YOUR EURO PACIFIC REPRESENTATIVE IF YOU NEED HELP, OR HAVE A QUESTION. 1-800-993-8350. Below, there is a link to the offering memorandum. You should read it carefully. It contains all the conditions of the Partnership (sometimes referred to as the "Fund"), including fees, liquidity, management, risks, et cetera. There is also a link to a simpler, PowerPoint presentation of the Fund. YOU CAN ALSO CALL ME DIRECTLY, OR YOUR REPRESENTATIVE AT EURO PACIFIC FOR MORE INFORMATION. 1-800-993-8350.

The partnership will effectively "short" the riskiest part of the mortgage market—the sub-prime, interest-only, adjustable rate (negative amortization), no-money-down loans. The monthly payments on the mortgages held by the asset backed securities that the partnership will "short" typically reset to a much higher level after 24 or 36 months. In some cases borrowers' payments can more than double upon the reset date. In many instances the borrowers have little or no equity in their property, or even negative equity, especially as the decline in housing prices accelerates. We believe that as mortgage payments reset in an environment of higher interest rates, curtailed lending and potentially declining home prices, many borrowers will find it impossible to refinance their mortgages and will thus default.

Technically, the partnership enters into credit default swaps (CDS) on sub-prime mortgage asset backed securities (ABS). The General Partner believes that the credit quality of these ABSs is far worse than the current market prices indicate. Through the use of CDS, the Partnerships will attempt to take advantage of this market inefficiency by creating short positions in the riskiest portion of sub-prime mortgage ABS. Thus, if prices of these sub-prime mortgages ABS should decline, the Partnerships will benefit in direct proportion to the size of the decrease.

A CDS is essentially an insurance contract, providing the buyer with protection against specific risks. The "protection buyer" (*i.e.*, the Fund) pays a periodic premium to the "protection seller," and in return, receives payments to cover losses from a default on a reference bond or ABS. The protection seller is in a similar position to a buyer of the bond, as they take on the bond's credit risk through the CDS, without having to fund it, or for that matter, find it. The protection buyer has an exposure similar to that of a short position in the bond (*i.e.*, it benefits if the bond loses value).

The riskiest tranche of a typical Collateralized Mortgage Obligation (CMO) is assigned 100 percent of the principal losses of the CMO before any higher rated tranches lose any principal! Therefore even with only a modest amount of principal loses in a CMO, the lowest rated tranche can be wiped out entirely. This would translate into nearly a 100 percent gain for the unleveraged fund and a multiple of that in the leveraged funds.

There are three partnerships. One with no leverage, one with two times leverage, and one with five times leverage. Obviously, the higher the leverage the higher the potential return, as well as risk. IF YOU ARE INTERESTED IN PARTICIPATING IN THIS PRIVATE PLACEMENT, YOU CAN GET MORE INFORMATION BY CLICKING ON THE LINK BELOW. It will take you to a password protected website, on which you will find:

1. Three separate Offering Memorandums (one for each partnership)
2. A PowerPoint presentation
3. Three separate Subscription booklets (one for each partnership)

Here is the link to our Private Placements site:

www.europac.net/private.asp

To open the site, you must enter your e-mail address, and the following password:

realestate

You should carefully read all the information, including risks, fees, and management qualifications. If you decide that you would like to invest, print out the Subscription Booklet for the partnership in which you would like to invest, fill in the appropriate sections and return either by fax to: 310-424-7121 (if you intend to wire money) or by mail (with a check) to: Lahde Capital Management, 2700 Neilson Way, Suite 1126, Santa Monica, CA 90405. Please make checks payable to the partnership in which you would like to invest, e.g. U.S. Residential Real Estate Hedge II, L.P. If you qualify and are accepted into the partnership, you will receive an acceptance letter from the General Partner. If you have sent a check, it will be held until just before the next acceptance date, which is typically the first of the month. If you have sent a fax, you will be required to wire funds just prior to the next acceptance date. Wire instructions are included in the subscription booklets.

Since each partnership is limited to 99 investors, the General Partner reserves the right to raise the minimum, or decline to accept an investment, at its sole discretion. If the General Partner declines to accept an investor, that investor will be notified as soon as practical.

Sincerely,
Peter Schiff
President and Chief Global Strategist
Euro Pacific Capital
pschiff@europac.net
1-800-727-7922

Appendix II: A Brief History of Money in America

ONE OF THE GOALS OF THE U.S. Constitution was the elimination of paper money. The Founding Fathers were very familiar with the evils of paper money, not simply because they studied history, but because they had just experienced the disastrous consequences of the Continental—irredeemable paper notes issued by the Continental Congress during the Revolutionary War. After the war ended the notes became practically worthless, giving rise to the expression "not worth a continental." With this experience fresh in their minds, the framers wanted to protect future Americans from a similar disaster.

The monetary provisions of the U.S. Constitution are established in Article 1: "No state shall . . . coin money; emit bills of credit; make any thing but gold and silver coin a tender in payment of debts." Bills of credit are how the framers described paper money.

So the Constitution clearly prohibits the states from printing money or making anything other than gold or silver legal tender. What about the federal government?

Article I, Section 8 authorizes Congress to "coin money, regulate the value thereof, and of foreign Coin, and fix the standard of weights and measures."

Washington, then, is not empowered to issue bills of credit, meaning print paper money, but merely to take money, which is defined in Article 1 section 10 as being gold and silver, and make coins out of it. After all, if the Federal Government were to coin anything other than gold or silver, the states would have no authority to make it legal tender.

Today it is generally accepted that "coining money" includes printing paper money. But if the Constitution intended to use "coining" to mean both, why would it have mentioned both separately in discussing state powers?

During the Constitutional convention a proposal to authorize the Federal Government to issue bills of credit was soundly defeated by a vote of nine to two.

As a final element in this case, consider the Tenth Amendment: "The powers not delegated to the United States by the Constitution, nor prohibited by it to the States, are reserved to the States respectively, or to the people."

So if the Federal government is not specifically granted a power it does not have it. If the states are not denied a power they retain it. Since the Federal Government is not granted the power to print money or establish legal tender, it does not have it.

Since the states are also denied the power to print money and to make anything but gold and silver legal tender, the Constitution was clearly written to prohibit paper money.

James Madison, considered to be "the father of the Constitution, wrote in *Federalist Paper* #10 of the "rage for paper money" as being an "improper and wicked project," and in *Federalist Paper* #44 he wrote "the prohibition to bills of credit must give pleasure to every citizen in proportion to his love of justice and the true springs of public prosperity." He further commented on "the pestilent effects of paper money" and noted that government "ought not to be at liberty to substitute a paper medium for coin," that "the power to make anything but gold and silver a tender for payment of debts is withdrawn from the States on the same principle with that of issuing paper currency."

The Supreme Court validated this as early as 1827. In *Ogden v. Saunders*, 25 U.S. 213 (Wheat) the court remarked that with respect to "issuing bills of credit, or making anything but gold and silver coin a tender in payment of debts" the Constitution "was intended to cut up paper money by the roots." The court further declared that the monetary provisions in Article 1 sections 8 and 10 "must obviously constitute members of the same family, being upon the same subject, and governed by the same policy." This caused the court to conclude, "that the prohibition, in regard to the state tender laws, will admit no construction which would confine it to state laws." In other words, the Supreme Court ruled that the restrictions on making anything but gold and silver legal tender or issuing bills of credit applied equally to the Federal Government as well as the States.

Pursuant to its constitutional authority, Congress passed the Coinage Act of 1792 that defined the dollar as either 24.75 gr. (troy) of fine gold or 371.25 gr. (troy) of fine silver, for an official gold to silver ratio of 15 to 1. The Act also established the creation of specific U.S. coins and specified their composition and design. In other words, the Act provided for the coining of money (gold and silver) with fixed standards of weight and measure, the value of which was regulated by Congress. Precisely as authorized by the Constitution in Article 1 section 8.

We followed the Constitution faithfully until the Civil War. The Legal Tender Act of 1862 authorized the issuance of "greenbacks," direct obligations of the United States Treasury fully payable and redeemable in gold and silver.

After the War there were several legal challenges to the Legal Tender Act of 1862, leading to a series of Supreme Court cases collectively known as the "legal tender cases." The earliest among them, *Hepburn vs. Griswold*, 75 U.S. 603, ruled the act unconstitutional in 1870. After noting "the long train of evils which flow from the use of irredeemable paper money" the Court held that "We are obliged to conclude that an act making mere promises to pay dollars a legal tender in payment of debts previously contracted, is not a means appropriate, plainly adapted, really calculated to carry into effect any express power vested in Congress, that such an act is inconsistent with the spirit of the Constitution, and that it is prohibited by the Constitution."

So even though greenbacks were redeemable in dollars, meaning a specific quantity of gold or silver, the Supreme Court still found them to be unconstitutional.

The following year, in a 5-4 decision, the Supreme Court in Knox vs. Lee, 79 U.S. 457, reversed *Hepburn vs. Griswold*, ruling the Legal Tender Act of 1862 constitutional. However in reaching that decision it is important to note that the court did not look to the monetary provisions of the Constitution. In fact the court conceded that Congress lacked the monetary authority to issue greenbacks. The Court instead looked to the dire circumstances that prevailed at the time, and ruled the Legal Tender Act constitutional only as it was necessary and proper to save the Union.

The nation was embroiled in the Civil War. Writing for the majority, Justice William Strong recounted:

Taxation was inadequate to pay even the interest on the debt already incurred, and it was impossible to await the income of additional taxes. The necessity was immediate and pressing. The army was unpaid. There was then due to the soldiers in the field nearly a score of millions of dollars. The requisitions from the War and Navy Departments for supplies exceeded fifty millions, and the current expenditure was over one million per day. The entire amount of coin in the country, including that in private hands, as well as that in banking institutions, was insufficient to supply the need of the government three months, had it all been poured into the treasury. Foreign credit we had none. We say nothing of the overhanging paralysis of trade, and of business generally, which threatened loss of confidence in the ability of the government to maintain its continued existence, and therewith the complete destruction of all remaining national credit.

It was at such a time and in such circumstances that Congress was called upon to devise means for maintaining the army and navy, for securing the large supplies of money needed, and, indeed, for the preservation of the government created by the Constitution. It was at such a time and in such an emergency that the legal tender acts were passed. Now, if it were certain that nothing else would have supplied the absolute necessities of the treasury, that nothing else would have enabled the government to maintain its armies and navy, that nothing else would have saved the government and the Constitution from destruction, while the legal tender acts would, could any one be bold enough to assert that Congress transgressed its powers?

So the Supreme Court ruled that during an emergency as grave as the Civil War, with the very fate of our nation and the Constitution itself hanging in the balance, that the government could temporarily issue paper notes payable in gold and silver. However, even under those extreme circumstances, four justices still found the Act unconstitutional!

With respect to the monetary authority given to the Federal Government in peacetime, the Court was crystal clear. It held, "The legal tender acts do not attempt to make paper a standard of value. We do not rest their validity upon the assertion that their emission is coinage, or any regulation of the value of money; nor do we assert that Congress may make anything which has no value money. What we do assert is, that Congress has power to enact that the government's promises to pay money shall be, for the time being, equivalent in value to the representative of value determined by the coinage acts, or to multiples thereof." The court went on to rule, "This power is entirely distinct from that of coining money and regulating the value thereof . . . It is not an attempt to coin money out of a valueless material, like the coinage of leather or ivory or kowrie shells. It is a pledge of the national credit. It is a promise by the government to pay dollars; it is not an attempt to make dollars. The standard of value is not changed."

So in overturning *Hepburn vs. Griswold*, the Supreme Court ruled that during a wartime emergency, Congress could issue paper notes provided they were ultimately payable in lawful money, meaning gold and silver. Yet despite this, *Knox vs. Lee* is this very case that lower courts now cite and upon which Congress relies to defend the constitutionality of modern Federal Reserve Notes. However, modern Federal Reserve Notes have nothing in common with greenbacks. They are not obligations of the United States but the Federal Reserve; they are issued in peacetime, and are not redeemable in anything. Federal Reserve Notes are unconstitutional and the very case the government relies on to support their existence proves it!

Another Supreme Court case the government relies on for a constitutional basis for Federal Reserve Notes is *Juilliard vs. Greenman,* 110 U.S. 421. This 1884 case however, can no way be used to uphold the constitutionality of Federal Reserve Notes. According to the Court "The single question, therefore, to be considered, and upon the answer to which the judgment to be rendered between these parties depends, is whether notes of the United States, issued in time of war, under acts of congress declaring them to be a legal tender in payment of private debts, and afterwards in time of peace redeemed and paid in gold coin at the treasury, and then reissued under the act of 1878, can, under the [110 U.S. 421, 438] constitution of the United States, be a legal tender in payment of such debts."

What do notes issued by the United States, during wartime, redeemed and paid in gold, have to do with Federal Reserve Notes? The answer is nothing.

Of specific interest are comments by Justice Stephen Field, who wrote the dissenting opinion. Field, citing from Bancroft's *History of the Formation of the Constitution of the United States,* vol. 2, p. 134, writes "when the convention came to the prohibition upon the states, the historian says that the clause, 'No state shall make anything but gold and silver a tender in payment of debts,' was accepted without a dissentient state. 'So the adoption of the constitution,' he adds, 'is to be the end forever of paper money, whether issued by the several states or by the United States, if the constitution shall be rightly interpreted and honestly obeyed.'" Id. 137.

Field also goes on to quote the recognized constitutional authority Daniel Webster, who as a United States senator said, "The states are expressly prohibited from making anything but gold and silver a legal tender in payment of debts; and although no such express prohibition is applied to congress, yet, as congress has no power granted to it in this respect but to coin money and to regulate the value of foreign coins, it clearly has no power to substitute paper or anything else for coin as a tender in payment of debts and in discharge of contracts."

Despite the clear language of both the Constitution and the Supreme Court, Congress began issuing "silver certificates" in 1878 and "gold certificates" in 1882. Direct obligations of the United States Treasury, the certificates issued during peacetime certified that a specific number of dollars in either gold or silver had been deposited in the Treasury of the United States of America and were payable to bearers on demand. The notes themselves were not originally considered to be legal tender, but were merely promises to pay legal tender. Gold certificates eventually achieved that status in 1920, as did silver certificates in 1933.

In the meantime, Congress passed the Federal Reserve Act in 1913. Pursuant to that Act, the Federal Reserve began issuing its own notes that originally circulated in tandem with gold and silver certificates.

In their original form, Federal Reserve Notes were not considered to be lawful money. They were "notes" redeemable in lawful money—meaning gold coins or gold certificates issued by the U.S. Treasury. The notes themselves contained specific language promising to pay to the bearer on demand a specific sum of dollars in gold. The notes further claimed to be redeemable in gold on demand at the United States Treasury, or in gold or lawful money at any Federal Reserve Bank.

So even though a Federal Reserve Note might have had the words "ten dollars" printed on its face, the note itself never claimed to be ten dollars. It merely promised to pay the bearer of the note ten dollars. That is why Federal Reserve Notes are called notes. A note is a promise to pay a sum certain. In the case of a Ten Dollar Note, the Federal Reserve promised to pay ten dollars. The note merely evidenced that promise.

The Gold Reserve Act of 1934 made it illegal for Americans to own gold. The Treasury stopped issuing gold certificates, and the gold redemption clause was removed from Federal Reserve Notes. The new clause read, "This note is legal tender for all debts public and private and is redeemable in lawful money at the United States Treasury or any Federal Reserve Bank." The note still contained a promise to pay a specific number of dollars to the bearer on demand.

The new language revealed two important changes. First, Federal Reserve Notes were now declared to be legal tender. Second, they were still redeemable in lawful money, meaning the notes themselves still did not constitute lawful money. Since gold was now illegal for Americans to own, the only lawful money U.S. bearers could be paid was silver coins or silver certificates. Foreign holders, of course, could still be paid in gold.

The Gold Reserve Act led to a number of Supreme Court cases involving the abrogation of gold clauses in contracts. *United States vs. Bankers Trust Co.*, 294 U.S. 240, *Nortz vs. United States,* 294 U.S. 317, and *Perry vs. United States,* 294 U.S. 330, were all decided simultaneously on February 18, 1935. A sharply divided Supreme Court ruled five to four in favor of the government. As a result all gold clauses in contracts were thrown out, and the right to include such clauses in future contracts was prohibited until the ability to do so was reinstated by an act of Congress in 1977. The legal limitation on gold ownership itself was repealed in 1974.

Writing for the majority, Chief Justice Charles Evans Hughes cites extensively from both *Knox vs. Lee* and *Juilliard vs. Greenman.* However, much of what he wrote was either misrepresented, taken out of context, or just plain inconsistent with the opinion he was citing. It's as if Evans had not even read those decisions, but merely added the citation to create the false impression that there was precedence for the decision.

His line of reasoning evidences such a complete lack of understanding of the Constitution that I find it hard to believe it represents an honest assessment. I find it far more credible that he was simply looking to create a rationale for upholding an obviously unconstitutional usurpation of federal power by FDR.

For example, citing *Knox vs. Lee*, Hughes writes, "The Power of the Congress to Establish a Monetary System. It is unnecessary to review the historic controversy as to the extent of this power, or again to go over the ground traversed by the Court in reaching the conclusion that the Congress may make Treasury notes legal tender in payment of debts previously contracted, as well as of those subsequently contracted, whether that authority be exercised in course of war or in time of peace."

First, neither the Constitution nor the Court in *Knox vs. Lee* mentions anything about Congress establishing a monetary system. The only constitutional monetary power Congress has over money is to coin it and regulate its value. Second, Hughes mistakes the *Knox* decision with respect to the wartime emergency powers of Congress, and those normal powers associated with peace.

Citing *Juilliard vs. Greenman,* Hughes makes the same misrepresentation. He writes "The broad and comprehensive national authority over the subjects of revenue, finance, and currency is derived from the aggregate of the powers granted to the Congress, embracing the powers to lay and collect taxes, to borrow money, to regulate commerce with foreign nations and among the several states, to coin money, regulate the value thereof, and of foreign coin, and fix the standards of weights and measures, and the added express power 'to make all laws which shall be necessary and proper for carrying into execution' the other enumerated powers."

Remember, in *Juilliard vs. Greenman* the court made clear that the only issue it was addressing was whether paper notes, redeemable in gold and issued pursuant to wartime emergency powers, could be reissued in peacetime once redeemed. There is nothing in that decision that would support the Court's opinion in this case. However, history is full of examples of government usurping powers during wartime, yet refusing to surrender them once the wars end. From that perspective it can be argued that since the revolution Americans have lost every war we've fought, since each one has resulted in more government power and less individual liberty.

In a scathing dissent, Justice James Clark McReynolds wrote, "If given effect, the enactments here challenged will bring about confiscation of property rights and repudiation of national obligations. Acquiescence in the decisions just announced is impossible; the circumstances demand statement of our views. To let oneself slide down the easy slope offered by the course of events and to dull one's mind against the extent of the danger, . . . that is precisely to fail in one's obligation of responsibility. Just men regard repudiation and spoliation of citizens by their sovereign with abhorrence; but we are asked to affirm that the Constitution has granted power to accomplish both. No definite delegation of such a power exists; and we cannot believe the farseeing framers, who labored with hope of establishing justice and securing the blessings of liberty, intended that the expected government should have authority to annihilate its own obligations and destroy the very rights which they were endeavoring to protect. Not only is there no permission for such actions they are inhibited. And no plenitude of words can conform them to our charter."

He concluded the opinion with the following blistering remark: "Loss of reputation for honorable dealing will bring us unending humiliation; the impending legal and moral chaos is appalling."

In 1963 the redemption clause was completely removed from Federal Reserve Notes. It was replaced with the simple claim "this note is legal tender for all debts public and private." Also removed was the promise to pay a specific number of dollars. Instead the notes merely stated a dollar amount.

At that point in time, all U.S. currency became fiat. It has little in common with either greenbacks, gold or silver certificates, or legitimate Federal Reserve Notes. They were no better than the Continentals the Constitution was specifically written to prohibit.

Technically there is no official name for modern Federal Reserve Notes. They clearly are not dollars. At one time they contained a promise to pay dollars, but now they simply have the word "dollar" printed on them. A dollar is still defined by the Coinage Act of 1972 as a specific weight of gold or silver. Simply printing the word "dollar" on a Federal Reserve Note does not turn a mere piece of paper into gold or silver. No more than the word "Washington" printed beneath his image on the note turns it into the father of our country.

In fact, Federal Reserve Notes are not even notes. A note must contain a promise to pay a sum certain, and since Federal Reserve Notes no longer promise to pay anything, they are not even notes. However, the fact that they are designed to resemble legitimate notes makes them counterfeit. My father named them "Greenies" in his 1976 classic, *The Biggest Con: How the Government Is Fleecing You.*

In 1965 Congress began removing silver from U.S. coins as well. Prior to 1965, dimes, quarter, and half dollars contained 90 percent silver (the government stopped making silver dollars in 1935). In 1965 all the silver was removed from dimes and quarters, while half dollars were reduced to 40 percent silver until 1970, at which time the remaining silver was also removed. In fact, the effort to make then new coins look like the older legitimate ones they replaced by plating copper with nickel rendered them counterfeit as well. So in effect all U.S. coin and currency currently in circulation are counterfeit.

In 1971, Nixon finally severed the last remaining link between Federal Reserve Notes and gold. After 1971, not even foreigners could get legitimate dollars for their Federal Reserve Notes. When Nixon took us off the gold standard, he claimed the move was only temporary. This was likely necessary to appease currency markets that would have reacted far more violently to a permanent suspension of gold payments. However, this temporary policy has now been in effect for over forty years.

The irony is that Nixon was correct in that the move will turn out to be temporary after all, just not on the terms Nixon or anyone else at that time would have imagined. We will likely return to the gold standard not out of a policy choice but out of necessity due to a complete economic collapse that will be brought about as a consequence of Nixon's actions.

Notes

1. *Where We Are and Where We Are Headed*

1. "Balance Sheet of Households and Nonprofit Organizations," Federal Reserve Board, December 8, 2011.
2. "Exports and Imports of Goods by Principal End-Use Category," U.S. Census Bureau.
3. Gross domestic product is the total monetary value of all the goods and services produced within the United States per year.

2. *How We Got Here: Government Is the Problem*

1. Christina Romer, "Spurious Volatility in Historical Unemployment Data," Princeton University, available at MinneapolisFed.org.
2. Quoted in Thomas E. Woods Jr., "Warren Harding and the Forgotten Depression of 1920," Lew Rockwell.com, October 19, 2009.
3. Woods, ibid.
4. Tom Woods, *Meltdown*, p. 96.
5. Murray Rothbard, *America's Great Depression*, p. 187.
6. Paul Krugman, "Dubya's Double-Dip," *New York Times,* August 2, 2002.

4. *Jobs, Jobs, Jobs: Government Can Improve Employment Only by Getting Out of the Way*

1. www.msnbc.msn.com/id/28590554/ns/business-stocks_and_economy/t/obama-stimulus-will-create-million-jobs/.

2. www.huffingtonpost.com/2010/07/14/job-stimulus-report-white_n_645541.html.

3. "Family Income of Unemployment Insurance Recipients," Congressional Budget Office.

4. Clyde Wayne Crews, "Ten Thousand Commandments 2010," Creative Enterprises Institute, April 15, 2001.

5. How to Fix the Financial Industry: Deregulate

1. Transcript of first presidential debate, CNN.com.

2. www.washingtontimes.com/news/2010/mar/19/bank-regulators-given-big-bonuses/.

3. Matt Apuzzo, "Govt rewarded bank auditors with big bonuses." AP, March 18, 2010.

4. Department of the Treasury, Budget in Brief, FY 2011.

5. *The Greatest Trade Ever: The Behind-the-Scenes Story of How John Paulson Defied Wall Street and Made Financial History* (Crown: 2009).

6. Richard Fisher, "Containing (or Restraining) Systemic Risk," Remarks, June 6, 2011.

6. Sound Money: Return to the Gold Standard

1. Alan Greenspan, "The history of money," January 16, 2002.

2. www.frbsf.org/currency/independence/history/text1.html.

3. "1998 vs. 2008: A Tech Retrospective," *PCWorld*, February 23, 2008.

7. Tax Reform: For Starters, End the Income Tax

1. "National Taxpayer Advocate Delivers Annual Report to Congress," Internal Revenue Service, January 5, 2011.

2. David Kocieniewski, "GE's Strategies Let It Avoid Taxes Altogether," *New York Times*, March 24, 2011.

8. Tear Up the "Third Rails": End Social Security and Medicare

1. Franklin D. Roosevelt, "Message to Congress Reviewing the Broad Objectives and Accomplishments of the Administration," June 8, 1934.

2. www.ssa.gov/history/ratios.html.

3. CBO's 2011 Long-Term Projections for Social Security: Additional Information, Congressional Budget Office.

4. www.ssa.gov/history/ratios.html.

5. The Social Security System, Hearings Before the Joint Economic Committee, May 1976, pp. 27–28, GPO, 1977.

9. Fixing Higher Ed: Time to Drop Out of College?

1. Adam Schaeffer, "They Spend WHAT? The Real Cost of Public Schools," Cato Policy Analysis, March 10, 2011.

2. "Inflation-Adjusted Per Pupil Spending, Staff-to-Student Ratio, and Achievement of 17-Year-Olds," Cato Institute.

3. Jennifer Cohen, "Examining the State Per Pupil Expenditures and State Graduation Rates."

4. Schaeffer, ibid.

5. Jacques Stenberg, "Is Going to an Elite College Worth the Cost?" *New York Times,* December 17, 2010.

6. Scott Cohn, "Student loans leave crushing debt burdens," CNBC, December 21, 2010.

7. see.stanford.edu.

8. All data, National Center for Education Statistics.

9. docs.google.com/viewer?url=http percent 3A percent 2F percent 2Fnces .ed.gov percent 2Fnationsreportcard percent 2Fpdf percent 2Fmain2009 percent 2F2010451.pdf.

10. nationsreportcard.gov/reading_2009/summary_g12.asp.

11. nces.ed.gov/nationsreportcard/pubs/main2010/2011467.asp#section4.

10. Health Care: Repealing ObamaCare Is Just the Beginning

1. "Plastic Surgery Procedures Rise . . . And Men Are Fueling the Trend," *Daily Finance,* March 23, 2011.

2. Chuck Smith, "Business of being beautiful soars," *Sacramento Business Journal,* February 20, 1995.

3. Organization for Economic Cooperation and Development, stats.oecd .org/Index.aspx?DataSetCode=SHA.

4. Kim Carollo, "Doctors Face High Risk of Malpractice Claims," ABC News, August 18, 2011.

5. Alex Nussbaum, "Malpractice Lawsuits Are a 'Red Herring' in Obama Plan," Bloomberg News, June 16, 2009.

12. America Is Bankrupt: Time to Admit It

1. Nicole Bullock, "States Warned of $2 Trillion Pensions Shortfall," *Financial Times,* January 18, 2011.

2. Tom Gantect, "State Employee Public Pension Liability Jumps $900 Million in One Year," *Michigan Capitol Confidential,* January 2, 2011.

3. Annalyn Censky, "Savings Rate Falls to Lowest Level Since 2007," CNN Money, November 23, 2011.

4. Robert P. Murphy, "Is Deleveraging Bad for the Economy?" Mises Daily, August 15, 2011.

5. Budget of the United States.

Index